the life of

ORSON F. WHITNEY

Orson F. Whitney (CA)

the life of ORSON F. WHITNEY

HISTORIAN
POET
APOSTLE

AS RECORDED IN HIS DAILY JOURNALS

DENNIS B. HORNE

CFI
An Imprint of Cedar Fort, Inc.
Springville, Utah

ISBN 13: 978-1-4621-1431-3

Published by CFI, an imprint of Cedar Fort, Inc.
2373 W. 700 S., Springville, UT 84663
Distributed by Cedar Fort, Inc., www.cedarfort.com

Library of Congress Cataloging-in-Publication Data

Horne, Dennis B., author.
The Life of Orson F. Whitney : historian, poet, apostle / Dennis B. Horne.
pages cm
Includes bibliographical references and index.
Summary: The history of Orson F. Whitney, a prominent early member of The Church of Jesus Christ of Latter-day Saints.
ISBN 978-1-4621-1431-3
1. Whitney, Orson F. (Orson Ferguson), 1855-1931. 2. Church of Jesus Christ of Latter-day Saints--Apostles--Biography. 3. Mormon Church--Apostles--Biography. 4. Historians--Utah--Biography. I. Title.

BX8695.W53H67 2014
289.3092--dc23
[B]

2014011652

Cover design by Shawnda T. Craig
Cover design © 2014 Lyle Mortimer
Edited by Kevin Haws

Printed in the United States of America

10 9 8 7 6 5 4 3 2

Printed on acid-free paper

To Chelsey, Renae, Annette, Helen, and Celia
My precious family

Other Books by This Author

Bruce R. McConkie: Highlights from His Life and Teachings

"Called of God, by Prophecy"

An Apostle's Record: The Journals of Abraham H. Cannon

Determining Doctrine

Faith to Heal and Be Healed

Latter Leaves in the Life of Lorenzo Snow

Contents

Acknowledgments

I **am grateful** to Clint Pumphrey of the Utah State University Merrill-Cazier Library Special Collections for kindly arranging to have the Orson F. Whitney diaries scanned and posted online at a very reasonable cost so that I could study them at my leisure. Such online posting gives access to all who wish to study Whitney's diaries. His colleague Dan Davis also assisted by providing me with photographs of individuals mentioned in the text. Publication of portions of the diaries and photographs is by their permission.

I wish to thank Christopher R. Greenwood, Dale Stokes, Neal W. Kramer (an Orson F. Whitney literary expert), Bill Slaughter, Glenn Rowe, Donald Q. Cannon, Sylvia Blight, Julia Naylor, and Ed Brandt for various kinds of assistance, counsel, or feedback.

The staff of Cedar Fort did their usual professional job editing the manuscript and preparing it for publication: Catherine Christensen, Shawnda Craig, Heather Holm, and Emily Chambers.

While perhaps not directly connected preparing the present work about Orson F. Whitney, I have benefited immensely during my life from the teachings, insight, wisdom, counsel, and sometimes even gentle rebukes, of a number of wise, faithful, loyal, and spiritually mature and experienced men, true disciples of Christ that have kindly taken their time to tutor me. Among these are Brit McConkie, Elder Glen L. Rudd, David H. Garner, Jerry W. Baker, Edward J. Brandt, Max Molgard, Robert Lund, Lee Donaldson, Roger Fluhman, and Dan Hogan.

Orson F. Whitney

Introduction

Orson F. Whitney—the great poet, prophet, and preacher of yesteryear—is all but unknown to most Latter-day Saints today. Such fading collective Mormon memory is a tragedy in need of remedy; hence, the present publication. A life as profound and influential as his needs an honest and fair recounting of both the good and the surprising.

Orson Whitney rubbed shoulders with some of the most prominent men and women of his time, leaders and thinkers both in the Church and out. A man of deep spirituality, he saw visions, conversed with the Spirit, entertained translated beings, healed the sick, prophesied, cast out devils, rebuked the elements, endured sickness and hardship, and sat in collegial council with prophets and apostles.

Whitney was doubly gifted of God. He could write with beautiful expression and moving lucidity, approaching the lofty standard of the Brother of Jared (see Ether 12:24). He could also speak with eloquence, persuasive power, and concrete conviction, again, perhaps approaching the sublime heights reached by Moroni and other Nephite prophets of old (see Ether 12:23, 25). Over the course of his life, Ort was magnified in these talents to the point that many of his peers thought him the very best the Church had. President Lorenzo Snow wrote a letter to Orson, adjudging that "there is not an Elder in all Israel, endowed with ordinary sense and ambition, though he were a millionaire, if he lacked what you possess, but would gladly give his entire wealth, could he thereby secure the gifts of oratory and argument, the talent and ability that the Lord our God has so abundantly bestowed upon my admired and beloved friend, Bishop

O. F. Whitney." President Joseph F. Smith likewise wrote to Elder Whitney, humbly acknowledging that Ort's abilities to communicate from behind the pulpit easily exceeded his own—and this while Whitney was still a young man. President Gordon B. Hinckley's father, Bryant S. Hinckley, while serving as a stake president, told Elder Whitney that he thought him "the most eloquent expounder of the Gospel in the Church."

As a contemporary of James E. Talmage, John A. Widstoe, and B. H. Roberts, Orson fit comfortably among the best and brightest of their generation. While the other men mentioned are better remembered today because of the longer-lasting impact of their (non-poetic) writings, Elder Whitney easily held his own with them. Yet, because most of his output took the form of poetry—a literary style of diminished use and popularity today—he and his works are largely forgotten and unknown outside scholarly circles. Even among historians, most of the unusual complexities and unexpected detours found in Orson's life have remained relatively unknown and unexamined, at least as far as I have been able to determine.[1]

This biography views the life of Orson F. Whitney largely through the lens of his diaries. Ort was a competent diarist, though not the most thorough and detailed. But his labors to record the important events of his life were steady, often insightful or provocative, and prolonged, lasting from the beginning of his first mission to within the last three weeks of his life. He indicated that his purpose (and therefore the substance of this volume) was to write "such things as are most important in my experience."[2]

By drawing heavily upon them as primary source material, I have followed the example of Orson Whitney himself, who filled his own biographical triumph, *Life of Heber C. Kimball*, with quotations from Kimball's diaries, thereby letting Brother Heber speak for himself as often as possible.

I also followed the example of Elder Matthias F. Cowley, author of *Wilford Woodruff: His Life and Labors*, who drew heavily upon President Wilford Woodruff's exemplary diaries. That classic volume states its main source clearly on the title page: "As Recorded in His Daily Journals." I have borrowed this phrase. Though it is too much to say that Orson made "daily" entries in his diary, especially in his last years, he did often meet that standard. When researching biographical material on Wilford, Elder Matthias Cowley had the privilege of closely examining Woodruff's record. He explained, "I was also honored after his decease, by approval of President Joseph F. Smith, to read President Woodruff's daily journals through from beginning to end, comprising over 6,000 pages, written by his own hand."[3]

As used herein, quotations from Orson F. Whitney's imposing diaries become the very foundation of the work and hold the most interest for readers. In preparing the present work, I read Whitney's journals closely, as written by his own hand, and transcribed much of them.[4] While I didn't count the pages, they also numbered in the thousands, covering thirty-five volumes, and contain many interesting narrations, explanations, episodes, anecdotes, and puzzling mysteries.

In 1930, as perhaps the last major project he completed, Orson F. Whitney oversaw the self-publication of his autobiography, *Through Memory's Halls: The Life Story of Orson F. Whitney*. This excellent volume, today very difficult to locate, reviewed the highlights of his life from his perspective, with his own explanations and interpretations, and also his omissions. With no fault or blame to him, he purposely ignored or glossed over significant portions of his life. Providentially, his diaries tell a more complete story. As Paul Harvey, the famous radio commentator said, they tell much (but not all) of "the rest of the story." In Whitney's case, what can be learned from the rest of the story is sometimes almost astonishing. Only a fraction of the full quantity of diary entries are used herein. As would be expected, these are the most important, interesting, enlightening, candid, and flavorful portions.

Some of the entries in Whitney's diaries pertain to matters that could be unsettling for some less-experienced or naïve readers of LDS biography. No man or woman, save One, has lived a perfect life. Just as it is known that Brigham Young himself sometimes taught some ideas out of harmony with the scriptures, Orson Whitney, despite the magnificent mind and gifts and inspiration that were his, also entertained for a time some strange notions in conflict with settled Gospel doctrine.

For a time, Orson Whitney, as part of a small secret group, rendered misplaced loyalty to one undeserving of it. This troubling period of his life contained many difficult learning experiences for him: trials of faith and fealty that provided necessary growth, correction, and introspection. Whitney's path to the apostleship was no smooth progression to high office; he had to enact and endure great revolutions and tribulations within himself to overcome some ideological obstacles before he was called to the apostleship.

Whitney courted several women with potential plural marriage in mind, some of them after the second 1904 manifesto. But as far as is known, he did not marry any of them as plural wives while he lived. He had but one plural wife and she became such in 1888, well before the first 1890 manifesto. Elder Whitney, an Apostle of the Lord, lived a life of virtue and moral purity. He lived chaste before marriage and practiced physical fidelity, at least, after. Some few other inexplicable matters are related as well and have no satisfying conclusion or explanation.

As a general principle of gospel safety and doctrinal wisdom, when it comes to the erroneous beliefs or teachings of individuals—even those holding prominent position in the Church—a modern Apostle has written: "What he [in this instance, Orson] did is not a pattern for any of us." And further, "As for me and my house, we will have the good sense to choose between the divergent teachings of the same man and come up with those that accord with what God has set forth in his eternal plan of salvation."[5] This counsel applies to any errant notions of Brigham Young, Orson F. Whitney, Amasa M. Lyman, Moses Thatcher, or any other leader, high or low, who believed or taught something out of harmony with the canonized standard works and the teachings of modern prophets and apostles.[6]

In addition, there are instances in the diaries where Whitney records his memory of the words of someone repeating to him their memory of something said to them (or in their presence) by the Prophet Joseph Smith. While Ort had a near-photographic memory and could record conversations with others in impressive detail, such third-hand accounts, especially when dealing with speculative doctrinal matters, are surely not the wisest foundation upon which to build a sturdy doctrinal house.

President Joseph F. Smith warned the Church about reliance on uncertain doctrinal linkage to Joseph Smith: "We fear that many things that are reported as coming from the Prophet Joseph, and other early elders in the church, by not being carefully recorded or told with strict regard for accuracy, have lost something of their value as historical data, and unwarranted additions have sometimes been made to the original facts, until it is difficult to determine just how far some of the traditions which have come to us may be accepted as reliable representations of what was said or what was done. Let those who feel impressed to make a record of facts, as they become acquainted with them, do so; but let them exercise the greatest care in obtaining accuracy of statement and in giving the authority for the statements they record."[7]

My belief is that Orson recognized the troubling issues or events that some of his diary entries recorded. With the past behind him, he decided to self-censor them, either by cutting out pages and lines of his diary or by scribbling out parts of them. The cut-out excisions are designated by brackets such as [text removed] and they, regrettably, obscure understanding of some difficult matters, leaving me to occasionally deal in probabilities and educated guesses. Readers should beware of making judgments or assigning blame or sin based on incomplete information. Some of the scribbled-out text is still decipherable and has been retained as ~~regular diary text, though crossed out~~. These portions of the diary give some indication of the kind of matters Orson sought to remove. There are two time periods when Whitney would most likely have done his diary-censoring: July 1916, when Orson indicates that he spent time "revising" his journal; and from 1925 to 1930, when he was using his diary, along with other sources, to prepare his autobiography. He also spent time in August 1916 destroying many letters he had written.

As for full assurance regarding my understanding and interpretation of some episodes recounted from Whitney's diaries, such surety is elusive. If one day it is found that I misunderstood some matters, such is entirely possible.

Outside of his early private ideological detours, Whitney's doctrinal presentations are sound, solid, insightful, and penetrating.[8] He was thoroughly conversant with gospel principles, from the beginning basics to the meatier matters. When he spoke or wrote about church doctrine, he combined logical progression of thought and argument with a sprinkling of wit. He wove in verse, stories, parables, scripture, and social commentary where it would be meaningful. As President Snow once assured Orson, "No man could lay a finger on a line of false doctrine" that he had written or spoken. Elder Whitney became a master teacher, solidly grounded in faith and true doctrine, and he preached by the power of the Holy Ghost. As his life journey progressed, he endured the refiner's fire and eventually came off the triumphant conqueror, performing a great ministry before the Lord and His people. His last years in the apostolic harness were marked by great doctrinal preaching and powerful influence for good in the Church. But it was a long, hard road to get to where he eventually got: to minister among the people as a prophet in Israel, beloved and esteemed by all the faithful.

I recognize Elder Whitney's marvelous doctrinal contributions to Latter-day Saint literature; however, space considerations have kept me from engaging and analyzing most of this material. His talks at funerals and stake conferences, as spread throughout the various newspapers of his day, if collected, would fill a volume by themselves. Such a work would constitute a treasure trove of gospel teachings and insights, but remains outside the scope of this biography. Indeed, there are probably a thousand items of interest mentioned by Orson in his diary, covering a host of subjects that, if always followed up and explained, would divert the reader from the main purpose and plot: to follow Whitney through his life as unfolded in his diary. Therefore, I have sought an equitable balance. Where life story constitutes the theme, it receives precedence. Where secondary items of special importance are encountered, they receive due notice, or else the notes contain direction to other sources giving further consideration. After Whitney became an Apostle, his diaries lost some of the flavor and intrigue that had previously characterized them. Much of his record became notes about stake conferences: travel to and from, who spoke, how often he spoke, whom he ordained, where he slept, and other like matters. The diaries must contain hundreds of such lengthy entries narrating these visits, indicating the sheer volume of such work he performed, but adding little of interest to his life's record. Unless something of exceptional interest occurred on such visits, they have been passed over herein; however, readers should be aware that stake conference visits constituted a major portion of his life and work after 1906.

Whitney left behind some correspondence and a few handwritten (formerly unpublished) autobiographical sketches. I have made good use of the autobiographical pieces, reproducing them in print as early chapters, but have drawn very little on the correspondence. Space limitations haven't allowed me to do equitable justice to his story as found in the diaries and still give full consideration to his other papers. Life history has taken precedence over all else.

Such is also the fate of his published writings. Unfortunately, his massive output of literary productions—deserving of expert analysis and commentary—has received meager and sporadic attention herein. Perhaps one day someone far more qualified than I will give Orson's poetry and historical works the fair treatment they merit.[9] Whitney loved writing poetry to near-obsession and he loved reading it to others just as much. Poetry, a beloved form of expression so common in bygone years, has lost its once-prominent place in society. The reviewer of an important compilation of the poetry of Eliza R. Snow (a friend and mentor of Orson Whitney), explained:

> The poetic traditions, the oral and textual worlds, and the theories and practices of poetry out of which Snow's [and Whitney's] poetry grew are largely lost to us now. These poems, once a regular feature of public discourse and a familiar aspect of private expression, have become historical artifacts in and of themselves—a fact which invites us to ask questions about the broader context for Snow's poetic practice. To begin with, what was the place, literal and figurative, of poetry in nineteenth-century Mormondom?
>
> Poetry was located within both public discourse and private reflection. Snow's published poems appeared primarily in official LDS publications; they were often recited or sung at public gatherings and offered as representations of Mormon opinions and theology. . . . This . . . speaks to the ubiquity and centrality of poetry itself in the lives of nineteenth-century people.[10]

What is said here of Eliza is also true of Orson. Readers will notice the many references to his poetry, whether writing, revising, publishing, or reading it. The manner it permeated his life and that of others is covered adequately, simply by continued reference to his diary. His poetry is rarely analyzed or critiqued, but its conception and reception are often noticed. He wrote two book-length poems: *Elias: An Epic of the Ages* and *Love and the Light: An Idyl of the Westland.* Elias was written as an aid to dispersing grief and depression and as a vehicle for teaching supernal and eternal gospel doctrines in an epic form. The other still substantial but shorter work seems to tell the story of a lady-friend's struggle with issues regarding science and religion, in dramatic and romantic form. Each becomes a major element within the course of Whitney's life. Many of Whitney's diary comments and allusions pertaining to his other lesser poetic efforts are mentioned incidentally or ignored. Those readers interested in his poetic writings can find them in online public domain editions.

The diaries themselves were donated by Orson's grandson Winslow Whitney Smith to the LDS Church Archives in 1971. Upon donation and by agreement, they were photocopied for the donor. Copies were then placed with other libraries, such as those at Brigham Young University and Utah State University. For the present volume, I worked from the copies located at USU that have been scanned and are available as of this writing on the USU Special Collections library website.[11] Also as of this writing, the LDS Church Archives originals are restricted to researchers. Because an error was made in the photocopying process (cutting off the bottom text line of the page for some entries), senior employees at the LDS Archives were kind enough to waive the restriction for me so that I could see the poorly photocopied entries in their entirety in the originals. Perhaps someday the access, resources, and technology will be available to view beneath the scribbled out diary entries and unlock more of the mysteries found in Whitney's journal. Further, there may be words or phrases illegible to me that a better handwriting analyst could decipher. I alone am responsible for errors of any kind that may be found herein. I have sought to render accurate readings of the diaries, but haven't gone to excessive lengths to ensure perfection in transcription. Nor have I gone to such lengths to ensure exact spellings of names or places; Whitney's handwriting was often so poor as to make such an effort a futile exercise. Readers interested in locating further information about many of the characters mentioned in Ort's dairies may desire to check the biographical registry section of the scholarly publication of his mother's diaries, *A Widow's Tale: The 1884–1896 Diary of Helen Mar Kimball Whitney*. Most of the people mentioned by Orson in his diaries are leaders or prominent members of The Church of Jesus Christ of Latter-day Saints; biographical information about them is found in the common LDS historical publications. See the bibliography and notes for further information about these sources.

Orson F. Whitney
(USHS)

Chapter 1

Early Years, 1855–1876

Most of this chapter consists of a previously unpublished handwritten autobiographical account Whitney wrote in early 1889 that he titled, "My Mortal Mission; A record of events in the life of Orson Ferguson Whitney; narrated by himself." *It contains similar, though much more candid and detailed, information on his early life to that found in some of the biographical sketches published in his day.*[1]

I opened my eyes upon mortal life in this dispensation on Sunday, July 1st, 1855, at ten minutes past 10 o'clock p.m. My birthplace was Salt Lake City, Utah Territory, U.S.A., where, at the date of commencing these memoirs—January 1st, 1889—I still reside.

My ancestors for three generations were members of The Church of Jesus Christ of Latter-day Saints, and I was born in the covenant and faith of my fathers.

My sire was Horace Kimball Whitney, eldest born of Newel Kimball Whitney and his first wife, Elizabeth Ann Smith.[2] My mother, Helen Mar Kimball, was the second daughter and third born of the household of Heber Chase Kimball; her mother being his first wife, Vilate Murray.[3]

I was the fifth child and third son in a family of eleven, whose names, in the order of their birth, are as follows:

1. Helen Rosabelle

2. William Howard
3. Horace Kimball
4. Vilate Murray
5. Orson Ferguson (blessed by Bp. L. [S.?] Young, March 6/56)
6. Elizabeth Ann
7. Genevieve
8. Helen Kimball
9. Charles Spaulding
10. Florence Marian
11. Phebe Isabel

The first three died in infancy; the fourth, my sister Vilate, at the age of sixteen; leaving me, in my fifteenth year, the eldest living of my father's children.

Helen Mar Kimball Whitney (1838–1896) (USU)

My grandfathers, Newel K. Whitney and Heber C. Kimball, were both natives of the state of Vermont. The ancestors of the former came from England early in the seventeenth century. The Kimballs also came from England, in time to assist in governing the independence of the Colonies.

The Prophet Joseph Smith, whose progenitors and those of my grandfather Kimball at one time inter-married, declared that my grandparents were of the lineage of Judah in the House of Israel. In a patriarchal blessing upon the head of Newel K. Whitney given by Father Joseph Smith Sen., he called him "a descendant of Melchisedek."

Grandfather Whitney and his family joined The Church in

Kirtland, Ohio, in November 1830. Heber C. Kimball and his household embraced the Gospel in Mendon, Monroe County, New York, in the spring of 1832. Both became bosom friends of the Prophet Joseph.

My father was born in Kirtland, July 25, 1823, and my mother in Mendon, on the 22nd of August, 1828. They were married in the temple at Nauvoo, Illinois, on the night of February 3, 1846, President Brigham Young performing the ceremony. Prior to my mother's marriage with my father she had been sealed to the Prophet Joseph Smith, as one of his plural wives, in the holy order of celestial marriage. This union took place in the spring of 1843, before the revelation on celestial marriage was written, and a little over a year prior to the Prophet's martyrdom. Heber C. Kimball pronounced the ceremony, which joined his house with Joseph's for time and all eternity.

A similar relationship had been established, some time before, between the Prophet and Newel K. Whitney, who gave to Joseph his eldest daughter Sarah, in the celestial order, her father officiating in the sealing ordinance. She was the first woman given in plural marriage according to the law of God, by and with the consent of both parents, in this dispensation. After Joseph's death she wedded Heber C. Kimball.

Horace Kimball Whitney
(1823–1896) (USU)

My grandfather Whitney, who was the second to the Bishopric at the time of his death in the year 1850, was the Presiding Bishop of The Church of Jesus Christ of Latter-day Saints, and was acting in the office of Trustee-in-Trust for the same. My grandfather Kimball was one of the original Twelve Apostles of the Church, and during the last twenty-one years of his life, the second of its First Three Presidents. Himself, my father, and my uncle, Orson K. Whitney, were all three members of the Mormon Pioneer band, which entered and took possession of the Valley of the Great Salt Lake on the 24th of July, 1847.

I was named Orson Ferguson for my uncle, before mentioned, who, at the time of my birth, was absent on a mission to the Sandwich Islands; and for my father's friend, James Ferguson. In temperament and disposition I am much like my mother, whom I also resemble in person. From her I inherited my religious nature, and a love for music, poetry, and the fine arts generally. My father gave me memory and love of books (which in him were remarkable) also music and a taste for the drama, of which he was one of Utah's earliest representatives. He was not of a spiritual turn of mind, but was honest, virtuous, and upright in all his dealings, and, though gifted above many of his fellows, was modest and retiring. Outside of his early vocation of actor, and his almost life-long clerkship in the President's Office, he had an absolute distaste for public life and official responsibility. Had he been ambitious, even to a moderate degree, he might have risen to prominence. He died November 22nd. On the other hand, my mother, who is still living, is intensely spiritual, and to her example and early teachings I owe much of what I now have of the knowledge of God and the Gospel of salvation.

My father obeyed the celestial law, or the polygamic part thereof, being the husband of three wives, viz: Helen Mar Kimball, Lucy Bloxum, and Mary Cravath. The second died before I was born, in bringing forth her first child, a son named Newel, who also died, and mother and babe were buried in one grave. Mary is the living mother of thirteen children, eleven of whom are alive and all are, or bid fair to be useful and honorable members of society.

One of my earliest recollections—I may say my earliest—was the "Move" in the spring of 1858, at the time of the entrance of Johnston's Army into the Valley. I was not then three years old, but I remember the exodus and the journey to Provo, where we resided for several months, very distinctly. Perhaps one thing that quickens my memory in relation to those early times and our sojourn in the "Garden City" was the impression left, not only on my mind, but on the back of my neck, by a shower of hot water from a dish-cloth wrung carelessly over my head by the "hired girl" while I was sitting one day on the doorstep of our humble domicile. We returned north the same summer, the War being over, and resumed life at the old homestead on City Creek. The house where I was born has long since disappeared; I know nothing of it except by tradition.

At a very early age—too early I think—I was placed at school. It was a favorite saying with my father, who was quite a scholar, that if he could leave his children nothing else, he would at least try to give them "a good common English education." This I may be said to have acquired, though I make no pretensions to scholarly attainments. I was an apt pupil, however, especially in reading, spelling, and writing, or in any other study that interested me, but in arithmetic, for which I had little liking, somewhat slower. I found myself from the first inquiring into the root and reason of things, not being satisfied with the simple *ipsi dixit* of my teacher, and because of my inability at that age to probe matters to the depths and grasp the why and wherefore, I became disgusted with some branches of study which in after years I learned to like. Anything in letters came naturally to me. At school I started in the First Reader, having mastered the alphabet and syllables at home, and when the teacher asked me where I had learned my letters, I innocently replied, "I never *did* learn 'em; I always *knew* 'em," it being my childish supposition that nothing could be "learned" out of school. I have since found that many older children are imbued with the same idea. It is my opinion, however, that the knowledge acquired *out* of school, or rather in the school of everyday life, the university of experience, is often of vastly more service to its possessor than that which colleges and academies impart. My memory in childhood was excellent. I would frequently amuse myself and amaze my fellow pupils by glancing over whole paragraphs, once, that were entirely new to me, and then, looking off the book, repeat them rapidly, word for word, without the least hesitation. Though naturally fond of fun, and prone to mischief, at times, for purely mirth-making purposes, I was generally studious and thoughtful, and at one time wore the teacher's silver medal for good conduct and attention to study. This, however, made me a target for the envy and spite of my playmates, and I soon learned to regard the wearing of the medal as a misfortune and a species of martyrdom. One of my teachers used to say, as she watched me with my eyes fixed on my book, while the boys on either side of me were laughing and playing, without once ever distracting my attention, that I had power of concentration which would be of great service to me in after life.

This teacher—one of the first I ever had—was Mary Ellen Abel Kimball, one of many wives of my grandfather, President Kimball. She taught school in a little adobe house of one room, situated on the hill near his residence, and afterwards in a new frame building erected by him for such purposes. Others of my teachers at the same place were Keziah Pratt, one of the widows of Apostle Parley P. Pratt, and Thomas Stayner, a brother to my present friends, Charles W. and Arthur Stayner. Later on, at different times and places, I attended schools kept by Huldah Barnes Kimball, another of my grandfather's wives, James Cobb, H. T.[?] Doremus, Alexander Ott, L. W. Peck, M. E. Randall, and others.

In the spring or summer of 1866, being then in my eleventh year, I was baptized and confirmed a member of The Church of Jesus Christ of Latter-day Saints. The baptism took place in a fall of City Creek, a little below the Kimball Mill, and near my mother's house. My uncle, David P. Kimball, who had but recently returned from a mission to England, officiated in the ceremony under the direction of Grandfather Kimball, a number of whose children and some others were baptized the same day. Of the month and date of my baptism I am uninformed. Charles S. Kimball, returned from England with Uncle David, informed me that they got back on the last day of the April conference. My baptism was shortly after, probably in April or May. I shall never forget the happiness that filled my heart as I realized that my sins were forgiven and washed away, and that God had accepted of me as His child. I had become, since the earlier days of my childhood, what I thought a very sinful and disobedient boy, which was probably the case, though conscience, which was ever quick within me, no doubt magnified the faults of which I knew myself to be the possessor. I was confirmed the same day that I was baptized, at Grandfather's house, under the hand of David P. and Charles S. Kimball (also a lately returned missionary), the former, I believe, being mouth [voice].

I had always evinced a fondness for elocutionary exercises and theatricals, and at Doremus's Academy in 1865; Ott's school in 1866; and at Peck's school in 1867–8, did considerable in the way of declamations, dialogues, etc. But it was not until I attended the last named school, in the seventeenth ward, that I took lessons in elocution. I once impersonated Albert, in a scene from William Tell; my teacher L. W. Peck, assuming the title role. Albert having carefully retired from the scene of danger, a literal bow and arrow were provided, with which my enthusiastic preceptor succeeded in riddling and ruining one of his best maps on the opposite wall of the school room. Those were merry happy days and many an hour did our class pleasantly spend in such sports and exercises. I was a great favorite with this teacher, who never tired of encouraging me, and predicting great things for my future. Under him I first studied grammar and book-keeping. The former became a favorite study with me, but the latter afforded me little delight, and I did not pursue it very far.

About this time I became what is termed "stage-struck." Organizing a company of amateurs, and procuring the use of the Widow Gibbs' barn, we presented the . . . border drama, "Nick of the Woods," with more startling effects, incidental and accidental, than we or the author of the play had ever dreamed of. I have written up the episode at length and published it in the *Herald* and *Contributor*. It is considered one of my best efforts in high literature.

In the summer (August 5th) of 1868, soon after the death of my grandfather Kimball, I left the parental roof for the first time—excepting a week's absence, a little while before, at my uncle William H. Kimball's in Parley's Park—and spent three months (100 days) in eastern Utah, working on the Union Pacific Railway, then in course of construction. I was in the employ of my uncle, David P. Kimball, a subcontractor, whose camp was situated, first on Sulpher Creek, then on Yellow Creek, and finally on Bear River. Quite a number of my grandfather's sons, the Kimball boys, were also members of the Camp. For the first two months I carried drinking water for the men who were working on the "dump" or grade, and during the last month drove team and scraper and helped to build the great highway, which now binds with a belt of iron the two oceans. I had my first experience in "roughing it" while absent from home at this time. From daily and hourly contact with rough men, I became almost as uncouth and semi-civilized as they were, and from a pale and delicate school-boy was transformed into a bronzed and weather-beaten urchin, with the manners and aspect of a tramp, and the strength of a young bear. At one time we were camped near Bear River City, a veritable den of wickedness, as such primitive railroad towns usually are, where all sorts of vicious and depraved characters, male and female, consorted and carried on their trades of iniquity. I frequently visited the place, but only out of curiosity, and then in the company of elder persons who exercised over me more or less of a guardian care. Though in the midst of wickedness and surrounded by the vile, I escaped unscathed, and by the blessing of God returned home as chaste, if not quite as innocent, as I went away.[4] I had learned some things that were beneficial to me, and others that were not, and had earned nearly $150.00, the largest sum of money I had ever possessed. We returned November 12th, the weather being warm in Salt Lake Valley, but where we had been it was bitterly cold. We had lived in "dug-outs" (underground huts) part of the time, they being much more comfortable than tents or wagons. While on the way home, we heard that Bear River City, the vicinity of which we had lately left, during a drunken riot and battle had been burned to ashes and many people killed. Thus perished in smoke and flame what might be termed one of the railway Sodoms of the Rockies, as wicked a place perhaps, according to its size, as the ancient doomed Cities of the Plains.

Soon after my arrival home, I was afflicted with a species of scurvy, or skin disease, contracted while away, which being neglected, and aggravated by improper treatment, kept me ill and confined to the house the greater part of the following winter.

Monday, February 8, in the year 1869, I began attending school taught by Sister M. E. Randall, in President Young's school house, but did not remain there long. I quit February 19th. The next fall I enrolled myself among the students at the University of Deseret. I little dreamed at that time that I would yet be the Chancellor of the institution, which is [illegible] at the date of this writing. I had now begun to appreciate the practical value of education, and though still fond of sport and somewhat prone to playing truant—for which propensity I hold partly responsible the fact that I was sent too early to school and wearied with its confinement while very young—made rapid progress, particularly in grammar and elocution. In the former I was second to none in the class. I won some reputation as a comic reciter, though why I can scarcely tell, as the comedy vein in my nature by no means predominates. I found myself hampered for lack of means, and unable to take the higher branches, which were extra, a fact I have often since regretted, as a classic education had been one of the dreams of my life. Poverty may sometimes be a blessing, but I could not recognize it then.

About this time, 1870, I commenced taking music lessons from Sister Lucy B. Young. I had always been musically inclined, singing and whistling from childhood for my own and other's amusement, and loved the divine art dearly, but prior to that had had no cultivation. My sister Vilate, who had also been taking music lessons of Mrs. Young, died that winter (February 5, 1970 at 8:45 p.m., aged 16 years & 9 months). We were learning to play the organ.

Young and Whitney's Minstrels, organized by myself and two of the sons of President Young, next made their appearance, and gave a performance at the President's School House, which was said to be very creditable for "the boys." I was the interlocutor, or centre man, and also sang a song, "The Little Octoroon," which I had learned while working on the railroad, and took part in the closing piece, a farcical sketch entitled, "Gissippins," borrowed by memory from Murphy and Mack's Minstrels, at the Theatre.

The University having closed (1870), during the absence of Dr. Park, its principal, in Europe, I sought for some kind of employment and secured a situation as express driver for H. B. Clawson, Supt. of Zion's Cooperative Mercantile Institution. Grooming horses and delivering goods were hardly congenial to my taste, but better far, I knew, than idleness, and I was not ashamed of honest toil.

I continued my musical practice, not upon the organ, but on the flute, my father's instrument, which I picked up at home and learned to play without a teacher.

Not being of a robust nature, or muscular frame, the work I was engaged at proved too heavy for me, and having previously suffered a severe sprain while playing at baseball, of which I was once very fond, and met with a similar accident while driving, I was obliged to seek labor of a lighter kind.

I was employed for some time as a clerk in the Produce Department of Z.C.M.I., George Teasdale, Supt, but soon resigned my place and left Z.C.M.I. altogether.

In the summer of 1872, I worked several weeks for a man named O. W. Easton, of California, who had come to Salt Lake and rented the old Kimball Mill property, and undertaken in a way of his own, as futile as original, the reduction of ores. Though energetic and persevering, he failed in his venture, and becoming discouraged, he departed secretly for the Pacific Coast, leaving his employees clamoring for their pay. This man Easton was a rank Mormon-hater. Men of his stripe generally are. It was after this that I worked for H. B. Clawson at Z.C.M.I., I believe.

It was about this time that I made my debut upon the boards of the Salt Lake Theatre, impersonating "Kit Bird" in the "Robbers of the Rocky Mountains," a dime novel dramatized by James A. McKnight, one of my youthful associates. The press spoke favorably of the performance, crude and juvenile as it was, and soon after I received and declined the offer of a regular engagement in the stock company of the Theatre, tendered by W. T. Harris, who was then manager of the house. I was very fond of the profession, but knew that my parents would be unwilling for me to embrace it. Between the acts of the performance above named, Harry Emery, one of my musical friends, and myself played a flute duet, which the papers said was well executed and quite artistic.

I next found myself a clerk in the music store of Charles W. Stayner, whose acquaintance I had formed while playing at parties; his instrument being the violin. I remained in his employment during the winter of 1872–73, and indulged my musical predilections to my heart's content. I had learned to play the guitar, and also to accompany myself in singing and whistling, on the banjo, piano and organ, all without a teacher.

On the 24th of March, 1873, I went through the House of the Lord and received my endowments, being ordained an elder the same day by William J. Smith, since a Patriarch in the Salt Lake Stake of Zion. This was my first ordination in the priesthood.

In May of the same year, in connection with Joseph O. Young, a school mate at the University, I took an agency for the Howe Sewing

Machine, from Thomas P. Miller of Salt Lake City, and travelled into Southern Utah, our agency comprising Beaver and Iron Counties. In Beaver, our headquarters, we made our home at President John R. Murdock's, whose family treated us with great kindness. I was there during the troubles with the land jumpers that year, in the fields west of the city. In the effort of the citizens, who owned the land, to dislodge the robbers, who were armed to the teeth and in possession of the property illegally seized upon, one or more of the marauders were shot and killed. The remainder, fearing a similar fate, abandoned their claim. Two lawyers named Hawley and Brown, bitter anti-Mormons, and men of little or no principle, were at the bottom of the nefarious business affair. Messrs. Hyde and Carrigan two non-Mormons commenced the publication of a paper in Beaver about this time. For some articles excoriating the land jumpers the lives of the editors were threatened, but they bravely stood their ground in defense of law and order, and the threat was unfulfilled. The editors were non-Mormons. During my absence south, I composed, one day in Beaver Canyon, my first effort in verse that I remember writing. It was a feeble attempt, and only interesting from the fact that it was the first trial my humble muse ever made of her wings. Returning north in the fall, improved in health, I travelled alone through Tooele and Davis Counties, still canvassing for the Howe Sewing Machine, but did not succeed very well, and during the winter following, quit the business in disgust, having been defrauded by various persons.

During the winter terms of 1873–74, I attended the University, which had reopened, and there my school days closed. My avocation was far from complete, so far as the sciences and the classics were concerned, but I had a pretty thorough knowledge of the common branches, and was an expert grammarian, insomuch that my tutor, Dr. Park, told me that he could teach me no more in that line, and advised me to next study rhetoric and English literature. This I have never had the opportunity of doing, except in the practical school of life, which was then opening up in all its stern and stubborn realities to my youthful view. I had connected myself with the Delta Phi and Zeta Gamma Debating Societies—concomitants of the University—but I was a slow speaker and cared very little for debate, devoting myself more to declamatory exercises and, to a limited extent, writing. I did not then dream that I would ever be regarded either as a speaker or a writer. I envied such young men as John T. Caine Jr., W. G. Snow, my half-brother Horace G., and others their fluency and facility with tongue and pen, but never deemed myself capable of emulating their excellence.

In the latter part of the winter, or early in the spring of 1874, was organized the Wasatch Literary Association, of which I was the principal founder. I was its first, and, four years later, its last president. The Wasatch had an interesting career.[5] It was a talented Society, and became the nucleus around which clustered the youth, beauty, and intellect of many well-known Mormon families, and forming a social coterie of its own. Its object was improvement in literary, musical, and dramatic exercises; an object faithfully adhered to for several years, when it degenerated into a society of mere pleasure seekers, beaus and belles, and its days were numbered. It was successful and enjoyable, but when bitter sarcasm and merciless satire took the place of good natured badinage, and the box became, as it did in many instances the vehicle of private spites and personal animosities, it came to be dreaded and feared and in the end tended no doubt to the disruption of the Society. Those Wednesday night meetings of the Wasatch are a bright spot in my memory. I derived much benefit and pleasure from our exercises and from the society of my friends, the young ladies and gentlemen composing the Association. Its organization I consider an important turning point in my career. I not only formed better associations than I had kept for several years—though my sought-out associates were never at any time bad—but I began to take more real interest in intellectual and elevating pursuits than I had ever done before.

My mind at this time was much wrought up and perplexed in relation to the choice of a profession. I saw many of my mates preparing themselves for the realities of life by setting aside its vain romances, going east to college to complete their education, marrying and settling down, or selecting and engaging in some sort of a pursuit in which to earn a livelihood. I saw that I was losing valuable time, but still I remained embarrassed and undecided. At one time I thought of devoting myself to music, for which I had evinced aptitude, but was restrained by the reflection that "music, heavenly made, was young" in our infantile community, and that musicians and professors, even the best, could scarcely earn their bread; then of studying law, but was dissuaded by my mother; and finally of becoming an actor, for which I was already pretty well prepared by study and private practice. Nearly all my friends disapproved of my choice, purely on moral grounds, without, however, suggesting any other vocation, or encouraging me in any way, and I was becoming almost desperate from suspense and indecision. I was unemployed, and no one offered to employ me. I would gladly have worked at anything, but was too diffident to push myself forward and ask for a situation; besides I was in debt and felt that everyone distrusted me. I imagined, at times, that I had not a friend in the world, and became gloomy and melancholy in consequence. My health was poor and my spirit almost broken. Those were the darkest days I have ever known. Many believed me idle from choice, which knowledge added to my torment, and I became almost mad with misery. Still I kept up my practice in elocution, mastered Bacon's manual of gesture, and went on preparing myself for the stage.

The summer my little sister Phebe died, 1874, I took part in a great Musical Tribunal at the Tabernacle, playing the flute, in the Theatre Orchestra, which appeared on this occasion, rendering the Overdue Poet and Beowulf. I had previously played the flute in the Orchestra just for practice. Professor C. J. Thomas, conductor.

During the latter part of the year 1815, just before winter set in, I went out to Bingham Canyon to try my fortunes in the mining camp. On the recommendation of S. W. Sears Esq., a relative of mine by marriage, I secured a situation as clerk in the store of I. Morris and Co., general merchants, and the low salary of $30.00 a month. I would have worked almost for nothing, so anxious was I to obtain employment, pay my debts, and close the mouths of gossips. I remained there during the winter and returned to Salt Lake early in the ensuing spring. I canvassed a short time for rubber stamps manufactured by L. Stenhouse and Co., and made good wages, but in a few weeks was again out of employment.

About this time the Decennial Philadelphian Society was organized, of which I was made the Vice President. It was a society for young men only. Its object, partly indicated by its name, was to promote brotherly feelings among its members, preserve the record of their lives, and to meet once in every ten years. Its first meeting was its last, and it soon went to pieces.

I had now firmly resolved to adopt the dramatic profession, and to leave home and go east, where I thought the prospect for a good start and regular employment was more favorable. The Salt Lake Theatre at that time was running very irregularly, and it was the only Thespian temple in the community. I was given a farewell benefit by my friends, in the Social Hall; when I impersonated "Robert McCaire" and sang and played the flute and guitar, in an olio; and had about completed my preparations for departure, when an event occurred which changed the whole current of my thoughts, turned over a new leaf in the book of my life, and formed the stepping stone to whatsoever of success I have since achieved. At the October Conference of 1976 I was called by the Church Authorities to go upon a mission to the United States.

The remainder of this chapter is taken from a previously unpublished handwritten autobiographical narrative by Whitney that he titled, "Autobiography of Orson Ferguson Whitney, written in 1885–6."

For several years I had paid little or no attention to religion, and though naturally of a spiritual turn and possessed of deep veneration, had become careless and indifferent, like many others, and had contracted a distaste for sacred things. This was due largely to the company I kept, but most of all to ignorance of the true meaning and import of religion. I had, for some reason, despite the best of teachings, come to regard meetings and sacred gatherings more as places of punishment than of instruction. I carried this aversion to such an extent that if I picked up a book and saw the word, "God" or "angel" or anything about religion in it, I would at once lay it down, as of no interest. All this time I never doubted God's existence or that I was one of His children, and would often, though not regularly, pray to Him. It was reported that I was an infidel, but this was not true; I was only reckless and disobedient. I never doubted the truth of "Mormonism," though I did not *know* it was true, and I believed that God would answer honest prayer. When quite a child, I remembered losing my knife, the first I ever had, and grieving bitterly over my misfortune. In the midst of my trouble I suddenly felt an influence of peace whispering comfort to my soul. I looked up to heaven through my tears, and it seemed as if a ray of light was resting down upon me. All at once these words of a well-known hymn, came into my mind:

> Judge not the Lord by feeble sense,
> But trust Him for His grace
> Behind a frowning providence,
> He hides a smiling face.

Where I had heard them, I know not, nor did I see clearly their relevancy at that moment, but somehow they had the effect of drying up my tears, comforting my heart, and giving me the assurance that I would regain possession of my knife. A few minutes after I walked down the path, from the house to the street gate, and there, glittering and half hidden in the dust at my feet, lay my lost treasure. This might seem trivial to some, but to me it was a God-send, and I thought then, and do now, that He who "watcheth the sparrow, and heareth the young raven when they cry," saw my childish grief, pitied me, and took this method of letting me know it, and inducing me to trust in Him.

Up to the time I was called on my mission, for several years previous, nothing seemed to prosper with me. If I got a position, it was only to lose it in a short time, and for long periods I was out of employment entirely. Being in poor health, and lacking confidence in my ability in practical matters, I forbore asking for work purely through fear of not being successful in obtaining it. As said before, I was all the time uneasy and unsettled in my mind as to what I had better choose as a regular vocation, and added to this unease was the mental torture of knowing that it was generally supposed I was idle from choice. Some of those who should have been my friends thought this, and I was too proud to deny it; at the same time I would have gladly accepted any situation offered me, or that I thought I could have had for the asking. Besides, I sought employment again and again, but could not obtain it. It was either not to be had, or people did not think me worthy of it.

As said before, I had decided on embracing the dramatic profession, and had put myself through a course of discipline—all the time that I was supposed to be indolent—to prepare myself for the stage. But one obstacle was in the way. I had not the money needed to take one to where I thought I might secure some kind of an engagement. My mother entreated me not to go, but finding me bent on it—for I was desperate, and I am not sure but I reproved her for seeking to discourage what I regarded as my forlorn hope—she finally said that, if she could sell a piece of land she had, she would give me enough money to take me away. But this she was unable to do. Everything seemed to be in the way of her disposing of that land. I began to feel discouraged.

It was now the fall of 1876, and at the October conference I was called on a mission to the States. I had no sooner signified my intention of going and fulfilling it, than plank came $150 into my hands, from the sale of my mother's property. This was to me another evidence of God's overruling providence. I had faith enough, even then, to recognize in it His all but visible hand.

There was a young man, a few years older than myself (I was 21 past) who was called to take a mission at the same time; but he asked to be excused, stating to President Young that he did not believe in "Mormonism" and would not like to feel called upon to preach it. The President readily released him and I have seen him go steadily downward from that day. He was then one of my associates, but it was not long before he dropped entirely out of the society we frequented and became one of a class I would not care to mingle with.

On the 12th of October 1876 I went to the Endowment House and stood proxy for my grandfather Newel K. Whitney, at the altar, where wives were sealed to him. Aunt Emmeline, Nella, his former wife, represented the women who were also dead, and Counselor Daniel H. Wells officiated.

The last words President Young said to me, for he died while I was away—were these: "Are you going on your mission?" "Yes, sir," I replied. "That's right," said he, grasping my hand warmly. "May the Lord bless you!"

Chapter 2

First Mission: Pennsylvania and Ohio, 1876–1878

Chapters two, three, and four consist of a previously unpublished handwritten autobiographical narrative by Whitney that he titled, "Autobiography of Orson Ferguson Whitney, written in 1885–6." *The notes contain further explanatory material from Whitney's diary that he started keeping on his first mission.*

On the 6th of November, 1876, I started on my mission to the United States, in company with Elder A. Milton Musser. I had previously been re-baptized and renewed my covenants with the Lord. My parting blessing, given me when I was ordained a Seventy and set apart for my mission, said, "You shall go in peace and return in safety," and I clung to the promise faithfully. Brother Musser left me at Council Bluffs and I went on to Chicago, where I stayed for two weeks at my cousins (Mrs. Susie Murray) and then rejoined Brother Musser in Pennsylvania.

I passed through Philadelphia at 4 a.m. and went on to Luzern County (missing the Centennial Exhibition) while my companion had preceded me. I was now among the coal mines and "Molly Maguires" (a secret society of a murderous character) in Northern Pennsylvania. The weather was bitter cold and I was very lonely. The sudden transition from society where I was so well known, to the strange world where I was scoffed at and frowned upon, and my natural melancholy disposition, made my experience for the first month cheerless and at times almost disconsolate. This was before I had learned to lean upon the Lord. I traveled the first few weeks with Elder James H. Straw, of Springville. We were surrounded by Josephites [members of the Reorganized Church of Jesus Christ of Latter-day Saints, now called the Community of Christ], whose cunning lies and captious, quarrelsome natures, full of anger and disputation, put me in a ferment whenever we met them. Brother Musser and his cousin Brother Neff had gone on down into Lancaster County.

My ignorance of the scriptures and the Gospel at first made me an easy prey—or so I thought—to the cunning and information of our opponents, particularly the Josephites, who all the time hung around us, like so many stinging insects, daring us to public discussion, especially on the subject of "polygamy." But this, instead of discouraging me, only served to rouse in me the spirit of inquiry, and I determined to know for myself whether or not plural marriage was a true doctrine, or whether my parents, who I knew were sincere, had been deceived and had taught me error, thinking it was truth. No one, I think, had ever heard me utter a disrespectful word concerning the principle, and often I had defended it when assailed, but I now realized that my attitude in favor of it was due more to tradition and lifelong familiarity with it, than to a positive knowledge of its divinity. I therefore asked the Lord in humility—for I was humble if nothing else—to give me a knowledge of whether it was true or not, and if it was to empower me to defend it successfully. I arose from prayer feeling well, and satisfied that I was heard and would be answered.

Shortly afterwards, I heard from Brother Musser that Brother Neff was sick and that either Brother Straw or myself would have to go home with him, and the other remain with Brother Musser. I secretly determined that I would be the one to remain; for going home after six weeks absence was to me more to be dreaded than a ten-year mission. So I told my companion, who had a family, and had more to draw him back than I did, that he could go so far as I was concerned, as I had no desire to. He did not seem displeased at the prospect, and accordingly went down to Lancaster, and soon after set out with Brother Neff (who was indeed *homesick*) for Utah.

I remained a day or two in Plymouth, Luzern County, and then joined Brother Musser in Lancaster. While in northern Pennsylvania I wrote some verses called "A Voice from an Absent One" and sent them to Aunt Emmeline Wells, editor of the *Exponent,* for which I sometimes wrote, to be published. While on my way from Luzern to Lancaster County, I was delayed overnight at Harrisburg and there wrote "Tis Only a Portrait," the tense of which, from present to past, I changed a year or two later.

We remained in Lancaster and the adjoining town of Strasburg until after the holidays. At the latter place we held a two or three nights discussion with a Presbyterian minister named John Wynne Martin. It happened in this wise. Having failed to obtain the free use of a public hall in Strasburg, Brother Musser, just previous to my arrival, had secured the Town Hall for one night at five dollars, the money being furnished by a gentleman who was an infidel [non-Christian], and whose name I forget. In the midst of the meeting, which was well attended, Brother Musser was interrupted by Mr. Martin, an old Scotch polemic, who disputed the doctrine advanced and dared us to discuss with him. He was politely invited up to the platform and was starting out to interrupt again, when the infidel who hired the hall for us, and who had just enough liquor in him to make him a trifle merry, shouted out from the body of the hall: "Go ahead, Mr. Musser; this is your meeting, we didn't come to hear that old duffer talk." The "old duffer" did talk, however, and the result was a public discussion was arranged for a night or two after. The Presbyterians present looked upon the coming of Mr. Martin, who was an itinerary preacher, as a godsend to put down error. We regarded him as "a ram in the thicket," sent to open up further opportunities for us to declare our message. The result justified our view, for he was most miserably put to rout and the truth again triumphed. I did little more than to carry the books to and from, and open and close the meetings, or sing, but my prayers for Brother Musser and against his opponent, I am satisfied did some good. I remember that as Mr. Martin arose to reply, I closed my eyes and prayed secretly with all my strength that he might be confounded. He had not spoken more than five minutes when, being somewhat deaf, he mistook for applause the noise of feet descending an outside stairway from some gathering in the room overhead, and to the surprise and mystification of his audience addressed them in these words: "At any other time, my friends, I would thank you, but you know it was agreed upon that no demonstrations of approval or disapproval should be permitted." The audience stared, looked at each other, grinned and snickered, and could not again be brought to order. Mr. Martin's speech was entirely lost upon them, and he disappointed and disgusted his most ardent supporters.

We strove in vain to get other opportunities to preach in Strasburg and Lancaster City, and after a short stay in the latter town, and preaching in one or two suburban places, we moved to Columbia in the same county and took a room in a private tenement house. We here issued some tracts and preached at one or two small towns in the neighborhood. While here, I read a book owned by Brother Musser called the "History and Philosophy of Marriage, or Polygamy and Monogamy Compared." The perusal of this book did more to enlighten me upon the subject of which it treated than any work I had ever seen, and it went far toward convincing me of the rightfulness of plural marriage. The Spirit of the Lord did the rest, and I became, and have ever since remained, a firm believer in the divinity of the doctrine, as preached and practiced by The Church of Jesus Christ of Latter-day Saints. Thus was my prayer answered, my mind convinced, and my testimony obtained. I saw many reasons to sustain it, not only from the scriptures, but from reason and daily observation.

During my residence in Columbia, I went down to Washington D.C. and spent two weeks in the nation's capital. I visited Mt. Vernon, the former home and burial place of George Washington, the Halls of Congress, Smithsonian Institute, and other points of interest, and sat one forenoon in the House of Representatives, occupying by his invitation the seat of Hon. George Q. Cannon, Utah's delegate to Congress. This was February 8th, 1877. On the night of the 11th I heard Dr. Newman at the Metropolitan M. E. Church, on "Jerusalem," the last of a series of lectures on the "buried cities of the world." I had previously heard him in Salt Lake City, in the Pratt-Newman polygamy debate. He was the same foppish, conceited pedant as ever. On the 16th in company with Bros. George Q.

Cannon, A. M. Musser, Henry Groesbeck, and John Q. Cannon, I visited the White House, but did not see President [Ulysses S.] Grant or any of his family. He was not to be seen often as he was busy getting ready to vacate for his successor. I returned to Columbia, PA., from Washington, a few days before the inauguration of President Hayes.

I now wrote my first newspaper letter, descriptive of sights and scenes in and about Washington, and sent it to the *Salt Lake Herald*, over the *nom de plume* of "Iago," my old soubriquet in the Wasatch Literary Association. I previously dispatched a note to Byron Groo, editor of that paper, asking if he would publish my correspondence, so little confidence had I that it was worth printing. I was proud to receive an affirmative reply, thanking me for the proposition, which to me was not only complimentary but encouraging. My first "Iago" letter was written March 14, 1877, and I kept up my *Herald* correspondence at intervals until I returned home. The letters were popular, and my success surprised no one more than myself. I began to cherish dreams of literary life. In fact I was becoming more interested in this than in my missionary labors. One night, or rather early in the morning I dreamed as follows.

I thought I was in the garden of Gethsemane. I saw the Savior and his Apostles, Peter, James, and John, enter from the direction to my right, and, leaving them there in a group, praying, He passed to the other side and also knelt down. He seemed to be in great mental distress and His face, which was turned towards me, was streaming with tears. He prayed to the Father, "Let this cup pass from me; nevertheless, Thy will, and not mine, be done." Finishing, He arose and crossing to where His Apostles were, shook them—for they had fallen asleep—and rousing them up, reproved them for neglecting to watch and pray. He then returned to his former place and, kneeling down, prayed again. Unseen of them I watched their movements from behind a tree. My heart was so full of sympathy for Jesus and His sorrow that I wept in unison with Him and my whole soul, as if melted, went out to Him. Pretty soon He arose and beckoning his companions to him, seemed about to take His departure. The whole circumstance of the dream then changed, though the scene remained the same. The only difference was in time; instead of before the Crucifixion, it was after, and the Son of God, having made the sacrifice required, was about to go to the Father, taking the three disciples with Him. I could stand it no longer, and rushing out from my concealment, fell down at His feet, clasped Him about the knees, and begged Him to take me with Him also. He gazed upon me with inexpressible tenderness, then stooped and lifted me up into His arms and embraced me with all the affection of a father or an elder brother. I could feel the beating of His heart and the warmth of His bosom against mine. With a voice full of sweetness and compassion, slowly swaying His head in denial, he said, "No, my son; your work is not finished yet. These have done their work and they can go with me, but you must stay and finish yours." These words uttered in all kindness only made me more anxious to go, though I did not repeat my request, but clinging to Him I besought Him further, "Well, promise me that I will come to You hereafter." Again he shook his head and sadly and sweetly said, "That will depend entirely on yourself." I awoke with a sob, and it was morning.

I was profoundly impressed and related the dream to Brother Musser. He told me it was from the Lord. Of this I had no doubt, for the lesson it taught was full of wisdom and warning, and it was stamped upon my mind eternally. I could not forget it, and hope I shall always profit by its instruction.

On April 8, 1877, I bade Brother Musser adieu and left Columbia for Ohio, where I had friends and relatives whom I desired to visit. I arrived in Elyria, Lorain County, Ohio, on the following day, and walked from there about three miles into the country to the farm of Truman Frink, who, with his wife, had been to Utah several years before. I had met them repeatedly at my mother's. They were members of the Church and very excellent people, and received me very kindly. Sister Angie Frink was a woman of great faith. She was especially glad to see me, not only on account of her friendship for my parents and her (?) to the faith, but because a neighbor of hers Mrs. Margaret Frink, wife of Truman's brother, and her daughter, Mrs. Emma Kirkbride, were investigating "Mormonism," and were anxious to hear it preached by an Elder from Utah.

Here was my first real trial. Hitherto, I had had Brother Musser to lean upon. Now I must lean entirely upon the Lord. My faith almost failed me, and when Sister Frink proposed to throw open her house and call in the neighbors for me to preach to them, the first thing I thought of was to send for Brother Musser. But he, alas, was far away, and a second thought convinced me that it was now or never with me, and I must gird up my loins, trust in the Lord, and face the music for myself. How I ever got through that meeting, or what it was I said, I do not know. Sister Frink, kind soul, said it was "splendid," and those present seemed well satisfied. I knew that a power not mine had helped me, for I was humble as a child, and as weak as one, and threw myself entirely upon the Lord. I spoke upon the first principles of the Gospel, and so far from having nothing to say, I had more than I could find words for and that too with my words falling like the patter of the rain. I preached several times in the neighborhood soon after, in meetinghouses and schoolhouses, and was always blessed in speaking.

My next trial was on the 24th of April, a few weeks after coming to the Frink Farm. I was called on to administer to Mrs. Margaret Frink, who had been suffering constant pain from neuralgia for several weeks, and was almost worn out with it. Her husband, Eli Frink, was a bitter hater of the "Mormons" and a foul-spoken fellow. I felt timid about going to his house, not only on his account for I was sensitive to a word of unkindness, but I doubted my own faith, and I trembled over the probable failure of theirs (Mrs. Frink and daughter) if the "signs" did not "follow" and she was not healed. I did not doubt the Lord's power, but I doubted that I was worthy to be its medium. However, I had faith enough to try, and having prayed with all my soul to my Heavenly Father I started with Sister Frink and her husband for their sister-in-law's house. We were met at the door by Mrs. Kirkbride, and shown into a room to the right of the hallway, where the sick woman lay. The coarse laughter of Eli Frink and his vulgar associates could be heard from the other side of the house. Fearing every moment that they would come into the room, but praying fervently in secret that they might not be permitted to do so, I proceeded to anoint the head and face of the sick woman with the holy oil which had (?). I then placed my hands upon her head, and what I then said I scarcely know. I sealed the anointing and rebuked the disease in the name of Jesus Christ, and

I remember that the moment I began to speak a power fell upon me which till then I had never felt. A burning sensation, not painful but almost oppressive in its intensity, filled my bosom, almost depriving one of speech, and ran like fire to the very tips of my fingers. I recognized the power of the Holy Ghost, and that I was right was proven a moment later when, "Amen" having been spoken Mrs. Frink exclaimed, "Thank God the pain is gone!" My joy and gratitude I cannot express. Tears welled to my eyes. I knew that the Lord was with me and had answered my prayers.[1] Many persons were healed after this under my administration.[2] My faith grew stronger daily, and I rejoiced in the God of my salvation.

On the 26th of April I started for Kirtland, Lake County, on a visit to my relatives—the Whitneys. I had written while in Pennsylvania to "Uncle Sam," my grandfather's brother, a Methodist minister, asking him what kind of a reception I might expect if I visited him, as I was "a Mormon to the backbone." He replied that I would be "welcome to the hospitality of his house," that he was "always glad to see his relations, and cared nothing about their religion." I accordingly set out for Kirtland via Cleveland. Next day I went on to Willoughby and lighting from the train walked from there to Uncle Sam's place, three or four miles in the country. I reached there early in the evening and was kindly received. Next day Uncle Sam took me in his buggy to Kirtland Flats, a few miles from his house, and showed me the temple, Gilbert and Whitney's old store, my grandfather's former residence, and other old landmarks. Uncle Sam habitually referred to Grandfather as "N. K." and though differing from us on religion, seemed to have a high opinion of him. A day or two after my arrival he took me down to Mentor Plains, where his son, S. F. Whitney Jr., and his daughter Susan Whitney Talbot resided. Both families made me very welcome and I stayed there several weeks. Cousin Nellie, Samuel Jr.'s daughter, and Fred his son, were congenial spirits in everything but religion, and we became mutually much attached. Fred and Nellie accompanied me to visit the temple, then in the hands of the Josephites. Afterwards I wrote a description of Kirtland and the temple for the *Herald*. While there I called on Guy Smith, a cousin of my father's, and other old-time acquaintances of my family, who received me with marked courtesy.

Having returned to the Frink farm, on the 28th of May, 1877, I baptized Emma Hamlin Kirkbride and her mother, Margaret Fowles Frink. The latter was the same one who was healed by the power of God, as related heretofore. The baptisms took place in Lake Erie, some miles from the Frink farm, and were the first I had ever performed. I shall never forget the joy I experienced that day. The Spirit of the Lord rested upon me, and my heart was melted by its influence, and I wept for joy and happiness.

On the 18th of June I received a letter from President Brigham Young, formally releasing me from the Pennsylvania District, over which Elder Henry Grow presided, and appointed me to labor in Ohio, under the presidency of Elder David M. Stuart, in St. Louis.[3] On the 3rd of July I received another letter from President Young, who had noticed my writings in the *Herald* at home, inviting me to correspond with the *Deseret News*, and giving me much valuable advice.[4] He especially urged me to cultivate my "gift for writing," that I might "use it in the establishment of truth and righteousness upon the earth." This advice I cherished, and formed the determination to devote myself to literature, instead of the drama, a choice I have never since regretted.[5]

On the first of August, I started for Akron, Summit County to visit a family by the name of Sharp, residing in the suburbs of that town. Luke Sharp, the head of the family, had written to President Young asking if there was an elder anywhere in his vicinity as he wanted to be baptized. This letter was sent to me from Utah, and I answered it. The result was this visit. I reached their place, about two miles from Akron, among the coal mines, early in the evening, having walked from town, and was kindly received by Mrs. Sharp, who with her children was at home, but her husband absent at his work in the mines. On his return he told me his story. He was a Scotchman and some fourteen years before, in his native country, was a member of the Church. He quarreled with his branch or conference president and became a back-slider. He did not know that he was ever cut off, but both he and his wife wandered away and came to America. He now wanted to renew his covenants and come back into the Church. His wife, while she too had some faith, was less eager, being of a jealous turn of mind and afraid of polygamy.

She, however, was praying for a testimony. The children, mostly girls, were almost converted, and most of them ready for baptism.

The next day, I baptized Luke Sharp, his daughters Celia and Joanna, and his sons William John, Luke Jr., and John. On the day following, Eliza, his other grown daughter, was baptized by me, and the day after their mother, Barbara Edgar Sharp, submitted to baptism. That same evening, August 4, I preached in a school house nearby and had a good audience and the best attention. The next day I preached in the afternoon and at night held a sacrament meeting at Brother Sharp's house and blessed his children, Barbara Ann and George, who, with a married daughter living some distance away, were the only ones of the family I had not baptized. The two children were not old enough, and the married daughter did not know of the opportunity offered, though she also believed in the Gospel.

On August 6th I returned to Elyria, and found the feeling very bitter against me on account of the baptisms I had performed.[6] Eli Frink was the main instigator and said and did all he could to my detriment in his false and malicious way. I heard of many threats to "tar and feather" me, but was not molested. A letter from a young man named Charles M. King, in Springfield, was awaiting me when I returned to Sister Frink's. He said he was searching for information on the "Mormons" from reliable sources. I wrote to him, sending "Spencer's Letters" for him to read. He answered and seemed much interested, and was on the point of coming to me to be baptized, but something turned him and I never heard from him afterwards. He did not even return the book I had lent him and I was forced to the conclusion that he was either dead or dishonest.

On the 30th of August I received a visit from Mrs. Dr. Chester, or Norton, with whom I had been corresponding for some time. She was an intelligent woman and a skillful M.D. Her ideas of marital relations corresponding, she said, with those of our Church. She had addressed a letter to President Young, asking him what chances there were among our people for her to practice her profession. She believed "polygamy" to be the natural marriage system, and that infanticide, feticide, etc., were crimes. She said that cherishing such views had made her unpopular where she resided—Warren Trumbull Co.—and she wished to live among those who could sympathize with her. Her letter to the President was sent to me, and I answered it. Arriving at Frink's on the date above named, she brought with her from Elyria a paper containing the sad tidings of the death of President Young. He died at Salt Lake City, Utah, on the 29th of August, 1877, at one minute past 4 p.m.[7] The death of our great and noble leader, and my personal friend, naturally filled us with sadness, but I had learned to take a stoical or "Mormon" view of such things and bore up with patience and resignation to the Lord's will.[8]

Dr. Chester remained at the Frink farm about a week, and on the 6th of September I baptized her. On the same day Brother Truman Frink and his wife renewed their covenants and were rebaptized.[9]

The feeling in the neighborhood had grown more bitter against me, and Eli Frink had done all he could to intensify it. When the news came of the death of President Young, he cut up all the capers of a madman. Assisted by a boy named Clarence Perkins, he procured a brush and some black paint and daubed upon the fences: "Brigham Young is dead; glory to God!" He also hung crape upon his doorknob in mockery. I was walking up the road one day, reflecting, when I heard a voice from one of the yards to my right, exclaim, "Mormon son of a b----h!" I turned and saw Clarence Perkins dart behind a wood shed near his mother's house. I was angry in an instant, but controlled myself and passed on. A younger brother of Clarence was lying ill at the time but was improving and it was thought he would recover. From that day, however, he grew steadily worse, and within a few days died of lockjaw. I know not whether it was a judgment, but Sister Frink thought so. The boy's mother was one who tried to induce a number of young men to mob me. As for Eli Frink, he was stricken down with rheumatic paralysis, and became a worse wreck than ever.

On the 7th of September I started on my second visit to Mentor Plains and Kirtland. Dr. Chester accompanying me as far as Cleveland. Arriving at Mentor at 6 o'clock p.m. and no one from Kirtland being there to meet me, as I had expected, I turned in the direction of "the Plains," and walked the 2½ miles to cousin Samuel's in the rain. I passed on the way the farm of General Garfield, which adjoined that of Cousin's. Arriving at the Whitney farm after dark, I was warmly welcomed by the family. I remained there six weeks, making a number of pleasant acquaintances, and visiting Cleveland, Painesville, and other places. While there I wrote "Lakeside Musings," the first poem of any particular merit that had come from my pen. It was pretty generally admired and I received various compliments. During my stay at the Plains, I visited Painesville and heard General Garfield in a political oration, and in Cleveland attended the Northern Ohio Methodist Conference and heard Bishop Mathew Simpson preach. Also heard Hon. Alfonzo Taft and Gen. Geo. Sheridan at a Republican mass meeting one evening. These last two events were on the 15th and 16th of September, respectively.

On October 10th, I visited Cleveland again and stayed most of the time at Henry Martyn's, a cousin of my father's, No. 62 Cross St. I attended the Woman's Congress on the above date and heard several noted women speak. At one of the sessions I met Mrs. Mandane North, Cousin Nellie's aunt, whom I had before met at the Plains, and at her invitation went home with her to dinner. There I met Mrs. May Van Camp, a widowed lady, young and intelligent, who afterward became very much interested in "Mormonism."

I returned in a few days to Mentor Plains, but on the 19th of October left there for Kirtland, Nellie's mother taking me there in her carriage. I had borne testimony to my relatives of the truth of Mormonism, but, while treating me very kindly they had rejected my warning message. In Kirtland I stopped at my father's cousins, Guy Smith, where I was kindly treated at first, but it did not last long. His wife behaved very rudely to me one occasion particularly, and grossly insulted me for daring to have an opinion of my own on politics and religion. While there I preached in the Kirtland Town Hall and was asked to preach again. I gave out an appointment for the Monday following—November 5th (October 29th was the other date) and in the meantime visited Uncle Sam's. On the 5th I walked to Kirtland to fill my appointment, but got wet through in a drenching rain, and it was too stormy for anyone to come out to hear me. I stayed overnight at Cousin Guy's and next day walked back to Uncle Sam's. During this visit to Kirtland I gathered the inspiration for my poem "The Land of Shinehah," which I commenced soon after returning to Elyria.

On November 19th I revisited Cleveland and witnessed Edwin Booth in Hamlet. It was the finest piece of acting I had ever seen.

Next evening I heard Mrs. Van Colt, the noted woman preacher, at a Methodist revival meeting, and on Wednesday the 21st attended a lecture by Wendell Phillips on "Woman—Labor—Temperance." Revisiting Mr. and Mrs. Worth I bore them and Mrs. Van Camp a strong testimony and bade them farewell. Mrs. V. C. was a convert to "Mormonism" through my preaching, but although she had said that if she could be convinced of its truth she would be baptized "if it was in a lake of living fire," when it came to the test, the sacrifice was more than she could make and she receded. We parted the best of friends, however, and she insisted on keeping the book I had lent her—"Orson Pratt's Works"—and has it to this day. Having bade my friends and relations in Cleveland, Kirtland, and Mentor Plains good-bye, on December 3rd I returned to Lorain County and was once more an inmate of the hospitable home of Brother and Sister Frink.

The feelings against me had abated some and I began to form acquaintances and make friends in the neighborhood.

On the 24th of December a man named John Good called at the Frink farm, on his way to Elyria to obtain some medicine. He had suffered much from a pain in his head, which the doctors said would eventually kill him, and was suffering from it then. Sister Frink asked him why he did not "get Orson to administer to him." He answered rather lightly, but seeing she was in earnest and having heard something of such things, he finally consented for her to ask me. I was called down from upstairs, where I was writing, and after we had prayed I anointed his head and administered to him. He arose and left the house and went home without saying a word. Sister Frink said he was as white as a ghost. A week later he came by and told Sister Frink that he had been healed and had had no pain since but begged her not to tell anyone lest he should be laughed at and ridiculed. Notwithstanding such a testimony, he would not be baptized.[10] During this month—December—I wrote the "Land of Shinehah."

January 5, 1878, I left Elyria for Akron, having been sent for by Brother Luke Sharp, who was in trouble. His daughter Joanna had eloped with a Chinaman and he had threatened to kill the heathen and his folks, taking sides with the latter, they had had a general family quarrel. On my arrival I found matters in a little better state, and did what I could to make peace all round. A day or two later Sister Sharp related to me the following: the night previous to my first arrival at her house while she was about getting into bed—all the family but her having retired—a tall shadow crossed the window curtain on the opposite side of the room. She had not yet put out the light, so that she discerned it distinctly, and feeling somewhat alarmed, she turned to her husband who was lying in bed and asked him to get up as there was someone in the house. He made light of her fear and said she was nervous as he had locked all the doors and none of the family were awake but themselves. She allowed herself to be persuaded and was just on the point of blowing out the light when the shadow again fell upon the curtain and crossed to her left. This time she saw it distinctly in the centre of the room, and it (the figure) threw its shadow upon the curtain.

To use her own words, "I felt very timorous. Having recently lost my baby, the thought flashed across my mind that this was a warning of my death also, and I thought must I die too and leave all my children? Then I remembered how I had prayed for a testimony of the truth of 'Mormonism' and I thought perhaps this is sent to me for that purpose. While thinking in this strain and trembling at the strange sight before me, the figure spoke: 'Sister Sharp, Mormonism is true, and you must be baptized for the remission of your sins, or you cannot enter the kingdom of God.' Then it went away. I made my husband get up and look all over the house, but he found no one, the doors were fastened, and all the family but ourselves were sound asleep. If I had seen what I did on awaking from sleep or if I had been dull and drowsy I would have given up that it was all in my imagination. But I had not been asleep and was wide awake and I saw and heard it with my own eyes and ears. I told Luke what I had heard. He had not heard it, but he finally believed it and said, 'Mormonism is true, and we will both be happier if we go back into the Church.' We then went to sleep, fully determined to join the Church once more, and praying the Lord to send one of his servants to baptize us." Sister Sharp said that the first words I spoke to her on my arrival next day, startled her by the similarity of tone to that of the figure which had appeared to and addressed her the night before.

The next day, as narrated, I baptized most of the family, but Sister Sharp was so afraid of the water and so nervous that it was decided to postpone it in her case until the following Sunday at mid-day. That same night, she said, she had another visitation and was told by the same messenger that she could not enter God's kingdom unless she was baptized. The next day her husband said, "Perhaps you had better wait till Brother Whitney comes again," but she answered, "No, I may not live till then, I must be baptized this time or not at all." Next day she was baptized. She also told me that the night previous to my arrival there on my second visit she saw the same shadow cross the room, but it did not frighten her a particle. She simply said to herself, "Brother Whitney's coming."

On Sunday, January 13th, in the afternoon, I preached to an attentive audience in Thomastown, not far away, and at night held forth in Sodom or Pleasant Valley, to another good hearing. This was the first time I had ever preached twice the same day. I walked back to Brother Sharp's, a distance of several miles, and was very tired and worn, but full of satisfaction that I had done a good day's work. While on this visit I interviewed Joanna's Chinese husband. She still adhered to the faith, but he, having secured her, did not care for her religion, and would not be baptized. A number of the neighbors, among them a miner named Thomas Bell were favorably disposed to the Truth, but did not care for some reason to take up the Cross of the Master.

On the sixteenth of that month I baptized Agnes Sharp Reese, Brother Sharp's married daughter, and blessed her three children. Her husband, suspecting her intention, had threatened to kill her if she was baptized, but she took advantage of his absence from home this day to come over to her mother's and have it done. The day was bitter cold and the water all but frozen over. I had laid aside me garments, having but the one pair with me, and deeming it wiser to put them on dry after changing my wet clothes, than to keep them on and have to dry them afterwards. As I walked into the water I could scarcely suppress an exclamation of pain, the water was so cold. I could grit my teeth and bear it, but I was afraid Agnes would not be able to, and standing there I offered up a silent prayer that the Lord would temper the water. All of a sudden it seemed to grow milder, almost warm, and I baptized Sister Reese without any difficulty. I am inclined to believe that instead of the water getting warmer, I was given strength to withstand it, but it was all the same to me; my prayer was answered and I gave God the glory. As soon as I reached the bank, I was seized with a pain in my left elbow. I recognized rheumatism, the first symptom I had ever felt. All that day it grew worse, and I began to reproach myself for leaving off my garments. At night I put some liniment upon my arm and went to bed hoping it would soon be well. It had not occurred to me that I could administer to myself, and in my ignorance I refrained from using holy oil as I ought to have done. I was amply repaid and taught a lesson I shall never forget, for the next day my arm was still worse. That evening I humbled myself before the Lord, and having great faith that the pain which had seized me had no business there, as it was while doing my duty that it came upon me, I carefully washed off the liniment, and having anointed my sore arm with consecrated oil I rebuked the pain in the name of the Lord Jesus Christ. As I turned to kneel down and pray before getting into bed, I found to my surprise the pain had gone, my stiff elbow was once more freely in use, and the soreness had all but left it. Next morning it was well. This manifestation, I need not say, greatly comforted me and strengthened my testimony.[11]

On Friday, January 18th, I left Akron and returned to Brother Frink's in Lorain County. A nephew of his, who had come from Missouri and was stopping there, became convinced of the truth of Mormonism during my absence in Akron, and in much the same way, according to his story, as Sister Sharp did.

On January 25th, I attended a lecture in Elyria given by John B. Gough. It was entitled "Blunders" and embodied a savage and brutal attack on "Mormonism," altogether unprovoked. It was the worst blunder, Mr. Gough will find, that he probably ever made.

About this time I received a letter from Mrs. Van Camp, inviting me to come to Cleveland and pay her a visit. She praised my poem, "Lakeside Musings," I having sent her one of a number of printed slips sent me from home by Aunt Em Wells. Nellie, my cousin, had also written me in relation to it, saying that her aunt Mrs. North had shown the copy given her to Mr. Adams, a noted lawyer of Cleveland, who said it was equal to Tennyson or Longfellow, and asked her permission to copy it. Aunt Em wrote me from Salt Lake, sending the slips and complimenting me on my "success as a poet." This was all very flattering, and I wish I had only deserved it.

On the second of February I visited Cleveland, and while there went with Mrs. Van Camp to visit a sick girl, Miss Timmins, who was bedridden from a severe burn received some time before. Her life was despaired of, but she recovered, and Mrs. Van Camp believed it was the prayer offered for her that saved her life. She accepted it as a testimony and was about to be baptized, but weakened and wept and said the sacrifice of friends, home, and social position was more than she could make. She still clung to the faith in her feelings, though, and said she hoped the time would come when she could enter the kingdom and call me "brother." I sympathized with her for she was an intelligent, noble soul, and sincerely believed in the Gospel. She had received an offer of marriage from Andrew Timmins, brother to the girl who was healed, but whether she finally accepted him and they were married I never learned, thought that she did is very probable. I talked to him on religion, but found him a worldling [uninterested], and could make no impression upon him.

On the seventh of February, I returned to the Frink farm, which was my home and headquarters, and on the 13th heard the celebrated Mendelssohn Quintette Club, of Boston, at a concert in Elyria.

On Saturday, March 16th, I received a letter from President John Taylor informing me that I was honorably released from my mission and at liberty to return home as soon as circumstances would justify.[12] On the 19th I left on a farewell visit to my relatives and friends in Kirtland, Mentor Plains, and Cleveland, and having seen and bid them all good-bye, returned to Brother Frink's on the 23rd. On the 26th I baptized in Black River Charles David Frink, and Mary Moulder Frink, the latter an adopted daughter of Sister Angie's. We held our last sacrament meeting together on the afternoon of the 27th and enjoyed much of the Spirit of the Lord.

On the 28th of March I bade the Saints farewell and amid much weeping and sadness at parting and started for Elyria, where I took the evening train for the west, homeward bound.

Before leaving I had finished a poem entitled the "Women of the Everlasting Covenant," which I afterwards published with the "Land of Shinehah."

I reached Salt Lake on the evening of April first, and thus finished my first mission as a servant of the Lord Jesus Christ, the experience of which was to me of untold value.[13]

Orson F. Whitney, an actor at the Salt Lake Theater (USU).

Zina Beal Smoot (USU)

Chapter 3

Employment, Bishopric, Courtship, and Marriage, 1878–1881

Continuing from Whitney's handwritten autobiographical manuscript.

Soon after my return I was asked by Bishop L. D. Young if I would act as a teacher in the 18th ward. I told him I would, and was accordingly sustained as a teacher of that ward. I was also appointed a home missionary and began laboring in that capacity. I had greatly desired and prayed that I might be kept in the harness of my religion, and not be permitted to go back into the old groove I had left, and thus my prayer was answered.[1]

Another thing that troubled me was the fear of becoming idle again, which I dreaded, and I had prayed before leaving Ohio that I might be able to find employment as soon as possible after reaching home. I had scarcely set foot upon my native city's soil when I was offered the position of local editor of the *Salt Lake Herald*, for which I had written while away. At first delighted with the idea, I soon had my spirits dampened by the thought that it would be night work, (the *Herald* being a morning paper) and consequently unhealthy; and as my physical condition was far from rugged already, I shrank in my feelings from endangering it still more. Besides I knew it would occupy my Sabbaths, which I wished to devote especially to the Lord. These reflections caused me such uneasiness, and even sadness, that I resolved to decline the *Herald's* offer and seek for a situation on the *Deseret News*. There was no opening there, but through faith and prayer and the kindly offices of Apostle Brigham Young and others I was foisted into a place in the business department, which I held until I succeeded Brother John Nicholson as city editor of that journal.[2]

On the 14th of July, 1878, the Bishopric of the 18th ward was reorganized, owing to the resignation of Bishop Young, and I was chosen to succeed him in that office. I was ordained a High Priest and set apart by President Daniel H. Wells. Apostles George Q. Cannon, Brigham Young, Pres. Angus M. Cannon and other Elders were present.[3] It was in President Young's school house, then used as a meeting house by the 18th ward. I was thunderstruck when I heard my name called. I had jokingly said to an acquaintance while on my way to meeting, in reply to an invitation to step into his room, "I must go to the meeting; they are going to put me in [the] bishopric tonight." But I did not dream that I was predicting a fact. I was so young, having just turned 23, and being unmarried, I had not the remotest idea of the choice falling upon me. My counselors were Robert Patrick and William B. Barton. *The new Bishop did not choose his own counselors.* I was too young and inexperienced, I suppose, to be entrusted with that responsibility.[4] *Though Orson chose to ignore the problems that developed with his counselors in his published autobiography, he soon learned that one of them especially would become a periodic strain in their bishopric.*

On the tenth of August I assumed the duties of local editor of the *Deseret News*, Brother John Nicholson, who held the position, having been called to go to England on a mission.[5] John Q. Cannon succeeded me on January 3, 1879, and I was appointed to go east as a business agent for the paper.

At this time, Ort's social life blossomed and, among other young women, he began actively dating Minerva Edmeresa Richards (1858–1936), a daughter of Franklin D. Richards of the Quorum of the Twelve. On the first of January, 1879, Orson wrote: Spent this New Year's in Farmington, Davis County, Utah. Took dinner with Miss M. E. R., an excellent young lady, whom to know is to admire. Attended ball in the evening.

I got all ready to go, but the Authorities decided not to send anyone east, and I was instructed to travel through the Territory instead.[6] Before leaving, I helped to bring out at the "Social Hall," a juvenile operetta, written by my brother Horace G. and myself, and performed by the children of the 18th ward Sunday School. It was a success and was performed three times to crowded houses.

On the seventh of February, I started on a business trip through the northern counties, in the interests of the *Deseret News*.[7] At Ogden I was offered an editor's chair on the *Junction*, but declined it.[8] I continued on through Weber County and Box Elder into Cache Valley, meeting with success and gaining subscribers for the *News* in Mendon, Wellsville, Paradise, Hyrum, Millville, Providence, and Logan. At Hyrum I made the acquaintance of Bishop Liljenquist, who gave me my first patriarchal blessing.[9] I had been feeling very sad and downhearted. Being in poor health, I had felt for some time that I was going to die soon and was very much depressed in mind. The Patriarch at first hesitated when I asked him for a blessing, and shaking his head said half smiling, half grimly, "Bishop and Patriarch don't go very well together." He told me, however, to come and see him next day and he would see if he had a blessing for me. At the appointed hour I went to his house. He met me with a smile and looking at me very earnestly said, "Brother Whitney, I have been wrestling with the Lord all night. I regard your coming as an admonition to me to magnify my patriarchal priesthood. I have turned so many away empty-handed who have come to me for blessings. I have been praying to the Lord, and there is a blessing for you." He then placed his hands upon my head and gave me a marvelous blessing.[10]

All of which, said the Patriarch, as he took his hands from my head, "I am just as sure will come to pass as though it had already occurred. It passed before me like a vision; and in greater detail than I have given it, but the Spirit prompted me to use general terms, covering it all, without being more explicit." Brother Liljenquist never sees me but he alludes to it. Just before leaving for Europe, on my second mission, in the fall of 1881, he met me on the streets of Salt Lake City and said, "Well, you're going on a mission?" "Yes sir," I answered. "Yes, and you will go on many of them," he rejoined, impressively. I have since been told by two persons that he said to them that the blessing he had pronounced upon me would lead to high honor and authority in the Church. God knoweth.

Ort continued courting Minerva, whom he referred to as M. E. R. and Nerva: March 4, 1879, Logan: Received letter from Nerva. Transacted some business for the *Deseret News, and* March 10, 1879: After breakfast, returned to Logan. Received letter from Nerva. Answered it. *On his return, Orson spent most of his evenings with Minerva.*

Returning to Salt Lake, after visiting and holding meetings in most of the settlements of Cache Valley, I resumed the position of local editor on the *Deseret News*, Tuesday, March 25, 1879.[11] I was repeatedly offered the editorial chair of the *Ogden Junction*, about this time.[12] During my trip up north I wrote a little poem called "The Voices" and dedicated it to Aunt Emmeline B. Wells. On the 7th of May following "A Second Daniel" inscribed to General Daniel H. Wells (imprisoned for refusing to reveal in open court the secrets of the Endowment House) appeared in the *News.*

That spring proved to be a very busy and emotional time for Orson's social life. He continued actively courting Minerva, but he also desired to be sealed to a deceased daughter of Daniel H. Wells, named Emma Wells, who had passed away a year previously.[13] Because Orson did not keep a journal before his first mission, we know little detail about their relationship, except that he considered her his girlfriend. It is apparent that Orson had deep feelings for her, feelings so strong that he wanted Emma to be sealed to him (by proxy) as his "priority" wife.[14] Minerva did not care for that arrangement and let him know it was over. May 20, 1879: Received letter from Nerva. She has weakened on the matter of Emma Wells's priority. Wrote to her declaring my affection for Emma, and releasing her from everything." *Then*, May 21, 1879: [I] Am feeling miserable and wretched, because I am the cause of unhappiness to another.

In the meantime, Orson had seen and taken notice of Zina Beal Smoot (daughter of President Abraham O. Smoot, a stake president and former mayor of Provo), and was in the same social group as May (or Mary) Wells, another daughter of Daniel H. Wells.[15] (He would later marry both Zina and May.) Within a day of breaking up with Minerva, he gave a priesthood blessing to a boyhood friend with Diphtheria who died the next day.[16]

In order for Orson to be sealed to Emma Wells, he had to get her parent's permission. April 21, 1879: Busy day in the office. Decided on going to Provo in the morning. . . . At night had a long talk with Aunt Emmeline B. Wells about Emma [Wells]. Asked her for Emma. She asked time for reflection.

With Minerva no longer in the picture, Orson dated several other girls, but Zina Smoot quickly became his priority. April 22, 1879: Took the 7 a.m. train for Provo. Arrived at 10 a.m. and proceeded at once to the Academy. Met Susa [Young Gates], Professor [Karl G.] Maeser, Hardy, et al. Spent the evening at Zina Smoot's singing, playing, etc. *And* April 23, 1879: Attended the Academy again. . . . In the evening, walked on the hill with a party of 7: . . . Zina Smoot and myself. Attended a social at the Academy. Zina looks prettier every time that I see her.

Zina Beal Smoot Whitney (USU)

Orson had not spent long pining for Minerva,[17] *but he was operating under a different paradigm than eligible bachelors would be after the 1890s. We cannot know how much he thought about it at this time, but he could consider the option of plural marriage—he was not restricted to one wife, and this may be why he became friendly with a number of eligible young women, both before and after his first marriage. He courted in an environment where he did not have to "lock his heart" against all others besides his eventual wife.*

Orson's courtship with Zina picked up immediately. June 15, 1879: Heard that A. O. Smoot and two of his children are in town. Zina said she was coming in her letter. *Then*, June 17, 1879: Arose early—could not sleep. Walked downtown. Zina went back to Provo this a.m. . . . Went home and slept, slept, slept. *And*, June 20, 1879: Took the 7 o'clock Train for Provo. Attended the Academy exercises. Also Zina—Sad! I'm wholly gone. . . . Took dinner at Zina's. Made a few calls. Spent the afternoon at Zina's. Went to dance in the Academy. *With his quick wit, ready social skills, phenomenal memory for recitation and poetry, ability to play various musical instruments and whistle, and not to mention his position as bishop, Orson was the life of the party, the quintessential catch. His options were many, but his eye was increasingly fixed on Zina. The relationship deepened:*

> June 23, 1879: Bade Zina good-bye. Wrote in her book.
>
> June 25, 1879: Found a letter from Zina on my desk at the office. Was surprised and blessed. . . . Answered Zina's letter.
>
> June 28, 1879: Sent portrait to Zina.
>
> July 1, 1879: Received letter from Zina. I am 24 years old today. Answered Z[ina]'s letter, dating it July 2.
>
> July 4, 1879: Arose early and after breakfast went to the depot and took the 7 o'clock train for Provo. . . . Met Zina and asked her to go to the party—"Certainly." Had an excellent time at the ball.
>
> July 5, 1879: Asked Zina to go walking tomorrow. "Certainly."
>
> July 6, 1879: After breakfast, Zina and I walked up to Grave's Gardens. Sat under the trees and I read "Out of the Question" to her. Returned to the house about 2:30 p.m. Got a mild reprimand and a good dinner. Stayed and whistled for the folks.

Perhaps it was because he was spending so much time in social activities and pursuit that the first signs of trouble showed with his counselors. June 24, 1879: Was warned against my counselors. *Although the reasons for this entry are not clear, later entries indicate that Orson did not get along very well with his first counselor, Robert Patrick.*

Early in July I began writing for the *Contributor*, a magazine established, edited, and published by Junius F. Wells. Also contributed articles to the *Salt Lake Herald*, such as dramatic reviews, etc. On September 25th I published the "Land of Shinehah" and distributed it among my friends. It was well received, and gained me some reputation as a poet. Soon after I had it republished with the "Women of the Everlasting Covenant."

By the end of the month, Orson and Zina had fallen in love. July 27, 1879: Zina loves me and our betrothal was sealed this night. *Yet there was still the matter of his love for the deceased Emma Wells to be settled.* July 28, 1879: Went with Zina over to Maggie's and returning, went over to the orchard to get some apples. Sat under the trees and conversed. Zina said she would marry me before New Year's. Asked me to see her father about it. She consented to Emma's right of precedence. Returned to dinner. She gave me a picture of herself. *Zina had done what Minerva would not in regard to Emma, but permission was still needed.* July 29, 1879: Spoke to Aunt Em about Emma's being sealed to me. She will see Bro. Wells [her husband] about it. *Ort's diaries do not then indicate whether consent was received, although the entry for July 13, 1888, strongly suggests it was not. The marriage to Zina moved forward anyway.* December 10, 1879: Saw Aunt Em about arrangements for my wedding. Wrote to Zina concerning the same.

On Thursday, December 18, 1879 I married Zina Beal Smoot, of Provo, daughter of Abraham O. Smoot, President of Utah Stake, and his second wife Emily Smoot. The ceremony took place in the Endowment House, Counselor Daniel H. Wells officiating.[18]

On the second Monday in February, 1880, I was elected a city councilor and held the office until the expiration of my two-year term, before which, however, I had started on a mission to Europe.

On April 1st, 1880, the Home Dramatic Club, of Salt Lake City, was organized, with myself as President. Its career was very successful, and during the next eighteen months much of my time was devoted to the stage. My last appearance on the stage was in "The Green Lanes of England" in October 1883, after my return from Europe. I then renounced the stage forever, finding that I could not do justice to my bishopric and my spiritual duties if I devoted any time to the drama.

Orson F. Whitney and Zina Beal Smoot Whitney, ca. 1879 (USU).

On the 24th of July, 1880, a grand celebration took place in the Tabernacle, Salt Lake City, preceded by a magnificent procession, commemorative of Pioneer Day and the Fiftieth Anniversary of the Church—the Year of Jubilee. I was appointed by the Committee of Arrangements to write a poem for the occasion, and the result was "The Jubilee of Zion," which was read at the celebration by the Col. David McKenzie. It was published in the city papers and in a pamphlet containing the day's proceedings, at the time, and afterwards in an amplified form in the "Woman's Exponent." This poem brought me still further into public notice.

On the 27th of October 1880, my wife gave birth to a son, our first child, whom we named Horace Newel Whitney, after my father and Grandfather Whitney. He was blessed and christened by President Joseph E. Taylor on the evening of November 4th, being then eight days old. I afterwards blessed him at fast meeting, myself.

On the 26th of June, 1881, I was appointed by the General Committee on Arrangements for the celebration of the 4th of July, to be orator of the day. President George Q. Cannon, chairman of the Committee, called at my house the next day, notified me of my appointment, and gave me some valuable advice in relation to preparing the oration. I felt very grateful for the counsel, as the task seemed a stupendous one to my un-experienced mind, and set about fulfilling it with a humble and prayerful heart. The Lord blessed me, and my oration, being completed, was accepted by the Committee. All was in readiness for the celebration when the horrible news of the assassination of President Garfield flashed over the wires on the 2nd of July. This put a stop to all the preparations and the city joined with the nation in mourning. It had been designed to celebrate the day in grand style at Liberty Park, which was to be christened at the same time. But man proposes and God disposes. Thus was my first oration "still-born."

On the 13th of September, 1881, I was informed by President Joseph F. Smith that it had been decided to send me on a mission to Europe, to succeed Elder Chas. W. Stayner as subeditor of the *Millennial Star*, at Liverpool. I had heard rumors of this for some weeks, and was not surprised when notified that it had been finally determined. President Smith gave me his blessing and best wishes.

I announced myself as ready to go and do my duty, as best I could, and as the Lord should give me strength. It was left to me to set the day for my departure and I named November 1st as the time for sailing per *S.S. Arizona* from New York.

On the 30th of September, I severed my connection with the *Deseret News* upon which I had been employed as city editor since August 10, 1878.

October 8th, 1881, in General Conference, I was formally called to go upon a mission to Great Britain, and on the 10th of that month was set apart by President Wilford Woodruff and Apostles F. D. Richards and Moses Thatcher, the first named being mouth.

On October 11th I received a patriarchal blessing under the hands of Patriarch William J. Smith, of Salt Lake City. The Patriarch has since told me that it was the greatest blessing he had ever pronounced upon any man. It certainly was a great comfort to me, corroborating as it did my former blessing, and buoyed me up mightily for the mission I was about to undertake. I have lived to see much of it fulfilled, and that it will all be, if I am faithful and do my part, I have not the shadow of doubt. "Be humble, Brother Orson," the Patriarch has often since said to me, "and you will be high enough."

Three days after receiving this blessing, I visited Provo with my wife for the purpose of bidding our relatives there good-bye, and on the evening of October 16th, I received another [patriarchal] blessing under the hands of my father-in-law, Patriarch Abraham O. Smoot.

After pronouncing the blessing, Father Smoot told me that if there was anything else I wanted I had only to mention it, but it seemed to me that his blessing covered every desire of my heart. I was again struck with the magnitude of the promises made to me, and marveled greatly that one so weak and undeserving should be thought worthy of so many and such mighty blessings as were those mentioned.

On the evening of Sunday, October 23rd, I preached my farewell discourse in the 18th ward meetinghouse (President Young's old school house). There was a large attendance and the Lord blessed me in delivering my testimony to them. After the meeting many of my friends assembled at my mother's house, where I was staying, and took final leave of me, wishing me success and prosperity on my mission.

Chapter 4

Second Mission: London and Liverpool, 1881–1883

Continued from Whitney's handwritten autobiographical manuscript.

I left for the east after a tearful parting with my wife and child, father, mother, brothers, sisters, and other relatives and friends. I was accompanied by Elders John Pickett, John T. Rich, and Joseph W. McMurrin, missionaries like myself. Also by a Mrs. Johnson and child, returning to England from a visit to relatives in Salt Lake. We reached New York Saturday morning, October 27th and registered at the Stevens House. After calling on Church Agent James H. Hart and writing letters home, I visited James Dwyer and his daughter Ada, who were at the Grand Central. We went to Booth's Theatre at night and saw Edwin Booth as "Shylock" and as "Petruchio." Next day, with the Dwyers, who were Salt Lake acquaintances, and a Mr. Horseman, of Brooklyn, I drove to Coney Island and for the first time gazed upon the ocean. It was a grand sight and one that impressed me deeply. Monday morning, I went with Agent Hart to buy my ticket to Liverpool and hose of my party. There was but one first cabin passage left on the *Arizona*, and it was with difficulty that even it was secured. I wanted it for Mrs. Johnson, but this was impracticable as it was in a room already secured by three men, and mine was the fourth or last berth. Besides, Mr. Gibson, agent of the Guion S.S. Line, stipulated that I use it personally and not transfer it to someone he had not seen. Thus it was that I was separated from my party, who took second cabin passage to Liverpool. I wrote a letter to the *Salt Lake Herald* over my old *nom de plume* of "Iago," and that evening took supper with Brother Hart at the Grand Central, and afterwards went to see the comedians, Harrigan and Hart, in a piece called, I believe, "The Major."

Tuesday, November 1, 1881, at 1:05 p.m., we steamed out of New York Harbor and in due time were on the broad, rolling bosom of the Atlantic. I experienced that common and terrible malady know as "sea-sickness" soon after luncheon, and after partial relief by means of the usual process, returned to my berth where I remained till next day. I need not go into details. Suffice it that the voyage, though rendered disagreeable by my sickness, the results of which were loss of appetite and a failure of physical strength, was prosperous and furnished an interesting and valuable experience. The sunlit cliffs of Old Ireland were sighted, early on the morning of the 9th and at about 4 p.m. the *Arizona* anchored off Queenstown, sent her mailbags ashore, and then steamed on toward Liverpool.

Elder Whitney did not know at the time that upon arriving at his appointed mission field of labor, he walked into an invisible hornet's nest that would try his soul to the utmost but would also strengthen and stretch him in ways he had never known. The European Mission was then troubled by strands of strange doctrine that entangled some of the elders (including Orson) and was presided over by a morally corrupt man holding the apostleship. The mission experience would affect Orson for both good and ill for two decades and would powerfully influence the course of his future. Some seeds were planted in him that he should not have cultivated; other seeds flourished within him in such marvelous manner that he eventually became perhaps the most accomplished man in the Church, in some respects.

Arising early on the morning of the 10th, I found to my joy that my sea-sickness had entirely disappeared though I was still very weak. For the first time I took breakfast in the cabin and enjoyed it very well. The vessel had anchored below the "Bar" waiting for the turn of the tide to carry her into port. At 10:40 a.m. we resumed our course up the Channel and entered the Mersey and one hour later were opposite the docks, and the steam tug from the shore came alongside. On board were Elders Charles W. Stayner, his wife, and Brother C. B. Felt from the Liverpool Office, 42 Islington, who had kindly come to meet us. I need not say the meeting was a cordial one. It was the next thing to home to see such friendly and familiar faces. After landing and reaching "42," I met President Albert Carrington, Brother R. R. Anderson, and others.

Mrs. Johnson had been met by her father and taken home to Waterloo, a small town a few miles from Liverpool. The brethren who came with me were assigned to their respective fields of labor the same day or the day following, but at the advice of the friends at "42" I remained there a few days to recover my strength. President Carrington asked me to what part of the mission I would like to be assigned, as it was the advice of the Authorities at home that I be permitted to spend a few months in the ministry, to get generally acquainted with affairs before assuming literary labors in the Office. Secretly, I desired to go to London where my friend, Elder John Q. Cannon, was laboring. I forbore saying so, however, and replied, "Just wherever you see fit to send me, Brother Carrington; I am entirely under your direction." Again he asked me to choose, and again I respectfully declined. "Well, will the London Conference suit you?" he finally asked. "Yes, sir," I replied eagerly, and thus the matter was then settled.

Albert Carrington (USHS)

On the following Sabbath, November 13th, I attended the

meetings of the Liverpool branch and addressed the Saints and visitors there briefly.

I had taken a cold on landing, and as it grew worse I became concerned and began to fear that the predictions of my friends at home, that I would not be able to withstand the English climate, might be realized. I remembered, however, the promises of the Patriarchs to me, and especially the words of Patriarch W. J. Smith, after he had done blessing me. Said he, "Don't you mind what they say about your health failing you. Go right along; trust in the Lord, and you will be all right. You are a lively spirit; there's no death in you; you will live to reap all these promises." I sought the Lord and reminded Him of these words, and asked Him to heal me. That was the last of my illness. My system gradually became acclimated, my lungs grew stronger, and I experienced no difficulty in discharging the duties incumbent upon me. While in Liverpool I made the acquaintance of Elder John Donaldson, President of the Liverpool Conference, a resident of Mendon, Cache Co., Utah. We became fast friends.

November 18th, 1881. After finishing and mailing my second letter to the *Herald* and other correspondence to the folks at home, I bade the friends at Liverpool good-bye and took the 11 a.m. train at Lime Street Station for London. The train pulled into Euston Station at 4 p.m. and I was met by "John Q." [Cannon] to whom I had written beforehand. We were mutually overjoyed at seeing each other after his absence from home of over three months. He took me to the Conference House at 23 Dorinda Street (off Bride Street, Liverpool Road, Islington) and introduced me to Elder John Cooper, President of the London Conference. I slept that night at the house of Brother George Cross, 22 Mt. Pleasant, Cold Bath Square, Clerkenwell; like Islington, one of the suburbs of London City proper. The next morning "John Q." called and took me out to show me the sights, which greatly interested me and gave me material for several newspaper letters. The next day, being Sunday, I attended the meetings of the North London branch and spoke at each time, in the evening about an hour.

The day following—November 21—I was appointed by President Cooper to labor in connection with Elder Newton Farr in the Whitechapel Branch, which took in the east end of the city and was probably at the time the largest, though not the most prosperous, district in the City. There were but three in all—the North London, the Whitechapel, and the Lambeth branches. Brother Farr and I attended a meeting of the Saints in Old Ford that evening at the house of a Sister Todd, where we each spoke a little while, and then went to a Bro. Spillman's in Stepney, where we stayed overnight. The next morning we called at the residence of Brother Joseph Atkinson, 19 Mile End Road, where we were asked to stay to dinner. They were a peculiar but interesting family, and treated us very kindly. They took an especial liking to me and I was always welcome to come and stay as I pleased.

The Joseph and Emma Atkinson family would become a subject of interest in Elder Whitney's diary and a looming presence in his routine mission life. He censored his diary, removing the most detailed references to them, and especially to their sixteen-year-old daughter Bertha, or "Dolly," as she was commonly called.[1] *He left in enough comment that an intriguing but incomplete story emerges. Orson's 1930 self-published life story briefly refers to the family, but it leaves out the drama of his infatuation.*[2]

I was now fairly launched upon the regular, or irregular routine of missionary labor. I preached and visited a great deal, and the Lord raised up friends to me on all sides. I was welcome wherever I went, and never wanted for anything that kind hearts and ready hands could provide for my comfort.

In December 1881, having become acquainted with Dolly Atkinson, Elder Whitney began showing an increased romantic interest in her. He found himself at their home often, blurring the line between fellowshipping and socializing. Dolly was not baptized and her parents were less active members. December 15, 1881: I . . . then called at Atkinson's. Did some writing and conversed with Dolly and her mother. . . . Recited [poems]. They were delighted. Remained there till nearly 2 a.m., and was asked to stay all night. Did so. Had my shoes repaired free of cost. *The day after Christmas:* In the evening we took the train for Aldgate and from there walked to Atkinson's, where we found Bro. Farr and a goodly company assembled. Spent the night singing, playing, reciting, dancing, games, [illegible], etc., etc. and left at 8:30 a.m. for "23." *The actions of these missionaries should not be compared to modern times with mission rule handbooks, strict hours, and companionships; such did not exist then. Even while on his mission, Orson lived with the possibility that he could secure a plural wife, and it seems that he tried with Dolly.*

One morning my companion, Elder Newton Farr, related a dream to me that he had had during the night, and asked me to interpret it. It was as follows: He thought he was standing with John Q. Cannon and myself upon a bridge. We were all leaning over the railing or curb at the side, looking down upon some men in the channel below, who seemed to diving after wounded ducks in the water. Just then a load of hay, on top of which was John Cooper, the President of the London Conference, crossed over the bridge. Cooper, seeing us, instead of driving to the other side of the bridge to avoid running over us, made directly for us with the remark: "I've got you now just where I want you." He drove so close that, to save ourselves, we got over the railing and leaned over the abyss, clinging only with our hands and feet. The wagon went by and we feared our knuckles would be skinned by the hubs, but only the hay scratched our fingers and the wagon passed on and we regained our places unhurt.

I interpreted the dream to mean that our [London Conference] President was jealous of our influence among the Saints, and would yet use his authority over us to remove us from the Conference. The bridge was the London Conference. The men in the channel were elders preaching the Gospel and baptizing. The wounded ducks were converted souls. The load of hay was President Cooper's office and authority and his remark, "I've got you now just where I want you," indicated the use he would make of it against us.

The dream was fulfilled to the letter. He did all he could to annoy us and lessen our usefulness; in fact so jealous did he become and so evident did it appear, that it was the common talk throughout the branches. The Saints became disgusted with him, and the more he tried to injure us the more his influence decreased, and ours increased. He was full of egotism and vanity, and also vulgar in his language and conduct. Some of the Saints were talking of leaving the Church, and other converts hesitated to join, on his account. It finally reached President Carrington's ears and he resolved to release him and send him home as soon as practicable, which he did.

This experience, though very disagreeable and painful, did me no harm. My influence increased rapidly with the people, and the Lord blessed me abundantly in preaching. One old lady told me "the mantle of Orson Pratt had fallen on me." Compliments were showered upon me from every hand, until it became almost tiresome to listen. I felt grateful to the Lord for it all, realizing, that He, not I, was the cause of the favor shown me, and strove to be humble and do my best to merit His great goodness.

Elder Whitney magnified his talent as an orator and public speaker. January 16, 1882: Spent the day at Atkinson's and in the evening attended a meeting at Old Ford. Spoke with more force than ever. The Lord's Spirit was upon me powerfully. There were strangers [non–Latter-day Saints] present. *As Elder Whitney's prominence and influence grew, the compliments and praise increased as well. He seldom neglected to record the accolades he received after speaking. Such may be the single most common notations in his diaries to the month of his death. He may have self-deprecatingly written that they got old, but in truth he never tired of them and often felt justified and enlivened by them. At the same time, his facility behind the pulpit was likely equaled by no one in the mission, so his local fame as a preacher and speaker spread, thereby enabling him to do much good and bear powerful testimony.* January 29, 1882: Stayed in the house till evening, reading and reflecting upon scripture. Attended night meeting in Whitechapel; spoke most of the time. My discourse was upon the Restoration and gathering. The Spirit of the Lord was upon me powerfully. Sister Widpin told me afterwards that the "mantle of Orson Pratt" had fallen upon me. Others highly complimented the sermon. Here as well as in North London it is the same. My preaching is much liked.[3] The Lord is blessing me according to the promises of my patriarchal blessings.[4]

Meanwhile, at home in Salt Lake City, Orson's wife, Zina, missed him terribly and also dealt with pregnancy and depression. Her letters to Orson occasionally voiced her struggles and tribulations. January 28, 1882: Received note . . . enclosing letter from Zina—a most unhappy one, full of gloom and foreboding. It made me very unhappy but I prayed and then answered it. Still my heart aches for my poor, lonely, suffering wife. Would to heaven I could see her for an hour! I can stand my separation from her well enough, but the thought that she is miserable nearly unmans me, and "I could play the woman with mine eyes." God bless and comfort her! She is with child and says she has a strong presentiment that she will not live through her confinement [pregnancy]. Prayed for her and then answered her letter, giving her all the comfort I could. God will do the rest.

The Atkinson family, especially Dolly, received his continued attentions. February 7, 1882: I went to Atkinson's. Remained there all night. Had a long talk with Sister Atkinson. She thinks a great deal of me. So do her husband and children. In fact, the Lord raises me up friends wherever I go. But we all have our likes or favorites, and the Atkinsons are among them. They are intelligent and musical, as well as kindhearted. *Meanwhile, Elder Cooper, the conference president, seemed to be making an effort to gain Orson's favor.* February 9, 1882: Cooper and I went home with Sister Godfrey and stayed all night. Cooper is "making up" to me for some purpose. He is a very shallow and deceitful being, more and more distasteful to me every day. *As he said, Orson had his likes and dislikes.*

President Carrington arrived in London and gave Cooper the transfer assignments. February 20, 1882: Found John Q. [Cannon] in. Remained with him till evening. Cooper came, having seen Pres. Carrington onto the train and off for Liverpool. He told us the program of changes as follows: I am to go to Liverpool in about a month, as Stayner leaves on the first ship. April 12th, John Q. goes to Germany about that time to relieve his brother Abram [Abraham H. Cannon] in Bremen. Farr goes home on the second ship, about the last of May. Will King, my old rival for Zina, takes John Q. Cannon's place in the office. Thus is Farr's dream completely fulfilled. Cooper no doubt inspired the changes. But mine is quite agreeable to me. I dislike to part with John and my London friends but then the parting must come sooner or later, and I am not at all sorry to leave Cooper's society. He, it is very evident, is equally or even more glad to get rid of me. He even offers to pay my fare to Liverpool. I know one thing, however, that I have won his ill will simply by winning the good will of the Saints over whom he presides, and therefore am well contented. It is mere jealousy—"only this and nothing more." John Q. and I attended the Old Ford meeting. . . . I went to Sister Godfrey's. She tells me that Cooper told Bro. Carrington I was waiting and ready to be called to Liverpool. The latter had then said he was glad of it and would send C. W. Stayner home on the first ship. Brother Carrington, it appears, had been waiting for me to manifest my desires in this respect. This I have not done, so Cooper kindly did it for me.

February 22, 1882: Farr called at Atkinson's for me. Dolly asked me to baptize her before I go to Liverpool. Told her to get her father and mother ready also and the three could be done together. *Orson was realizing that he would soon be parted from Dolly and had done some planning of his own, though following through with it would prove difficult.* February 26, 1882: Dolly is becoming a beautiful girl. I can't help but be interested in her. Her mother is determined she shall never marry, however, and eyes very jealously anyone who approaches Dolly. The latter [Dolly] however will yet have something to say on the point of matrimony, and her mother's efforts to place barriers in the way will only defeat her own object. Whoever gets Dolly will get a nice little wife anyhow. *Not long after this,* March 6, 1882: Found my photographs had arrived. Gave one to Dolly. She says she will write to me when I get to Liverpool. It will be good practice for her.

Sunday, March 12, 1882: I baptized Bertha [Dolly] Atkinson and re-baptized her father and mother, Joseph and Emma Atkinson, in the Pentonville Baths, North London. The same day and at the same place I was re-baptized by Elder John Q. Cannon, and he by me. We were reconfirmed in meeting the same evening, he being mouth in my case. *Almost two pages were cut from the handwritten autobiography at this point.*

On Saturday, two days later, Elder John Q. Cannon left England for Germany. Brother Farr had been released to return home, and I was summoned to Liverpool to succeed Elder C. W. Stayner in the "Star" Office. These changes, I suspected, and afterwards learned as a fact, though all in contemplation, were hastened by President Cooper through misinformation, harmless but annoying, volunteered to the President of the Mission who was made to believe he was consulting our wishes in the premises. This was true in one sense. We were all willing enough to get out from under Cooper's jurisdiction, though sorry to part with each other. Thus we were pushed off the "bridge," and yet clung to it and were unharmed by the "load of hay," which passed on and was seen no more. Brother Cooper's subsequent lot of obscurity, after being sent home in the May Company, a subordinate, whereas he had boasted that he was being "kept for Captain of the big June Company" of emigrating Saints, fulfilled the dream of Brother Farr still more completely.

Elder Donaldson, president of the Liverpool Conference, came to visit his new friend Elder Whitney in London. During this visit, Orson learned that Charles W. Stayner, working as a sub-editor at the mission office on the Millennial Star, *claimed great prophetic revelatory powers.* March 16, 1882: Elders John Q. [Cannon], Donaldson, Jones and Farr called on me . . . Donaldson, whom I like very much, told me many things of Brother Stayner, his revelations, etc. Donaldson believes in him. *Orson was being introduced to some doubtful matters that he would grapple with for many years to come.*

On Sunday, March 20th, I preached my farewell discourse in the Whitechapel meeting hall, the largest one in the London Conference, and took affectionate leave of the congregation to which I had become so much attached. Brother Donaldson also spoke some of the time. After meeting we spent the evening at Brother Atkinson's and at Brother Donaldson's suggestion I reconfirmed Bertha, or "Dolly" as she was called, and added a blessing thereto, the confirmation at the meeting by one of the local elder's having been faulty and improperly worded.

The next morning, having taken leave of my many kind friends in London, I took the noon train at Euston Station for Liverpool, accompanied by Brothers John Donaldson and Wm. R. Jones Jr., who were returning to their field of labor, the Liverpool Conference. We reached our destination at 5 p.m. and I was warmly welcomed by the brethren at the office. Robert R. Anderson, the chief clerk, speaking of a poem I had written in London, and which had been published in the *Star* and in the *Woman's Exponent* at home, said it was one of the grandest things of the kind that he had ever read. To my utter amazement he told me that even President Carrington, who cared little or nothing for poetry, had said it was one of the few poems that he liked. The piece referred to was the "Poet's Prayer."

I commenced at once assisting Brother Stayner on the "Star" and began my first editorial: "What Is the Use of Religion?"

At this point another page and a half are removed from Whitney's mission autobiographical review. However, vague as they are, his diary entries fill in for some of the missing material. Ort became immersed in the prophetic claims of Charles W. Stayner and his belief in reincarnation, or what was sometimes referred to as multiple probations for one spirit:

> March 22, 1882: In the afternoon, went with Bro. Donaldson to the Lime St. station to see him off for Newton. He told me something very interesting pertaining to myself, but enjoined strict secrecy.
>
> March 23, 1882: In the evening had a long conversation with Bro. C. W. Stayner. He told me many things about himself, how he became possessed of the gift of revelation, etc.
>
> March 24, 1882: In the evening spent some time with Bro. Stayner in his room where he read me several of his revelations. I am praying for a testimony of their truth.
>
> March 25, 1882: Received letter from Bro. Farr, London, in which he told me some things of interest about the London Saints: the Atkinsons, Larkins, Roberts, etc., and of Dolly. Spent the evening in Bro. Stayner's room.

On Sunday, March 26th, by invitation of President Carrington, Brothers Stayner, Felt, and myself went with him to Manchester to attend a conference. The meetings were held in the Hulme Town Hall. There we met President Moroni Brown, President Donaldson, Elder Ben E. Rich, and quite a number of others. After the elders had made their reports, Brother Donaldson used the residue of the time of the morning meeting. In the afternoon I was the sixth speaker, but had not spoken long before I was interrupted by a man in the body of the house, who denied the truth of my testimony [that] Joseph Smith was [a] prophet of God. I continued without noticing him, President Brown having left the stand and taken a seat in the congregation just behind my interrupter and he was warned to be quiet. In a few minutes, however, he broke out again with

"You're a liar," and other insulting language. Brother Brown then seized him by the collar and lifted him out of his seat and carried him, kicking and struggling, out of the hall. The meeting was now in an uproar, the fellow having many sympathizers who objected to his being handled so roughly, and others taking our side and justifying his ejection as perfectly right and proper. The man was a Spiritualist. He had come to the meeting purposely to disturb it. While he was being put out he drew a loaded club, or "billy," and tried to hit Elder Brown over the head with it. It was wrenched from his grasp, however, and he was afterwards fined heavily for attempting to use it. A bit of British justice. After I had ceased speaking, the meeting hav[ing] quieted down without any further disturbance, Brother Stayner and President Carrington addressed the congregation. The latter was the only speaker at the evening meeting, which was quiet and orderly. We returned to Liverpool the same night by train. *Part of a page is missing from Whitney's account here.*

Wednesday, the 12th of April, 1882, was the day set for the sailing of the first company of the season's emigration taking away Brother and Sister Stayner and Brother Donaldson, in whose society I had spent so many happy hours. *Another page missing here.*

Orson discussed Stayner and his doctrines with a new missionary. April 13, 1882: Talked a while with Bro. Ormsby. He is strangely interested in what I have told him. We prayed and he asked me to administer to and bless him. Did so. *The next day Elder Whitney wrote to Zina and Dolly, and not long afterward he received a birthday card from Dolly. The two had decided to keep up a correspondence, secret from her mother.*[5]

I entered upon my literary work with great zest, and was much interested in making the "Star" shine as brightly as possible. I had the entire work to perform, writing the editorials and selecting or furnishing the other matter as well. The weekly editorial I always read to President Carrington the nominal editor, but that, aside from the "releases and appointments" of missionaries, was the extent of his labor upon the journal. I also prepared the matter of the *Journal of Discourses*, read the proofs, etc., the same as for the "Star." My labors, which were very congenial, and in which I felt abundantly blessed of the Lord, were varied from time to time by visits to some of the conferences, either on invitation of President Carrington or the Elder presiding over the Conference, and occasionally an open air meeting in the streets or in the parks. The Spirit of God would often rest upon me powerfully and under its influence I felt that I could roar like a lion and soar like an eagle.[6]

On May 2, Orson wrote a long letter to President Joseph F. Smith. The content of this letter is partially known from President Smith's reply. Elder Whitney was troubled by a thoughtless and unkind remark about him traced to President Smith, which reached his ears through a mutual friend. Orson wrote asking for clarification (really an apology) and received it expressed in humble terms and sincere goodwill. After apologizing, President Smith wrote: "We will regard each other as brothers. I may be the eldest, but you the most favored, by stature and opportunity. I boast of no gifts but those of an honest heart and an earnest and humble desire for the triumph of God's great latter-day work. You have all this and rare gifts of mind and tongue besides. God give you the strength and wisdom, Bro. Orson, forever to use your talents and all the gifts of God within you for the salvation of man, in the . . . channels which He has dictated." *Evidently Elder Whitney also referenced the subject of "congeniality of spirits," since President Smith also wrote:* "I heartily endorse your sentiments respecting congeniality of spirits. Our knowledge of persons and things before we came here, combined with the divinity awakened within our souls, thru obedience to the gospel, powerfully affect, in my opinion, all our likes and dislikes, and guides our preferences in the course of this life, provided we give careful heed to the admonitions of the Spirit." *The letter continued on with an explanation of the Atonement and seeking to become like our heavenly parents by obedience to the Gospel.*[7]

On Sunday afternoon, May 14th, I preached in Wavertree Park, the first open air meeting I ever attended. Elder C. B. Felt and a number of the Saints of the Liverpool Branch were with me. We had a moderate-sized hearing, and quiet and respectful attention. The following Sabbath, however, we were insulted and abused and our meeting brought to an untimely close. Brother Felt was the first speaker and was interrupted by a man who, I was told, belonged to the Baptist Church, and was a chronic disturber of "Mormon" meetings. He first bribed the policeman in charge of the grounds to move off to where we could not appeal for protection, and then he commenced the disturbance. He said: "Are you Mormons?" "If you are we don't want to hear you." "Why don't you preach Mormonism?" etc., etc. I told Brother Felt to proceed and not notice him at all. This made the fellow angry and he became more vociferous and abusive. A gentleman and lady took up on our side and urged him to be quiet. Just then, three or four other men commenced on us, and polygamy. "How many wives have you got?" "Tell us about the five wives." "One wife's enough." and other cries of like character resounded through the crowd. Not one word had been said of polygamy by us, but this was the unfair method adopted by our Christian friends, for they were preachers and church members, to stifle freedom of speech and prejudice the crowd against us. When Brother Felt had ceased speaking I addressed the multitude, which had grown considerably since the services commenced, and by appealing to their patriotism, fair play, and sense of justice [I] succeeded in awakening some sympathy, and the mobocrats were for a few moments quelled. But as soon as I began speaking upon the principles of the Gospel, they renewed the clamor and we were compelled to close the meeting and leave the Park, followed by the taunts and jeers and insulting remarks of our persecutors. That evening I addressed the Saints in our regular meeting hall in Oldham Street, and being well-wrought up from the event of the afternoon, I enjoyed much freedom and power.[8]

Matters related to the Atkinsons: Dolly and her mother continued to haunt Elder Whitney's thoughts. He received a letter from Sister Emma Atkinson inviting him to stay with her family again. He spent time visiting with a missionary serving in London, discussing the situation. Evidently Sister Atkinson was causing some kind of trouble among local Latter-day Saints.[9] *One evening, Orson* dreamed of Zina and Dolly. Thought the latter [Dolly] went home with me. *Orson was becoming infatuated and determined to make an attempt to secure Dolly for himself. On an early June trip to London, Elder Whitney recorded:* I then called at Atkinson's and after talking with Dolly and her father I went downstairs and tried to take a nap. Could not sleep but reposed. Arose and prayed, asking the Lord for an opportunity to tell Dolly my feelings torward her. Her mother watches us like a lynx. Attended evening meeting and on returning, lo! Dolly and I were left behind together and my prayer was answered. I told her what I had learned about our mutual destiny. She seemed pleased. I told her I loved her and she said she did me, etc. Spent the evening at her house, and slept at [the] Larkins.[10] *What Orson meant about their "mutual destiny" is not explained, but it probably meant he believed she would become his plural wife. Matters became worse after his visit.* June 21, 1882: Got a note from Brother West. A mess in London. Sister Atkinson is rampant worse than ever, and Sister Larkin does not deliver my [secret] letters to Dolly. All right, or it will be sometime. I shall not bother my head about it. *Whether Elder Whitney realized his part in the mess is unclear. Because of the pages missing from the manuscript, much detail is unrecoverable. During all this time he continued receiving letters from and writing to Zina, other friends, and relatives, and he occasionally corresponded with Charles W. Stayner.*

Tuesday, June 20th, I received a letter from my mother, informing me that Zina, my wife, had given birth on the third of that month to a fine boy, our second child. He was named Heber Kimball Whitney, agreeably to my suggestion in case the anticipated birth should be that of a boy.

During the summer I visited London several times, attended conferences and other meetings there, both in and out of doors, and also conferences and district meetings in Nottingham, Birmingham, Derby, Bury, Merthyr Tydfil (Wales), and later on the Leeds Conference, besides visiting various towns and villages adjacent to Liverpool.

In September, Elder Whitney received the aforementioned answering letter from President Joseph F. Smith. Orson was again able to visit London and see Dolly, but the full extent of their relationship is not known. In mid-October he received a letter from Dolly containing her photograph.[11]

In early November a new group of missionaries arrived at Liverpool, one of them bringing a welcome gift and news from home: S.S. Wyoming arrived bringing 49 missionaries from Utah, in charge, George C. Lambert. He had for me two parcels—one a case containing likenesses of my babies—and another with album, having my wife and several other portraits. They were a very welcome gift from my darling wife. George informs me that Apostle John Henry Smith is on the way to Liverpool to succeed President Carrington. He also tells me that the two apostles chosen to fill the vacancies in the present quorum are Heber J. Grant and George Teasdale, amen! The Lord's will be done.[12]

On the night of Saturday, November 11th, 1882, I had the following dream: I was in the Tabernacle or Assembly Hall, Salt Lake City, on the occasion of a conference or some other large meeting. I had taken an obscure seat in the body of the hall, where I could hear but could not see the speakers. The chair I had taken was an easy one, working upon a spring and pivot, enabling one to turn round or lean backward very readily. There were several such chairs around me, each placed at the end of a long bench. I had not sat for many minutes when Brother C. W. Penrose, chief editor of the *Deseret News*, came up to me and invited me to take a seat at the reporter's table, in sight of the stand, but still on the lower floor of the building. The request seemed to be seconded by Brother John Nicholson, the local editor, who appeared in the background. I complied therefore and leaving my easy chair went forward to the table, where I was given a hard, rough seat, half bench, half chair, much less comfortable than the one I had left. I mentally drew the contrast, but took the seat nevertheless. I had no sooner touched it when President John Taylor, who had entered the building, passed by and tapping me on the shoulder, said, "Brother Whitney, come up into the stand." He then passed on and I arose to follow. I felt greatly embarrassed, every eye being upon me, and was weak and half-dazed as I ascended the flight of steps leading to the President's stand. I took hold of the railing several times to keep from falling. Finally I got there and was waved to a seat at the President's right hand. He then said to me, "Brother Whitney, announce to this congregation that I will occupy the afternoon in speaking." I arose to comply, and was again seized with trembling and dizziness. Everything seemed shaky and unsteady also, and I was again obliged to catch at and hold on to various objects as I passed. I did not fall though and succeeded in planting my feet firmly in the front pulpit, when I shouted at the top of my voice, "If the congregation will give their attention, we will listen, this afternoon to a discourse from President John Taylor."

This was the full thread of the dream, as far as I remember. The congregation seemed scattered and disorderly, and were reproved from the stand several times for their misconduct. The apostles sat with their hats on, and Brother Franklin D. Richards, who had on a soft hat somewhat slouched, or bent, stood up on the breastwork of the pulpit with an open Bible in his hands, and censured the congregation in an ironical way—such as: "That's right; make all the noise you can," etc. The dream made a vivid impression on my mind. I thought I could interpret the first part of it to mean that I would have to go back to the "News" Office to work, the idea of which was distasteful to me. I was consoled, however, by the thought that I would not stay there long.

Soon after this I had a remarkable answer to prayer, which to me was nothing short of a miracle. My health had not been very good for some time, owing to close confinement in the office and lack of fresh air and exercise. I worked hard and too long at a time, and neglected my general health. I was engaged on an editorial, the second of two entitled, "Is Talmage also Among the Prophets?" It was Tuesday, November 14, and I had to finish the article and submit it to President Carrington and give it to the printers next day. It was an extended commentary on one of the sermons of the [anti-Mormon] Rev. T. Dewitt Talmage, entitled, "The Degradation of American Politics," and I took great pains to get out a creditable piece of work. But I was worn out and exhausted, and struggle as I might I could not get it to suit me. I knew what I wanted to say, but could not say it as I wished. I sat at my desk nearly all day, writing and tearing up as fast as I wrote. My mind absolutely refused to work; it was completely tired out. I felt greatly discouraged, but after "tea" and a short walk returned and went at it again. No use; I could do nothing, and flinging down my pen [I] burst into tears of chagrin and despondency. Just at this moment a spirit seemed to whisper to me, "Why don't you pray over it?" "I do pray," I replied, "and often; why cannot I be helped?" (I was then in the habit of kneeling [and praying] to the Lord five times a day.) "Ah!" said the Spirit, "but pray now and for this especial thing." I hesitated not a moment, but sinking down sobbed out a humble entreaty for help. I arose feeling like a new creature. The change was instantaneous. My mind was full of life and vigor. I sat down and wrote, wrote, wrote, without a moment's hesitation until I had finished the article—one of the most vigorous that ever came from my pen. My mind was as clear as could be; I arranged my thoughts and clothed them in words without any difficulty, and I felt perfectly the master of the situation.[13] It taught me anew a lesson I shall never forget; and that is to ask the Lord, in praying, for the precise and particular thing that you want, just as a child would ask its parent. High-sounding rhetoric and long petitions, stereotyped and hackneyed by use, are not prayer. "Prayer is the soul's sincere desire." "Ask and receive" is the whole thing in a nutshell.

Elder John Henry Smith (USHS)

On Sunday, November 19th, Apostle John Henry Smith landed in Liverpool from Salt Lake, having come to succeed Brother Carrington as President of the European Mission.[14] His coming was a godsend. Things had not been as they should be at "42" for some time. Brother Carrington had been acting very unwisely with women in the office, although I had no idea then that he had criminally committed [adultery] himself with them. There was a bad spirit there, a fact I had recognized for months, although ignorant of the depth of the cause. Judge of my astonishment to learn, and my horror to realize, some years afterwards, that he was an adulterer and was practicing his lecherous sins in the very house where I resided, while all the time preaching and exercising, or at least holding the apostleship, and presiding over that great mission. No wonder his preaching was always harsh and repellant, and without the Spirit of God. No wonder he was tyrannical and selfish and cruel to those under him, particularly to Brother Stayner, whose "revelations" he rejected and denounced as from the devil. Whatever may have been Brother Stayner's faults and errors, I bear solemn testimony that the Spirit which he enjoyed and manifested was as different from that of Albert Carrington and Robert R. Anderson, who both treated him so cruelly, as day differs from night, and heaven from hell.

I will here say that some time before this we had received word from Salt Lake that Brother Stayner had been tried by the High Council of the Salt Lake Stake of Zion, for disseminating false doctrines, and that the High Council, presided over by Angus M. Cannon, David O. Calder, and Joseph E. Taylor, had sat in judgment upon him and his teachings and decided that he had been led astray by the evil one. They required that he renounce his belief in the reincarnation of spirits, in his own calling as "One mighty and Strong," and in short in everything connected with his revelations; to call in his writings, revoke his teachings, to get re-baptized and "sin no more." This, Brother Stayner agreed to do, and did so to the best of my belief and knowledge; and I kept my word in regard to setting them aside if the Priesthood should decide against them; plighted to Brother Stayner on his leaving England. The arrival of Apostle Smith, who had attended the trial of Brother Stayner, confirmed previous reports, and after several conversations with him upon the subject,[15] I reiterated my position and took his counsel in regard to Brother Stayner's doctrines, which was to lay them aside as incorrect and banish them from my mind as far as possible. Brother Smith, having assumed the Presidency, and his predecessor having sailed for home, affairs at "42" were straightened out, a better influence prevailed, and new life was infused into the mission. He treated me with marked kindness in every respect.

~~I will now cite some of the reasons I had for investigating and crediting, so far as I did, the doctrines advocated by Brother C. W. Stayner~~. *Orson had a change of heart and did not give his reasons for his belief in Stayner's revelations and doctrines and crossed out the introductory sentence. Notwithstanding Orson's stated attempt to lay aside his views about Stayner and reincarnation and banish them from his mind, he was unable to do so and they followed him home from his mission.*

Meanwhile, over the Christmas holiday, Orson helped the new mission president, John Henry Smith, investigate a case of fornication committed by one of the mission home servant-girls. With this unpleasant chore behind him, he could concentrate on writing editorials for the Millennial Star *and begin preparations to visit London. On arrival, the first thing Elder Whitney did was visit the Atkinson's, and other old friends who were members of that conference. He spent part of January there and then returned to Liverpool.*[16]

In early February Elder Whitney bought a valentine but found himself internally debating who to send it to. He finally decided on Zina.[17] *This same month Orson went back to work as editor of the* Millennial Star *and the* Journal of Discourses. *Elder Whitney found himself reading old sermons found in early volumes of the* Journal of Discourses *and was so taken with certain deeply doctrinal sermons of President Brigham Young and Heber C. Kimball that he quoted from them at length in his diary.*[18] *They dealt with the nearness of men—such as Joseph, Brigham, Heber, and the Twelve—to God and how such men weren't truly known by the people.*[19] *It may be that he saw evidence of the reincarnation of spirits in them, though such an interpretation would have been his alone.*

On Saturday, March 3, 1883, I left Liverpool for London, having been released from laboring in the office and appointed to preside temporarily over the London Conference, during the absence of Elder Joseph A. West on the continent. This fulfilled a dream I had had about a year previous.[20] It was Brother West's desire that I should succeed him, we being very good friends and close confidants.

During March, Elder Whitney found himself in doctrinal discussions regarding reincarnation with some of his fellow missionaries. March 5, 1883: Had an interesting talk with Brother West on the principle of plurality of probations. *Whitney was also highly pleased to get some nice and complimentary mail from home*:

March 13, 1883: Arose late as is usual in London. After breakfast walked out, returning found letters from Zina, Mother, and Brother Nicholson. Soon after got one from Hebe Wells and a package containing photographs of my children, Race and Hebie—very good ones. The letters were all excellent and cheering. Ma's contained this passage, "Eliza (Eliza R. Snow Smith) asked Em (Emmeline B.

Wells) if she had read your 'sermon on canvas.' She thought it the greatest and most sublime of anything that had ever been written. It was nothing less than inspiration. I never saw her more enthusiastic over anything. She pronounced you the 'greatest writer that we have in our midst.' Well, in fact, says she, 'He's beat himself.' Why, said I, do you think that he wrote that? George Lambert is there in his place now. 'George Lambert never wrote that,' says she. 'Nobody but Orson Whitney wrote that article.' I had not read it, only the first of it, and supposed that Brother Lambert had done it; but I read it last night and hope you are the author. . . . Aunt Em and others said they would not give much for the paper when you left it. You see how you are valued and I am sure Sister Eliza thinks a good deal of you. She said she wondered if you remembered how she once talked to and counseled you when a boy."

The reincarnation discussion continued, this time with George C. Parkinson, a missionary from Idaho. March 22, 1883: Cold and windy outside. Stayed in all day. Writing on newspaper letter revise and talking to Parkinson. Gave him list of names given me by Brother Donaldson nearly a year ago, of persons who have lived in this and former dispensations.

Most of Elder Whitney's time presiding over the London Conference was spent speaking in meetings and meeting with members and investigators (called "strangers").

After his [West's] return from Italy he and I took a two weeks tramp without purse or scrip through the counties of Essex, Hertford, Bedford, etc., described minutely in correspondence published in the "Star."[21]

During the night of May 4, Elder Whitney had another dream, which he recorded in his diary:

May 5, 1883: Awoke with the vague recollection of a dream to the following effect: I seemed to be in the temple block, on the north side of the Salt Lake Temple, which had just been completed. At my left side stood President George Q. Cannon. There seemed to be a vast multitude around. Suddenly a light burst from the east like a pillar of fire and from it seemed to extend on an inclined plane to the temple a grand avenue or stairway and ascending up, from the temple towards the horizon was a numberless concourse of fleecy forms, radiant and angelic, some of them of giant size and all marching upward in a grand [a few words missing] said I to Bro. Cannon: [a few words missing] the angels"? It seemed to be the glory of God resting upon the completed temple and I thought that the light from the east was the precursor of the Second Coming of Christ. The scene changed and I was within the temple holding communion with the spirits of the departed. Among those who came to me was Emma Wells and Nettie Culmer, her half-sister, (the latter still living). Nettie extended her arms entreatingly toward me and said something like this, "Oh, Ort, come, do come, you don't know what a beautiful place it is." But Em, with a wiser look, seemed to advise me to stay. I turned to her and said: "Do you love me? She said, "No," but said so archly and with such apparent reluctance that she seemed to mean "yes," as women often do. I do not remember any more but it was a glorious dream and left a weight upon my waking thoughts.

On Wednesday, May 9th, a letter from my father-in-law, President Abraham O. Smoot, apprised me of the death of my little son, Heber K., who expired at 9:40 a.m., April 20th. A few days later I was honorably released from my mission with the privilege of going home in the May Company. I preferred the June Company, however, and President Smith very willingly gave me permission to wait until it sailed. *End of Orson F. Whitney's handwritten autobiography, 1885–86.*

During the same week in May that Orson learned of his newborn son's death, a son he had never seen in person, he and Brother West, who had both come under the influence of Charles W. Stayner, resolved to fast and pray until they received an answer from the Lord as to whether Stayner's revelations and doctrines were true.[22] *Orson also suffered from a severe toothache. Their fast passed the fifth day:*

April 13 and 14, 1883: Sixth day of our fast. Dreamed last night I was in Palestine. Prayed with Bros. West and Brown and afterwards with West alone. We have continued to earnestly supplicate the Lord for the knowledge we desire, but while receiving of the Spirit while doing so, [we] have not yet obtained what we are after. Called at [illegible] told them of my going away, and made an appointment to stay there tonight. Then rode on the Mile End. Called at Atkinson's, saw Dolly and her father. . . . Bade all farewell. Took tea at

Atkinson's, saw Bro. Larkin also. Bade them good-bye. Started for North London. Arrived in time to bear my testimony in the open air meeting. . . . Bade many friends good-bye. . . . Arose early and bidding the family farewell. Returned to the office. Continued fasting and praying.

On the morning of the seventh day he ate breakfast, thus ending the fast, and said farewell to the departing members and missionaries, going with the May company to Salt Lake City. Since Orson himself wasn't leaving for a month, he made preparations to travel and see Scotland and France, accompanied by George C. Parkinson. Remaining diary entries do not indicate if Orson felt he received any kind of answer to his prayer, but his subsequent actions decisively demonstrate that he believed Stayner to be a prophet and that reincarnation was true doctrine. This decision would deeply influence his life for almost two decades to come.

On May 20, Orson recorded another dream: Dreamed of Rosa Hawks, that I was courting her. Something about Oliver Cowdery in connection therewith, as if she was or had been his. She did not seem averse to my suit [attentions]. The other night [I] dreamed of Dolly Atkinson. She came to me and gave herself to me, but her mother as usual was in the way. *Rosa Jane Hawks, who suddenly appears in Orson's diary, was another young lady Orson had become interested in, but to no avail. Just before sailing for home, he sent her a postcard.*[23]

As far as is known, Orson never saw Dolly again.[24] *He heard from another missionary that her father Joseph Atkinson had been struck by lightning and killed, and that Emma had been forced by necessity to go to work.*[25] *The Atkinson family sold and repaired boots and shoes to earn their keep. Six years after Orson's departure ended his designs, Dolly (twenty-two years old in 1888) married a man named Earnest Tomlin. He was also in the shoe business. They had at least five children, naming a daughter Dolly. In later years Dolly worked as a florist while her children learned the shoe trade or sewing. They lived next-door to her mother, Emma, for much of her life. Bertha died at Leytonstone, London, in 1938.*[26]

On June 20, Elder Whitney boarded the Nevada *and began sailing for home. In no time at all, he was again besieged with miserable seasickness that stayed with him most of his return trip. On July 1, his twenty-eighth birthday, he found himself in New York Harbor, disembarking for the long train ride to Salt Lake City.*

He reached home on July 7, 1883, enjoying an emotional and welcome reunion with his family and wife—"finally took Zina in my arms"—*full of joy to be home again.*[27]

Orson F. Whitney
1879 (USU)

Chapter 5

Earning a Living, Shepherding a Ward, and Doctrinal Detours, 1883–1886

When Orson returned from his mission and began regular life anew, the first things he did were further investigate reincarnation and renew mission friendships, along with seeking a way to earn a living. The very day he stepped off the train at home in Salt Lake City he sought out an older friend and "had a long talk concerning [Charles W.] Stayner and his revelations."[1] The friend, John Nicholson, was a locally prominent literary man working on the *Deseret News*, *Millennial Star*, and *Juvenile Instructor*, and with the Genealogical Society of Utah. He also wrote poetry and hymns. His name often appears in Whitney's diary as something of a father figure and counselor.[2]

On Sunday while Orson sat down for services in the Salt Lake Tabernacle, he "was asked to speak a portion of the time. Did so, but only occupied a short time. The Lord was with me however, and though badly frightened I did not fail."[3]

Evidence suggests that within a week he had shared his new notions about reincarnation with Zina, who initially reacted negatively. Orson also started spending time with Charles Stayner at his home, bringing Zina with him.[4] At some future point she appeared to have followed Orson and accepted Stayner as some kind of prophet and revelator.

Stayner himself was a native of London, England, converted to Mormonism as a youth upon immigrating to Utah, returned to England twice for missions, served as president of the Northern States Mission, and was a lawyer, a judge, an investor in the Utah sugar beet business, and a false prophet.[5] Stayner had a brother named Arthur, who was a leading founder and entrepreneur in the Utah Sugar Company, energetically pushing sugar beet agriculture and business prospects with Church leaders and prominent businessmen in Utah.[6] The brothers practiced a specialized ("Mormonized") form of theosophy, which meant that by extended periods of fasting and prayer they sought to learn the secrets and mysteries of the universe and to receive revelations, visions, visitations, manifestations, and interpretations.[7] It was their belief that Charles Stayner would someday become the prophet and President of the Church.

Orson also had some long personal and religious conversations with his mother and revealed to her his interest in a young lady he met on his mission, Rosa (or Rose) Hawks, evidently having her in mind as a possible plural wife.[8] The record is unclear, but Orson's "Ma" Helen may have accidentally let Zina know about Rose.[9] Zina herself had a dream she understood to be a testimony to her relating to the truth of plural marriage doctrine.[10] But Rose is never mentioned again.

In late August, Orson took his family on a trip to Idaho where he visited with missionary friends he had met in England: Dr. Ormsby, John Donaldson, and George C. Parkinson. They had long discussions, sang, recited, read poetry, and Orson whistled. Then he visited the Donaldson's, where reincarnation became the topic of conversation. At this point he recorded in his diary a theory he had developed concerning Elias, one that he would offer as scriptural proof of reincarnation on many occasions:

> Called at Donaldson's[:] the following from the Doctrine & Covenants. Section 27, Verses 6 and 7. "And also with Elias, to whom I have committed the keys of bringing to pass the restoration of all things spoken by the mouth of all the holy prophets since the world began, concerning the last days." "And also John, the son of Zacharias, which Zacharias he (Elias) visited. (Luke says Gabriel hence Gabriel and Elias are one; and as Joseph Smith says Gabriel and Noah are one, then there are three in one) and gave promise that he should have a son, and his name should be John, and he should be filled with the spirit of Elias (hence 4)."

> Section 110. Verse 12. "After this Elias appeared, and committed the dispensation of the gospel of Abraham (as Abraham stood at the head of his own dispensation and none but he had the right to deliver the keys thereof to another, then it follows that Abraham and Elias are one) saying that in us and our seed (Abraham's promise) all generations after us should be blessed."
>
> Bade them farewell and returned to Logan.[11]

Orson next visited his mission friend Bishop Newton Farr and was introduced to another local bishop, Thomas Wallace, who related to Orson a dream that he felt revealed to him that he (Wallace) was reincarnated, that in a past life he had been a Nephite. Orson recorded the narration in detail in his diary, feeling it to be further evidence of reincarnation—a subject about which he was becoming obsessed.

He soon had another conversation with his mother, Helen Mar, relating that

> Ma, who went to Farmington yesterday with Aunt Prescinda Kimball, told me this morning of something Prescinda said to her in relation to plural probations. They were conversing upon the subject rather indefinitely when Ma, after expressing her belief in it, asked her companion her view of it. Aunt Prescinda confessed that she too held the same idea and related in confirmation that Joseph Smith the Prophet also [illegible] a [illegible] man named [illegible] (who afterwards apostatized) [most of two pages are illegible because of smeared pencil lead].[12]

This is one of a few entries in Whitney's diary where belief in reincarnation is linked to Joseph Smith.

It was within this same diary entry of September 30, 1883, that Orson Whitney first chose to record a dream of the Savior in the Garden of Gethsemane that he had received on his first mission. A few words of preface to the account is all there is to indicate his reasons for timing and placement, but because of the importance of the dream, it is here given,

> Right here I will record a dream which I had in 1877 while in Pennsylvania on my first mission. It was the last of winter or the beginning

> of Spring. I was rooming with Brother A. H. Musser in Columbia, and I had not been paying much attention to religion, not being thoroughly aroused and converted, but thought more of writing for the press and reading secular works. One morning I had gone to sleep in my second nape before getting up when I had the following dream. I was in the Garden of Gethsemane and standing behind a tree, from which position I could see without being seen. The picture before me was most vivid. At my right a group of four persons appeared, whom I recognized as the Savior and His apostles—Peter, James, and John. He left the three disciples at the right in a group to pray and He himself crossed over to the left and knelt down also. I could see His face distinctly with the tears coursing down His face as He implored the Father to "Let this cup pass." My feelings were so wrought upon by witnessing his agony that I wept also. Just then He arose and walked over to His apostles, who had fallen asleep, and reproved them for so doing. The circumstances then seemed to change, though the scene remained the same. The four were at my right and seemed to be about to take their departure. It was no longer before the crucifixion but afterwards. I thought they were going up to heaven and I ran out and fell at the Savior's feet, clasped Him around the knees and begged Him to take me with Him. He reached down tenderly, raised me up and embraced me very affectionately and with a most tender and sweet expression, mingled with sadness, shook His head and exclaimed: "No; my son, Your work is not finished yet. These have done theirs and they can go with me, but you must stay and finish yours." "Well, promise me," I said, "that when I have done it, that I will come to You." Again He shook His head sadly and sweetly and with the most angelic voice said: "That will depend entirely on yourself." I woke up with a sob and it was morning with the sunlight streaming in at the window. Over six years have elapsed since then, but the dream and everything connected with it is as fresh in my memory as if it was but yesterday I dreamed it. It had a deep effect upon my mind and stirred me up to reformation and diligence in my missionary labor. It was the first [illegible] evidence I had and the initial of a long series of spiritual manifestations. It seemed after I awoke that I could still feel the warmth of the Savior's bosom against mine, while His words of wise warning, "That will depend entirely upon yourself," I shall never forget.[13]

Soon after his return Orson received an offer to do some theatrical acting. He reluctantly accepted after having cleared the matter with President John Taylor. Money problems had quickly confronted him on his return and he had to scramble to make ends meet.

He received an offer from friends and his father-in-law, Abraham O. Smoot, to become editor of a proposed newspaper in Utah County, but he declined, not wanting to relocate his family to Provo. At general conference in early October, President Taylor told him that he needed to resume his former position as local editor of the *Deseret News*. He did not enjoy journalism and did not want the job, but the financial pressures of supporting his family compelled him to accept. He worked for the *Deseret News* until November 1884 when he was offered the position of Salt Lake City Treasurer by the city council, filling out the unexpired term of the previous treasurer, who had died. He had to post a bond of $50,000 with several prominent and wealthy friends acting as sureties.[14] Orson commented on the change of pace, "I was not sorry to forsake the hurry, worry, and drudgery of newspaper life, for a position where I had time to think, and in spare moments to achieve something higher in the realm of literature."[15]

Whitney also busied himself with his duties as bishop, constantly blessing the sick, speaking at funerals, and conducting ward meetings. In November he learned of the death of an uncle under extraordinary circumstances: "We received particulars from my brother Charles, (who went home with Uncle David in the latter part of this month) of Uncle David's death. He died two years almost to the hour from the time he was found on the desert after a terrible experience with bad [evil] spirits and a wonderful experience with good. His father Heber C. Kimball appeared to him and wanted him to go with him. Uncle David plead for two more years and it was granted. He died at the end of the time he asked for."[16]

Along the same lines, he recorded a manifestation given to his wife,

> Last night, my wife Zina had a vision. She was very sick and had been thinking of her dead mother, whose birthday it was, when, about 3 o'clock in the morning of the 26th, as she was lying on the [lounge] in Aunt Mary's [illegible] room, [illegible], she suddenly became aware that her mother stood at the back of her bed.

> Zina was awake, but had her eyes closed, and saw with her spiritual vision. Her mother looked pale and sick as in life, and was dressed as usual while here. She said "Zina, what's the matter?" Zina, who felt no fear, replied that she was sick, telling the cause—miscarriage. "Where is Race?" (our boy) the spirit asked. "In the bedroom with Orson," (myself) said my wife. The vision [visitor] then turned to go out at the front door, where a balcony overlooks the ground. "Let me go with you," said Zina. "No, you can't go," said her mother. Zina repeated the request. "Not this time," said her mother. "When can I go?" asked Zina. "Be patient a little longer and you can go next time," was the reply. "When?" repeated Zina. "In a few days," was the reply and the spirit then opened the door and went out, closing the door after her."[17]

Zina did not pass away at that time, but she did die relatively young only seven years later, at age forty-two.

Orson continued writing poetry, perhaps the greatest passion of his life, and soaked in the compliments, especially from those he revered. Regarding one poem he wrote, "Put the finishing touches on my poem 'A Christmas Idyll.' It is the best I ever wrote, and I acknowledge the Spirit of God as my inspiration. . . . President Taylor, to whom it was read by George Reynolds, said he liked it better than Whittier's poetry. . . . Wilford Woodruff [said]: 'It's the best thing I ever read in my life.'" Such compliments encouraged him to continue with zeal. Of President John Taylor, he wrote, "President Taylor was always kind to me. A poet himself, he took an interest in my verses, and encouraged me to write. He also commended my public discourses."[18]

In March of 1884 Orson was appointed to the honorary (non-paying) position of Board of Regents and then Chancellor of the University of Deseret (Utah). He served in this capacity until a different political party took over the city government; he was dropped and the position was later abolished.[19]

In April President George Q. Cannon invited him to attend the dedication of the Logan Temple, but since others at the *Deseret News* office had also been invited, he had to cover the city desk for them. Over the summer he wrote articles for the *Contributor* magazine run by Junius F. Wells, who would later become his brother-in-law. That

November his father, Horace K. Whitney, died. Regarding the causes, Orson wrote that it was "of the heart, with dropsy and rheumatism following. He has been sick since last June. He was born at Kirtland, Ohio, July 25, 1823."[20] Horace's passing made Helen Mar a widow, and since she lived in his ward, Bishop Whitney felt responsible for her economic welfare. He quickly inquired about his mother's finances. Orson and Zina soon moved in with her.[21] Helen's financial situation would be a continual worry for her son, who did his best to help as he appropriately could, both personally and as her bishop.

The day after Christmas Bishop Whitney

> attended a meeting of bishops in the Social Hall, to consider the advisability of organizing special police forces in the various city wards to protect ourselves against burglars, night prowlers, and sneaks of all descriptions. President George Q. Cannon was there and also the presiding bishopric: Preston, Burton, and Cannon. I was asked to open by prayer. Speeches were made . . . and a motion was carried that a special force be organized of 12 men in each ward to be captained by a special officer chosen by the City Marshall.[22]

The new year brought the birth of another child. His first daughter was born while he was in the very act of administering to Zina.[23] Money troubles often occupied Orson's mind and caused him great anxiety. After a few long talks with him, his mother Helen wrote, "He feels anxious and troubled about how he is to get along—no house or home of his own, and paying tithes and donations, etc."[24]

In April Orson was appointed to a committee to help write a document protesting the persecutions that the federal government, and some local appointees, were imposing on Latter-day Saints because of the practice of plural marriage: "Appointed one of a Committee of 22 to frame a Protest of Declaration of Grievances to the President and People of the United States in Behalf of the Latter-day Saints, and have worked on it up to this date, Sunday, April 26, 1885. It is about finished. We hold a mass meeting in the Tabernacle next Saturday, May 2, at 1 p.m. Held the meeting and I read the protest."[25]

Orson was able to move out of his mother's house and into his own rented home in June. Helen's parlor had been the scene of much of his writing. During their stay Helen had grown very attached to Orson's new baby, and their absence caused her much loneliness.[26]

Later that year the Salt Lake stake presidency asked Bishop Whitney to initiate Sunday school services at the Utah Territorial Prison where a number of men were serving time for plural marriage offenses as part of the persecutions inflicted on the Church and its members by the government. The U.S. Marshal approved the proposal and Orson became the first bishop to visit and teach. Of the visit he wrote, "We shook hands with all the brethren in silence, but were privileged to have an interview with Bro. John Nicholson."[27] Word of Orson's spirit-filled preaching occasionally reached the ears of family. After one sermon his mother recorded: "Understand that Orson preached today—they say he was filled with inspiration."[28]

The year 1885 was also the year that Albert Carrington's adulterous transgressions, as noted by Elder Whitney in chapter four, finally caught up with him. It seems that some missionaries like Elder Whitney, who lived in the mission home, knew that Carrington had acted unwisely with female mission home staff members. But it was later found to be much more than foolish or imprudent behavior. Rumors of Carrington's liberties with some of the office women had come to President Taylor first and he had interviewed Carrington about it, but had been lied to. By late October and November proof of Carrington's adulterous affairs had come to Church authorities. As part of their investigation they not only spoke with Orson, but they asked him to help. "One evening about this time, had an interview with President George Q. Cannon who commissioned me to gather up certain information in the case of [Albert Carrington]. A few days after, Apostles John Henry Smith and John W. Taylor called on me and took down my testimony." Orson recorded the results of the apostle's investigation, "[Albert Carrington] excommunicated by the Quorum of the 12 for 'lewd and lascivious conduct and adultery' Nov. 10, 1885."[29] There remained one last act in the play where Orson's life intersected Carrington's.

Sometimes Orson became reflective in his diary. Suffering from episodes of deep depression on occasion, he was quick to take stock of his successes and the prominence he was gaining in the community and Church. He wrote, "Had a remarkable answer to prayer," but did not elaborate. Then, "Within the last few months [I have] preached many times [words removed], at funerals, etc.—three of my sermons were published in the [*Deseret*] *News*. Also lectured on 'What Is Education' at 14th ward meeting. . . . Among the last things said to me by Brother [John] Nicholson who went to the Penitentiary [for plural marriage] Oct. 13, 1885—were these: 'Your future will be glorious. Remember what I say, for it is a fact. The Lord will open up a broad field for you yet.' He said it very positively and emphatically, as though perfectly aware of its truth. In fact he uttered it as a prophecy, as he said. I answered that the Lord had done more for me already than I deserved, and I hoped I would be worthy of all He should do for me in the future."[30] Orson organized a special social program at his own home for John before he went to serve his sentence, inviting many mutual friends and at least one apostle. Orson and others spoke so highly of him that he broke down and cried.[31]

With thoughts of the future still very much on his mind, Bishop Whitney recorded: "Returning last night from North Jordan Ward (Taylorsville) where I had been to attend meetings at the invitation of Pres. Joseph E. Taylor. I related to Apostle John W. Taylor, who was with me, a dream I had in Liverpool, Nov. 11, 1882, the first part of which was fulfilled in my going back to work on the [*Deseret*] *News* on my return from England. He said: 'The other part will be fulfilled also. I can give you the interpretation. You will yet be called to be an apostle of the Lord Jesus Christ, and it will be at a time when all things that can be will be shaken,' etc. I answered: 'I had not dared to think that, although it was a good dream and I supposed it meant some call or other *up higher*. But I will remember your words.'"[32] These were critical years for Whitney—marvelous, almost unthinkable portents awaited him, but other matters intervened and interfered.

Meanwhile, Orson was part of a movement by Church Authorities to create associations in stakes and wards that would hold Church property, this being an effort to keep it out of the hands of the federal government's appointees tasked with confiscating it. During one meeting the marshalls surrounded the meetinghouse, but they were unable to capture the high-ranking Mormon men they sought.[33]

In March 1886, Orson received another patriarchal blessing, his fourth. Charles W. Stayner wrote it down as the local patriarch spoke the words. A few days later he received a fifth blessing, this time under the hands of the Church Patriarch, John Smith. Obviously, Orson was trying to determine a course in life. At about the same time he recorded another dream,

> I dreamed last night that the city of Washington was undermined and laid with dynamite, gunpowder and other explosives and that the mine had been fired. Being among those who were forewarned, I fled hastily from the scene, expecting every moment to hear the explosion. I prayed as I ran for protection. Zina, my wife, was with me at first, but I afterwards found myself alone. After climbing over a mountain and putting it between me and the city, I heard the explosion, which was terrific; blocks and fragments of buildings were hurled into the air and came pattering to earth for miles around. One piece just touched my finger, but did not hurt me. My most painful thought was that I had left my wife and children behind, the latter being forgotten. Death and disaster spread abroad and I awoke with feelings of terror and dread. The city of Washington, seemed to be in Salt Lake, or else Salt Lake in Washington, and I thought President [Brigham] Young was in the midst of the Saints mustering them. The city was also besieged, (I think by dynamiters) and soldiers were in our midst. I wore a uniform and was allowed to pass freely. The rest of the dream was vague and uncertain. . . . In my remarks at the Tabernacle I said the explosives shown in my dream were unconstitutional laws against the Latter-day Saints which would redound to their enemies disadvantage.[34]

The polygamous persecutions were becoming more and more intense. Most of the members of the leading Quorums of the Church, being polygamists, were in prison or in hiding on the "underground," as it was called. Taking this scenario into consideration, as well as Orson's ability as a gifted speaker, he became something of a de-facto voice for the Church. For instance, at the April 1886 general conference held in the Provo Tabernacle, with the First Presidency absent, he received an assignment: "I read the Epistle of the First Presidency to the congregation. That is, I read about ½ of it—Bro. James E. Talmage finished it. I had a cold and my voice would not permit me to finish it. It required two-and-a-half hours to read it." Later, "The same day I met Father O. N. Liljenquist, Patriarch, on the Utah

Central Railway Platform of Provo. Said he, 'Well, are you going to be called into the Quorum tomorrow?' meaning the Quorum of the Twelve. 'On no,' said I, 'I guess not.' 'Well, you will be someday,' said he, 'if not tomorrow.' 'It seems too high for me,' I replied. 'I am not a prophet nor the son of a prophet.' 'Well, you are as near to it as can be,' said he, 'you are grandson to two prophets, ain't you?' 'Perhaps,' I said. 'Well, you will be there someday,' said he. Many tell me the same but God knoweth where he wants me; I am in His hands to do as seemeth Him good."[35]

Orson's mother, Helen, noted how her son prepared to speak: "Attended meeting at Tabernacle. Orson preached the best sermon I ever heard from him, and I heard a number of others say the same. I prayed for him, knowing that he'd fasted as he always does when he expects to preach."[36] Orson found himself in a difficult position. He was highly regarded and his gifts for speaking and writing were blessing and influencing the Church, yet he was becoming more and more involved with Charles W. Stayner, secret prayer meetings with his England-mission friends, and reincarnation. The two paths were incompatible and placed him in untenable situations that would grow in complexity and stress as the years passed.

Cryptic entries begin to show up in his diary, such as "[I] spent the fore part of the afternoon at Brother C. W. Stayner's and then went to the Tabernacle. Read some interesting things in the Book of Esther and about Gideon in the Book of Judges." And, "Have recently heard some interesting things about my life, past and future. Also about the First Counselor to the President of the Church [George Q. Cannon], and the mission of the ones like unto Moses & Aaron."[37]

Some explanation for these and other increasingly mysterious entries was inserted by Orson in his diary in early October 1883. A list of prominent biblical names was adjacent to a column of initials (given backwards) on the left. It may be that this list was adapted and enlarged from one created by John Donaldson in England.[38] The list identifies names of family, friends, and associates that he believed were reincarnated and that had lived (as mortals) in former dispensations as prophets, apostles, and other prominent figures, both men and women.[39] This list becomes valuable when deciphering the diary because he began using initials and the ancient names as code words in diary entries that identified a person who he believed had once been in a former mortal life. He used this codename system most often when referencing his friends as they met in secret prayer meetings and sought for revelations. Whitney's use of codenames in diary entries also introduces an element of uncertainty into decipherment of events he narrates. Often there is no way to tell to whom Whitney is referring because the identity of the person is unknown and because the most mysterious and secretive entries have been scribbled out or removed from the diary. Between the list and some entries that still remain and can be read, a reasonably strong probability exists that many, but certainly not all, mysterious diary entries can be understood sufficiently.

Based on a careful examination of the diaries, it is fairly certain that Charles W. Stayner is referenced as "Joshua" and also as "Elias," or "E," and that Arthur Stayner, Charles's brother, is "Moses." John Donaldson is likely "Nephi." Since some of the names are not identifiable, it often becomes impossible to know whom or what Ort was talking about. It is likely that group members used their codenames when talking to each other at their meetings. (To assist readers, where known, names of the probable identity of persons have been inserted in brackets next to their codename.)

Whitney did his best to keep the group meetings with his friends secret. He was busy serving as bishop, working as Salt Lake City Treasurer, and filling speaking engagements of various kinds, with funerals commonplace. He also became a more frequent speaker at the Tabernacle, where Sunday services were held for the public, and consequently where his local prominence and visibility increased. He recorded another dream: "Last night I dreamed that I was addressing a congregation, either at a funeral, or on some other solemn occasion. I had a little dead bird in my right pants pocket; it (the bird) having been chilled to death or frozen, or killed in some way. As I warmed to my theme the bird came to life and I took it out of my pocket and, holding it up, I said to the congregation: 'Thus does the Spirit of the Lord revive and lift up the drooping soul.'"[40] Poetry was a theme in many talks. "Lectured in the 14th ward hall before the Salt Lake Co. Teachers Summer Institute on 'Poets and Poetry,' occupying an hour and ten minutes. Had a large and refined audience and excellent attention. Received a hearty round of applause on closing and a vote of thanks. Received many compliments from individuals and glowing press notices. The *Salt Lake Herald* wants my lecture entire for publication next Sunday. The Lord was with me in delivering the lecture, as He was in my composing it. To Him be all the glory."[41]

Public speaking, or oratory, gradually became one of Orson's greatest talents. Demand for his services grew as the years passed, and he did his best to meet the many requests. "Preached in the Tabernacle, occupying whole of time, on faith, repentance, baptism, and laying on of hands for gift of Holy Ghost. Had the blessing of the Lord and much freedom and power. Dwelt especially on need of faith and repentance in Church. Many remarked 'that's the word of the Lord.' Bishop A. H. Raleigh told a friend of mine that I was growing and would be a great man eventually. Said the cross between Kimball and Whitney was good stock and that I was inspirational, etc."[42]

Bishop Whitney was soon sent back to the territorial penitentiary Sunday School to speak again to the Mormon "co-hab" inmates. It was on this occasion that he met an apostle that would become one of the great mentors of his life. "Went to Penitentiary in afternoon with Bishop John Q. Cannon. Held services—I preached. Had a fine Spirit and splendid attention. Afterward had interview with Apostle Lorenzo Snow and other Brethren. They were delighted with services. Bro. Snow said, 'Bro. Whitney, I very much enjoyed your remarks; I was entranced. You are getting on famously.' I prophesied to Apostle Snow that he would not finish his term in prison."[43] The prophecy was fulfilled when Lorenzo Snow was released many months early, the United States Supreme Court having intervened in local unconstitutional, anti-Mormon court proceedings.[44]

Ort then spent a month on a camping vacation with his family, seeking to avoid the summer heat. It was during this trip that the family learned of the suicide of his younger brother Charles.[45] The event devastated the family. Helen Mar wrote,

> I could not believe that Charley was dead. It seemed like a dream that I must awake from. But, oh it was a bitter reality, and in my silent agony I wondered what I have done, or what I had left undone, or if

> I was doomed to suffer this that I could know how to feel for others under like trials who's suffering I could not know in any other way. How I cried to the Lord to help me bear it if needful, and acknowledge His hand in Charlie's taking his own life. I could not weep but oh the agonizing though; how a boy like him could have given way; what could have brought him to commit such an act? Had all my prayers for his eternal salvation fallen to the ground unheeded?
>
> When arriving at the Depot I was hardly able to walk. . . . Bro. Farrington, who nearly carried me to the Hack, and helped me in with my Orson's assistance, who was there with Zina & Gennie to receive me and brother Sol. We were driven to my home of wretchedness, and to my surprise it was surrounded, and filled with sympathetic and anxious friends. My children strove with all their might to be calm for my sake. As soon as all was quiet, Orson, Sol, and George administered to me. Sol anointed my head; he wept, and could hardly speak. Orson then gave me a great blessing; many wonderful things were pronounced upon my head. Orson had previously offered a prayer, and all present thought it the greatest they had ever heard. The first thing he'd said when we were on the way from the Depot was that Charley was not accountable for the act, and he had gained this testimony by fasting and prayer. I told him if I could know this I would never murmur. He prophesied that I should know it and that very soon. . . .[46]

Helen Mar Kimball Whitney
(USU)

A few days later on she recorded, "I accepted Orson's invitation when he came down that afternoon with Arthur Stayner. He said that he had glorious things to tell me. . . . Took breakfast and said good-bye. Sol and Orson carried our bedding, etc. to the Street Car, and my spirits were much improved by the . . . consoling words from Orson which flowed from his lips from the time we started till we were met by Zina and Race as the train stopped. . . . We breakfasted the 2nd time and Orson read to us from the Book of Mormon. We spent a very pleasant day hearing it, and teachings from him."[47] Orson and the Stayner brothers also gave Helen a blessing, as they had visited the Whitney family on the camping trip. Then a few days later, "Orson called; had a splendid time; [he] told me some glorious things concerning Charley and the past, present, and future."[48]

That month Orson also attended a Whitney family gathering. "Held family reunion at mother's at which all my father's family were present. We had an excellent time. I spoke to them and prophesied and speeches were made by [my] brother Bud, my mother, Mary, Uncle Sol, Kimball, George Pyper, etc. A beautiful Spirit prevailed and our hearts were drawn nearer to each other and the Lord. Angels were in our midst and the Lord was pleased with what we did."[49] Helen Mar recorded some of what Orson said on this occasion:

> Orson opened with prayer; then addressed us, and his teachings were sharp and to the point. He made a prophecy, at the close, that if we would turn over a new leaf, and obey God, honor His Priesthood, keep the word of wisdom, etc., we should be able to stop the destroyer from this time, etc. But if we continued to break over His laws, and did not keep the Sabbath day holy, etc., we would have something worse than Charley's death, and these things he prophesied in the name of Jesus Christ. He invited Sol, who gave some excellent instructions. Then he asked Bud, and he spoke very humble and was desirous of being more united in the future; that Charley's death had set him to thinking of these things, and how much more he had been united, and associated, with those outside of his father's family than with his own brothers and sisters, etc.[50]

Two weeks later the reunion continued, but Zina did not feel well enough to go. "Zina arose suffering from indigestion, very severe spells. We were to attend the Whitney reunion at Aunt Mary's at night, but Zina thought she was too sick to go, as the spells came upon her every little while and she did not want to be away from home when they came upon her. I was very anxious to have her go and felt led to say to her, 'If you will go, you will not be troubled by them.' She clung to the promise in faith and sure enough felt not another pang all day nor all that night. Thus the Lord honors the words of His servants uttered in faith and in faith accepted."[51]

The next day, he "spent the afternoon at Charles W. Stayner's. Moses [Arthur], Joshua [Charles], and Sarah [Charles's wife] were there. Had a splendid time; exercised the gift of prophecy."[52] Whitney found himself spending a considerable amount of time with the Stayners. His diary becomes increasingly filled with references to them, to meetings, and hints that he may have started giving Charles money by this time, though that timing remains unclear (the edits to the diary eliminate surety).[53] Helen Mar again described one of the prayer or blessing meetings, which she seems to have attended occasionally on invitation, "We had an interesting time; conversed upon the two powers who were working for the victory, and related incidents of faith, the power of God and the evil one, and struggles which we had experienced in our own lives. Orson asked me to tell some of my experience and others with the evil spirits, which I did. We had a very interesting meeting."[54]

At some point in their meetings, Orson came to envision himself as someone that would open or prepare the way for Charles's rise to preside over the Church. The secret meetings would grow in number and purpose, with Whitney as the most prominent member. "At Joshua's [Charles's] in the evening," he wrote. "He saw a woman's hand pointing to me. The hand was beautiful and shapely and the sleeve was black. The interpretation was that I was 'a marked man' in the Church, and the Church, typified by the woman who was in mourning, was pointing at me and looking with favor toward me—and that ere long I was to be the recipient of favor at its hands."[55] Orson was subject to flattery, and Stayner's revelations probably helped to strengthen his influence over Ort.

Orson's old love for his first girlfriend remained with him, and he dreamed of her. "Dreamed last night of Emma Wells. It was very vivid. She stood in white at the top of the stairs at her old home, and looked beautiful and angelic. I rushed up to her and tried to embrace her. She put out her hand as if to restrain me, as though suffering from her old ailment—the pain in her side resulting from an accident—and afraid in my impetuosity I would hurt her. She was nevertheless kind and affectionate. The scene changed and we were out of doors. It was winter and I stood snowballing with John Q. Cannon, he being below me in a courtyard and I on an elevated parapet with a wall as a bulwark before me. We were not angry. One of the balls I threw hit Emma, who was near me on the parapet, on the shoulder, and she made an exclamation of pain. I desisted and threw no more."[56] Two more dreams followed in the weeks ahead. "Last night I dreamed that I was appointed at conference to carry the Gospel to Russia and found a mission there. This repeats a dream I had some weeks ago, wherein I was appointed minister to Russia for the government—that is for a government that seemed to have superseded the U.S. though identical with it. It afterward appeared in the dream that the offices of minister and that of missionary were blended or identical. About this time was shown in a dream L. & B. as my w[ives?]."[57] Whitney did not elaborate further and we are left without explanation. Plural marriage was on his mind, as shown by the fact that he eventually took a plural wife, but the identities of those he dreamed about are not given.

Orson F. Whitney (USHS)

Chapter 6

A Rising Influence in the Church, 1886–1887

In the fall of 1886, Orson bought a home in Salt Lake City and moved in. He continued meeting with the Stayners on a regular basis, often weekly. In January Elder John W. Taylor asked Ort to accompany him on a trip through some of the northern Utah stakes. When Elder Taylor could not go at the last minute, Charles Stayner went with him instead.[1] Sometime after their return, Whitney encountered Elder Lorenzo Snow, recently released (early) from the Utah Territorial Penitentiary by the United States Supreme Court. This chance meeting was to become the first of many and the beginning of a remarkable and dear friendship to them both. "Heard Apostle Lorenzo Snow in Tabernacle—his first public address after coming out of prison. I reminded him of my saying to him last July at the Pen. 'Bro. Snow, you won't stay here 18 months,' at which time he replied 'I came prepared for it.' When I asked him if he did not remember it he said, 'Yes,' and added, 'You are a prophet—you are a prophet.'"[2]

At the April 1887 general conference, Bishop Whitney, at the direction of the First Presidency, read to the assemblage an epistle they had prepared, reviewing plural marriage persecutions and counseling Church members.[3] The recitation took an hour and a half.[4] Not long afterward he preached to a mixed group at a relative's funeral: "A large gathering was present, Saints, gentiles, apostates, etc. All seemed deeply impressed. I am told that Rev. T. W. Lincoln, Methodist minister, said, 'If that is Mormonism, it is a grand religion.' David Evans, an apostate, said 'That's the kind of Mormonism I once believed in.' Others said it was a most impressive and eloquent address. . . . It was therefore the Lord's doing, and I was surely the medium. It is sufficient glory for me if the Lord is with me. To Him be all the honor."[5] At the next funeral, the reaction was phrased a little differently. "The widow, Kate Ferguson Burton said, 'I shall always love Orson Whitney; how can he talk like that and be a Mormon?' She little knew that it was all because I am a Mormon."[6] Others thought so as well; "Lillie went to evening meeting at our chapel; came home happy, had heard Orson preach the best sermon she'd heard. He came to see me and spent a while yesterday," wrote Helen Mar.[7]

That spring he began an endeavor that would become perhaps his most well-known literary work. "Last month . . . commenced *Life of Heber C. Kimball* for which I am to get $1000 from the Kimball boys [children of Heber]."[8] Shortly thereafter, he "received of Sol. F. Kimball $250, first payment on *Life of H. C. Kimball*."[9] In a letter to President Joseph F. Smith he wrote, "I am now writing the *Life of Heber C. Kimball*. The family [will] hold a reunion on his 86th anniversary, June 14—at Fullers Hill. . . . I will write a sketch for the reunion, simply, and finish the history afterwards."[10] To do the work, he borrowed some items from his mother, Heber's daughter. "Orson called at evening to get some of the items from my writings in the [*Women's*] *Exponent*; took home one book and some of Father's small journals."[11]

Miracles continued to follow his ministry as bishop. "Administered to Bessie, Shirley, and Nellie Clawson, children of Emily Clawson. They were healed. This fulfilled a dream I had last winter."[12] He next preached a powerful sermon in the Salt Lake Tabernacle, receiving many compliments, and ascribing the glory, and his gratitude, to God.[13]

Intimations that a higher office in the Church awaited him continued. He recorded, "Last night I dreamed I was at a great feast where many were assembled, and where I was the chief topic of conversation. Pres. Angus M. Cannon, who was present, exclaimed, 'Let a crown of gold be placed upon his brow, and in his hand the Word.' Everyone then turned to his or her neighbor and said, 'He's going to be an apostle.'"[14]

By June Ort had prepared his sketch far enough on *The Life of Heber C. Kimball* to read an outline of it at the Kimball family reunion.[15] He also qualified to vote, and to attend local state constitutional conventions. Church leaders were continually striving for Utah's statehood, trying to get out from under the thumb of corrupt and anti-Mormon federal appointees for governor and the territorial supreme court.

Comments on his public speaking prowess continued to reach his ears. Because Orson never saw a pulpit he did not like (with the possible exception of political stump speeches), he was hypersensitive to both compliments and criticisms, which sometimes amounted to backhanded compliments. For example, that summer he wrote, "In the fusion of elements for the 4th of July celebration, I was wanted as one of the speakers, but . . . others objected, because I would 'outshine them all'—I was told this by a friend. P. L. Williams said to James Sharp that anyone who objected to Bishop Whitney as orator of the day or orator on any occasion was a ... fool for he (I) was the only natural orator in this part of the country. Heber M. Wells told me this."[16] His recording of others' reactions to his public preaching and lectures constitutes one of the larger elements of his diary, in concert with references to and reactions regarding his writings. Occasionally he explained the effort he expended.

> Preached at the funeral of Elder Feramorz Little. . . . Heber M. Wells told me it was a fine address, and that he had heard many compliments for me, and from "solid men." City Councilor John Clark said I was "wonderfully gifted," that the chief charms in my speaking were originality and suitability to the occasion. He had heard me speak several times and it was always fresh and new and appropriate. It was a marvel to him that a man could speak so often, so lengthily, so eloquently, and yet never say a thing that jarred the feelings at funerals. Ex-Mayor James Sharp said there was not a man in the Church who was as good for all occasions, as a speaker, etc.
>
> Heber Wells heard these comments and told me of them afterwards. I told him they little knew how I had to pray and struggle and

> wrestle with the Lord for those blessings, and how, when I was told I had done my best, was when, just before speaking, I had felt my worst. It was the power of God that helped me, not my own ability, except as the Spirit played upon it. To God be all the glory.[17]

Speaking and writing was his life, where his ego and self-esteem resided. Because he was so good at it, it raised his spirits out of depression, which was a trouble he battled throughout life. His fame and name were growing. Reading epistles written by the First Presidency at general conference helped legitimize him. Speaking at endless funerals placed him before diverse audiences. Accounts of his public addresses were often printed in the newspapers. Ort was becoming a leading figure in Utah and the Church. He explained the developments, "So many of the leading Brethren were in prison or 'on the underground'—as their enforced retirement was called—that I was bought to the front more and more, especially as a public speaker, and for a time was the most frequent occupant of the Tabernacle pulpit. 'Unduly prominent,' some said, and seemed to hold me personally responsible for the many calls that came to me. The logic of it was of course unanswerable."[18]

Not all went his way, however. Along with an occasional rumor reaching him about his views on reincarnation, and worry over his friendship with the Stayner brothers, he had a first counselor in the bishopric, Robert Patrick, that he struggled to work with. Bishop Whitney felt it was mostly a matter of jealousy. Patrick was older and more experienced while Whitney was young, inexperienced in business affairs, and becoming more popular and influential every year. This difficult relationship taxed Orson's patience. After leaving a meeting in which the leading Church authorities had recommended a divisive political direction, feelings arose:

> Going home from this meeting I was conversing with Bros. John Nicholson and Robert Patrick and we were all commenting on the meeting; Brother [Patrick] was quite ugly and spiteful in his criticism of those who upheld the statehood venture. I kindly said, "Brethren, we must be careful and not allow any bitterness to rankle in our hearts toward our brethren. We must pray for them, and feel

kindly towards them." At this, much to my surprise, Bro. Patrick took offense and insultingly accused me of rebuking him. I said, "You are putting the cap on yourself; I haven't spoken your name. I am speaking as much for my own benefit as anyone's." He again told me insolently that I was "losing time" in rebuking him. I then said, sternly a little, "Well, if the cap fits you put it on; if you feel the rebuke you're welcome to it." Bro. Nicholson parted with me in kindness for he recognized that I was in the right, but Bro. Patrick went off angry and muttering. The Lord judge between us. It's only a sample of his ill-temper and unreasonable and rude conduct that I have put up with patiently for years, he being my 1st counselor. God will humble the proud![19]

In truth Bishop Whitney was no more pleased with the push for statehood and the accompanying state constitutional provision outlawing polygamy than his counselor. He struggled mightily with the various steps taken by the First Presidency to end polygamy.

At the [stake] meeting in Orderville, John W. Taylor, after I had spoken, said to the people "I like to hear Bro. Whitney speak, it makes me feel happy for he tells the truth and he tells it by the Spirit of God. It does me good and makes me [repent?] . . . Whenever I am in doubt as the which of two or more things is right or what of two or more things I should do, I choose the one that gives me a happy feeling." So do I! But it should be prayerfully considered before action be taken. After prayer the Spirit of God makes things clear.

I have been greatly tried and tempted about the statehood movement. It seemed to me to be a relinquishment of power. [Illegible] receding from our position as Latter-day Saints, and God forbid, our doing anything of that kind!

But the First Presidency and Twelve sanction it, I am told, and the counsel of the Authorities is to vote for the constitution, anti-polygamy clause and all. Here's the rub! How can [illegible] more the Priesthood and be justified? How can we take the dead letter and with it condemn or sit in judgment upon the living apostles? If we can honor God's servants and sustain them, will not God honor us and justify us? I prayed over the matter much, for I was troubled. Like dews from heaven came that steady answer, "Yes my son, those who honor my Priesthood, those will I honor. Therefore, trouble not yourself about this matter, but go and do as my servants counsel you,

> and all shall be well with you. [Illegible] the issue," saith the Lord, "and I will judge men by their motives and the desires of their hearts and consecrate their action for my own glory [illegible] Amen."[20]

Two days later, Bishop Whitney learned that President John Taylor (John W. Taylor's father) had passed away. Ort expressed his feelings with vigor,

> Heard, this afternoon, that President John Taylor died last night at five minutes to 8 o'clock. Salt Lake papers confirm the tidings. Funeral Friday at noon in Tabernacle, Salt Lake City.
>
> At my house . . . about three months ago, I prophesied in the name of the Lord that the time was near when President John Taylor would be at liberty and would sit in the congregations of Israel. Also that he was not long for earth, but would soon pass away, being typical of "old things" to be done away, and that the Lord was about to "make all things new." I said [scissor snip excision several lines] away and the Lord will from henceforth make all things new. Mark it! Mighty changes are at hand. The proud will be brought low and the humble exalted. The hypocrite will be known and the unbeliever and ungodly cast out. Merit will be recognized, wherever it is found; nepotism will die out, and favoritism in due time disappear. God will speak! And bring forth the deliverer of Zion! [End of entry removed].[21]

President Taylor died at Kaysville, Utah, in exile on the underground, never having regained his freedom to move among the people. Unless Orson meant his passing into the spirit world would grant him his freedom, at least part of this did not come to pass. Because Orson took care to remove some of the diary entry, it seems likely this prophecy was uttered during a meeting with the Stayners. About the same time, Whitney learned that his father-in-law, Abraham O. Smoot, also died. And to make matters even more complicated, his wife gave birth while he was away from home. As soon as he could reach her, he gave her a blessing, promising that the baby would be healthy and strong. He also noted that "previous to this we prayed and Zina saw some visions, which I interpreted."[22] Orson also received another payment for his work writing the biography of Heber C. Kimball for the Kimball family.[23]

The question of whether to register to vote continued to plague Ort. Though he was not yet a polygamist, he believed in the principle, but the test oath put to Mormons required that they have nothing to do with polygamy. He shared his thoughts and how he was blessed on what to do:

> The last day of the registration came: June 11. I had prayed much upon the matter, but was still undecided. I wanted to obey counsel, and honor the Priesthood, but not to do anything wrong. I had a talk with Apostle Franklin D. Richards and he said, "You will not relinquish any principle by registering and voting. You take the oath as a condition precedent to voting or holding office [and] that is all. If your object is to take it so that you can vote, you can [illegible] sacred until after the election, and you are then relieved of the obligation assumed. If you take it to hold office, you should keep it until your official term is expired. That's the way I view it; and that's what I should do if I were in your place.
>
> I went home at noon and prayed that something might occur before night to throw me upon the right track. I called the Lord to witness that I was willing to do either thing—to register or not register—that He would show me [which] was according to His will.
>
> I left the office at 5 p.m., determined to register if nothing prevented. I went home and got to studying and actually forgot all about the matter. At about 6 o'clock or half past, a knock came at my door, and on my opening it there stood the registrar, Duncan Noble, who said, "Mr. Whitney, I understand you wish to register. I am going home a little early tonight and I thought I would call on you." I was amazed, not only because I had forgotten all about the matter, but because of this action of the registrar, an anti-Mormon or at least a non-Mormon, not interested at all in the registration of Mormon voters. Yet, instead of my calling on him (he had been sitting in our meeting house a little way from my house) he had actually called on me. I at once recognized it as a dispensation of providence, a testimony, the "sign" in fact that I had asked for, and inviting him in. I registered in my own house. He did not ask me to raise my hand and swear but signified to sign my name to a printed form beginning "I swear or affirm," etc., "not a bigamist or polygamist," "will not aid or abet others to practice" [the] same. Will keep laws of U.S. especially laws of [illegible] & 1882 relating to bigamy or polygamy," etc. On August 1st I voted for the constitution forbidding bigamy, polygamy,

> with the same motive that prompted me to register—to honor the Priesthood and sustain their measure for the cause of Zion, for such I understood it to be.
>
> Is it not the highest moral ground a man can take, to sacrifice his own convictions, the result of reason, at the promptings of a still higher conviction, based on faith, and sustained by a clear conscience and by what he believes to be the Spirit of God, the peace of which "passeth understanding?" Is not faith superior to reason? Yes. Is not faith the highest grade of reason? I believe so.[24]

Still seeking affirmation of his troubled feelings and thinking, he met with a friend that he respected and admired above all others. "Had an interview with Bro. Joseph F. Smith who was very kind and glad to see me. First time I have met him since he went into exile. He thinks the prospect for statehood was never so bright—and that we give away nothing in the transaction—it being in his view a political settlement and not a religious compromise. A few days later had a very enjoyable interview with Apostle Moses Thatcher. He confided to me that he had more hope than faith in the success of the statehood movement. He said many other things some of which it would not be wise to put down. He agreed with me that the key to the whole solution of the problem of Zion's redemption was in that we place the spiritual above the temporal and seek God's kingdom and his righteousness first of all things."[25]

At the October general conference, Bishop Whitney was accorded a favor, demonstrating his growing prominence.

> Opened Conference with prayer this a.m. in the Tabernacle and was appointed to read Pres. Woodruff's epistle this afternoon. Read the epistle 1 hour & 45 minutes long. My voice held out wonderfully, Bro. Nicholson said; adding—"Very few men in the Church could do that—their voices could not endure the strain." I had asked the Lord to strengthen me according to my need and He did so.
>
> On Sunday, [the] 9th in the afternoon, the speakers were President Wilford Woodruff, Apostle H. J. Grant, Elder John Nicholson, myself, and Apostle F. D. Richards. It was the first time I ever spoke at a General conference of the Church. Bro. Woodruff had me called up. I occupied about 12 minutes. Bro. Woodruff's appearance in public after his long retirement in exile was the signal for a demonstration.

> The congregation applauded him to the echo. He waved back salutation. This was before he had spoken. Apostle Erastus Snow spoke Saturday morning. He also has been hid up for two or three years. Bro. Woodruff said he was not long for this life, or words to that effect, and he looked pale or ethereal as he spoke. We all rejoiced to see him and I to be among the few to grasp his faltering hand.[26]

Ort had another dream involving President Joseph F. Smith,[27] and was invited by President Lorenzo Snow, who recognized the unusual ability in his new protégé, to speak at the Box Elder Stake Conference. He recorded the incident that became one of the great miracles of his life,

> At Box Elder Stake Conference on the invitation of Apostle Lorenzo Snow. My wife and children were sick and I had about given up going, but Zina, my wife, urged me to go and seeing her faith I resolved to fill my appointment and had no reason to regret my trust in Providence, for the Lord healed my loved ones, and blessed me abundantly. . . . Sunday afternoon, in meeting, I had a little bouquet of flowers given to me by Bro. Burbank. It occurred to me to bless the flowers and send them home by R. W. Sloan, who was going to the city that evening while I was to remain till next morning. I therefore laid hands on the bouquet and in the name of Jesus Christ and by virtue and authority of the Holy Priesthood blessed them that the flowers might be instrumental in healing anyone who touched or smelt of them, especially little Helen Mar, our sick baby. Bro. Sloan delivered the flowers and my message that night. When I arrived home next day the baby was sitting up bright and quite herself again, although she had had a severe spell of sickness, and Saturday and Sunday, both, were very bad. Zina on getting the flowers had let her hold them in her hand and she was healed according to my prayer—and the blessing pronounced upon the flowers.
>
> Apostle Snow was absent at the Bannock Stake conference. I was entertained by Sister Minnie J. Snow, his wife. I have never had a pleasanter time than at this conference. The Spirit and power of God were there, certainly.[28]

In mid-November, Orson had a dream that he interpreted as support for his reincarnation beliefs. He wrote that "last night, in a dream, a beautiful woman, angelic in appearance, was shown to me as in a vision. She told me she was my wife, that she lived in heaven, and that I left her in change of my home there when I came down upon the earth. Her face was entirely new to me, so far as recollection went, and she was very beautiful. This dream illustrates a doctrine I have believed for several years."[29]

Meanwhile, Ort noticed that President Snow's sister Eliza was not looking well, and mentioned the fact in a letter to President Joseph F. Smith. "Sister Eliza R. is wearing the look of another world. It looks as though her long and useful life were drawing to a close. Well, she has nobly won the right to rest, and is to be almost envied by the weary. However, I am one who wants to live—yes as long as she has, if God wills, and do as much for Him and His holy cause. Peace be unto her, living or dead."[30] Some six months later she was gone and President Snow asked Orson to prepare the remarks given at her funeral for publication.

Eliza R. Snow (USHS)

It was during this time, late 1887, that President Snow and Orson began having long private talks together, mostly regarding deep or speculative Church doctrine and history. Much of the material is lost because Orson removed pages or lines from the diaries, but what remains is of interest. The account begins with Orson receiving a priesthood blessing from Pres. Snow:

> [At least one page missing] hands were upon my head he predicted that I would be "lifted up and occupy places high and glorious in

> this life," and when he sat down he said that the Lord had shown him some things concerning me that he did not dare tell. "But," he added, "they will all come along in due time."
>
> During our talks he told me that his sister, the late Eliza R. Snow Smith was a firm believer in the principle of reincarnation and that she claimed to have received it from Joseph the Prophet, her husband. He said he saw nothing unreasonable in it, and could believe it, if it came to him from the Lord or His oracle. He said [two lines missing], that I had a revealing mind, and was wonderfully gifted in the power to reach after and grasp the mysteries. He said he loved to talk with me, but that I must be careful to whom I talked for most men did not care anything for these principles, being "darkened in mind," that as I grew and increased in the knowledge of God men would become jealous of me and seek to injure me. "But I will befriend you," he said, "and I want you to feel perfectly free with me." He told me that he heard Joseph Smith tell a man once that he would become a God and reign in glory, but that before that he would have to be crucified as Christ was. That man is still living [one line missing].[31]

Other such visits would follow as the years passed. Orson regarded his friendship with men like Presidents Snow and Smith, and other such Church leaders, as one of the greatest blessings of his life. At a social function near the end of the year, he found himself in their presence. "Attended a supper at Heber M. Wells. . . . President Wilford Woodruff, George Q. Cannon, and Joseph F. Smith were there. We had a splendid time. A feast of fat things, but the fattest of all was the sight of our dear leaders' faces. My heart went out in affection toward them, hunted and driven and obliged to conceal themselves from their own people, because of ungodly persecution. I felt as though I could shed my blood in their defense if necessary. Bro. Woodruff was very kind to me, and paid me marked attention. I learned from Joseph F. that my friend Rudger Clawson, lately released on the President's pardon after three years in the penitentiary for polygamy, is to be the President of the Box Elder Stake of Zion. Good!"[32]

The year closed with Whitney once more recording someone's reaction to his speaking: "I heard today that Apostle John W. Taylor, in the 19th ward meetinghouse last night, said in his remarks that five or six men were made to do all the preaching in the Tabernacle nowadays and it was wrong. He added—'I don't want you to think I am referring to Bishop Whitney. If all our preachers were like him, the congregation would always be interested. His sermon today was one of the best I ever heard in my life. Furthermore, I have traveled with Bishop Whitney, and he is not only a gentleman but a man of intelligence and information. I never enjoyed myself better, or learned more in the same length of time than I did while traveling a few days with him, through some of the settlements of this territory. I don't mean him.' Bishop James Watson told me this. I was glad to hear the straight of it for it had reached my ears first that he said nobody but Bishop Whitney could get a chance to preach in the Tabernacle nowadays. How a lie will gather bigness, like a snowball, as it goes!"[33]

Chapter 7

Of Wives and Doctrine, 1888–1889

The year 1888 began with Orson Whitney's continued rise in prominence as a public speaker, strengthening of his friendships with men like Charles Stayner and Moses Thatcher, and learning of a misguided attempt to lobby for his inclusion in the Quorum of the Twelve. Of this last incident, he wrote,

> B. Y. Hampton, the other day, handed me the copy of a letter written July 11, 1887 to the First Presidency, wherein he referred to a sermon I preached in the Tabernacle a day or two before and said he went home strongly impressed that I was the right man to fill the vacancy in the Quorum of the Twelve. He therefore recommended or nominated me for that office and hoped it was the Lord's will, etc. I had heard of this several months before and was a little vexed, for though Brother Hampton's motive was good and he is my friend, I thought it possible the Authorities might think I had inspired it. My friend Heber M. Wells told him that he would hurt rather than benefit me by such things, and Hampton then said he hoped not, as it was far from his intention. He had influence with the Quorum and other brethren in high places and had often nominated men for civil offices and they got them. I heard nothing more of it until B. Y. H. handed me the letter the other day.[1]

Orson continued working on *The Life of Heber C. Kimball*, and filling many speaking engagements. He was elected to take the minutes for various sessions of the Utah legislature, a position that did not last long because, as he reported on February 9: "This day I was elected Chief Clerk of the House of Representatives of the 28th session (or the remainder thereof) of the Utah legislature, succeeding Joseph A. West who resigned yesterday. I was the unanimous choice of the Committee on nomination, and was unanimously elected in the House. I resigned my office of Minute Clerk to which I was elected first one month ago today."[2]

He continued having dreams and recording them, though leaving an element of mystery in them. "Dreamed last night that Salt Lake City was filled with soldiers and under martial law. The Tabernacle was closed and no preaching was allowed there. Our people had taken to the mountains and woods and were camped in various places, in the most primitive manner. I saw some that are now in good circumstances, living in mansions, sitting round campfires, driven from their homes. I am told that my grandfather President Heber C. Kimball predicted such things. I had two dreams a little while ago corroborative of the above in which a certain young lady friend of mine was connected."[3] The young woman's identity remains unknown, unless he was referring to the plural wife, May Wells, whom he would marry later in the year.

One day he found himself at his mother's home. She explained, "Orson came in this forenoon; said he was on his way home and the Spirit said to him, 'Your mother wants to see you, go and see her.' He turned his face and came as directed. I was filled with gratitude; knowing of a surety that the Lord had heard my prayers and told him I knew that it was the right spirit that spoke to him. 'I know it too,' said he. [He] wanted to know if I have anything new to tell him. I told him no, but I'd longed to see him, to have a little visit. He is working hard to finish my father's history and said he had felt nearly disheartened he found so little time."[4]

At this point in his life, with the secret prayer meetings continuing and his alliance with the Stayner's deepening, Whitney begins referencing a "cause" and what he thought to be his place in it. Based on later diary entries, it seems that Whitney saw himself as a forerunner to Charles Stayner becoming the prophet of the Lord to the Church. Commenting on public compliments that mentioned one of his talks quoted in a newspaper, he wrote that "I'm afraid such eulogies win me as many enemies as friends. All I am I owe to my Heavenly Father, and without Him I am nothing. That I have a mission I believe; I know; but it is not to lead Israel. I am only a forerunner and the humble representative of a cause. There cometh one after me mightier than I, the latchet of whose shoe I am barely worthy to unloose, as he the Master's."[5] Stayner's influence over Whitney would increase as the years passed, with a plan formulated for Charles to one day become President of the Church. Stayner's flattery continued working on Ort: "Preached in the Tabernacle occupying all the time (1 hour). Had felt much unlike speaking and for fear I might be called I decided not to go; but as I was leaving the yard, after circle meeting I was sent for and returned. The Lord was with me and my words were with power. Arthur Stayner said it was the profoundest discourse I ever preached, full of meat and instruction."[6]

Helen Mar recorded in her diary a glimpse of some of the things her son shared with her about his meetings with the Stayners, "Orson came to see me and told me some experience of his own and others in grappling with the powers of the evil one, and [of] gaining the victory and receiving great blessings from above, etc."[7]

February saw Whitney re-elected as City Treasurer and continuing as Chancellor of the University of Deseret. He also kept serving as bishop. One day Elder Moses Thatcher, who had been hiding on the underground, made a surprise appearance in his ward sacrament meeting and spoke. The next day Orson ran into Elder Thatcher again and they had a long visit together; the substance of what they discussed was not recorded.[8]

At the April general conference, Whitney again "read the Epistle of the Twelve at the conference, which commenced last Thursday 5th, and afterward, by request of Pres. Lorenzo Snow, addressed the congregation. Was tired from reading, but the Lord blessed me."[9] John Donaldson, Whitney's missionary friend from England, visited during the conference and joined with Ort and the Stayners: "We had some fine times while he was here. He and I went on top of the Mount first to the east of the city cemetery and prayed and dedicated the spot to the Lord for the redemption of Zion. Met several nights at Joshua's [Charles Stayner's] and had splendid times."[10]

During spare moments, Orson was able to continue working on Heber C. Kimball's life story. "Orson had father's history uppermost in his mind," Helen Mar wrote, "and searched through some of the bound [*Woman's*] *Exponent's* for my historical sketches, taken from my father's journal."[11] The work was progressing well.[12]

In May, Whitney was able to attend the dedication of the Manti Temple, south of Utah County toward Central Utah. President Snow asked Whitney to speak with Elder John Henry Smith, his former mission president, at the Manti Stake conference, previous to the Temple dedication. He called it "a splendid meeting."[13] He was thrilled with the dedication service itself: "Attended the dedication of the temple, the first one I ever saw dedicated. Sat in the bishop's seats at the south side of the central stands devoted to the Aaronic Priesthood. During the dedication some saw Haloes of light about the speakers heads and heard singing from an invisible chorus. I heard music and felt a very vivid impression of the Holy Spirit. Apostle Lorenzo Snow offered the dedicatory prayer. The grand shout of 'Hosanna' [illegible] the entire congregation. It was the most animated and inspiring spectacle I ever beheld. After the ceremonies which, with the addresses, lasted about five hours, all formed in twos and the line went through the temple examining and admiring its beautiful interior."[14] The temple had previously been dedicated by President Woodruff in a private service, before the public dedication presided over by President Snow.[15]

In early June, Orson gave one of his more well-known lectures, stating, "This morning I delivered my lecture on Home Literature in the conference. It is published in full, or will be in tomorrow's [*Deseret*] *News*. It is said to be my best effort of the kind. I fully realized Bro. Thatcher's blessing, given me April 29th."[16] Orson also participated in blessing some family members. His mother wrote, "Orson and Bro. Charles Stayner called . . . to administer to Lillie and bless the babe. Orson was sick, the cause of his not coming yesterday; Lillie was first anointed and blessed, and then her babe. They received great promises by the Spirit. Orson then proposed my being blessed. He anointed me and Brother Stayner administered, and pronounced the most encouraging blessings upon me, and that I should enjoy that of health, and begin to mend from that time, etc. I asked them to administer to Sister Paramour, as she was feeling poor in body and mind. Although they had stayed longer than they felt that time would allow they did so, and afterward Bro. Stayner testified that there was a heavenly spirit here, and Orson said the same. I told them it was comforting to hear it from them though I'd felt it."[17]

On July 1, Ort turned thirty-three years old, and for a surprise birthday present of profound and selfless love, his wife Zina gave her consent to his marrying, as a plural wife, Mary (or May) Wells, a daughter of Daniel H. Wells by his plural wife Lydia Ann Alley Wells. She was also a sister of Emma Wells, the young deceased woman Orson had desired to be his first wife, in precedence to any other. Whether May knew anything of these circumstances regarding her sister is not known. On his birthday, Orson came home to find May in the living room of his rented home, and Zina cooking a family birthday dinner in the kitchen.[18] In his original diary entry, Orson wrote, "Today I complete my 33rd year. Zina gave me a present which I cannot name. She is a brave and noble girl." Some unknown time later, he added the words, "Zina gave me her consent to marry May."[19] This marriage was kept secret from Zina's children and from the public until Zina's death.

That same day, Orson wrote of finishing his first extensive historical project. "I also celebrate today the completion of my book—*Life of Heber C. Kimball*—my first literary work issued in book form, upon which I have been engaged for about one year. I have received for it $1000 from the Kimball family. This has been no adequate payment, but I agreed to do it for that and have kept my word. It has been a labor of love, not of money, and I dedicate it to His memory of my noble grand-father and the great Cause of Truth for which he lived and died."[20] The book became a classic, then and today. Orson felt pride in its reception, and noted special compliments: "My uncle, Solomon F. Kimball, tells me that Pres. Joseph F. Smith told his brother Andrew Kimball that whenever he had the 'blues' or felt dejected, he picked up *The Life of Heber C. Kimball* and read in it; he said it always gave him a good spirit. This is one of the highest compliments my book has had."[21] Also, "My friend George C. Parkinson from Franklin, Idaho, is in town. He told me that during a recent visit to his stake of Apostles John Henry Smith and Heber J. Grant;

these Brethren, speaking of the respective merits of *The Life of Joseph the Prophet* and *Life of Heber C. Kimball*, said they would lay down the former (George Q.'s book) any time to take up the other. [Text removed] told George C. [text removed] been brought into prominence, not particularly on his merits, that Orson Whitney had got there on his own merits. I thought this was very generous of Bro. Grant."[22]

Some fifty-five years later, when Andrew Kimball's son, Spencer W. Kimball, became a member of the Quorum of the Twelve Apostles, he was also elected president of the Kimball family organization. As part of that responsibility, Elder Kimball's biographers stated that "he set about reissuing the long out-of-print *Life of Heber C. Kimball*, which had been out of print for some years, hoping with this book 'to bring the immense Kimball family together . . . that they will lean to the Lord and His work as they follow grandfather.' Although the many miracles, prophecies, and visions in the *Life* were thought by some to be too loosely documented and by others too sacred for general publication, Spencer decided that, except for a handful of changes, it was 'wise to leave the new [edition of the] book in the masterful form given it' by his cousin Orson F. Whitney in 1888."[23]

Now that Ort had received from Zina, and from Church leaders, permission to marry a plural wife, he still had the matter of his strong desire to be sealed to the deceased Emma Wells to consider. It seems he did not receive permission from her parents to be sealed to her before he married Zina. He now took measures to resolve the longstanding issue. In his diary he recorded,

> July 13, 1888: This day, in the temple at Manti, were sealed to me for time and all eternity Emmeline Wells, daughter of Daniel H. and Emmeline B. Wells, and Fannie Adele McBride, daughter of David and Orpha McBride. Both these are dead. Emma's mother (Emmeline B. Wells) stood as heiress in one case and proxy in the other. The officiating Elder was President Daniel H. Wells, Emma's father. Witnesses: John Alder and Christian J. Christianson. Emma was born in Salt Lake City, Utah, Sept. 10, 1853, and died there April 8, 1878. Fannie was born in Oberlin, Ohio, March 11, 1853, and died in Salt Lake City, January 7, 1881. I went through the temple and had endowments for and in behalf of James Woodward, Emma's uncle, brother to E. B. Wells, her mother.

> I had written to Pres. Wells two or three days before, asking his consent to my union with Emma. He gave me consent last evening on my arrival here, and told me I had his blessing and heartiest approval. Thus is fulfilled the word of the Lord to me through his servant [Charles W. Stayner] in Liverpool over six years ago. The Lord said, "Verily, thus saith the Lord, it is my will that my servant (Orson F. Whitney) should take my handmaiden (Emma) but it must be according to the order of heaven and not of earth." This is the gist of it as I recollect it. I thank thee, O my Father, for these precious blessings conferred upon me this day. Help me to merit them and all that I have yet received or shall receive from Thee; for Jesus sake, Amen![24]

With his sealing to Emma finally accomplished, he started a long trip to Diaz, Mexico, where he could be sealed to May Wells. He traveled with Zina and their baby Helen, but he does not mention whether May traveled with them or took another route. May and Orson were married by Elder Moses Thatcher on July 24, 1888. They then returned home by the same route, and upon returning kept the sealing a secret, even from their children.[25] The federal raids and persecutions were in full force, and it was thought better to keep the union secret rather than risk a prison term for Orson.[26]

Orson was only home for a couple of weeks when he came down with typhoid fever, a malady that put him in a bed-ridden, near delirious condition for much of two months. By October he was still unable to work, but had been able to give a few talks, and meet with friends. John Donaldson had again visited, and the group "had some very happy meetings."[27] One of the funerals he spoke at was that of the wife of his old friend Heber M. Wells. Heber Wells would later become the first governor of Utah. On November 10, Orson Whitney was proud to see the first copies of his book *Life of Heber C. Kimball* come from the bindery.[28] This was a special moment for him, but one he would experience many times during his life.

Later in the month Orson again traveled to Brigham City, this time with the Stayner brothers, to visit President Lorenzo Snow and speak in meetings. "We arrived the same night and were quartered comfortably at the house of Sister Minnie Snow. Had an interview after supper with Apostle Lorenzo Snow at the house of Bp. Nichols, where Bro. Snow has a room."[29] The next day, "after a brief and interesting interview with Apostle Snow, Arthur and I attended a missionary meeting at the Box Elder Stake Academy, where we each addressed the little assembly. C. W. [Stayner] remained with Bro. Snow. Myself and Arthur spoke to the meeting in the Tabernacle at 2 p.m. And C.W. [Stayner] and I at night had a splendid time. The Spirit was with us powerfully. The meetings were crowded."[30] Of the visit, Ort noted, "Bro. Snow was much pleased with our visit. He seems to think a great deal of me and takes much interest in my welfare. He warmly commended and endorsed my remarks yesterday and also those of the other brethren, and in a private interview told me several things of great interest. One of the things he said he had kept [confidential] for 50 years. It pertained to the lineage of my grandparents Newel K. Whitney and wife and Heber C. Kimball, who, he said, the Prophet Joseph told his sister Eliza, were descendants of the Savior."[31]

After Christmas, Whitney reported another dream, this time involving his old friends and mentors, Presidents Brigham Young and John Taylor:

> I dreamed last night that I went into a meeting of some kind at which President Brigham Young was the presiding authority. As I entered he came toward me and taking me by the hand gave me a kind and cordial greeting. His manner was hearty and whole-souled, and his face beamed with pleasure. His look and action seemed to say: God bless you, my boy, you are doing well, and I am watching you with interest and satisfaction. He appeared to be in the full rigor of manhood, and replete with spiritual power. The impression left by the dream was happifying. The full meaning will doubtless appear hereafter.
>
> Some months ago I dreamed that President John Taylor came into a room where I was and shook hands with me and several others. He was bent and worn and emaciated, and wept as he greeted us. He took both my hands in his, and while the tears coursed down his cheeks, said with deep feeling: "God bless you, Brother Whitney."[32]

The new year, 1889, began with Orson signing notes (cosigning on loans) with the Stayner brothers for a thousand dollars, to help them pay some debts. He also preached, at President Wilford Woodruff's request, at the funeral of Woodruff's brother Azmon.[33] This led to a visit the next day with President Woodruff. "In the course of our conversation he said, 'Well, Bro. Whitney, you're doing a great deal of good. You are preaching sound doctrine and comforting the hearts of the Saints, and the Lord is blessing you in your labors.' He was referring to my sermons, etc."[34] Orson was careful to record such comments, since they helped balance out the anxiety he felt because of the rumors that reached his ears about his dealings with the Stayners and reincarnation.

The Stayner brothers asked Whitney to invest in a sugar beet company they were organizing and serve as a director.[35] (Nothing is mentioned again of that enterprise.) Orson also put some thought into what he felt to be Charles's future. His diary states, for February 8, 1889, "It occurred to me today that Elias [Charles W. Stayner] would be the 7th President of the Church in this dispensation. Therefore, that having had three already and Pres. Woodruff being the 4th, there are two more to intervene before Elias takes the seat of Presidency."[36] No further reasoning or commentary is given, but at the time, it was planned that Whitney would try to help Charles Stayner up the ladder to the apostleship, and then he would become President of the Church. However, things did not work out as they anticipated. Elder Heber J. Grant, who did not care for the Stayner brothers, became the seventh president of the Church after the death of President Joseph F. Smith.

That winter, Whitney learned that a small settlement in Idaho had organized and received permission to name their town and ward after him. Some of the leading residents had enjoyed newspaper reports of his sermons and lectures, and had requested the naming. "Pres. George C. Parkinson, of Oneida Stake is in the city. He told me today that the name 'Whitney' had been given to the little settlement between Franklin and Preston, in accordance with the intention of the inhabitants and their desires expressed to him about a year ago, and related to me last March. . . . He wants me to visit the place and I told him I certainly would [at] the first opportunity. I considered it an uncommon honor, the christening of this town after so unworthy a person as myself."[37] The fact that George C.

Parkinson, the stake president in that area, was one of Orson's best friends and a member of his prayer group, probably helped it happen.

Orson's rise as a speaker continued, and he recorded his success. "This night I delivered a lecture in the sixth ward meeting house under the auspices of the Mutual Improvement Association of said ward. My subject was 'Mormonism, the Misunderstood.' There was a full house; I spoke an hour and ¾ and was listened to with rapt attention. At the expiration of about 1½ hours I apologized for keeping them so long, and remarked that 'Mormonism' was not a subject that could be presented in a nut-shell—when voices cried out 'go on, go on' and so I continued another 15 minutes. The Lord blessed me abundantly, and out of my weakness brought forth His own strength. It is a night I shall never forget."[38]

The same day Orson, with a friend, called at the Gardo House to see President George Q. Cannon, just released from the penitentiary. Orson commented, "He is looking and feeling fine, a picture of health and brimming over with good nature." The next Sunday, Cannon and President Woodruff both spoke in a packed Tabernacle—"His words were spirited and powerful and visibly affected the multitude." Whitney gave the closing prayer.[39]

Early March found Ort with the Stayners. "At Joshua's [Charles's] this afternoon I exercised the gift of revelation, pure and simple, for the first time. It came in fulfillment of Joshua's words at a previous meeting. Moses [Arthur] already had it and exercised it at the former meeting."[40] Again, so further explanation is noted.

At this time, Bishop Whitney found himself embroiled in a minor doctrinal controversy. He explained,

> Was called on to speak in the Tabernacle this evening, during the stake conference; occupied about an hour. Theme: The living oracle in preference to the dead letter, and the progressive character of Mormonism as the work of God. Apostle Moses Thatcher followed for a few minutes, and the meeting then came to a close. My remarks were in two sections. I preached a discourse in which I showed the progressive character of the Lord's work, and the necessity for an inspired Priesthood at the head of the Church—the living oracles, and that it was the duty of the Saints to honor existing authorities through whom God communicated His will to His people, and that unlike

the Christian world we must not deify the dead letter and deny new revelation; not lose confidence in the leaders of the Church today, which Joseph Smith said was the first step to apostasy. But, as it was evident that much more remained to be revealed to the Church—and greater things than had ever yet been revealed—it was necessary that we not only have living prophets, seers, and revelators, and always would have them, but must honor them, uphold them, and pray for them that they might be abundantly inspired to deliver unto us the word of God as fast as we are able to receive it, etc. I testified that God was with this people and that His word was not going backward, or standing still, as some supposed, but was going on and was preparing to take the grandest leap of victory the world had ever beheld.

After I had sat down Apostle Moses Thatcher asked me to explain that I did not mean that the written law could be done away with until it had fully subserved the purpose for which it was instituted; an explanation I hardly thought necessary in view of the fact that I had said in the beginning of my remarks that we accepted as divine the Bible, the Book of Mormon, Doctrine and Covenants, etc. And that God's laws were eternal and Himself unchangeable, though circumstances were continually changing and that of necessity there must also be changes in regulation, and law, etc., when obsolete, to suit the times, etc. However, at his request I emphasized my meaning, showing that while the Gospel's principles were eternal, and even such laws as that of Moses was or might be eternal in one sense—that is whenever applicable in this world or future worlds—that regulations and laws that became obsolete were superseded, and God's work progressed, by higher laws and more suitable regulations. That the law of Moses was an instance, not destroyed but fulfilled in the coming of Christ, and hence set aside like a kerosene lamp after the introduction of the gas light, etc.

Bro. Thatcher then made his remarks endorsing what I had said and laying it down that the living oracle must speak according to the written law, as long as that law was in force—a position I had not in the least questioned. My only motive was to uphold the authority of the Holy Priesthood, and show that a living prophet, inspired of God, was superior to a dead book though filled with written truths, as a leader and guide on to perfection—a position taken yesterday at priesthood meeting by Pres. George Q. Cannon, by Pres. Brigham Young in his lifetime, and by many other prophets of The Church of Jesus Christ of Latter-day Saints. And I know that my position is right, for so speaks the Spirit of God to me.

> William B. Dougall and wife told me, when I asked them if they thought I had put my foot in it that they thought Moses had done so, not me; that my position was correct, and it was not right for him to break the force of my testimony or detract in the least from what I had said.
>
> B.Y. Hampton said he thought Bro. Thatcher imagined I was aiming a rebuke at him for his course and attitude in the Quorum of the Twelve, which is said to be in opposition to some of his seniors, and, said Hampton: "You gave him a terrible scoring for his remarks of the [afternoon?], and he felt it; that's all. You were all right and he deserved all he got." The remark Bro. Hampton referred to was a eulogy of Pres. Brigham Young in which Bro. Thatcher had said, "Would to God we had another Brigham Young." "Israel, where is thy wisdom?" As much as to say Pres. Woodruff was not only unwise, but was not the man for the place he holds. Hampton thought this was "a bad break" on Moses's part, and that my discourse in the evening was a fitting answer to him. And yet, I had not intended it as such. I simply spoke what the Lord gave me, purely unpremeditated, and without an intent to reply to him, or aim at anyone. I am certain I am right, and shall stand by my position which I believe to be invulnerable. I uphold God's Priesthood, the living oracles. Let those who will fight against them; I dare not.[41]

The exchange with Elder Thatcher at the pulpit caused some local stir, and Bishop Whitney soon found himself talking with a friend (whose name he deleted from the entry, but was likely John Nicholson) on the matter.

> In the afternoon I had a long conversation with [name removed] in which he took the ground that it was wrong to obey the Priesthood [brethren] unless you felt that what they directed should be done was the correct thing to do; that a man should be the judge himself of the rightfulness of the thing ordered done, and that if he did not see its rightfulness he ought not to do it, no matter who told him to; for if he did he would violate his conscience, morally injure himself, and in effect "stunt his growth" and spiritual development. He took the position, substantially, that unless the living oracle, i.e., the revelator and mouthpiece of God at the head of the Church said, "Thus said the Lord," in requiring a thing done, that he would not do it, and that the living oracle must speak in

consonance with the written word, i.e. the letter of the law, or he was not to be obeyed.

I held that God's Priesthood to me was the same as God, for they represented him and held His authority. That they had the right to direct and govern and give counsel, and that it was the duty of the Saints to honor them and uphold them and to follow counsel, even though they might not at all times see the wisdom of that counsel. That the Priesthood was placed in the Church for that very purpose: to see for those who could not see for themselves, and that those who obeyed counsel would always be justified, and those who gave the counsel were the ones who were responsible in the premises. I held that while it was to be hoped that a necessity for choice between the written word and the living oracle would never come, that if it did come the safest plan was to heed the living oracle.

Bro. [name removed] in conclusion, said he used to think as I do now but had got past it and would hate to take such a position at the present time. I answered him that I used to feel as he does, but was a happier man since I changed my views and adopted my present position. This difference of sentiment, I find, is spreading all through the Church, some being for the living oracle, some for the dead letter. It will probably be the line on which the Church will divide in the great "falling away" that is near at hand. Oh, my God, and Father in Heaven, preserve me in the true way with thy Spirit as my guide, that in that day of choosing I, like Mary, may take the better part.

Charles H. Wilcken told me today that Bro. Thatcher's remarks and mine at the Tabernacle [on] Sunday had created quite a sensation. In relation to mine and Bro. Thatcher's qualification Sunday night, Wilcken said all that he had spoken [and?] thought that what I said was correct, and that no "explanation" was necessary.

Bro. Nicholson told me today that Bro. Thatcher assured him that he had no personal feeling in what he did, and that if he heard me intimate anything to that effect he was to make me the same assurance for him. I can say that Bro. Thatcher's treatment of me since the meeting has been very kind indeed. What I have put down that would seem to convey the opposite impression concerning his feelings, are the opinions of others and not my own. Bro. Moses and I have always been the best of friends and I hope we may continue to be.[42]

That night Whitney had another dream that he viewed as a presentiment of greater things to come in his life, at some future time.

> I dreamed last night that I was in the President['s] Office?, some text removed] side, and was moving toward the door southward. As I was passing the west door that opens and from the inner office, where the Apostles hold their councils, I noticed President Wilford Woodruff, seated just to the north of said west door and in the same room where I was. At his right sat Apostle Moses Thatcher and someone whom I did not recognize, or do not now remember, on his left. Angus M. Cannon, President of this stake, was also present. President Woodruff held out his hand to me as I passed, and, in a kind fatherly, benevolent way, said, as he grasped my hand, "They tell me you are to be the President of the Church." I blushed and stammered and was covered with confusion, as I saw the eyes of Bros. [Thatcher and Cannon?, text removed] fixed upon me searchingly and I thought half enviously, though no ill feeling was expressed. I tried to reply but could think of nothing to say except to remark in jocular manner that it was more likely I would be the President's son-in-law. Not heeding this, nor my embarrassment, Bro. Woodruff went on, "Well, you would make a very nice President." I had it on my tongue then to reply: "Why, Bro. Woodruff, I don't feel worthy of being a bishop, much less a President." But before I could form the words, I awoke.
>
> This dream may possibly foreshadow a promotion in the Priesthood of some kind, though precisely what it means I am not prepared to say. Perhaps they intend to make me a President of some kind in the Church, it may be of a stake. But it is not for me to say what is in store for me. Whatever the Lord sends I will accept and try to honor and magnify as He shall give me strength. Amen![43]

Orson also recorded further impressions and conversations he had had with his friend,

> A few more thoughts on the dead letter and living oracle controversy. If it [text removed] man's right and prerogative to stand by the written word in preference to the living oracle, it is also another man's right to do the same, and the prerogative of any number of men to do likewise. If, then, the interpretation of the written word vary, we have as many opposing positions as there are diverse interpretations, which would bring confusion and discord, entrenched behind a show of principle. Now, there must be of necessity, some oracle at the head of the Church to decide which position or interpretation is correct. Hence I say that oracle is of more importance than the

dead letter and should be deferred to in preference to said letter or written law.

During the conversation with Bro. [text removed] that I referred to yesterday, he said, "I was not present at Sunday night's meeting in the Tabernacle, and hence did not hear you, but I am told that you said the Priesthood had the right to change a law of God, and that it was on that point Bro. Thatcher asked you to explain." I answered that I certainly held that view, for, said I (as Bro. Nicholson was preparing to deny it) the Law of Moses was a law of God, and yet it was changed when it became obsolete and was superseded by a higher law. "Yes," said Nicholson, "but God did [text removed] course he did."

I answered, "But what difference does it make whether God or His Priesthood do a thing, do they not represent God? Christ was God's [text removed] and it was Christ who fulfilled the Mosaic Law and did away with it. To make God one thing and the Priesthood another is to make the latter an empty shell, a hollow sham; for what is Priesthood without authority, and who gives that authority but God? Therefore, they are identical and are not to be disassociated. Only when the Priesthood apostatizes are they shorn of authority and power entirely. And as long as they are not apostate they hold power and authority that must be honored and obeyed. I notice, said I, to Bro. [text removed] that the men who do as they are told by the Priesthood are the men who prosper. "They get all the fat offices," he replied, sarcastically.

Bro. [text removed] said there was no freedom unless a man had the right to decide for himself what was right and wrong and stand by his own convictions in place of yielding to authority and yet he admitted that he would do what the Priesthood [brethren] said if it came with a "thus saith the Lord." No freedom in this, though, according to his first affirmation.

I will stand by and sustain the truth, said he. Well, said I, is it not the word, or a portion of it, to stand by and obey the Priesthood? It is low ground, he said, to surrender one's own convictions. I said it was high ground to surrender one's own opinion in deference to superior authority.

I remember when Bro. [text removed] little boy [text removed] was dying that he [text removed] said in his grief and desperation, "I protest against any power, Omnipotent or otherwise, taking that child away." This was said in my presence. It shows to what a dangerous extreme that idea of "independence and unfettered freedom" can

> be carried, when men can thus insist on their own will being done instead of the Father's, and protest against the Almighty fulfilling his own purposes. This was not the Spirit of Job, nor of Christ. "The Lord gave, and the Lord hath taken away; blessed be the name of the Lord" [Job 1:21]. "Thy will, O Lord, be done, and not mine" [Jacob 7:14]. Such is the true feeling of a Saint. Anything more or less cometh of evil.[44]

Orson did not refer to the controversy again. Within a day or two, Orson was again assisting in an administration to the sick. "Bro. Nicholson called for me this morning to go and administer to her. We did so and later in the day Bishop James Watson of the 19th ward went with me to bless her again. She was better afterward, but Bro. Nicholson feels very anxious about her."[45] Bishop Whitney soon met Bishop Watson again, and they found themselves in deep discussion,

> As I was going into the Tabernacle, Bishop Watson was ascending the steps just ahead of me. He greeted me cordially as I overtook him and said, "Bro. Whitney, I have been thinking a great deal about you lately. (By this time we had taken our seats.) And I said to myself this morning I wonder if I will see Bro. Whitney at [the] meeting today. I want to ask you a peculiar question which you may think "cranky" but I have a reason for asking it. Do you ever receive revelations?
>
> I answered that I had at different times in my life, not only in dreams, but by the voice of the Spirit speaking to me directly—that is to my inner consciousness. Why do you ask? He replied, "Because I dreamed about you the other night; and I saw that you were *en rapport* [speaking] with your grandfather [Heber C.] Kimball; I talked with him and he told me that you were pleading with the heavens to learn certain things and I inferred that you had received them."
>
> When was this, I asked? Last Thursday night, said he. "I seemed to be in a room where your grandfather was, and I saw you on your knees pleading to him. He turned to me and said: 'Do you see Bro. Whitney?' 'Yes,' I answered. 'Well, he is so full of faith that he can see me any time he wants to. I can't hide myself from him. But his spiritual organization is greater than the physical, and the strain is so heavy that he must be careful or it will draw him to the other side of the veil.'" Bishop Watson said that in his dream he resolved to get to me as soon as possible and give me the warning. He said that when Grandfather told him that I could see him at any time, and that he

> could not hide from me that he compared me in his mind to the Brother of Jared, whose great faith enabled him to see the Lord, to enter within the veil and comprehend the mysteries of the kingdom of heaven concealed from human eyes. During our walk up to Bro. Nicholson's I told the Bishop some things that the Lord had revealed to me, which caused him to rejoice.[46]

Whether Whitney referred to Bishop Watson as being reincarnated, or meant something else is not stated. A few days later, he "met Bishop James Watson and had a long conversation with him, during which he told me that he had long had an impression that I would be one of the Quorum of the Twelve. 'I believe,' said he, 'that eventually the Twelve will all be of the royal stock—the lineage of [text removed] that, I belong [excised text] lineage [excised text] exercise a spiritual influence in the Quorum, and it is needed at the present time.' I told him some things the Lord had shown me, about him and myself, in which he took much interest."[47] The missing text likely referred to the lineage of Jesus Christ, meaning that Bishop Watson believed Whitney to be a direct blood descendant of the offspring of Jesus. Such a belief, that Jesus was married and had a mortal posterity, was and is believed by many in the Church.[48] Exactly what it was that Bishop Whitney believed the Lord had shown him about Bishop Watson is, again, not stated, but likely it referred to past lives or probations. A friendship developed between the two men that lasted until Watson's death. A few days later Orson recorded,

> Bishop Watson, at my invitation, walked home from the Tabernacle and took dinner with me. I told him more of the things the Lord had shown me—especially on [one word removed]tion and the spiritual era of the Latter-day work ahead of us. He received my testimony—and said that his wife had some views similar to mine to the effect that [three short lines removed]. He told me that Bro. Moses Thatcher had been reprimanded by Pres. Woodruff and Bro. George Q. Cannon for what he said at the stake conference: "O Israel, where is thy wisdom; would to God we had a Brigham Young," and that Pres. Woodruff had said to Moses at the time, "I am a weak servant of the Lord, Bro. Thatcher, but the Lord can speak through me all

> the same." The reproof was kind and gentle, but very effective. The Bishop said he had this from good authority.[49]

As March neared its end, Whitney found himself in another doctrinal dispute, though of a much more private nature:

> In the [*Deseret*] *News* Office today I had an argument with Elders Charles W. Penrose (who is again at liberty from underground retirement on a pardon from Pres. Cleveland) and John Nicholson, in which they took the ground that the Holy Ghost was not a personage in the sense of being an organized entity, but was a diffused spirit or essence only. I claimed that the Holy Ghost was both an organized entity, that is a personage of spirit, and a diffused essence pervading all things. I claimed that I had seen words attributed to Joseph Smith to the effect that the Holy Ghost was not only a personage of spirit but one who had "not yet received a tabernacle," thus implying that he would yet receive one, and consequently was an organized spirit now. This they doubted and denied, saying that the word "personage" (which they admitted was used) was a misnomer, and that someone unauthorized must have added the words "who has not yet received a tabernacle." I know I had read them as Joseph's words, however, and held to my position.[50]

Being strong-willed in his views, Whitney felt the need for more positive proof than his memory alone, to buttress his position, so the next day he "conversed with Apostle Franklin D. Richards, on the subject of the Holy Ghost being an organized spirit, and he agreed with me; he said that Joseph never taught anything more plainly than the personality of the Holy Ghost. He remembered the phrase I had quoted to Elders Penrose and Nicholson about the Holy Ghost having 'not yet received a tabernacle,' and said he would find it for me. He knew it was so recorded somewhere. At this interview Bro. Richards employed me to condense certain portions of his published biography for Tullige's *History of the Northern Counties of Utah*."[51]

Chapter 8

Learning from Lorenzo Snow and Others, 1889–1894

With April came general conference, where Bishop Whitney gave an opening prayer and spoke. He also met with Elder Franklin D. Richards of the Quorum of the Twelve, informing Orson that he had finished work on a biographical sketch that Orson had condensed and edited for him. At this general conference the newly organized First Presidency of Woodruff, Cannon, and Smith were formally sustained in a solemn assembly. President Woodruff had sought to do so some two years earlier, but issues of disunity prevented earlier attempts.[1]

Also at this time Ort formalized an agreement with President Lorenzo Snow for a biographical project. "Before the [priesthood] meeting commenced, Apostle Lorenzo Snow came over to where I was sitting and told me he would accept of a proposition I made to him some time ago to write an appendix to his published autobiography—300 pages print for $1,000, and would get his papers ready for me to begin. He thought my terms were reasonable and had no doubt my work would please him."[2] The "published autobiography" mentioned was Eliza R. Snow Smith's *Biography and Family Record of Lorenzo Snow,* a classic tome first published in 1885. Whitney's idea was to prepare an update or sequel to Lorenzo's sister's impressive work.

Because the new First Presidency was created out of the Quorum of the Twelve, it created three vacancies in the Twelve, vacancies that were not filled to the surprise of those in attendance. In reference to the question, the next day Orson wrote, "Aunt Emmeline Wells told me this evening that Pres. Daniel H. Wells (her husband) had informed her very privately that the reason the other vacancies in the Quorum of the Twelve were not filled at conference was that President Woodruff wanted more time to think about it. Two names had been agreed upon—Charles W. Penrose and Orson F. Whitney, but the third was being considered. William Budge, John Morgan, and B. H. Roberts had been thought of for the place, but it was not settled as to whom the choice would fall upon. It will be as the Lord wills in relation to all of them and there's no telling what will occur except the Lord make it known beforehand."[3] If this unconventional communication ever had any legitimacy, it was not to remain so. At the next general conference, Anthon H. Lund, Marriner W. Merrill, and Abraham H. Cannon were chosen to fill the vacancies.[4] Some weeks later Orson heard further rumor: "In a conversation today with Elders John Nicholson and Robert Patrick, the latter informed me that the wife of Apostle Erastus Snow told him that my name was mentioned for the apostleship as far back as when John W. Taylor was chosen to that Quorum—October 1883. It was also mentioned, I am told, along with those of Angus M. Cannon and William Budge, for the office of presiding bishop at the time Bishop William B. Preston was chosen."[5] Between the rumors and the dreams and the patriarchal blessings, Whitney was kept in a state of perpetual expectation.

Soon Ort decided to risk bringing one of his best friends, nicknamed "Bid" Young, a grandson of President Brigham Young, into his inner circle of friends that believed in reincarnation. "Had a ride with Bro. Brigham S. Young in his buggy and a long conversation with him on the subject of [some text removed] to him, but he drank it in eagerly and believed."[6] After this, "Bid" began attending the secret prayer meetings, and he would often be referenced in Orson's diary by a codename. They met two days later. "Met at Joshua's [Charles Stayner's] and began another series of prayer meetings, this time with two objects in [excised text] received word from the Lord. The Church and kingdom is to be universal before Christ comes, etc. Thursday and Friday continued the prayer meetings."[7]

On April 30, Bishop Whitney and his wife went to Provo, where he spoke in the Provo Tabernacle on the 100th anniversary of the inauguration of George Washington as president of the United States. As usual, he was elated at the burst of applause that met him as he finished.[8] Then another rumor found his ear: "On the train going to Provo I conversed with Sister Susie Young Gates, just returned from the Sandwich Islands. She told me, among other things, that while Pres. Joseph F. Smith was on the Islands in exile, before Pres. Taylor's death, that correspondence passed between him and Pres. Woodruff relative to the filling of the vacancy that then existed in the Quorum of the Twelve, and that both Bro. Woodruff and Bro. Smith were in favor of my selection, but that others more influential advised delay for wisdom's sake, so as to be sure when the choice was made that it would be all right. Pres. Taylor's death dissolved the First Presidency, Presidents George Q. Cannon and Joseph F. Smith resumed their places in the Twelve, and in lieu of a vacancy then there was an extra apostle—13 in all—until the death of Erastus Snow. The last election of the First Presidency created 3 vacancies which have not yet been filled."[9]

At this point some pages are missing from Whitney's diary, but it is apparent that the rumors about a possible call to the apostleship were affecting him, as was the fact that he had not been selected. Part of a conversation remains, evidently with a member of the First Presidency or Twelve, and from this it is clear that Orson learned he was under scrutiny because of his association with the Stayners. "We parted very kindly and he told me he loved me and only spoke as he did on account of his interest in my welfare. He asked me about [Charles W. Stayner] and his belief in [text excised] things, and I answered that I knew [Stayner's] position was that he honored the [disciplinary] decision of the Priesthood in his case, and that he never expected to take up those things unless the Priesthood commanded it. A few days ago Apostle Moses Thatcher, in a conversation, told me that so far as he knew there was no member of his quorum [of the Twelve] that did not hold me in the highest esteem. And, says he, if you meet any other feeling you can put it down to just one thing—jealousy. I will prophesy that if God makes you what I think He intends to, you will have plenty of that to meet; and is of [text removed] some of the best of men."[10]

Reincarnation doctrine was becoming thoroughly ingrained in Whitney, and his loyalty to it occasionally showed in his diary to the point that his private thoughts betrayed a hint of defiance toward those above him ecclesiastically that he disagreed with. These private thoughts, however, remained private, or within the secret prayer group. He did not teach reincarnation publicly. He was strictly circumspect in that regard. He wrote,

> Today I picked up a copy of the [*Deseret*] *News* containing a discourse by Pres. George Q. Cannon at the last general conference. Sunday a.m., April 7, 1889; in which the following passages occur: Speaking of Jesus Christ, the Son of God, he says, "Who is this divine Son? Jesus Christ. Was He, the Son of God, born of a woman? Yes. Well, then, if one god be born of a woman why not other gods be born of women? Is He the exception to the entire race?" In another part he says, in relation to the power that full grown spirits have of being compressed within infant bodies: "It is a strange thing to state; but because we do not understand all things, shall we reject truths?"
>
> Now if Bro. Cannon had gone a step farther he would have said right out, "Brethren and Sisters; we are not all equal as sons and daughters of God. Some are gods who are undergoing reincarnation, and some perhaps are only children of God, incarnate for the first or second time or such a matter. Some belong only to this planet, others have lived on other planets and been glorified therefrom to the celestial worlds." And yet Bro. Lyman and other apostles declare this to be a false doctrine. I declare it to be true, for God has shown it to me as being true and Pres. Cannon touched on things in that sermon that I have believed for the last seven years. The Church will yet accept reincarnation, of gods and sons of God, in this and other worlds as true.[11]

A week later, "At 4 p.m. met at Joshua's [Charles's] with Moses [Arthur] and Mathias [George C. Parkinson?]. Had a precious time. . . . This evening I heard that Pres. Woodruff, in a meeting at Manti a few days ago, publicly declared that the doctrine of reincarnation, that is, one spirit having several bodies, to be false; that he was Wilford Woodruff and no one else, etc. All right, Bro. Woodruff, if you really said it, it is ~~[illegible]~~ you ~~must account for~~ between you and the Lord. I believe it to be a true doctrine, and have for the last [seven] years [text removed]."[12] Whitney's stubbornness regarding reincarnation would become a growing source of stress and complication for him as the years passed and would long delay the fulfillment of prophecies relating to his future.

Several days later Ort "left Salt Lake for Brigham City on a visit to Pres. Lorenzo Snow, who has engaged me to write some supplemental chapters of his history. Arrived . . . and after taking breakfast at Sister Minnie J. Snow's, went across the road to a house where Bro. Snow stays, separate and apart from his family. We had a very interesting conversation this day and the three days following, on 'the mysteries.' He told me he had never unbosomed himself to mortal man as he had to me, [and] considered me a close friend and a brother. He blessed me the day before [I left and] set [me apart to write] his history. While [two pages missing]."[13] The main purpose of Orson's June 8 to 12 visit was to obtain papers and records pertaining to President Snow's life and ministry: "Several days since I commenced writing the book for Pres. Lorenzo Snow, in the interests of which I visited him at Brigham City recently."[14] The two men remained close the rest of President Snow's life, and Lorenzo unknowingly became a part of Orson's and the Stayner brothers' plan to elevate Charles to the apostleship.

Lorenzo Snow (USHS)

The end of the month brought the death of Orson's friend Bishop James Watson, a man with whom he had shared spiritual thoughts and experiences in recent years.[15] On his birthday, Orson commented, "Calls for preaching, lecturing, etc. are so numerous upon me that it is impossible to comply with more than half of them. It has been so for years, more especially since 1885."[16]

His nighttime dreams continued,

> Several nights ago I dreamed of Emma Wells, my wife, deceased; I thought she was dead and I took her in my arms and laid her upon a bed and then, standing before her, made a sign of the holy priesthood . . . and she came to life. She was bustling around as busy and full of energy as I ever saw her, and we seemed to be going on a journey somewhere, she ahead of me walking along briskly. Afterward I dreamed that I woke up and found her gone, and I had a little mirror set in marble saved to her memory.
>
> Aunt Em, her mother, to whom I related the dream, thinks it means something I will be called to do for the Church, such as the opening of a mission or some such thing. It may be that she represented the Church and my bringing her to life signified that I would yet do some work toward the spiritual resuscitation of the Church. It also may prefigure the resurrection, when by the power and authority of the priesthood I will call her forth from the grave."[17]

That August Zina gave birth to their fifth child, and Ort gave a priesthood blessing to their sick dog, which he concluded was thereby healed. Then came a victory of the local anti-Mormon Liberal political party, with them gaining control of the Salt Lake City government, an event Bishop Whitney lamented but viewed as part of God's plan. He dreamed of it.

> Last night I dreamed that all Salt Lake Valley was submerged in water. I thought my wife woke me from sleep, saying, "Ort, the water is nearly up to our window" (we were sleeping upstairs, in my house on the hill). I arose and looked out and as far as I could see was one mass of water, seething and foaming and splashing like a great lake lashed by the storm. The water was turbid and roily. The wife wanted to run at once and escape from the house, as the waters were rapidly rising, and threatening every moment to come in at the windows. But I caught her and made her kneel down with me in the center of the room, where we held up our hands to God and I exclaimed, "O Lord preserve us, through Jesus Christ, Amen." We then took up our children and ran for the hills, higher up, toward and beyond Anderson's

> tower. We succeeded in escaping, though we left all else behind us. In a short time, looking back, down toward the valley, I saw that the waters had abated and the valley was empty, but oh, the wreck and waste that met my gaze. I can imagine how Johnstown must have looked after the flood, from what I saw in my dream. In the morning the interpretation came clearly and suddenly to my mind. The water is the world. The power thereof will overwhelm temporarily the Church in this valley, perhaps to begin at the next city election, in February 1890. The Liberals will wreck and waste things, as they have ever done, but their reign will be short and their power soon be broken. The Church will be saved, as I was in my dream, by taking "higher ground."[18]

When Albert Carrington, Whitney's former, disgraced European Mission President died, he was asked to speak. "Preached at the funeral of Albert Carrington at his residence . . . today. It was at the request of the family and also, I was told, the request of himself prior to his decease. I had a free flow of the Holy Spirit, and I know I spoke by the power of God. Apostle John H. Smith and Elder John T. Caine followed each with a few words well chosen and charitable. Bro. Carrington died at 18 minutes to 4 o'clock p.m. on the 17th. Fifteen minutes after his death several elders arrived at his house for the purpose of ordaining him an elder before he died, at the direction of Pres. Woodruff. He had been rebaptized some time before. He was formerly one of the Twelve Apostles of the Church, but was excommunicated for adultery several years ago. Peace to his ashes! God is just and merciful."[19]

At the October general conference, Bishop Whitney was again called upon: "The first speaker this afternoon was Pres. Lorenzo Snow," he wrote. "I was then called on and spoke about 30 minutes. . . . The Spirit of God dictated the remarks." Orson gave an account of his dream of the Savior to the conference.[20] Three new apostles were called, one of them being President George Q. Cannon's son, Abraham H. Cannon, who had been both a friend and rival to Whitney. As the conference came to a close, Bishop Whitney wrote, "Attended a special priesthood meeting in the tabernacle. Apostle Francis M. Lyman dwelt upon false doctrine, including the one of reincarnation, and Pres. Woodruff declared it to be a false [entry ends]."[21] Word that some members believed in reincarnation had reached the ears of Church leaders, and they wasted no time trying to stamp it out. Whether Whitney liked it or not, his views on reincarnation were doing him no favors; others were talking and coming to conclusions: "Bro. W. A. King took me on to Springville from Provo, and on the way we amicably adjusted a little difficulty arising from the report that I had heard that he said the reason I was not chosen an apostle last conference was because I had been 'preaching false doctrine.' He denied saying so, but admitted he had spoken to Apostle Lyman about my views and his own (King's) on the principle of reincarnation. He said he had been indiscreet but not malicious and asked my forgiveness, which I granted."[22] Where one rumor reached Orson's ears, others might not have, though people might draw the same conclusions and there was no end of trouble in sight. Most significant for Whitney, it is reasonable to conclude that some of his personal beliefs were indeed hindering him from becoming an apostle.

In November, Whitney paid George Q. Cannon and Sons, a publishing company, to issue a book of his poems, *The Poetical Writings of Orson F. Whitney*. The money came from his wealthy father-in-law, Abraham O. Smoot, whose generous gifts to his daughter Zina and to Orson had been of considerable financial assistance on occasion.[23] The book just missed release for Christmas, coming out on December 28, and was reviewed favorably in the local papers.

That February the Anti-Mormon Liberal party won the election for local government. Ort commented, "The election was quiet, but some arrests were made for illegal voting. The Liberals carried the day. That is, they stole the election by fraudulent voting. The election is one of the blackest blots in American politics, but it fulfills my premonitions. My dream of the water filling Salt Lake Valley, recorded in my journal several months ago, is being fulfilled. And the end is not yet."[24] With the Liberals taking over, Whitney was replaced as Salt Lake City Treasurer, a position he had held for some six years.[25] A secondary consequence was that Orson was removed from his other elected office. He explained,

> Governor A. L. Thomas, a day or two since, emboldened by the decision of the U. S. Supreme Court in relation to the right of the Territorial Executive to appoint certain territorial officers "by and with

the consent of the Legislative Council," appointed the Chancellor and Board of Regents of the University of Deseret and other officers, to serve for the ensuing terms.

Of course, off went my official head as Chancellor of the University, an office I have held continuously since the legislature elected me to it in 1886. I am too much of a Mormon to suit His Excellency and his *Tribune* cabinet of advisors. My successor is Robert Harkness, of Salt Lake, a Gentile. Only a few Mormons were made regents, and they mostly half-hearted ones; the rest of the places—the majority—were given to Gentiles and apostates.

Personally, I care not a fig. It relieves me of just so much public service, care, and anxiety, for which I have never received a cent of salary. I was wondering how I was going to prevent my re-nomination by the legislature, if they adhered to their precedent of electing the Board in joint assembly. However, the governor has saved me any trouble, and the legislature today confirmed his appointments.

I had very good reasons for declining the nomination as Chancellor, which I should have done had it been made.

Without regular employment, Whitney was able to devote time to his current literary project. "Am busy at home, since going out of [public] office, working on Bro. Lorenzo Snow's biography. Am making rapid progress: have written 18 or 19 chapters in the last three weeks. I hope to finish by conference time."[26] Yet being out of full-time work and the sole provider for two families gave Orson considerable concern, worries he shared with Lorenzo.

Today I was feeling quite sad and dejected and stood gazing out of my library window at the snowflakes first falling, whirled hither and thither by the fitful gusts of wind, and comparing myself to a snowflake whirled before the wind of destiny when, a few minutes later, the postman rang and the following letter was brought up to me by the girl:

Brigham City
Mar. 25, 1890
Dear Brother:

I find I was mistaken in your having the papers and letters [needed for the biography]. I have them, and will take them with me when I go to the city the last of this week or first of next.

> I shall look for a visit from you after conference when we will take the opportunity to sit down by ourselves and exchange thoughts and views confidentially on matters and subjects that I trust will prove mutually interesting and of no common import.
>
> You must not lose heart nor suffer yourself to lose courage because of financial pressure. There is not an elder in all Israel, endowed with ordinary sense and ambition, though he were a millionaire, but would gladly swap his entire wealth and be reduced to beggary, could he thereby secure the gift of oratory, argument, talent, and ability the Lord our God has so wonderfully and so lavishly bestowed upon my admired and beloved friend, Bishop O. F. Whitney; and a moderate exercise of gratitude on the part of my aforesaid sweet friend, I trust will ever fortify him against discouragement or despondency.
>
> With kind regards,
> Lorenzo Snow
>
> It was like a message from heaven. It cheered my soul like a burst of sunshine. I was happy and serene all the rest of the day.

Whitney then "read the letter from Bro. Snow to Joshua [Charles] and Moses [Arthur] at the latter's home today. They rejoiced. Joshua said that L[?]. had told him I would soon have an interview with Lorenzo Snow and that it would lead to one between Lorenzo Snow and him [Charles]. Joshua has lately returned from Washington, D.C."[27] This scenario, with Orson seeking to set up a meeting with President Snow, to persuade him to call Charles as an apostle, became a critical piece of their plans. Orson sought to do just that for Charles some eight years later.

Receipt of the letter from President Snow reminded Orson of one he had received from President Brigham Young near the beginning of his first mission. The memory inspired him to record its contents.

> Here, while I remember, I will quote from a letter written to me by President Brigham Young while I was laboring as a missionary in Elysia, Ohio in 1877, the year he died. The words made a deep impression on my mind. I have never forgotten them:
>
> "I am pleased to see that you are doing your best to spread the truth wherever opportunity offers, etc.

> "Never condescend to argue with the wicked. The principles of the Gospel are too sacred to be quarreled over. Bear your testimony in humility and leave the result with the Lord.
>
> "I have read with pleasure your letters to the *Herald* of this city, and am pleased that you are cultivating the gift for writing that God has given you and trust that you will use it for the establishment of truth and righteousness upon the earth.
>
> "I invite you to correspond freely with the *Deseret News*."
>
> This letter from Pres. Young, who wrote to me twice while on that mission—the only two letters I ever had from him—encouraged me greatly and probably did much to [illegible] me to a literary career for which I was just then beginning to discover that I possessed some aptitude.[28]

Just before general conference, Orson visited his mentor: "Had an interview with Pres. Lorenzo Snow at his daughter's, Sister Dunford's; he cordially renewed his invitation for me to visit Brigham City after conference and paid me $250 on acct., leaving $200 still due for my labor on his book after completion."[29] At the conference, Charles W. Stayner was called to be the president of the Northern States Mission, leaving in April. Whitney left no commentary on his friend's assignment.[30]

During May, Ort took advantage of President Snow's offer to visit him. "Left for Brigham City with my little son Horace, [carrying?] the Mss [manuscript] of *Latter Leaves of the Life of Lorenzo Snow*, finished and ready for his inspection. While in Brigham City preached the funeral sermon of Sister Harriet Snow, who died Monday, May 12th, at 20 mins to 3 a.m., aged 71. The funeral was on Tuesday at 10 a.m. Bro. Snow and his family were much [illegible] by the discourse which was warmly commended by all. Apostle F. D. Richards also spoke." The manuscript was in handwritten form at the time, but Snow had his son LeRoi type it up in a first draft form. It was mostly complete but lacked a few documentary items where Orson had left space to be filled in later. President Snow never published the manuscript, possibly because it was filled with material defending plural marriage, and President Woodruff issued the manifesto that same summer, signaling the beginning of the end of polygamy.

In a 2012 publication, I condensed Whitney's manuscript, removing many items related to legal matters. I added many chapters based on new research and had it published under the title, *Latter Leaves in the Life of Lorenzo Snow*—thus finally providing interested parties the long-overdue sequel to Eliza R. Snow Smith's book, *Biography and Family Record of Lorenzo Snow.*

Along with delivering the manuscript and preaching at President Snow's wife's funeral, Orson and Snow again talked privately together:

> At Brigham City on my last visit, Apostle Snow told me that Pres. Woodruff thought as much of me today as he ever did, and that all prejudice occasioned by Bro. Lyman's talk had passed away. I asked him if I had done anything to cause him to lose confidence in me. "No, indeed, my dear brother," said Lorenzo. "I regard it as a great blessing that the Lord has thrown us together. I have defended you to the Brethren repeatedly when these things have come up and told them that I knew your views and your spirit, and that no man could lay his finger on a line of false doctrine that you had ever written or spoken, and that there was no cause to condemn you whatever. But you must be wise and not express your opinion, even in private, etc." I asked him if he remembered the blessing he gave me a year ago. "Yes," said he, "I remember it, and I may yet have it in my power to help fulfill my prediction."
>
> I told him the story of Elias, etc. with which he was much interested and surprised—did not put credence in it exactly, but said it might be true, etc.[31]

The fact that President Snow had to defend Whitney to the other Brethren in the leading councils was not a favorable development, nor was the talk about false doctrine and the counsel that Whitney should be careful to whom he expressed his unusual doctrinal opinions. One of the things that protected Whitney the most over the next decade was just that—though he continued his relationship with the Stayners, the secret meetings, and belief in reincarnation theology—he kept his views within the group and did not speak of them publicly.

President Snow's blessing given the year before had hinted at an eventual call to the apostleship, as did his hint that if he became Church president himself he may yet have the power to fulfill his own prediction. Orson's relating of his "Elias" theory, that the spirit personage named Elias had inhabited a number of mortal bodies, let President Snow know of his ideas regarding reincarnation. But exactly how much President Snow knew of how enmeshed Orson had become with reincarnation and the Stayners is hard to know. It is at least unlikely that President Snow knew that he himself had become part of their plans to have Stayner called to the apostleship.

At the October 1890 general conference, where President Wilford Woodruff issued his famous manifesto, Orson participated prominently: "I opened the meeting Sunday afternoon and Monday morning, read to the congregation at the request of the Presidency the Articles of Faith and the President's recent manifesto, which were endorsed by the conference. The proceedings, that morning, were reported by the [*Deseret*] *News*."[32]

Whitney's diary entries in the latter half of October are very brief, using initials, and a crossed-out note mentioning Charles W. Stayner's disciplinary court [now council] before the Salt Lake Stake High Council some years before.[33]

Two days after Orson turned thirty-six, his son Charles Byron Whitney was born. Byron would later be Whitney's first child to serve a mission. In August of 1892, Orson and Zina went camping. On his return he met Miss Maude May Babcock, a pretty, single, well-educated Episcopalian. "Miss Babcock . . . is from New York . . . and late from Harvard University. Sister Susa Young Gates became acquainted with her at Harvard during the same year of 1892. She was teaching physical culture there, after having graduated at the Philadelphia School of Oratory. She is a very fine reader and teacher and a very amiable and pleasant little woman—a perfect lady. Zina, my wife, is taking lessons [from] her both in

Maude May Babcock (USHS)

elocution and physical culture. Susa Gates brought Miss Babcock to our Sunday School and afterwards to our house on November 27, 1892. That was my first meeting with her. She has since joined my Bible class, which I have been teaching in Sunday School for some months."[34] By the end of December, the twenty-five-year-old Miss Babcock had been baptized, with Bishop Whitney confirming her.[35]

After the confirmation meeting, Bishop Whitney wrote, "During the meeting Zina had a vision—a star shaped diamond which while she gazed upon it and was about to reach out for it, flashed into a sun whose brilliance almost blinded her. I interpreted the vision."[36]

In time, Maude May Babcock would become part of Orson's social circle and secret prayer group, and an object of his romantic interest. She never married, but she would later become a professor at Brigham Young University and then at the University of Utah, a woman of prominence and influence in Utah's educational circles. She became a leading matron of the arts and theatre in Utah, writing many plays and mentoring hundreds of students in the drama.[37]

In April of 1893 Bishop Whitney "attended the dedication of the Salt Lake Temple—the opening service. The dedicatory prayer was offered by President Wilford Woodruff and the Hosanna Shout was led by President Lorenzo Snow. Remarks were made by Presidents Woodruff, Cannon, and Smith. It was a glorious occasion. We entered the building about 10 a.m. and the ceremonies closed between 12 and 12:30 p.m. The dedication was a continuation of the April conference."[38] While other sessions of the dedication services were still underway, he "received word from Presiding Bishop Preston that my presence was desired at the dedication services which have been repeated from day to day, since the 6th, and that there was a seat for me above the Aaronic stand." The Aaronic stand was the pulpit area opposite the Melchizedek stand area in the large assembly room of the fifth floor of the temple. "Went to the temple, as desired, and was given a seat by Bishop Preston and his counselors; Bishops Burton and Winder with them upon the Aaronic stand. Attended the services from day to day until completed, missing only one or two of the meetings. On Monday, April 17, at the close of the morning meeting was requested to dismiss by prayer. These honors were not for anything that I had done, but were in memory of my grandfather,

Newel K. Whitney, once Presiding Bishop of the Church."[39]

With general conference and the dedication of the temple, Charles Stayner had come in from the Northern States Mission where he was president, to attend. The reunion of friends was notable: "My friend Joshua [Charles] is here from the east and we have had some glorious times with him, Moses [Arthur], Nephi [John Donaldson], Mathias [George C. Parkinson?], Bid S. [Young], and myself."[40] Whether word of these prayer meetings (timed to be incident to general conference) escaped their group or not, by May some of the Brethren were discussing the subject. "[I had a] long talk with Elder Lyman while in bed on a variety of subjects . . .", recorded Elder B. H. Roberts of the First Council of the Seventy. "Reference was made to the Stayner brothers, and Bishop Whitney."[41]

After seldom being invited to speak in the Salt Lake Tabernacle, June and July saw Bishop Whitney occupy the pulpit there several times.[42] He also "had a friendly talk with President George Q. Cannon, and afterwards at 11 a.m. attended a special meeting in the Assembly Hall where the financial condition and situation [of the Church] were freely discussed. The speakers were Presidents George Q. Cannon and Joseph F. Smith and Elder Angus M. Cannon. The Church is in a great strait financially. We pledged our all to support it. The United Order begins to loom as a probability of the near future."[43]

In September, Miss Babcock returned to Salt Lake City with her mother, and Orson was pleased to be their guide. "On the 8th I met Miss Babcock at the Utah building and was by her introduced to her mother, brother, and Miss Lizzie Waugh of Binghamton, N.Y. I acted as their chaperon for a day or two and had many pleasant conversations with them. Mrs. Babcock, who felt much hurt at her daughter's conversion to Mormonism, will go back home, I think, with much of her prejudice dispelled."[44]

At the October 1893 general conference, during various meetings, Ort was not pleased with one of the subjects treated. "Attended all day p.m. Pres. George Q. Cannon followed Pres. Woodruff in speaking. He denounced as false the doctrine of reincarnation."[45] Also, "at a priesthood meeting held in the Church University building, which was this day dedicated, the First Presidency, I am told, all three condemned the reincarnation doctrine as false."[46] Having the First Presidency unified in condemning reincarnation did not sit well with stubborn Whitney, who held it as a favored concept. But more public and forceful denunciations would greet his ears with increasing frequency. But chafe as he did, he remained sufficiently wise, and when an opportunity arose to talk to intelligent non-Latter-day Saint inquirers about his views, he refrained from the temptation and chose his words carefully. This is as close as he ever came to publicly teaching reincarnation doctrine:

> About a month ago . . . W. K. Wright, vice president of a club composed of university and college graduates, all non-Mormon, invited me to deliver an address before his organization which has rooms in the McCormick Block, this city, and meets for the purpose of having "talks on all sorts of subjects" each Saturday night. He suggested as my theme "the Origin of Mormonism." I agreed to speak if it could be put off for a few weeks as I was then very busy. He named Saturday evening, March 10, and I acquiesced. At 8:30 p.m., I put in an appearance and President E.B. Critchlow, a prominent attorney, called them to order, introduced me and I delivered my address. It was altogether the most remarkable occasion of the kind I ever experienced. In fact nothing exactly of the kind ever before occurred in my experience. About 75 persons were present, all intelligent and many of them learned gentlemen, and the interest they displayed in my "talk" was extraordinary. After speaking a full hour, during which I was listened to with rapt and most respectful attention, and at the close given a generous round of applause, I sat for nearly another hour answering questions from all parts of the house. All the inquiries were pertinent and polite and ranged over all points of doctrine and history connected with Mormonism. Lient Wright and others told me they had never had any lecture that had excited so much interest or as prolonged a discussion, and he (Lient) said he thought I had been speaking less than half an hour. Others also congratulated me and thanked me for "a very pleasant evening." Among those most interested in questioning me were Mr. Critchlow, Leint Wright, Prof. Matthews, and . . . Colonel Donellan. The last named said, "Bishop Whitney, would you care to say anything about polygamy?" "No sir," said I, laughing. "It's against the law." (General laughter and applause.) One gentleman asked me if the Mormons believed in reincarnation. I answered that individuals did, but

> that the Church had not advanced it as a doctrine. They were much interested in the idea of God being man perfected and man God in embryo and asked me many questions, some of them heading into "deep water." But the Lord was with me to a remarkable degree and I was surprised at the readiness with which the Spirit enabled me to answer every query. Prof. Millspaugh wanted to know if these were my own ideas. "No sir," said I. "They are the teachings of Joseph Smith." I told them I had advanced but one idea of my own during the evening. They seemed surprised that Mormonism contains so much. I regard it as a rare opportunity to meet so many intelligent gentlemen and I feel assured that God will bless the words I spoke for good. They invited me to attend their Saturday night lecture and to come to the clubrooms whenever I felt inclined. I would always be welcome.
>
> It is an interesting fact that at the stake conference a few days ago I was led to speak upon the subject of the youth of Zion preparing themselves to meet the intelligent and learned of the world and teach them the truth. I little thought then that I was to meet them so soon, and in this way, for until 2 days before my lecture I did not know that the University Club was of that character at all.[47]

As usual, Orson basked in the afterglow. "My friend Heber M. Wells told me this morning that my lecture before the University Club had created a decided sensation among the members. Several had spoken to him about it all in terms of warmest praise, saying it was 'immense' and the 'most interesting lecture of the series' given at the club. E.B. Critchlow and Mr. Haviland both had said that it was one of the most entertaining evenings they had ever spent, and that the lecture was 'a revelation' to them, not only as to the facts set forth in relation to Mormonism but as to 'Bishop Whitney's scholarship and ability.' Critchlow said it was 'tongued and grooved,' meaning that the words and ideas fitted each other, etc."[48]

A few days later Orson heard a lecture given by Charles W. Penrose, commenting, "His remarks were chiefly versus reincarnation."[49] Later that August, Orson "went to Park City, by appointment of the First Presidency to preach in place of Elder B. H. Roberts, who had been expected to speak to the Saints of that locality, but had suddenly been called elsewhere. My wife Zina and Miss Babcock accompanied me. We went via Ogden and Coalville. It was a long and tedious ride, but on arriving at the Park were made more than welcome and hospitably entertained. Spoke twice, afternoon and evening."[50] Ort was now occasionally finding himself, by assignment, doing the work that a General Authority usually did. It was good preparation, but other obstacles remained in the way.

Chapter 9

The History of Whitney's *History of Utah*, 1890–1908

By the latter half of May 1890, President Lorenzo Snow's promise to Whitney was fulfilled, that "means" (money) would flow to him as he had need of it, when he learned that he had been chosen as author for a new literary project of expansive scope. "Today at a meeting in the Gardo House, I was appointed to write a history of Utah. The publisher is one Dr. Williams, formerly with Bancroft, who puts up the money and will be the proprietor of the work—he to employ me as the author of the same. Pres. Woodruff, Joseph F. Smith, Franklin D. Richards, George Reynolds, Prof. Maeser, Dr. Talmage, Dr. Williams, and myself were present. Dr. Williams proposes to pay me $200 a month while I am working on it, plus 25% of the net proceeds from sales. The history is to be written from a Mormon standpoint and has the full sanction and approval of the Authorities of the Church. I begin work next month."[1]

This taxing and time-consuming endeavor would become Orson's most voluminous work, and would rank with his *Life of Heber C. Kimball* in importance. A few days later, he noted: "[I] wrote my prospectus of the proposed *History of Utah*, and a few lines of Chap. I."[2] Then he recorded,

> Had interviews with Dr. Williams. He says Judge Goodwin of the *Tribune*, who is getting out the Gentile history of Utah told him

> Orson Whitney was the only man the Mormons had that could write the history of Utah from their standpoint, and that he was a very able writer. Williams went east this evening and is to be back in a week or two to begin canvassing. Zina and the children went to Provo today for the summer. I am at home all alone with my work.
>
> Am [illegible] forward the "Pioneer Women" so as to be ready to begin on the [Utah] history June 1st if possible. Judge Goodwin also told Dr. Williams that he needed no contracts with the Mormons, for they would keep their word. Said he, "Your work will be a big success, with Whitney as author and the Church Authorities at your back to help sell it. I shall do all I can to help you but when the book comes out I'm going to 'roast it.'" All right, Goodwin! So it's not a roasted chestnut. We can stand it. We take our roasting here. You may get yours hereafter.[3]

But worries about Dr. Williams's financial stability and some of his employees arose:

> There's being some delay in the *History* project, owing to the derogatory reports concerning Dr. John W. Williams, the publisher, [illegible] which now think advisable the appointment of a committee of seven by the Presidency, to investigate, etc., and said committee having rendered its report. I stopped today at the Gardo House to ascertain definitely whether I want to go on with my work or not.
>
> Pres. George Q. Cannon was present this time. He said, "I am thoroughly in favor of the work and thoroughly in favor of Orson as the writer of it." "Your style," said he, "is admirable for the purpose but you should be concise." I told him I should aim at it. Finally he made the motion, which carried, that if the Committee were satisfied with Dr. Williams and would make suitable preliminary arrangements, that the work be promoted without delay—thank the Lord! Williams will give a bond for $50,000, and the work will at once begin.[4]

Conciseness in writing was never Orson's strength, and because President Cannon knew it he counseled him to adjust his style early on in the process. The month Whitney turned thirty-five he began his work on the *History of Utah* in earnest. He signed a contract with Dr. Williams's publishing company on July 12, with Elder

Heber J. Grant and Francis Armstrong as his sureties (legal financial guarantors that Ort would do the work he was being paid to do). An announcement about the project and its author appeared in the *Deseret News*,[5] and other local newspapers,[6] and Orson was given a desk near the relevant historical materials. "Spent my first day in my new office in the west room of [the] President's Office—between the Beehive and the Lion House, where I am permitted by the Presidency to [sit?] and write for the present. Wrote a description of Salt Lake Valley as it doubtless appeared to the pioneers [on] July 24, 1847. A few thoughts jotted down for my *History*."[7] He was given free railway passes, helping him travel with less financial burden as he collected historical data.[8]

This mammoth project would occupy Whitney on and off for fourteen years, and would be viewed as a seminal historical endeavor. It consisted of at first three, and then later four, very large volumes with three reviewing the history of Utah in narrative form and a fourth containing brief biographies of Latter-day Saints and other prominent citizens of Utah. Sets were priced by contract at $30 each—or $10 per book—with the final volume to be given as a free reward to subscribers who bought the other volumes. Orson originally determined not to accept any payment from people for their life sketches included in the biographical volume, but his noble intentions became impractical so he was forced to accept remuneration.[9]

To assist with sales of the very expensive sets, promotional endorsements from leading Authorities were distributed, including those of the First Presidency. They wrote,

> No want has been more keenly felt for a number of years past than a thoroughly trustworthy history of Utah and the surrounding regions. Regrets have been frequent that no such work exists. The man and the opportunity have now appeared. Orson F. Whitney has undertaken the work. We know of few men so capable of worthily performing the task. His ability as a writer, his long experience, [his] being a native of Utah, his deep acquaintance with the subject, his sterling integrity, all combine to fit him most eminently for the undertaking. He occupies the unique position of being the son of one of the pioneers of 1847, who helped lay the foundation of Salt Lake City, and the grandson of another distinguished member of

> that heroic band, and the history of Utah is the familiar theme of childhood, youth, and manhood. Dr. John O. Williams, a gentleman of wide experience, will publish the history here in Utah. We heartily commend the project, and hope the author and the publisher will meet with that support and encouragement from our citizens and the general public, which we feel assured their labors and the results thereof will abundantly deserve.[10]

Some of the Apostles and the Presiding Bishopric also wrote commendations of the proposed volumes. Whitney was obliged to have the work completed in two years, and was to be paid on the 15th of each month. The publishing contract provided for a first edition of 2,000 sets.[11] Even so, as Whitney moved forward with the research and writing, numerous complications and delays arose, with financial troubles looming largest. He wrote, "The inner history of this period would tell for author and publishers a tale of protracted toil, with many interruptions and suspensions, and a final triumph over obstacles and discouragements innumerable. . . . The undertaking was gigantic. To carry it to success required years of hard labor on the part of the author, as well as the business heads of the concern; fighting against adverse conditions which were at times almost overwhelming."[12]

Early 1891 found Whitney hard at work on the history: "I have done little of interest for the past several months but work hard upon the *History of Utah*. Have written 12 chapters, concerning the Church narrative from the birth of the Prophet to his martyrdom."[13] Several weeks later he again wrote, "Am too busy with my *History* to desire much speaking."[14]

By June, reports of misrepresentation by the canvassers (door-to-door salesmen) employed by the publisher had reached the ears of some of the Apostles, who worried. Elder Abraham H. Cannon, the son of President George Q. Cannon, an apostle himself and the general manager of his father's publishing company, became involved. Elder Cannon wrote, "Bro. Heber J. Grant and I went to the Gardo House . . . and in the course of the conversation the Whitney *History of Utah* and Dr. Williams's management of its issuance were discussed. The Brethren felt fearful, from reports that [had] reached them, that there is a chance for a big swindle of the Saints in this affair, and, at any rate, the [First] Presidency do not approve of the way their names are used to secure subscriptions to the book. Bishop Whitney was sent for, and asked in relation to the work. He seems to have confidence in the integrity of John Williams, but feels desirous that a committee should give the matter attention, and so arrange the affair that we all feel secure. I was appointed a member of such committee."[15] The committee met the next day:

> At 4 p.m. I was at a meeting of the committee on publication of Whitney's *History of Utah*. The members present were John R. Winder, Chairman, F. S. Richards, O. F. Whitney, George Reynolds, C. W. Penrose, and myself. We considered the charges made against Williams and his agents, which come from various parts of the territory, and Bishop Whitney said that whenever complaints had reached Dr. Williams they had been investigated and corrected. He had made personal visits to settle some feelings which had been created by an agent in Sanpete County.
>
> To allay our suspicions concerning the honesty of Dr. Williams, a number of letters were read testifying to his good character, and the bond of $25,000 which he has furnished as security for the faithful performance of his labor has been fully verified.
>
> It was finally resolved to have Bishop Whitney get an extension of time on his bond for the completion of his part of writing the history. The history was to be completed within two years from its commencement, or about one year from today, the bond for which is $5,000, but the author has only done about one half of the first volume up to the present. An extension of time was, however, proffered him. This done we decided to invite the publisher, Dr. Williams, to be present at a meeting and hear the charges made against him, after which we will request him to increase his bond to $50,000 as he originally agreed to do.
>
> My fears concerning this matter are very much calmed by the conversation of today.[16]

It seemed the sales agents had long been using the names of members of the First Presidency to sell the books in a manner beyond that originally envisioned, and the Presidency resented it. Worse than that, certain people were representing themselves as salesmen working for Dr. Williams's publishing company that did not work for him and were taking subscribers money for themselves, or selling other history books as Whitney's. This problem led to a warning circular being sent to stake presidents and bishops. It read,

> Beware of Frauds
>
> Information has reached the undersigned that certain parties are traveling through the territory taking orders for a *History of Utah*, and that in many instances the people are led to believe that they are purchasing the history that is now being written by Bishop Orson F. Whitney.
>
> To guard the public against imposition, we will state that all authorized agents for Whitney's *History of Utah* will be the bearers of autograph letters to that effect from the author, and that as they enter the various fields proposed to be canvassed for subscriptions, their names will appear in the papers as the accredited representatives of the publisher and promoters of this work. Be careful whom you do business with. Let it be distinctly understood that Whitney's *History of Utah* is not yet published, and that any book now being offered to the public purporting to be such a work is a fraud. Whitney's *History of Utah* is the only history now being endorsed by the First Presidency and the Apostles of the Church. The accompanying letter just received from the First Presidency speaks for itself. Salt Lake City, Nov. 14, 1890.

The referenced letter from the First Presidency noted that Whitney was "engaged in preparing the *History of Utah*," and that they, the stake presidents and bishops, had "probably received the author's prospectus with accompanying testimonials from ourselves and other citizens." They continued, "We wish it understood that we are heartily in sympathy with the project, and that it has our entire support. The author of the proposed work is a native of Utah, one in whom we have great confidence as an able writer and a conscientious historian. We believe his history, which is to be published in three large volumes, will be complete and reliable, and should be in the possession of every family; and [we] can recommend it to the general public who desire to know the truth about our territory and its people. We trust that the Latter-day Saints will give it their support and encouragement. Wilford Woodruff, George Q. Cannon, Joseph F. Smith, First Presidency of The Church of Jesus Christ of Latter-day Saints."

With the letter was a note from Whitney that read, "It is the purpose to issue the first volume of our history, which was begun in May 1890, in about six months. It will be printed on super-calendared paper and handsomely bound, with gold gilt edges, profusely illustrated with steel engravings, type matter running from 700 to 800 pages. Very respectfully, Orson F. Whitney, Author."[17] In his autobiography, Ort explained further, "My duties were purely literary. At no time did I have anything to do with the business management; yet my name was used, without my consent, as if I had been the very head and front of the enterprise. Certain agents employed by Dr. Williams were reprimanded by him and discharged for this and other irregularities."[18] By this time, Dr. Williams had also heard negative comment about his handling of the business, and he decided that he wanted out. Elder Abraham H. Cannon recorded the meetings and deliberations:

> I . . . then had a conversation at my room with Bishop O. F. Whitney concerning the *History of Utah*. He says that Dr. Williams has become so annoyed at the numerous reports which have been circulated concerning his trustworthiness, and his character has been so maligned, that he is determined to get out of the business if Bishop Whitney can find someone who will be congenial to him to buy his interest, which is 45% of the whole enterprise; 5% is owned by F. S. Richards, who is the attorney, 25% by O. F. Whitney, who receives $200 per month as an advance on his share for writing the work, and 25% by Mr. Webster, who is the secretary. The Bishop thinks there is big money in the enterprise for anyone who will buy it. He thinks the Dr. will take $10,000 for his share of a business which he feels is worth $30,000. Orson is very anxious for George Q. Cannon and Sons' Co. to take the business, and thus reassure the doubting people of the certainty of the issuance of the work. We together laid the matter before Father and then before the First Presidency. After considerable talk on the subject, on suggestion of Pres. Joseph F. Smith it was decided that O. F. Whitney and F. S. Richards make another effort to get Dr. Williams to continue in the business, but

if he refuses to do so, then I had better investigate the matter and, if the results warrant it, buy out his share.[19]

Three days later;

At 9 a.m., I met O. F. Whitney and Dr. Williams and had some conversation about the *History of Utah.* The latter is very desirous that we purchase his interest and thus reassure the people of Utah that it will be issued, though he expresses a desire to continue with the thing and work to make it a gigantic success. I presented the matter to the First Presidency who told me to investigate the affair, and if everything was satisfactory to engage in it. Two of Dr. Williams's agents, Waterman and Clark, called to see me in the afternoon, as they had heard rumors of the pending sale, telling me of claims which they hold against the concern for canvassing services. The former spoke as though Mr. Williams is a rogue, but he was very desirous that I should not tell the latter of his visit to me. Mr. Clark said Mr. Webster had always treated him in the best possible manner. Their claims are really not due until the first volume is issued and delivered. Father's principal objection to the enterprise is the length of time required by Bishop Whitney to complete the manuscript—5 years from the time it was commenced.[20]

The next day;

At 11 a.m., Frank [Cannon] and I met with Dr. Williams, Mr. Webster, and O. F. Whitney. We spent several hours in looking over the accounts of the Utah Historical Society [the name of the business] and inquiring into the details of the publishing arrangements. The proposition finally made was that the Dr. remain with the business and receive 33⅓% commission on all orders for books and pictures, and that he sell us 70% of the business with his already accrued commissions for $15,896. The actual orders taken for the book amount now to over 2,500 at $30 per set. Available notes would be turned over to us in this deal to the amount of seven or eight thousand dollars. As pictured by Williams and Webster, there is big money for us in this undertaking, but it also means a considerable outlay before returns are had. We presented the matter to the First Presidency and they decided to consider it for a day or two.[21]

Three days later;

> I . . . wrote a letter to Dr. John O. Williams making him a proposition in regard to the purchase of his interest in the *History of Utah*. I submitted the letter to Father and Joseph F. Smith before sending it and they approved it. The offer is that we give him $12,000 for all his right, title and interest in the work to date. He is then to receive 33⅓% commission on all book and picture orders. The amount is to be paid as follows: $6,000 cash down, $3,000 when the first copy of the first volume is issued, and the remaining $3,000 when 2,000 copies of the first volume are issued. In the afternoon he came in the office and accepted our offer with these changes, that he be engaged as canvasser for at least three years, and that a certain date be fixed for the payments of the two latter notes, at such a time as we think the conditions of our proposition are fulfilled. We agreed to these modifications.[22]

Five days later;

> About five hours of today I was engaged in my room with Dr. Williams and Mr. Webster checking up the *History of Utah* business. I found that about 2,700 bona fide contracts for the work have been obtained. Notes for about $7,500 are on hand. There are time commissions due agents when the books are delivered to the amount of about $7,000. Judging from what appears on the books the business is in a very good condition. We agreed to meet F. S. Richards tomorrow to prepare the legal papers necessary to the transfer.[23]

The next day Elder Cannon attended the meeting: "At 11 a.m. I met Dr. J. O. Williams and Mr. Webster at F. S. Richards's office where we talked over with the latter the terms of our agreement in regard to the publishing of Whitney's *History of Utah*, and instructed him to prepare the necessary papers for the transfer."[24] Two days later;

> F. S. Richards, Frank Cannon, and I had a conversation with him [President George Q. Cannon] in relation to the Utah history, and read him the papers in relation thereto. He approved of them

> with two or three slight changes. At 2:30 p.m., F. S. Richards, O. F. Whitney, Dr. Williams, Mr. Webster, Frank, and myself met in the office of the first named and consulted about the agreements for the transfer of the Utah history business. We had considerable talk about their receiving their full commissions out of the first collections on the books, and finally compromised by their agreeing to accept ¾ of their commission out of collections on the first volume, and the other ¼ when the second volume is delivered and paid for. We adjourned till Monday to finish the business, as we could not do it today owing to the changes to be made in the papers.[25]

Two days later, the business transfer took place, with George Q. Cannon and Sons taking ownership. "I was engaged in the office till 10 a.m. at which time Frank and I met Dr. Williams and the others of Saturday's meeting and made final arrangements for the payment of the money ($6,000) and notes ($6,000) this afternoon and the transfer of the business to us. This was done at 4 p.m. when all the papers, etc., were completed and properly signed, and with the very best of feelings we started out on our new venture."[26]

Whitney's diary condensed the meetings of June to their conclusion: "The 29th of this month George Q. Cannon and Sons assumed the management of the *History* business, buying out Dr. Williams and Mr. Webster—who owned 70 percent of it—and the latter returning the contract to canvas for the works."[27]

Some three months later, as Orson worked furiously on the history, he noted, "Today the first type was set and the first galley of proof sent me of the *History of Utah*. It is being published by George Q. Cannon and Sons in Salt Lake City. Only 19 chapters are completed."[28]

In December, a history question arose that Whitney wanted help with. Elder Cannon recorded, "In the afternoon I attended my Quorum meeting at which were present all the First Presidency, Franklin D. Richards, and myself; George Gibbs, clerk. . . . Bishop Orson F. Whitney was present to obtain information concerning the object in settling this territory when the pioneers came here, as he desires to make a statement concerning it in the *History of Utah*. He had prepared something in which he affirms that the Mormons came here to found a new state for the United States. This is incorrect, as it was the expectation when the people arrived here to establish an independent state, and it was only when this western tract of land was ceded to the United States by Mexico in the Treaty of Guadelupe Hidalgo (February 1848) that the Mormons began to seek for admission into the Union as a state, and saw therein their success and destiny."[29]

By the next spring, Whitney finally reached a major milestone. "About the time I finished the first volume of my *History of Utah*, a banquet in honor of the event was given me at the Templeton Hotel by my friend Heber M. Wells and C. S. Burton, et. al. The first copy of the *History* arrived from St. Louis, where a few are being bound, on the 21st of April, 1892. Twenty more came a few days later."[30]

That July he found cause to celebrate: "On the 1st of July this year I completed my 37th year. Am in excellent health, weigh 182 lbs and am about halfway through Vol. II of my *History of Utah*, much of which is already printable."[31]

He finished volume two nearly a year after finishing volume one. "Completed the second volume of the *History of Utah*. This volume was begun last February."[32]

Whitney worked hard, but the financial ceiling was about to fall in on the project. When the business first began things had looked promising, largely because no one knew that in 1893 a severe financial panic would hit the nation, lasting for several years at its worst. This meant that George Q. Cannon and Sons, the publishers, no longer had the financial viability needed to pay the publishing costs, including payments to the author. Whitney recorded, "Had an interview with the First Presidency about the *History of Utah*. Messrs. Cannon and Sons being unable to proceed with it for the time being owing to their inability to make collections, the Church authorities have consented to lend aid—that is to pay me for writing the mss [manuscript]. I am to complete Vol. III within a year from date and receive $2,700 for it. Andrew Jensen [is] to assist me in collecting facts whenever necessary. This mss will belong to the Church from whom Cannon and Sons will afterwards purchase it if they are able. Cannon and Sons owe me $750 back salary from May 15 to Aug. 15, 1893."[33]

The main problem was the depression was so bad that people who had signed a note to buy the set could no longer afford it. Food and clothing suddenly became more important than expensive history books, marvelous as they were. President George Q. Cannon himself explained the situation in greater detail:

> At the meeting this morning with Bishop Whitney and Elder A. H. Cannon, to take into consideration the question of continuing the preparation of the *History of Utah*, in manuscript, upon which Bishop Whitney has been engaged some years. [The financial stringency rendering it impracticable for George Q. Cannon and Sons Co. to continue the publication of the third volume; and Bishop Whitney having prepared the manuscript to the extent of between a third and half of this volume.] The question arose, whether it is advisable to have him continue the work until the volume is completed or suspend the publication of the work where it is? The Presidency felt that as Bishop Whitney's mind was full of this work, and he had his data in hand, that it would be better for him to continue until it was finished, and then, when the time shall come, for the publishers to continue the work, the manuscript will be on hand. There is a fourth volume also contemplated which is to be given gratuitously to subscribers by the publishers. This fourth volume is to contain biographical sketches and brief sketches of the history of the cities and counties of the Territory.
>
> The question was asked Bishop Whitney, what it would cost to do this work—that is, finish the third volume? He answered that the publishers have been paying him $200 a month, and his wife $50, and that he had been engaged on the part already written between seven and eight months. President Smith made the estimate that the part already written had cost $1,750. Bishop Whitney said he thought he could do the remainder for $3,000, which would make the manuscript for the volume $4,750. The Bishop was asked if Brother Andrew Jenson could assist him in furnishing data and save his time, as he claimed it would take him a year or thereabouts to complete the work. Bishop Whitney thought Bro. Jenson could be of assistance to him. President Smith then suggested that as Bro. Jenson's time and assistance ought to be worth $300, to Bro. Whitney, he was asked whether that would be satisfactory—that is, the Bishop to receive $2,700 for the work, with the liberty, of course, to finish it as much earlier than the year, with the assistance of Bro. Jenson, as he pleased. He agreed to do this. A motion was made that $2,700 be given to him for finishing the remainder of the manuscript, carrying

> the *History* down to the end of the volume, which he intimated would be at the issuance of the manifesto. President Woodruff was quite pointed in remarking (which he did at least twice) that he [Whitney] must not expect cash for his work, as the Church was unable to pay cash now; that even the Apostles who drew their pay from the Church had to take it in tithing office pay. Bishop Whitney said, that which is due him now he ought to have in cash to meet his obligations, which were cash. But as this was a matter between himself and the publishers, the Presidency had nothing to say about it.[34]

Whitney had now passed his original contract time allotment of two years by over a year, with only two-and-a-half volumes finished. His perceived slowness in finishing the work was frustrating to those with a vested interest in his finishing as soon as possible, such as President and Elder Cannon, owners of the publishing company. Orson himself felt the pressure, literary as well as financially. Regarding his pay, he wrote, "Drew from James Jack, [Church financial] clerk, on above account $225; only $50 of it being in cash. The rest tithing orders and a little store pay."[35] He finished the third volume a year later (August 1894), an agonizingly slow rate for all involved. And Whitney's woes continued. He needed to approach the First Presidency to collect pay the publisher owed him. President Cannon explained,

> [The] $750 appropriated favor of Brother Orson F. Whitney. Some time ago $2,700 was appropriated also in favor of Bro. Whitney as compensation for his services in producing the third volume of his *History of Utah*. The firm of George Q. Cannon and Sons Company having made representations to the First Presidency through President Cannon of their inability to go on with the *History* in consequence of the financial loss of the enterprise. This $2,700 was appropriated to enable Bro. Whitney to complete the third volume of the history, it being understood by the Presidency that the manuscript of the third volume should become the property of the Church by reason of this appropriation. Bro. Whitney now represented that at the time this appropriation was made the publishing company owed him $750 which they had since failed to pay him and that he himself was in debt fully to this amount at that time and was obliged to settle with his creditors out of the $2,700 appropriation.

> He represented that the publishing company was still unable to pay him this amount and he asked that the Church be kind enough to assume it so that he might be enabled to continue his labors on the third volume. President Woodruff at first expressed himself averse to doing this but afterwards consented and it was agreed with Bro. Whitney that he draw it in provisions at the rate of $75 per month.[36]

The Cannons' frustration with Whitney's work began to show. Their publishing company was barely surviving, struggling under heavy debt. Elder Abraham Cannon recorded, "We [Abraham and George Q.] had a talk with the Presidency about the *History of Utah*, and they gave Bishop Whitney notice that they were through with him so far as writing on it is concerned, now that he has finished the third volume. I suggested that we hire a cheaper man, and a better worker, to write the biographies for the fourth volume. It was thought that this will be the best thing to do."[37] But Elder Cannon's idea to change authors did not pan out, and Whitney was used as planned for volume four.

There are no further entries in Ort's diary mentioning the project until mid-1897, likely meaning that even though volume three had been written, the tough financial conditions prevented anything being done with it (except revising and improving the manuscript) for almost three years. By July 1897, the publisher's financial position had improved sufficiently that they could finally have the manuscript turned into a book. Orson wrote, "[I] ran down to Salt Lake [from Logan] to take the last chapter of mss [*History of Utah* Vol. 3] to the printer."[38] Some weeks later he recorded, "The final proofs of Vol. [3] of the *History* are read and all printed but the index which I am now getting ready. The book will be issued shortly."[39]

Volume 3 finally found life when it was issued in January of 1898. The *Tribune* did their usual hatchet job reviewing it: "I don't know whether to attribute the *Tribune* assault [on Whitney for a published poem about Utah volunteers] to Judge Goodwin, or to Col. Nelson. The latter hates me and all Mormons, and has never got over the dressing down I gave him in the *History of Utah*, Vol. III, which he so bitterly attacked when it was published. The 'dressing down,' however, was only a plain statement of what Dr. Clinton, a prisoner in Nelson's custody, said in court about his treatment by that venomous Mormon-hater while U.S. marshal. Still, it may have been Goodwin."[40]

While the publisher was turning his manuscript into a printed book, Orson learned (to his relief) he was still on the job: "Today it was told me that final arrangements had been made for me to go to work on the 4th Volume of the *History of Utah*. Cannon and Sons will devote $1,000 to it and the Church $400. The latter in scrip."[41] Following that, "Tuesday, the 19th, [I] began work on Vol. IV of the *History of Utah*. Jacob Pearts's biography was the first one I prepared. Then came Joseph Perry's."[42] Orson finally had found a source of income. "In Salt Lake again. Got another $100 from Cannon and Sons on acct."[43] Also, "Have received from President's Office $100 Church script on acct."[44] Whitney had to coordinate with about three hundred and fifty prominent Utahans to obtain their biographical information that he would then write and edit. Those too busy, lazy, or slow to work with had their life sketches left out.[45]

The work progressed in starts and fits: "U. S. Senator Rawlins called on me today and made arrangements with me to prepare his biography for the *History of Utah*. Paid me next day $100 on acct. Gave ½ to Elias [Stayner]. U.S. Senator Frank J. Cannon has also arranged with me to prepare his biography, offering me $100."[46]

Nine months later, "A few days ago I resumed work on Vol. 4 of my *History of Utah*—the biographical volume—suspended since last fall. I have completed Willard Richards's biography, revised A. W. McCune's and submitted it to him, and am now on W. M. Budge."[47] Further, "This is Monday and the beginning of another year [1900]. I find myself in good health, firm in the faith of the Gospel, the bishop of the 18th ward and employed in the Church Historian's Office. For the past three months I have been engaged upon the 4th volume of my *History of Utah*, the biographical volume. I have just completed a sketch of the life and character of Pres. Lorenzo Snow to be published in the New Year number of the *Juvenile Instructor* and afterward in this *History*. [I] have been asked to prepare an address on the life and character of the late Pres. Franklin D. Richards, to be delivered before the State Historical Society and afterward published in the *History*. Spent most of today in my office."[48]

The work continued, with some humorous exchanges with those whose opposition to the Church was omitted: "Judge Goodwin, of the *Tribune*, sent me back the biographical sketch I had prepared for the *History of Utah*—his sketch, which I had submitted to him and which was rather complimentary to him, with this line upon the margin, 'Bishop, is there any forgiveness for lying in your religion?' To which I answered by postal card, 'Judge: Yes, there is. Come along, Bishop.'"

Along with his own work, Whitney was asked to help President Cannon with the preparation of *History of the Church*: "I have just about completed my 4th volume of Utah history, and it is almost ready for the press. I am assisting (with John Q. Cannon) his father, President George Q. Cannon, to prepare for publication the autobiography of the Prophet Joseph Smith. . . ."[49]

A year-and-a-half later, the publishers' finances reached a point where they could proceed with printing: "Started today to get out Vol. 4 of the *History of Utah*—biographies—which the Cannon Sons are now preparing to publish. The mss [manuscript] has been ready for a year or two, waiting their action; all I need now to do is the part or the finishing touches and [illegible] issue it through the press. The *Deseret News* office is to do the printing."[50]

Issuing the work became a time-consuming undertaking. "Am very busy getting out my 4th Volume of Utah history—the first form is printed containing the biographies of Presidents Brigham Young, Heber C. Kimball, and Willard Richards; and Orson Pratt and Wilford Woodruff are partly in type." For his part, Whitney was aware of the impatience concerning the completion of the history, but he felt he could do no better, stating, "To complete it required several years, during which I had many other duties to perform, and responded, as usual, to numerous calls for extra service in various directions. I was in love with my task—which lightened it greatly—but still it was strenuous and exacting, as anyone must know who has ever brought out a work of that character and magnitude."[51]

Elder Abraham H. Cannon died in the summer of 1896, and management of the daily operations of George Q. Cannon and Sons passed to a relative, Brigham T. Cannon. He oversaw the publication of the fourth biographical volume from 1902 to 1904. He also had to deal with the remaining unsold one thousand sets of the original two thousand printing. The financial panic of 1893–1895 had kept subscribers from being able to pay for their sets.[52] Brigham Cannon proposed that the Church buy them. In a letter to the First Presidency, which no longer included his father (the deceased George Q. Cannon), he wrote,

> December 11, 1902
>
> Dear Brethren:
>
> In accordance with a conversation had with President Anthon H. Lund, we beg to submit to you a proposition to sell 1,000 complete sets of Whitney's *History of Utah* in four volumes. About 1000 sets, possibly a few more, would be the entire residue of the only edition of this work ever published. Originally, the complete *History* was to be written in three volumes, and subscriptions were taken at $30 per set, or $10 per volume. As the work was proceeded with, however, it was found that a fourth volume would have to be issued to make the work complete, and bring it up to date. This fourth volume is now in press, and is to be given gratus [free] as a premium to all paid up subscribers. The materials and workmanship in these books are the best that can be obtained. As to the letter press and the steel plate work, nothing of a higher class can be obtained anywhere.
>
> Mr. Horace G. Whitney [Orson's brother], manager of *Deseret News*, states to us that considerable inquiry about the *History* is made at that establishment and of its agents, and believes that many sets of the *History* could be sold by these agents, as a mere incident of their other work. We feel sure that in a comparatively short time, this *History* will be at a premium, not only here, but elsewhere in the United States, as the publication of the second edition will involve a very great outlay of money. In fact, at present, there is quite a steady demand for sets of *History* from various public libraries throughout the country.
>
> We offer you 1,000 complete sets, or thereabouts, unbound, at $12.00 per set.
>
> We would like to have you give the matter consideration at your convenience, and let us know if you desire any further information on the subject.
>
> Yours respectfully, Brigham T. Cannon.[53]

Despite Brigham Cannon's best efforts, it took two more years for the final volume to be issued. "It [the rights to the project] was purchased by the present proprietors at a time when the whole project was imperiled, and their purchase was virtually a rescue of the enterprise. They are now about to make good their pledge to the public by the issuance of this gift volume, even though it entails upon them a heavy financial sacrifice."[54] The economic difficulties of the mid- to late 1890s had been formidable, the chief cause of delay. Yet Whitney was able to make use of the last unavoidable lull. "The major portion of this volume was written several years ago, and was ready for the printer, but financial disappointment, encountered by the management, prevented the publication, and Bishop Whitney, in the interval caused by the unavoidable delay, has re-written the whole book and brought it down to the present [1904], thus making it a more valuable work than it would otherwise have been."[55]

The change in management of George Q. Cannon and Sons had improved the relationship between author and publisher: "In conclusion, the author desires to express his appreciation of the pleasant relations that have always existed between him and the publishers, and to give a word of due praise to Mr. Brigham T. Cannon, the present manager, whose energetic labors, loyally backed by his company, the publication has been brought to a successful issue. Nothing further need be said, except that the author and the publishers are perfectly satisfied with the reception accorded their work."[56]

Whether the First Presidency agreed to some kind of arrangement with Brigham Cannon is not clear. Evidently he and Horace G. Whitney again overestimated the sales potential in 1904 for Whitney's *History of Utah* because by 1908, the *Deseret News* bookstore put it on sale:

> Whitney's *History of Utah* at Half Price:
>
> The *Deseret News* takes pleasure in announcing that it has secured the sole rights to the *History of Utah* by Orson F. Whitney, originally published by the George Q. Cannon & Sons Co. . . .
>
> In the three volumes are included 235 full-page steel plates, mostly portraits of leading figures in the history of the state, originally obtained at a cost of many thousands of dollars. The volumes each contain approximately 800 pages, a total of 2,351 pages in the three. The binding is quarto size, full morocco with gilt edges, no other style of binding being issued. . . .

> The *News* having obtained the unsold copies of the edition, will sell to first comers at half the original price, or $15.00 for the three volumes. . . .
>
> The low price at which this rare work is offered will undoubtedly exhaust the edition in a short time. The work will then be out of print, so that every book-lover should avail himself of this last chance.[57]

After the last sets were sold, it did indeed go out of print and after decades became an expensive collector's item. Because Whitney wrote from the perspective of a strong believer and defender of the faith, reviews of the *History* were mixed. Mormons thought it marvelous and Mormon-haters despised it.[58] Such has been the fate of most histories of Utah written since then.

Orson F. Whitney
(USHS)

Chapter 10

Professor, Politician, and Private Speculator, 1895–1898

As 1895 began, Ort found himself in further conversation with his friend Elder Moses Thatcher of the Quorum of the Twelve. Thatcher was struggling with painful stomach ulcers, for which he had taken and become addicted to morphine. Between that and minor feuds with some fellow Apostles, he became largely inactive in the Quorum. He seldom met with them, instead concentrating on recovering his health and on business and politics, where he had ambitions to become a senator.[1] Orson maintained his friendship with Thatcher despite all this. "Went to Logan, Zina accompanying me, and stayed overnight at Apostle Moses Thatcher's. Next morning, coming back to Salt Lake, had an interesting interview with him in the [train] cars. Interpreted a dream for him and told him of my belief in certain things."[2] Whether this conversation included Orson confessing his belief in reincarnation is not stated, but it is likely, in view of later developments. Thatcher was known to have his own peculiar doctrinal theories, and he and Orson would have had a lot to talk about. Thatcher's influence on Orson was probably not all positive. Thatcher was dropped from the Quorum of the Twelve in 1896.[3]

Bishop Whitney also kept up his friendship with President Snow: "In February had several interesting conversations with Apostle Lorenzo Snow at his rooms in the S. L. Temple."[4] President Snow had been called as the first president of the newly dedicated temple and had to move from Brigham City to Salt Lake City. He often lived in the temple, having a room that he could eat and sleep in behind the sealing rooms and Holy of Holies.[5]

That month Orson attended the birthday party of his father-in-law, Abraham O. Smoot, and the next month he attended Abraham's funeral.[6] He also attended President Woodruff's 88th birthday party, held in the Salt Lake Temple, as had become tradition.[7]

At the Constitutional Convention in 1895, Whitney was chosen as a member of a committee that wrote the "Preamble and Declaration of Rights of the proposed State Constitution. . . . I acted as Secretary of the Committee and penned most of the document. The preamble is mine, practically entire."[8] Further, Orson explained, "My most conspicuous service was in championing the cause of equal suffrage. I was among those who advocated the placing of an article in the State Constitution enabling the women of Utah to vote and hold office." In his autobiography, he wrote, "In defense of the proposed article, I crossed blades with the most redoubtable forensic warrior in the Convention, Hon. B. H. Roberts of Davis County—in my opinion the greatest natural orator that 'Mormonism' in the past fifty years has produced. Opposed to woman's participation in politics, he spoke against it and was answered by several members, notably by Hon. Franklin S. Richards, who read a scholarly paper in support of the pending measure. I had not intended to say anything upon the subject, but was urged by Mr. Richards and others to take the floor and reply to the gentleman from Davis County. Accordingly, on Saturday, March 30, I made my plea for equal suffrage."[9] Whitney's later glowing praise of Roberts's oratorical ability contrasted somewhat with his thoughts at the time:

> The sensation of the hour is the woman suffrage debate in the Constitutional Convention. I made my first speech in favor of suffrage on Saturday, March 30, answering B. H. Roberts, who spoke against it. He replied on April 2nd and I spoke again on the 5th.
>
> Bro. Roberts in his reply, intimated that my speech was a deliberately planned assault, and that in the silence of private study I prepared the arrows and dipped them in bitterness. Nothing of this was

> correct. I felt no bitterness. My speech was not planned but entirely spontaneous. I thought to speak only about 10 minutes, but held on for an hour.
>
> Following are some of the comments on my speech: . . .
>
> Heber M. Wells (to my brother Bud), "Orson took Roberts by the nap of the neck and the seat of his pants, swished him three times around his head, mopped the floor with him, and then took him up to a third story window and dropped him!"
>
> The speeches that I made are being published in pamphlet form by the "Utah Woman's Suffrage Association."
>
> The Convention adjourned on May 8 at about 2:15 p.m. The constitution was signed by all the members and by the president and secretary and placed in the keeping of Secretary of the Territory, C. C. Richards.[10]

The conclusion, "One of the first to congratulate me was Roberts himself. We had always been friends, and continued to be in spite of this rather sharp encounter—sharp, though good-natured throughout. . . . Other speakers followed, and after a stormy battle the equal suffrage plank was placed in the state constitution. . . . My able opponent could doubtless furnish a long list of eulogies evoked by his splendid oratory. It had but one fault—it was on the wrong side of the question."[11]

Becoming known as a champion for women's suffrage, Whitney was introduced to two leading proponents of women's rights, Dr. Anna Shaw and Susan B. Anthony, who heard him speak in the Tabernacle.[12] He gained friends among civic-minded women. But other than the compliments Orson received after giving the occasional speech, he did not care very much for politics. "Have been repeatedly solicited to take part in the current political campaign, but have as often declined. I care nothing for politics and the glory of 'the stump.'"[13]

Orson's diary had one of its more cryptic entries (that partially survived his censoring) that May. It had to do with the secret prayer meetings and codenamed members: "~~Thursday, May ?, 1895: Began a seven day fast with Joshua, Moses, David, and others, and revealed great things. Nephi~~ [John Donaldson] ~~came down from the north during our meetings, There was now seven more of our mystical~~

~~number, viz: Joshua, Moses, Nephi, David, Ishmael, Mormon, and Gideon.~~" The identities of all attendees are not known, but over the years Orson had been adding others to the group like Miss Babcock, Lyman R. Martineau, and John Beck, the wealthy majority-owner of the infamous Bullion-Beck and Champion Mine.[14] Reincarnation was a common belief among members, but it was not the only glue holding them together. Members were Mormon "theosophists," meaning they believed that if they fasted long enough, prayed with enough faith, and lived righteously enough, the mysteries of the Gospel and the secrets of the universe would be revealed to them. Ort removed most of the details of these meetings from his diary before he died, or he never recorded them at all, so the full extent and involvement of members and what they thought they obtained is unknown.

One detail that is known is that Orson decided to give Charles W. Stayner a lot of money. Stayner had returned from his mission, and somehow money began to be a prominent part of their relationship. For example, Whitney wrote, "Borrowed $2,000 of Col. E. Sells, through Glen Miller of this city. Paid off Kansas City mortgage—$1,236 including some interest—and realized a little over $600 on the new loan. Gave $300 to Joshua [Charles]. Have given him five or six hundred dollars since he came from W."[15]

A few days later Orson's wife, May, gave birth to a son that they named Wendell.[16] It was around this time that the Quorum of the Twelve discussed Bishop Whitney and rumors they were hearing. They wished to forestall troubles for him but seemed to have had no idea how deeply enmeshed he was. In a meeting of the Twelve, "Heber J. Grant was told to warn Bishop O. F. Whitney against carelessness in regard to attending meetings, as also to urge him not to become too intimate with Miss Babcock, or the Stayner brothers."[17] Some weeks later another similar discussion ensued: "We had some talk about reincarnation, which doctrine it is feared is entertained by Orson F. Whitney, George C. Parkinson, and others. It was felt that these and any other persons who believe in this false idea, should be corrected."[18]

Elder Abraham H. Cannon (a son of President George Q. Cannon), a member of the Quorum of the Twelve who was about the same age and had been something of a minor rival to Orson, helped investigate the reincarnation allegations. He discussed the situation with some locals when visiting Idaho.

> At noon we had a talk with Sol. Hale and M. F. Cowley [counselors in the stake presidency] about the reincarnation ideas of George C. Parkinson. The former had never been approached by his president on the subject, but Bro. Cowley said he had learned from Bro. Parkinson's own lips that he entertained some belief in this false doctrine, for he had brought supposed proof from scripture to sustain his position. At the time the Stake Academy Building was dedicated during the present year Pres. Parkinson had his house dedicated, and though Apostle Merrill was there, he was not asked to offer the prayer, but Orson F. Whitney was. Orson thereafter blessed Bro. Parkinson and his family, and was in turn blessed by Bro. Parkinson. George C. Parkinson has told his counselors that he [Orson] will yet be one of the Twelve Apostles, and Orson F. Whitney said that the only reason he was not made an apostle when I was chosen was because he violated the Word of Wisdom. For he had been selected, but when it was learned that he was guilty in this respect, he was voted down. This was not the case; his name was mentioned, but he was never chosen for the place."[19]

Elder Abraham Cannon had been friends with Orson in their youth, but he had grown frustrated with him and his work on the *History of Utah* project. As an apostle, his job was to investigate and help resolve what was seen as a growing problem with this group of former missionaries from Liverpool, England—the "Stayner crowd." The rivalry would not last much longer. Only a year later, Orson "Wrote John Q. Cannon letter of condolence on death of his brother Abraham."[20]

That December, Whitney decided to accept one of two teaching offers he had recently received from in-state colleges, taking a professorship at the Brigham Young College (later Utah State University). Salt Lake Stake President Angus M. Cannon saw to it that he was not released as bishop, but was only on loan to his new location. Whitney was upfront to confess that "I had had no experience as a teacher when I went to Logan."[21] He taught reading and theology first, but soon fell sick with something he called "cerebral congestion," which may have been severe anxiety or nervousness because of his new duties.[22] Further, his troubles regarding theosophy and reincarnation followed him to Logan.

> Under date of the above [March 7], the *Salt Lake Herald* reported remarks made by President George Q. Cannon at the S. L. Stake Conference, in which he stated that theosophists believed in reincarnation and that it was "a damnable doctrine." Some, he said, held that Brigham Young was St. Peter reincarnate and Joseph Smith someone else reincarnated. He condemned it all as false. The following, in reply and rebuttal, appeared in the *Herald* of March 11th:
>
> "Reincarnation: A Theosophist Replies Briefly to President Cannon's Criticism. To the Editor of The *Herald*:
>
> "I find in Monday's *Herald* a report of the remarks of President Cannon delivered at the Tabernacle on Sunday last. I was especially pleased that he spoke upon theosophy. It is immaterial whether in praise or censure, if only it serves to set people thinking upon the problems of life for themselves. However, we were surprised at the statement that theosophists claimed that Brigham Young was a reincarnation of Saint Peter and that Joseph Smith was somebody else reincarnated, since the large majority of theosophists do not claim to have any knowledge of the former incarnation of anyone; very few indeed claim to know anything of even their own previous lives. Those theosophists who accept the doctrine of reincarnation do so only because it logically and scientifically appeals to them. They claim no power to identify any personality with any particular previous one. The farthest they would go would be to refer an individual to a class or stage of human development of which he was a 'type.'
>
> "While the majority of theosophists accept the doctrine of reincarnation, logically and scientifically presented, yet it is in no sense a dogma nor is it incumbent upon a theosophist to believe it. He may believe it or not and still be a theosophist. Above any tenet or doctrine they hold that 'there is no religion higher than truth.' Therefore to those who revere truth above everything else it would be profitable to learn the reasons which impelled Mr. Cannon to pronounce reincarnation a 'damnable' theory. Perhaps Mr. Cannon may have felt it [un]necessary to enumerate the points of evidence against the theory, thinking that, given the authority of his word, it would be sufficient

and relieve the people of the necessity of investigating and thinking for themselves. However that may be, we hope that Mr. Cannon may speak further and elucidate the 'damnableness' of the theory and thereby remove error from many minds. [Signed] A Theosophist."

I suppose my friend George C. Parkinson is partly responsible for Pres. Cannon's assault. He informed me a short time ago that he related to Francis M. Lyman his dream or rather vision at Liverpool, in which Brigham Young appeared to him and told him he was St. Peter. Apostle Lyman doubtless told the Presidency about it; also of Arthur Stayner's having admitted to him (Lyman) a belief in reincarnation.

Lyman R. Martineau told me today (March 11) that Mathias F. Cowley, Parkinson's counselor in the Oneida Stake, Idaho, said today that F. M. Lyman told him there were some in Logan who believed in reincarnation, and that when it took hold of one, as it had of C. W. Stayner, that he never got over it.

I guess he's right. I would like to hear some of Pres. Cannon's "strong reasons" myself. "Damnable Theory" doesn't dispose of the matter at all. They will kick the mustard plant and scatter its seed the wider.[23]

Orson's stubborn pride occasionally showed in his private diary. Whether it also manifest itself in their theosophy meetings is unknown.[24] As the months passed, he visited family and friends, conducted 18th ward business in Salt Lake City, and then returned to Logan. Then he received bad news:

On my return to Logan, an unpleasant surprise awaited me. Pres. Kerr informed me that the Board of Trustees had set my salary for the [coming] year 1896–7 at $100 per month instead of $150, which he (Kerr) promised would be given me and upon which proposition I declined an offer of $125 made me by Pres. Paul of the A. C. College and engaged with the B. Y. working temporarily for $100 per month until now. I was shocked, and at first blamed the Board, but later found out that Pres. Kerr was to blame, for he had deceived me in the matter. The Board had never heard of his agreement with me and would not stand by it. On my presentation of the same they finally made my salary $1,300 for the year, with a promise of better things hereafter. They would have made it $1,500 but the President of the Board, George W. Thatcher, objected, fearing, he said,

> jealousy among the other professors. I think my attitude in behalf of the [illegible] had something to do with his opposition, however, I reluctantly accepted the offer—because I had to—until I could do better, but I consider myself wronged. I cannot live on such a salary, but I can struggle along till something better comes.[25]

Whitney determined to improve his abilities by taking classes from the more formally trained and educated professors. "Since the 25th of June this year (1896), [I] have been attending the summer school at the B. Y. College, or Prof. J. A. Langton's rhetoric class thereat, with a view to perfecting myself for next year's work in the college. Have also been reading a course in the history of philosophy—the survey proscribed in the guide to the *Encyclopedia Britannica* for a similar purpose."[26] While taking these various classes from other professors, Ort met one of their number that would in later years become one of his closest friends—Josiah E. Hickman.

Hickman's journal states, "School has begun again. Orson Whitney has been added to our faculty. He takes my theological class."[27] Only two weeks later Hickman had turned his advanced theology class over to Whitney to teach, preferring his work in chemistry.[28] An amiable friendship began. "I had a long talk with Bro. O. F. Whitney last Thursday evening and received from him a copy of *The Nauvoo Expositor*; also his three speeches he delivered in [the] Constitutional Convention in behalf of women suffrage."[29]

That November, Orson's mother, Helen Mar Kimball Whitney, died. He was designated executor of her estate by his sisters and eventually was able to amicably settle matters between her heirs.[30] January 1st found Whitney summing up the current events of his life:

> This day, Friday, I spent at my [rented] home in Logan, having returned the day before from a visit to Salt Lake City. I find myself in good health and spirits, firm in "the faith" and hopeful of the future.
>
> I am still bishop of the 18th ward of the Salt Lake Stake of Zion but can only go down occasionally to visit the people and my friends in the city, owing to my profusion of duties in the Brigham Young College at this place. This year I am teaching Theology 3 & 5, also a class in grammar (winter course). I occasionally give lectures to the students as well.

> Outside the college [I] am engaged in revising [the] mss [manuscript] and reading proofs of the *History of Utah*, Vol. III of which is going through the press. Owing to this and other labors I am obliged to decline many invitations to lecture and preach in Utah, Idaho, Wyoming, and other parts. My lecture on "Oratory, Poesy, and Prophecy," delivered last winter, has just been published (for the first time) in the Christmas issue of the *Logan Journal*. I have been tendered the editorial chair of that paper. I may accept if the college authorities do not object.
>
> Mary Houston Kimball, one of the widows of my grandfather, Heber C. Kimball, has recently died, leaving me sole executor of her estate. I am also to inherit ¼ of her property. The will is dated March 24, 1896. I am also acting as agent for the heirs of my mother, Helen M. Note—one of the members of my class in systematic theology is the Rev. N. E. Clemenson, a Presbyterian minister, who has just written to me expressing his appreciation of my lectures.[31]

Eventually, Orson saw the question of his taking the editorial reins of the local newspaper disappear, and for good reason.

> I shall probably not become editor of the *Journal*. Am informed that a cabal has formed against me among some of the stockholders, headed by George H. Thatcher. They have nothing against me personally and do not question my ability, but fear I would not be radical enough to suit them, that is, I would not assail the Church leaders, I suppose, as Mr. Warrum, the present editor, has been doing. They are right. I would not; not for ten thousand a year or any other consideration! And I feel relieved at the thought that I am not to take a position where a collar would be around my neck, and I would be the tool of a clique. I am a Democrat, but my religion is, and I hope always will be, above my politics. Amen![32]

In March Whitney exchanged letters with Elder Lyman over a perceived slight. "Wrote to Apostle F. M. Lyman concerning a remark he had made about me to Apostle Brigham Young [Jr.], who had repeated it to his son, my friend and informant, Bid S. Young."[33] Then, "Received a kind answer from Bro. Lyman, acknowledging that he had been in error."[34]

Orson had been teaching in Logan for just over a year when he received a proposition from Charles W. Stayner in which he was offered a sizable salary. He decided to accept. "I am offered $300 a month in the [Salt Lake] City. Here [at B.Y. College in Logan] I get $108, or $1,300 a year. I shall probably accept [Stayner's offer]. Told President Kerr before I went to Salt Lake this last time that I was about to sever my connection with the college. He expressed regrets, and said he was sorry matters had not been more pleasant to me here. I told him I had no complaints to make. I enjoyed my work, but had too little time in which to do it, and was too much rushed—that was all."[35]

Stayner's offer was probably connected to possibilities of working as a company director in the sugar beet business, an idea that did not work out. Within two years Orson Whitney signed, along with the Stayner brothers, John Beck, and many other prominent businessmen and church leaders, the articles that incorporated the Utah Sugar Company.[36] During Whitney's brief association with the company, it struggled and was unprofitable, but in later years the Utah-Idaho Sugar Company became a very profitable source of income for those investors that continued backing it, including the Church.

The April general conference saw another condemnation of reincarnation by President Cannon: "Conference closed today. Heard that President George Q. Cannon denounced reincarnation, secret meetings, etc. this afternoon and Pres. Woodruff endorsed his remarks."[37]

In June, Whitney officially resigned his teaching position at the Brigham Young College and spent some weeks at the home of Charles W. Stayner. Orson's diary contains a cryptic note, "Charles W. Stayner to Zina: 'We are the two best men on the earth' (Joshua & M. M.). Joshua to Jepthah: 'They don't make better men,' meaning M. M." With Joshua being Charles, and Zina being Jepthah, it seems likely that M. M. was Orson. The initials probably stood for Mahonri Moriancumer, the name of the brother of Jared in the Book of Ether in the Book of Mormon. The comments from Stayner imply another case of his flattering Whitney.

It was an extended visit;

> Returned today to Logan, from a three weeks absence in Salt Lake and Bountiful. At the latter place celebrated my 42nd birthday [on] Thursday, July 1st. My friend, Judge Stayner, gave a party at his home

> in my honor, and at night took us (Zina & myself) to hear [William Jennings] Bryan . . . at the Salt Lake Theater. It was very entertaining. Had heard the great silver orator once before but not since his famous Chicago speech where he was nominated for president. . . . During my recent visit to Salt Lake [I] spoke in the Salt Lake Temple and at the Salt Lake Stake priesthood meeting. President Snow told me that it was "a most lovely discourse." My remarks at the priesthood meeting were also favorably commented upon. It was Sunday, June 20th, that Zina joined me at Bountiful and she remained to return with me July 5th. June 21st was Judge Stayner's 57th birthday. We took dinner with him and a few select friends at Bountiful and spent the day at his home.[38]

On July 24, the "Pioneer Jubilee" (now known as "Pioneer Day"), Orson "was awakened by a call from Elder George F. Gibbs who informed me that Pres. Woodruff, who is quite feeble, wanted me to read his prayer at the ceremonies of unveiling the primary statue, at 10:30. Arose and went to the President's Office. Received the mss. Was on hand at the time appointed and read the prayer. The President sat in a chair during the delivery. . . . While on the stand was introduced to William Jenning Bryan, who attended the ceremonies."[39] President Woodruff seemed to love Orson's oratorical talent, often taking advantage of it. The next day he formally resumed his position as active bishop of the Salt Lake 18th ward.[40]

At this point, Whitney spent some time living at the Hotel Roberts in Provo, a rooming establishment then run by his sister, Maggie, who had also employed Ort's son Race as clerk. Because he had left his teaching position, he was again out of work. Further, Charles Stayner's employment offer never materialized. "Came to Provo (where I now am) with Zina and the children. We will sojourn here for a few weeks and then—I know not what. God knoweth. He 'is my Shepherd'—'I shall not want.'"[41]

Bishop Whitney's stake president, to whom he reported directly in ecclesiastical matters, was Angus M. Cannon, a brother of President George Q. Cannon. Orson seems to have developed a good and amiable relationship with him. He wrote, "Had an interesting interview with Pres. A. M. Cannon, who showed himself (not for the first time) my friend. Had some good meetings with Joshua, Moses, and other friends."[42] It's probable that Angus, the most influential stake president in the Church, was visiting with him about rumors of his secret meetings and reincarnation, or perhaps something related to plural marriage and Maude May Babcock. Ort would not say. "Returned to Provo. Remained all the week; preached in the Utah Stake Tabernacle [on] Sunday afternoon. Suffered terribly in my feelings during the week and shed many bitter tears. Why, I cannot tell here."[43]

The enigmatic entries continued, "This evening I had a most singular experience, painful and joyous, illustrating vividly the principle of sacrifice, or at all events how we are blessed and rewarded when we are resigned and acknowledge the Lord's hand in our sorrows and troubles."[44] No further explanation was given.

That same month, Orson and his friend Moses Thatcher, who had by then been dropped from the Quorum of the Twelve and was no longer an apostle, exchanged correspondence, with Orson "congratulating him on his course before the High Council. Received [a] good letter from him in reply."[45] Moses had swallowed his pride, confessed his wrongdoing sufficiently, and narrowly averted being excommunicated.[46]

Then Orson found himself discussing the mysteries with an acquaintance:

> This afternoon, at the residence of Aunt Zina D. H. Young, 18th ward, I had an interview with her brother, Oliver Huntington of Springville. It was at his solicitation. He told me, among other things, that he heard Joseph Smith the Prophet say that the Holy Ghost would yet have a body. The substance of this statement was this: The Prophet had said that no man knew who he was, nor would men know until he was weighed in the balance, etc. One of his wives said, "I know who he is; he's the Holy Ghost." Joseph, on hearing of this, said, "No; I am not, for the Holy Ghost hasn't a body, but," he added, "he will have."
>
> I told Bro. Huntington that I had read somewhere words of the Prophet to the same effect, but he thought I must be in error. Said he, "I heard the Prophet say that. I wrote it for the *Young Ladies Journal* and it was suppressed, so I want now to tell it to you that it may be remembered and perpetuated." He said he had given it to Susa Y.

> Gates, with the request that it be submitted to the Authorities. It was given to Joseph F. Smith and he heard no more of it.
>
> Bro. Huntington believes firmly in the principle of reincarnation; said it was revealed to him in the temple 12 years ago. He said he heard Brigham Young speak of it in such a way as to cause him to conclude that he believed it. And he even thought the present Authorities believed it, but for prudential reasons discountenanced it. I told him I did not think they believed it; one or two might, but not the most of them.[47]

Ort was always willing to discuss reincarnation with those who shared his views. After the October general conference, he found himself again speaking in the Tabernacle: "Had a large and attentive audience and was blessed of God in addressing them. My subject was sacrifice and consecration. Apostle Brigham Young [Jr.] presided. In pronouncing his benediction he declared the discourse to be the word of the Lord. Many spoke of it. It was said that I never spoke better."[48] At the conference, Matthias Cowley and Abraham Owen Woodruff were called to the Quorum of the Twelve Apostles.

Whitney had entered one of the more unfathomable stretches of his life. He was out of a job and his only source of income were the payments he was receiving for his work on volume four of his *History of Utah*. He was regularly meeting with his theosophy group at the homes of the Stayners and Miss Babcock. He became as enamored with Charles W. Stayner—whose codename he changed in his diaries from "Joshua" to "Elias"—as he ever would be. Such a condition found him making inscrutable personal decisions that placed him in an increasingly precarious position spiritually, emotionally, and temporally.

> Sold my house in Salt Lake—No. 155 Second St. to Dan D. Spencer for $2,450. In other words, he assumes payment of the mortgage of $2,000 now on the property (3X10 rods with house, assessed at $2,840) and pays me $450. Eighty dollars of this I paid as interest on mortgage to October 18, and $78.10 taxes for 1897. The residue [$291.90] I laid before Elias as an offering and it was divided as follows: Elias [meaning Charles Stayner] - $144. M. M. [probably Whitney] - $120. Moses [meaning Arthur Stayner] - $12. Naaman

> [probably John Beck] - $12. The balance of $3.90 was returned to me. This was given as an example of such things.
>
> Heber C. Kimball was seen by Moses to lay his right hand on my left shoulder, standing to my left and a little in the rear, and say, "Orson, this is a good thing that you have done."
>
> I had said some days before that if the Lord would give me a blessing in money I would lay every dollar of it before Elias and let the Lord [decide] how it should be disposed of. I had simply kept my word—my covenant.
>
> The other day at Babcock's I gave my last ten dollars to Elias as an offering—$10 of $15 that he had given me. Two or three days later, $10 was given to me by Dan Spencer. I regarded it as my offering returned. I have made offerings to Elias at different times aggregating hundreds of dollars; and that when I was in great need myself. Zina and I gave our house to him (this same house) but it was returned. She joined with me in this offering also.
>
> This evening we all met at 717 [Maude Babcock's address] and received each a blessing from the Lord [through Elias] in the following order: Keturah, myself, Esther, Ishmael, Moses, Nephi, Tamar. It was a grand meeting. ~~The Angel Raphael appeared and delivered a message~~.[49]

Almost ten years would pass before Whitney recovered financially from the sale of his home and the struggles from giving so much money to Stayner, but he was not alone. From various diary entries, it seems evident that John Beck (codenamed Naaman), an owner of the Bullion-Beck and Champion Mine, was invited into their growing group and told what would be expected of him. Whitney stated, "[I] Read this morning of a [silver ore] strike in the Bullion-Beck Mine. Glad news! It fulfills predictions made by myself and others at Bountiful last Monday. I told Naaman if he would pay Elias what was required, first of all it would turn the key in the lock of his prosperity and he and his family should never want. Nephi and Elias confirmed it. Naaman agreed to do it. This looks like the result."[50] John Beck became a millionaire, but eventually, due to bad investments and mismanagement of his personal finances, he went bankrupt.[51] It is unknown how much money Stayner collected from the entire group.

The meetings continued, and a new year dawned, with Orson missing Zina and worrying about the future. "And so passed my

New Year's. Was sad in the evening and longed to be with my dear Zina and the children in Provo. I expect she was just as lonesome for me. I feel that affairs are approaching a crisis."[52] He did not name the crisis, but one possibility is he meant family finances. Another interpretation is he meant the fate of the secret prayer group. He would have been right on both counts.

Meanwhile, Ort heard of another dream involving him. "Tuesday, Sister Mary Stayner related to me a dream she had had the night before. She thought I was dead and my funeral conducted by Horace G. Whitney and John D. Spenser. Was in the old B.Y. school house where, in July 1878, I was ordained a bishop. The coffin did not fit. Sister Stayner protested against my being buried in that manner and a better coffin was then provided. At length I arose and said 'I want to tell you a few things before you bury me,' etc. This probably means that I shall lay down my bishopric and pass into another sphere of labor. Amen! If the Lord wills."[53]

If Orson was hinting that he was tiring of his calling as bishop, or was hopeful of a change ahead, he would have to wait most of another decade.

Matters were not going Orson's way. The main problem with secret prayer groups is that the larger they get, the harder they are to keep secret. Rumors were leaking out and reaching the ears of high church authorities: "[I] had an interview with Brother Dan Collett at the Historian's Office. He showed himself my friend. He told me of reports that had reached the President's Office about me and others and of a remark made by President George Q. Cannon, asking, 'Why the Presidency of the [Salt Lake] Stake did not ferret out these secret meetings, oath-bound organizations, etc.'"[54] Whitney's private life was becoming more complicated by the month, and he struggled to keep things together. Later he "had another interview with Bro. Collett. He told me more of the rumors that had reached the President's Office."[55] A worried Ort impetuously shared his growing problems with a friendly and understanding but ill-chosen confidante. "Had an interesting interview with Elder Joseph E. Taylor. Answered some of the lies that have been floating around about me and my friends. Have had several interesting interviews with Moses Thatcher of late."[56] Thatcher was himself in the middle of a public feud with President Lorenzo Snow and other Church leaders.[57]

That January, both Orson and his wife had dreams that he felt important enough to preserve, but not explain:

> Went to Provo and staid till Saturday. Friday night dreamed that President John Taylor had presented me with a hat as a New Year's gift. It was new, black, of Alpine shape, and home-made. It was presented, for the President, by Elder C. W. Penrose, one of the presidency of the Salt Lake Stake of Zion. He invited me into a carriage prior to or first after the presentation. I remember saying to myself, I'll lay off the hat I am wearing—a Stetson—and wear this one every day. Zina dreamed the same night that I had returned from a mission, or some absence, and that she was hunting for me. [Illegible ~~searching/something~~] ~~directed her to a~~ [~~house~~?] ~~where she found me with~~ [illegible].[58]

No date is given for the below narration from Whitney's autobiography, and he was evidently not at home when the episode occurred, but he still felt it to be a precious incident connected with his immediate family:

> Among the many interesting incidents connected with our little home on the hillside, there is one that should always be cherished by the members of my family. It will be better understood after reading what the Book of Mormon has to say upon the subject of the Three Nephites. My wife [Zina] thus relates the incident:
>
> It happened many years ago. My husband was away, and the only members of the family in the house besides myself were three of our little boys. It was early spring, and I was busy house-cleaning. Hearing the doorbell ring, I opened the door, and there stood an elderly man, with white hair and beard, clean, neatly dressed, straight as an arrow, and altogether respectable in appearance and respectful in manner. He carried a cane and held his hat in hand. He asked me if I could help him. I told him that I had no money, but if he needed food I would gladly give him some. Said he, "I would be very grateful."
>
> The unusual answer somewhat surprised me, but being much occupied, I paid slight attention. Showing him down into the dining

> room on the basement floor, I spread before him what food I had, and left him sitting at the table. The little boys were playing there at the time, and I told them to stay with the stranger and wait on him, while I returned to my work on the floor above.
>
> After a while I heard the patter of feet running up the stairs, and here came the boys, all breathless and excited, the oldest (Murray) exclaiming, "Mama, I bet that was one of the Three Nephites!"
>
> "What makes you think so?" I inquired.
>
> Here spoke up the second boy (Bert), who had a toothache when the stranger arrived. "I was holding my hand to my face, and he said, 'Son, what is troubling you?' 'My tooth aches,' I said. 'It will trouble you no more,' said he. And it stopped right then and hasn't ached since."
>
> The boys told me that the visitor, when departing by a back door, spoke these words, "Peace be unto you and your house." They likewise related how they rushed out after him, not seeing him pass the windows, and looked up and down the street and through the back yard, but could catch no glimpse of him.
>
> I do not think that I am over-credulous regarding such matters. But the impression made upon my mind by that venerable stranger and his pleasing address, coupled with the excitement of the boys and their expressed conviction as to who he was, caused me to marvel. I have never been able to entirely banish the thought that possibly the boys were right.[59]

Soon Bishop Whitney and his friends found themselves hosting a prominent visitor to the city, manifesting curiosity about Mormonism. They lost no time enlightening him: "Met at the office of Judge Stayner. . . . Doctor John M. Reiner . . . who spoke in the Tabernacle last Sunday afternoon and is now the guest of Elder John Beck. There were present, besides the Doctor and Bro. Beck, Judge Stayner, Arthur Stayner, John Donaldson, B. S. Young, and myself. We had a most interesting conversation. Dr. Reiner said we were the first Mormon elders who had given him any satisfaction about Mormonism. He had met Elders Talmage, Roberts, Penrose, and others. Wednesday we were at Bro. Beck's at Waterloo to dinner, the Doctor being the guest of honor. A fine time!"[60]

Orson later related a conversation that he and the learned Doctor (a Catholic) had had about the strength of the position of Mormonism in Christianity:

> One day he [Dr. Reiner] said to me, "You Mormons are all ignoramuses. You don't even know the strength of your own position. It is so strong that there is only one other position tenable in the whole Christian world, and that is the position of the Roman Catholic Church. The issue is between Catholicism and Mormonism. If we are right, you are wrong; if you are right, we are wrong, and that's all there is to it. The Protestant sects haven't a leg to stand on; for if we are right, we cut them off long ago as apostates; and if we are wrong, they are wrong with us, since they were a part of us and went out from us. If we have the apostolic succession from St. Peter, as we claim, there was no need of Joseph Smith and Mormonism. But if we have it not, then such a man as Joseph Smith was needed, and Mormonism's position is the only consistent one. It is either the perpetuation of the gospel from ancient times or the restoration of the gospel in latter days." This clear and concise statement I answered as follows, "Doctor, I agree with you in almost everything that you have said; but don't deceive yourself with the notion that we 'Mormons' are not aware of the strength of our own position. We know it better than anyone else can know it. We have not all been to college; we cannot all speak the dead languages; and we may be ignoramuses as you say. But we know we are right, and we know you are wrong." I was just as frank with him as he had been with me.[61]

Another unusual situation involving Bishop Whitney took place when a member of his ward forsook Mormonism for theosophy. Since the Bishop himself was involved in a kind of theosophy, he found himself walking a very fine line, one that if improperly understood would smack of hypocrisy. The woman, a Dr. Ellen Ferguson, may have known about Bishop Whitney's theosophy group and was trying to use that fact to injure him. Whitney noted, "Heard today that the proposition that I should call Dr. Ferguson to account for theosophy was a trap."[62]

As Bishop Whitney explained to his congregation at her excommunication, Ferguson's brand of theosophy excluded faith in Mormonism. What he did not mention was that his own brand embraced Mormonism, and in this he saw all the difference. "On Friday evening last the Bishop's Court of the 18th ward sat upon the case of Dr. Ellen B. Ferguson, charged by the teachers (T. A. Clawson and

John A. Evans) with apostasy. The charge was sustained and she was excommunicated."[63]

Bishop Whitney was able to avoid being caught in a tight and compromising place, at least for the time being.

Chapter 11

Whitney's Watershed Years, Part 1, 1898–1900

Historian Ronald W. Walker, in his narration of major episodes in the life of Heber J. Grant, entitled one chapter "Grant's Watershed," meaning it told the story of how a young and sometimes overly ambitious Elder Grant humbled himself, fully harmonized with the Quorum of the Twelve, and changed the course of his life. This positioned him to eventually become the President of the Church.[1] Orson F. Whitney endured a similarly humbling watershed experience, or defining period of life.

For Whitney, 1898 through 1900 were momentous years. He found some financial stability, but, at his own volition, did not benefit much from it. The plans that he and the Stayners had patiently promoted for almost two decades finally came to a head. Thereafter, as the dust settled, he found his life shaken to the core and forever altered. His passage through these years tried his soul deeply, resulting in a more stable and submissive soul. In the end, he finally earned for himself the unqualified trust of the Brethren.

In March of 1898, Ort was approached by Spencer Clawson, the chairman of a special "Utah Semi-Centennial Commission" created by the governor and tasked with having a book prepared and published as part of Utah's fifty-year celebration of the July 24th arrival of the pioneers in the Salt Lake Valley. The original compiler, Henry

W. Naisbitt, had fallen short in the quality of work desired by the commission. Whitney was asked to revise and improve it.[2]

Also that month, Whitney endured something that he did not fully explain: "This evening I put into effect a principle taught by the Savior and emphasized and explained by Elias [Stayner]. The principle of the golden rule, and of turning the other cheek. Satan raged and for a time destroyed my peace, but not permanently. It turned out all right, and I know I did the proper thing."[3]

The April general conference saw the beginning of events that, after intensifying, would eventually culminate in Whitney changing his views on those matters he was not in harmony with Church leadership on. At that time Orson "spoke to President Joseph F. Smith about [receiving further temple blessings] and he kindly told me he thought me worthy. He said he would like to have a private talk with me, however."[4] Joseph F. Smith's conference talk that weekend provided Orson with a chance to make his feelings known to an individual that he knew to be a source of rumors about him. "At the conference, President Joseph F. Smith complained of anonymous letters of a threatening character sent to the Presidency and said that the writer of an anonymous letter was as bad as a sneak thief; he was a coward and one of the meanest of God's creatures. Bishop Beatie, who sat in front of me, nodded his head approvingly to those about him, and we all agreed that it was so. I then said that the man who slandered his brethren to the Authorities was almost as bad, just as sneaking and just as cowardly. He did not nod his head at this."[5]

Shortly thereafter Bishop Whitney was able to have what he viewed as an opportune visit with his friend Joseph F. Smith:

> From 5:45 p.m. to 6:45 p.m. this evening, I had a very interesting interview with President Joseph F. Smith, in much of which Apostle Heber J. Grant and A. O. Woodruff took part. I was asked about my connection with Bro. Charles W. Stayner and if I sympathized with his views, those formerly held by him at Liverpool, and which he was strongly suspected of having revived.
>
> This gave me an opportunity of refuting the falsehoods put in circulation by W. J. Beatie and others (who told the Sears family, my relatives) that Bro. Stayner, myself, and others were founding a new Church, had an oath-bound organization, a regalia, etc. I told the

brethren that these were outrageous falsehoods, that Bro. Stayner was one of the most loyal men I knew, that we were Latter-day Saints firm in the faith, and that the Church of God was the only Church we wanted anything to do with.

I did admit, however, to having had faith in reincarnation, or rehabitment of spirits, though I had never sought to spread it, but had said, in private, that I could believe it if the Church Authorities sanctioned it (Connie Thatcher incident) because there were evidences enough in the Church books to justify such a belief. "It is thought," remarked Bro. Grant, "that you and the brethren associated with you claim to have received advanced truth and we are behind the times."

"I never heard such a remark," I replied. "If I or anyone else taught any doctrine, true or false without authority, it would be premature, we would be ahead of the times, not you behind them."

President Smith finally said, "Well, if there is anything in our books that justifies a belief in reincarnation I would like to know it; for to me it seems opposed to the fundamental principles of Mormonism." I answered that I would take great pleasure in citing him to those passages in the books that contain the doctrine, and he invited me to do so. This was a great point gained, as [line missing] to listen to a statement of that kind. [Six lines scribbled out and illegible.]

The brethren were all very kind, manifesting the deepest interest in my welfare, anxious that I should not "get off," etc.

President Smith told me that Heber Grant thought as much of me as one man could of another, and assured me of his own warm personal friendship and brotherly love. He said it was President George Q. Cannon and Apostle F. M. Lyman, who most frequently brought this matter up about myself and Bro. Stayner, which did not surprise me, as that is in fulfillment of a vision had by Bro. Donaldson in Bro. Stayner's house (20th ward) years ago. The vision of the brick throwing, Bro. Lyman throwing them, and Bro. Cannon behind the shrubbery watching or directing it. The effects of attack, myself and Arthur Stayner; Charles W. being in a house nearby and us going to him walking on in the "calmness of the gospel, in the placidity of truth and in the self-possession of the Holy Spirit." Such was the language of the interpretation by revelation through Charles W. [Stayner].

President Cannon opposed my having my [further temple blessings] on account of my association with Bro. Stayner. President Smith said that personally he hadn't the shadow of a doubt as to my integrity and devotion to the Gospel.[6]

Ort had not been as forthcoming during this visit as he might have been. Instead, he used the occasion to set the stage for what he hoped would be his chance to persuade President Joseph F. Smith to accept reincarnation as doctrine. He had minimized the extent of his involvement in the rumored matters and said nothing of the groups' plans for Charles Stayner to become the prophet of the Church. But now the long awaited opportunity seemed to have arrived and he took as much advantage of it as he could. "Began a letter to President Joseph F. Smith, to accompany the statement regarding reincarnation."[7] As Bishop Whitney reached for the opportunity with both hands, other issues arose to distract and trouble him: "My 1st Counselor in the bishopric [Robert Patrick] acts very cold and distant. He is not friendly and has not been for some time. He has heard the rumors about Bro. Stayner and myself and thinks himself solid with the Authorities; [he] treats me with positive unfriendliness at times. I think he is jealous and I believe he wants my office. Will see."[8]

As the rumors spread, others reached his ears. "Last Sunday evening (May 1) Moses Thatcher told me a man had asked him if we (the Stayner crowd) ought not to be "hauled up" and made to stop our meetings. Moses Thatcher answered, "No." Lon H. was the man. Aunt Em denied to me the other day that she has said to anyone that I talked like an apostate. J. Q. [Cannon?] told it in the President's Office."[9]

Orson's life was becoming highly complicated, with more serious entanglements than he could safely navigate. But he moved forward with writing the reincarnation statement and letter that he hoped would be so overwhelmingly convincing as to change the doctrine of the Church. "At Bountiful today read to C. W. [Stayner], Arthur [Stayner], B. S. [Young], Sis. Stayner, and Miss Babcock my statement and letter to President Smith. It pleased them highly. Only a few alterations were suggested. Shall copy it and send it in as soon as possible; reserving a duplicate."[10] A few days later he "spent part of the forenoon at the office—305—copying the letter and statement—Dan A. Collett typewriting it at my dictation."[11] The same day, he "attended [the] Tabernacle in the afternoon and preached. President George Q. Cannon was present. I occupied all the time. My theme was Moses, Christ, [and] Joseph Smith, the three greatest teachers that the world has seen. Had a good spirit. It was voted 'a glorious discourse.' Thank God!"[12] It seemed that despite the rumors, his talent for teaching the fundamentals was still recognized, utilized, and appreciated.

A couple of days later he had the letter and statement typed and copied, and then "at 20 minutes past 4 this afternoon I handed to Secretary George F. Gibbs at the President's Office the letter and statement to President Joseph F. Smith. The latter was not in the Office, but Elder Gibbs promised to lay the document on his desk. This day is historic with me; or will be from this time."[13]

Now that the statement regarding reincarnation had been given to President Joseph F. Smith, Whitney pursued another part of the plan—to convince President Snow of reincarnation as well. Whitney recorded their conversation;

> Conversed with President Lorenzo Snow, at the Salt Lake Temple, on the subject of the letter and statement to President Smith, a copy of which I left with him (Lorenzo Snow) for perusal a few days ago. He said he had read it, but wanted to read it again. The first part was perfectly clear to him; He fully believed that Christ had two bodies, but what was the need of Elijah having more than one? We talked the matter over. I told him about himself and Ezekiel the Prophet, and bore testimony to the worth and wisdom of Elias [Charles Stayner]. He said my letter breathed a good spirit and he did not believe that I could be led astray by man, or that I would believe a doctrine without good reasons. I thought, "Bro. Joseph" [Joseph F. Smith] would have something to study over in the statement, for there were things in it that could not be contradicted. He talked also of obedience to counsel, in which I acquiesced, and said I had no thought, neither had Bro. Stayner, other than to honor the Priesthood. I had not sought to spread this doctrine, and had made the statement only at President Smith's request. He said he wanted to study the statement, so that if the subject came before the Council of the Twelve and the Presidency he would be prepared to speak a word for me, etc.[14]

What President Snow thought about Orson's announcement that he (Lorenzo) had once been the Old Testament prophet Ezekiel is not given. President Snow, who had in former years discussed many deep and speculative doctrines with Orson, was open-minded almost to a fault with his young protégé. Also, the very fact that President Snow had to defend Orson to the other Brethren was not a good sign. Other developments were worse: "I heard a few days later that Bro. J. N. had been a secret enemy; that the [18th] ward had been canvassed for complaints against me, but none could be found upon which to base an effort for my removal; that I had had a talk with President Joseph F. Smith and all had been made right, etc."[15] Bishop Whitney found himself sinking deeper into the rolling seas of rumor and distrust.

Because Orson had sold his home and given most of the profits to Stayner and others, he had to move into another house that he signed a lease for.[16] Then at the June 18th Ward Conference, to his relief, he was sustained "as usual" as the bishop.[17]

That summer, Charles C. Richards asked Orson to consider running for the state senate as a Democrat. Orson thought about it, talked it over with Charles Stayner, and then got permission from the Brethren. "Saw President Joseph F. Smith about the legislative candidacy. He said, 'Go ahead and God bless you.'"[18] Before Bishop Whitney could do anything further politically, sad but hopeful news reached him: "President Wilford Woodruff died at 6:40 this morning at the home of Col. Isaac Trumbo in San Francisco. This dissolves the First Presidency and makes Apostle Lorenzo Snow the virtual head of the Church. Pres. Cannon, who was with Pres. Woodruff when he died, is a sick and feeble man. Other changes are evidently at hand."[19] With President Snow quickly being sustained and set apart as President of the Church, Orson's plans to influence President Snow regarding selection of a new apostle could be tried when the right opportunity presented itself.

Meanwhile, even though Orson now had permission to run for a state senate seat, he needed to be nominated as a candidate. To resolve this, he enlisted his friend and uncle, J. Golden Kimball. "Bishop Orson F. Whitney asked me to nominate him as senator to the State Legislature from this district tomorrow at the County Democratic Convention." Golden Kimball's reflections on his own and Orson's lives as Mormons is noteworthy:

> It's a peculiar life a Latter-day Saint leads. He is a laborer, a hewer of stone, then a missionary to the world, traveling without purse or scrip. Next, perhaps, a president of a mission. When promoted in the Church, he preaches, prays, gets angry, speculates, attends funerals one day, the next in a political function or convention and is nominating men to office. Then family troubles, next a giving away to the weaknesses of the flesh. I can think of no people on earth that have such a varied experience.[20]

One of the Whitney family's "varied experiences" was being robbed.

> During the night (about 3 a.m. of Monday, [the] 5th) a burglar entered our house and ransacked several rooms, taking a watch and chain and a pin (all of gold) belonging to Mrs. Hampton, a friend from Logan who was staying with us. He went into Zina's room, but she saw him and screamed, frightening him away. I ran to her room from the next room, but the burglar had fled downstairs and out the front door before I could intercept him. I saw him plainly as he went out of the gate and could have shot him if I had had a gun. No one but Mrs. Hampton lost anything.[21]

Having survived that adventure, the day of his nomination came. Golden Kimball recorded, "Nominations for state senator were made. I nominated Bishop Orson F. Whitney as state senator. … R. K. Thomas and Orson F. Whitney were elected on first ballot. I was very much pleased as Bishop Whitney is a man of honor, intelligence, a rising young man, and a faithful LDS and is loyal and patriotic. He has been kept back, and I felt very pleased indeed with his nomination."[22] How Kimball knew Whitney had been kept back, and if he knew why, is not recorded.

Orson made his own record of the day's events: "At the Democratic County Convention, held in the Salt Lake Theater today, I was nominated on the first ballot a state senator. J. Golden Kimball made the nomination and it was seconded by Bernard Stewart. Both made fine speeches which were well received. . . . My wife Zina was a member of the Convention."[23] Further, he noted, "I was offered the nomination for County Clerk by Judge Powers, and that for County

Treasurer by others, but declined them as I had entered the race for state senator. . . . The Convention lasted two days and late into the nights. I was nominated the first day."[24] Ort needed the paycheck he received for his service, but the extra work was burdensome, and the political opposition to his speeches was unpleasant to him. He eventually decided not to run for a second term. Other matters intervened that directed his energies elsewhere.

Despite the rumors swirling around him, and with his reincarnation beliefs under consideration by the First Presidency and others of the Twelve, Orson showed no signs of curtailing the secret prayer meetings. In fact, evidence indicates that Alfred W. McCune had joined the group, and perhaps others as well. They moved the meetings from home to home, so each member had a chance to host the group. In September, Orson noted, "Attended a very important meeting at '313.' Details too sacred for mention here."[25] Not long afterward, Elder Heber J. Grant, still feeling concern for his old friend Bishop Whitney, tried to counsel him to be more cautious. Orson was not very receptive. "Had a conversation with H. J. Grant on the subject of the Stayners, McCune, the statement, etc. He told me he loved me, but did not like some of my associates and urged me not to injure my reputation by associating with certain persons. I answered that I could not go back on a friend because others were down on him, but thanked him for the good feeling he had for me."[26]

The General Authorities seemed to be vexed with what to do about Orson. In him, they had the services of an asset of tremendous worth to the Church, one who wielded influence almost equal to their own; one who publicly taught sound doctrine and righteous living in a powerful and persuasive manner. But at the same time he was beset by rumors that bordered on scandal because of private and secret activities that he stubbornly refused to cease. Instead, he was pushing them boldly before the Brethren, putting his plans into operation to get Stayner (or "E.") called as an apostle while a vacancy in the Quorum existed and his friend President Snow had the final say in who would be called.

As September passed into early October, Bishop Whitney arranged three private meetings with President Lorenzo Snow in order to advance his goal of Charles W. Stayner one day becoming the prophet. "Had a pleasant interview with Pres. Lorenzo Snow, at his house on Canyon Road, 18th ward (Three Priesthoods)."[27] Then, "Had a very important interview with Pres. Snow, paving the way for one between him and E. [the] next day. Bore testimony that E. was a prophet of God and that I had been sent of God in his behalf. (Mahonri—H. G.—Next planet)."[28] And lastly, "Had another interview with the President in the temple. He was kind as usual, but has no faith in E."[29]

Stymied in his efforts, Orson was deflated, and as the months passed, he would become devastated, depressed, and miserable. The grandiose plan had not worked; President Snow had not accepted Whitney's "testimony" that Stayner was a prophet. Orson had been the forerunner of nothing. Two days later, Orson noted, "Elder Rudger Clawson was chosen to fill the vacancy in the Twelve."[30]

During President Snow's later years, his two closest and most loved friends and protégés were Orson Whitney and Rudger Clawson. Among other reasons, it may be that because of Whitney's imprudent strategy to push Stayner's name as the new apostle at this critical time, he himself was also passed over. The Prophet looked to Rudger Clawson instead.

But all was not yet lost. While neither he nor Stayner had been called to the apostleship, Orson remained a powerful public influence, and he still had hopes of converting the Church to reincarnation. "Went to Tooele to attend stake conference with Francis M. Lyman. Had a splendid time. Spoke Saturday afternoon and Sunday morning and afternoon. The people were moved to tears. Bro. Lyman told me he was delighted with my remarks, and in his benediction thanked the Lord for 'Bishop Whitney's expressive and [illegible] words.' Afternoon on Sunday had a talk with him and Apostle John W. Taylor on reincarnation."[31] Whitney's reincarnation statement had let the cat out of the bag and, with it no longer a secret, he was free to try to persuade others of the Brethren to see it his way.

In addition, he continued giving half of his hard-earned money to Stayner: "Gave half the $25 to E. according to agreement. Got $50 from B. T. Lloyd for campaign service. Gave ½ to E. Also gave E. half of $5. This makes in all to date $1,250 that I have given him under the recent arrangement."[32] The Brethren remained kind and merciful to Orson. He was still President Snow's friend, and his political work and candidacy turned out to be successful. "The *Herald* this morning announces a Democratic victory. Roberts, Baskin, and the whole Salt Lake County ticket elected. This means that I am to sit in the state senate next January, and also in January [of] 1901. Herriman, the Republican stronghold, went Democratic! B. T. Lloyd, the County Chairman, told me that I did more for Democracy in the county than any other speaker. B. H. Roberts said he felt more indebted to me than to any other speaker for his election."[33]

Success in politics gave him confidence, and the day after the election he tried another idea;

> Started out this morning to see Pres. Lorenzo Snow and ask him to give me Charles W. Penrose's position as Assistant Church Historian; the latter, as I learned from Apostle Heber J. Grant, the other day, having been appointed editor of the *Deseret News*, and Pres. Snow having said to me some time since that he would "do what he could for me," etc. On my way met F. S. Richards, who, on learning of my purpose and being asked by me to use his influence with his father, the Church Historian, told me he had anticipated me and had strongly urged his father to use his influence for me. Thanked him, and went up to the President's Office, meeting Apostle Francis M. Lyman on the way. Asked him to say a good word for me in the Council this day. He did not say he would or would not. Found Pres. Snow in. He welcomed me with a cordial smile and said, "The very man I want to see." He asked me if I had had any help from the Cannons to assist me to complete Vol. 4 of the *History* (referring to a former conversation in which I had told him I had 3 months work yet to do, and no income, the $1,400 for which I had contracted to finish the *History* being exhausted. I told him I had laid the matter before Hugh Cannon. "Well," said the President, "I don't think you'll get any help from that quarter. But I've found a position for you and just the thing." He then told me that Apostle Richards had been to see him and wanted me for his assistant in the Historian's Office. At his suggestion I then saw Bro. Richards and made an appointment with him this afternoon after he gets away from the temple (Apostles Meeting). I asked Pres. Snow what Pres. Cannon thought of my being Assistant Church Historian. He smiled and said, "Well, it don't matter what he thinks of it. We'll fix it up for you."[34]

Being friends with the President of the Church had its benefits. However, Orson had been out of steady employment for so long and was in such need that he had to sell his watch—giving half the proceeds to Stayner as usual.[35] Orson seemed unable to recognize how splitting his income was affecting him: "My friend Alfred W. McCune sent me by the hand of Joseph Wells $250 with the proposition to write his biography. Gave ½ to E. ($125) which with $30 given the other day makes in all $250 that I have given him since I began to share equally with him my earnings."[36] It is not stated clearly in the (censored) diaries why Whitney had covenanted to give half his income to Stayner. He seemed to see it as an offering of spiritual import that would bless him in return. Whether such was the case is open to serious question. He found employment as both a state senator and an Assistant Church Historian, and this helped to rescue him and his two families from more serious economic severities, but parting with half his earnings was deeply consequential. He soon had to accept a charitable gift from his financially-wiser brother Horace in order to be housed. And he also had to struggle with a long slow decline in his wife's health.[37]

As the new year began, Ort explained his new job,

> Assumed my new office of Assistant Church Historian. Spent the day at the Historian's Office getting hold of the routine of my labors. I have taken Bro. [Charles W.] Penrose's place, he having gone back to the [*Deseret*] *News* as editor-in-chief with my brother Horace G. Whitney as Business Manager, and I have as an assistant Bro. Dan Collett, as typewriter, and a good fellow in general. . . .
>
> My duties at the Historian's Office are the keeping up of the daily journal of the Church, a record of all events affecting its interests in any part of the world. The current history of the Church, in fact. The work is behind hand some months. I began with the date of May 18, 1898.
>
> I have to correct [edit] the minutes of meetings held in the President's Office; the record of missionary appointments and returns; the daily papers, etc., and dictate a condensed account of affairs to the typewriter, Bro. Collett.[38]

The daily journal Orson worked on became known as the *Journal History of the Church*, begun by Andrew Jenson, another

Assistant Church Historian, and would eventually become a large and valuable source of information on the Church over most of its history. After Whitney's day it slowly degenerated into little more than a collection of newspaper clippings on Mormon-related topics, but during part of the time he oversaw its production, it contained unusually valuable information, such as condensed minutes of meetings of the First Presidency and Twelve Apostles.

A week later he was present and participating as the Utah State Legislature, convened for only the third time.[39] In the legislature, which at that time elected the United States senator, Orson voted for his friend Alfred McCune. "The [*Salt Lake*] *Herald* of today publishes my speech on McCune in full under the sub-heading 'An eloquent tribute' and refers to it as 'a ringing speech.' It was the talk of the town last evening. The *Tribune* of course (Anti-McCune and Anti-Whitney) made light of it and cartooned me, as I expected; though it credited me with 'well turned phrases'. . . . A few days later I drew $120 from the state secretary, my first month's pay, as a senator. Gave E. ½, also ½ of $15 marriage fees . . . making in all $355.75."[40] Things did not go smoothly for the new legislature: "The deadlock in the Joint Assembly over the election of a United States senator continues. Today the 105th ballot was taken without producing an election. I delivered my third speech [illegible] Representative Jackson who on Wednesday last had assailed Mr. McCune and his supporters. It was my last speech since the Constitutional Convention and created a sensation. I was loaded with compliments from all sides. The *Tribune* of course castigated me."[41]

As the Assistant Church Historian, he also began attending meetings of the new Utah State Historical Society, that then had Franklin D. Richards, Church Historian, as its president.[42] He wrote articles for various periodicals, encyclopedias, and in answer of incoming correspondence, as assigned by the Church Historian and the First Presidency.[43]

During general conference, Whitney expected to hear his name read for a sustaining vote: "In the list of names presented at conference on Sunday the 9th, mine was omitted as an Assistant to the Church Historian. Pres. Snow told me it was an accident. He was surprised and said he would see Bro. Richards about it. The latter, I think, was responsible for it."[44]

Orson continued his close friendship with President Snow, noting, "This afternoon I had a very pleasant visit with President Lorenzo Snow at his house on Canyon Road, this city. We talked of many things. He assured me again of his friendship and [illegible]; could talk to me as to but few men and the memories of our first conversations were among the most precious of his life, etc. He told me he had a photograph of himself for me if I would call at his office for it."[45] Rejecting Stayner did not mean President Snow rejected Orson, though it was apparent the possibility worried Orson greatly.

Orson used his influence to have his oldest son, Race Whitney, accompany President Snow on his famous trip to St. George, Utah, at the time he received a revelation reaffirming that all faithful Church members should pay a full tithing. "Introduced my son Horace to President Snow, at the latter's home, and seconded a request from the *Salt Lake Herald* that he be allowed to accompany the President and his party on their contemplated trip to St. George. The President kindly consented."[46] On their return, Orson heard the report on his son: "Pres. Snow and party returned from the South today; my son Horace included. Apostle F. M. Lyman and Pres. Richards both told me that he was asked to speak at Scipio and made a nice little address of five minutes which very much pleased the whole party and the congregation. Bro. Lyman says Race was 'white as a sheet,' but every word was in place. He patted him on the back for it. Race says Bro. Lyman said to the congregation, 'This is the son of Bishop O. F. Whitney, and he is the worthy son of a worthy father.' Pres. Smith spoke next and said it was remarkable that a young boy who had never spoken in public before could evince so much composure and speak so fluently. 'Just the kind of young man we want to defend the truth,' he added."[47] Ort even heard about it from President Snow himself, "After [the] meeting [I] met President Snow and wife (Minnie) and son (Roi). They were enthusiastic over Horace and his speech at Scipio. Sister Snow said, 'He has taken his first step in the footsteps of his father.' Pres. Snow said, 'I don't believe anybody else ever spoke that well the first time; we were quite proud of him. I saw you in him at every word, and that is saying a good deal.'"[48]

Race reported the activities of President Snow's traveling party as a newly hired reporter for the *Salt Lake Herald*. He had worked for a couple of other newspapers previously, and was becoming a good journalist with natural writing ability.[49] However, he did not follow his father's footsteps in spiritual matters as hoped, and after experiencing some hard times he died young (see chapter 15).

That year Orson and Zina became the proud parents of boy-girl twins whom they named Paul and Virginia.[50] He also received the portrait that President Snow had promised him.[51] On his birthday he summed up his circumstances, "I am 44 years old today. Am in good health, firm in the faith of the Gospel, and anxious to do all the good I can before passing on to the great beyond. I am still bishop of the 18th ward, an Assistant to the Church Historian, and a resident of Salt Lake City, my native place. Last evening I was at the lake with my daughter Emily. Today I had some friends, Bros. C. W. Stayner and D. F. Collett, up to my home to dinner. The Judge presented me with Dr. Talmage's 'Articles of Faith.'" Then followed one of Orson's mystical mathematical conclusions. "When I was 11, I was baptized (1866). When 22, converted to Mormonism (1879). When 33, obeyed the celestial law of marriage (1883). When 44—what? (When I was 44 I lost by death my dear wife Zina S. Whitney, May 20, 1900.)"[52]

Being a bishop in Salt Lake Stake, Orson was invited to the momentous (and first) Solemn Assembly (held in the Salt Lake Temple), called by President Snow to ensure all Church leaders knew about his revelation regarding tithing, and would not only live it themselves but teach their people to do so as well. Orson described the occasion,

> Attended the "Solemn Assembly" in the Salt Lake Temple. The celestial and terrestrial rooms were thrown into one large hall, thronged with representatives of the Priesthood from the various stakes and institutions of Zion. Pres. Snow presided and he, his counselors, the Twelve Apostles, Bishop Preston, and Le Roi C. Snow, the President's son, were the speakers. The Law of Tithing was the main theme. All present voted to obey it strictly and induce the Saints to do likewise. Pres. Snow said the Lord would not forgive us if we did not (He would forgive the past) but would bring trouble upon us if we were disobedient in [the] future. Cyclones, earthquakes, and other judgments were hinted at, as well as driving, like those from Jackson County and Nauvoo.

Pres. Snow said we did not know Joseph Smith; that we did not know ourselves; that we might learn many things from the Lord if we had sense enough to keep them to ourselves.

Pres. Cannon said there were descendants of the old prophets and of the Savior himself in the congregation.

The "Hosanna Shout" was given three times at the close. It was a grand meeting. All fasted. It lasted from 10:30 a.m. till 7:30 p.m. During recess at 3 p.m. I stepped out to attend a funeral . . . and returned at 6 p.m.

Apostle R. Clawson, in his remarks at the temple meeting, compared Pres. Snow to the Prophet Ezekiel.[53]

Chapter 12

Whitney's Watershed Years, Part 2, 1898–1900

Late 1899 and 1900 saw heart-rending episodes that changed Orson Whitney's life, and consequently altered his thinking. His friends Arthur and Charles Stayner died unexpectedly within four months of each other, and his wife Zina passed away some five months later. With their deaths, Orson was forced to reconsider his doctrinal beliefs. His secret prayer group meetings disbanded and his familial arrangements were permanently altered. He found himself humbled as he had never been, facing the possibilities of a future different than he had anticipated. Such changes, however, repositioned and reoriented him so that he could fulfill predictions of a great work and mortal destiny.

In September of 1899, the first domino fell. Whitney wrote, "Brother Arthur Stayner died today at 1:30 at his residence in the 20th ward. I was sent for last night to go and administer to him. I did so, and dedicated him to the Lord. He expected to die. He said I was the one man on earth that could do him justice in history, and I told him I would do it whether he lived or died. I shook hands with him, blessed him, and bade him good-bye."[1] Three days later he spoke at Arthur's funeral.[2]

As Ort dealt with the loss of one of his best friends (sometimes codenamed "Moses" in his diary), he was also forced to watch his wife's health decline. Stomach problems had plagued her for years, annually getting worse. The arrival of twins had not helped, with a difficult birth causing her great physical pain. They finally decided on an operation, a risky proposition for that day. "This morning I took my wife Zina to St. Mark's Hospital opposite the warm springs, to undergo tomorrow an operation which we hope will be for the benefit of her health. It is a womb and stomach trouble from which she has suffered for years, at times most troubling."[3] The exact nature of the operation is not recorded, but the next day Orson noted, "The operation was successfully performed at about ½ past ten this morning . . . and this evening Zina is resting quite comfortably considering all things. . . ."[4] They celebrated their 20th wedding anniversary with Zina in the hospital. "It is remarked that we are more like lovers than husband and wife."[5]

The Christmas of 1899 would be the worst of Whitney's life. His wife was recovering from surgery in the hospital (and racking up medical bills); he had some pain and distress of his own, and things got worse: "Christmas again. I spent the day in a quiet manner, visited Zina at the hospital in the morning and in the evening called there again. She is recovering nicely. I am weak from the effects of a second attack of renal colic (same as I had a year ago) which [seized?] me Saturday forenoon. Dr. Bossam was summoned and took me home in his buggy. I was in agony for several hours but a hypodermic of morphine gave me relief. Next morning there was a return of the pain, but not so severe. Stayed indoors and in bed all day. Saturday afternoon while lying prostrate, received a note from my friend Judge Charles W. Stayner to the effect that he was ill. He was expecting me to visit him at his home in Bountiful, so I had dropped him a postal card Friday that I was coming up by the 3:30 train next day. Only my sickness prevented it."[6]

Then Orson learned the worst;

> Early this morning while I was yet in bed, the terrible tidings reached me that Bro. [Charles W.] Stayner was dead, and that I was wanted immediately at Bountiful. I caught the first train that I could . . . and though weak and half sick went; the family were overwhelmed with grief but felt more peaceful after I arrived. Bro. John Beck and wife Tillie, Miss Babcock, and others were there comforting

> Sister Stayner. . . . Bro. Beck and I carried out the last wishes of the departed in relation to his remains and then turned them over to the Undertaker. Bro. Stayner died at half past 4 a.m. Returned to the city at 7:15 and went to Bro. Stayner's office and sorted his private papers, taking charge of some of them at his wife's request.[7]

The *Deseret News* listed pneumonia as the cause of Charles's death. Whitney gives no hint as to what was so important about his private papers or why they needed to be sorted and some removed. Whether they contained a will, or perhaps writings related to his self-appointed status as a prophet, is unknown. Members of the prayer group were present, and Whitney did all he could:

> Busy with others making arrangements for Bro. Stayner's funeral. We wanted to bury him in the Salt Lake City Cemetery and B. S. Young and I went there and selected a lot for him, but afterward, owing to the presence of scarlet fever in the family of Bro. Stayner, we were compelled to change our plans. The health office advised and required a private funeral and Mr. Simon Bamberger, who has kindly offered a special train free for the funeral, withdrew the offer of necessity on the announcement of the decision of the health officers. We therefore (Bishop Stoker, Miss Babcock, B. S. Young, and myself) got together and arranged for a private funeral and burial at Bountiful.
>
> Wednesday morning the 27th we discovered at home that my little son Byron has a sore throat and at night it was pronounced scarlet fever. We isolated him from the rest of the family by putting him in the library and I was out till nearly midnight hunting a nurse for him.
>
> Thursday evening I took Zina home from the hospital. Her bill for 3½ weeks was $[70?] kindly advanced by her brother Reed.[8]

Charles Stayner died at age 59. To those within his inner circle he was believed to be a prophet of God, awaiting the call to step up and guide the Church. Such had not happened. Instead, Whitney endured sorrow (and probably some confusion) at the loss of his friend. "This day I spent at Bountiful attending the funeral of my dear friend Bro. Charles W. Stayner. It was held from his residence at

1 p.m. Bishop David Stoker conducted the services, but I had charge of the arrangements. The speakers were Elder B. S. Young, Bishop Stoker, myself, Elder John Beck, Arthur Winter, and Thomas Briggs. I rode to the cemetery in the same carriage with the widow Sister Mary Stayner, Miss Babcock, and Isaac Whitney Stayner, the little son of the deceased. Zina and I had sent a beautiful flowery pillow with letters REST and at the cemetery I dedicated the grave."[9]

About the time that Stayner died, Elder John Henry Smith somehow came into possession of a letter written by John Donaldson (codenamed "Nephi") to Orson, that evidently referred to the idea that resurrected women would give birth to resurrected babies, as part of the continuing reincarnating probationary experiences among immortal beings. Elder Smith wrote, "I read a letter today [written] to Orson which establishes the fact that O. F. Whitney is mixed up with C. W. Stayner in the baby resurrection theory. The letter was signed by Nephi."[10] Elder Smith, who rejected reincarnation and the baby resurrection theory, knew Orson well from their days together in the Liverpool mission office in England, and had also been present at Stayner's stake high council disciplinary court. But exactly how much he knew of their activities then and since is unclear, as is whether he knew whom "Nephi" was.

After the funeral, Orson had time to reflect on his friend's life. Coincidentally, his position as an assistant Historian for the Church enabled him to see some documents otherwise unavailable to him.

> Today Bro. Dan Collett, my assistant in the office, turned over to me certain documents left by Bro. Charles W. Penrose, my predecessor, in this department, and which he (Collett) found some time ago under the cover of his typewriter on a shelf nearby. He did not know what they were at first, but reading a few lines disclosed the fact that they were the papers turned over by Bro. Charles W. Stayner to President John Taylor at the time he was called before the High Council in 1882. Those papers are the revelations he claimed to have received in England. I sorted them and put them under lock and key for safe keeping, holding them subject to the demand of the General Authorities.
>
> The first of these papers is dated Nov. 15, 1880 at about 4 p.m., at 42 Islington, Liverpool [England]. 17 in all are dated in

> November; 9 in December; 16 in January 1881, and 9 in February of that year—51 in all. The last one is dated Feb. 17, 1881. A blessing by Elder C. W. Stayner upon Elder Lyman R. Martineau of date July 19, 1881, and a blessing by the same Elder upon his brother Arthur—the latter given at Salt Lake City June 6, 1882 (after C. W.'s release from England). Also certain letters by C. W. to Arthur written in England are likewise among these papers. Nothing mentioning reincarnation appears in the first revelation, but many great promises are made to C. W. S., the recipient—one to the effect that he shall be a prophet, seer and revelator to the Lord's people.
>
> I find that during this past year I have given to Bro. C. W. Stayner upwards of $2000, in different amounts. I gave his widow, Sister Mary, $30 the day of his death. In all since my acquaintance with him, I have given him sums aggregating about $5,700 or nearer $6,000. His wife, since his death, has presented me with his century dictionary, a fine work in 6 or 7 volumes, and a bookcase for it.[11]

Whitney's self-censoring of his diary prevents full disclosure of his relationship with and personal views concerning Stayner. That they had a plan for Stayner to one day preside over the Church is abundantly clear, as is the notion that Stayner believed he was undergoing another mortal probationary experience, after having been reincarnated in ages past to live the mortal lives of many legendary men and prophets. That he was the center and ringleader of the secret prayer group is also certain. The details of most of the revelations he allegedly received are unknown. He seemed to be able to conjure them at will, and at least some of them seemed meant to flatter his friends, especially Whitney, with promises of grand designs to come. But it was all for naught.[12]

After the typhoid fever scare and the death of his friends, Ort sought to resume a normal life. One step was to return to activity in his temple prayer circle group, because he had "left it to go to Logan in January 1896. Abram H. Cannon was then President. George Q. Cannon is now."[13] He also held a social affair at his home with a specific purpose in mind:

> Last evening we had a little party at our home, 45 E. 1st North, and had the place dedicated. The guests present were Presidents Lorenzo

> Snow, George Q. Cannon, Joseph F. Smith with his wives, Bishop William B. Preston and wife, Pres. Angus M. Cannon, . . . [and] my counselors . . . and we had a very happy time. After supper at 6:30 we all assembled in the parlor and after I had made a brief address, to which Pres. Snow responded, Pres. George Q. Cannon, at President Snow's request, offered prayer. It was very feeling and very comforting. The rest of the evening was spent sociably. Miss Babcock and B. S. [Young] reciting as well as W. B. Baxter and I myself singing several songs, jokes, and stories.[14]

Orson's wife recovered her health enough to occasionally go out with him to a few parties and the theater, but this burst of hopeful health did not last long and, within a few months, Zina went into a steep decline and died. Whitney was devastated;

> The date under which I inscribe these lines is that set for the funeral of my darling wife, Zina Beal Smoot Whitney, who died last Sunday, May 20th, at 2:40 p.m. at our home . . . in the 18th ward. She was just three months past 41 years of age. She was conscious up to the morning of the fatal day and knew me and kissed me and loved me to the last. Her death is deeply and widely [illegible] some idea of her enviable and beautiful character and [illegible] may be gleaned from the following press notices, which are absolutely true and correct: [news clippings announcing her death follow]
>
> *Deseret News* [clipping] written by my brother H. G. Whitney the present manager of the paper. It was Zina's request, uttered to me two days before her death, that Bud write her obituary. She also gave me full directions about her funeral and the disposition of her effects. My right hand was on her head when she breathed her last, my left holding my watch. Her brother Reed Smoot the Apostle was in the room, I think, when she died and we two had repeatedly blessed her. The night before she died she asked me to pray with the family at her bedside. I did so and also prayed with others beside her, dedicating her to the Lord and asked him to release her spirit, about two hours before death put an end to her sufferings. I am glad she is at rest, though I shall really miss her and the world will be dark and lonely without her. I never knew sorrow till now. . . . One of the most pathetic of incidents was the appearance of the twins, Paul and Virginia, at the upstairs window laughing and prattling in innocent glee as the hearse with the remains of their dear mother drove away.

> Poor little things; they could not realize their loss. What a blessing they could not! Zina's grave, covered with flowers, looked like the Gate of Paradise.[15]

President Joseph F. Smith and George Q. Cannon spoke at her funeral, along with Brigham S. Young and James E. Talmage. President Snow attended but did not speak.[16] Orson spent the days following the funeral reflecting on their life together.

> May 24, 25, and 26, I spent at home working over old letters. Zina's and mine to each other, etc. In those three days have lived over the past twenty years. It was twenty years ago last December 18th, since my darling and I were married. We were sealed by God's authority for time and all eternity, and that is why I shall meet her again. She is mine forever! God be thanked! Now to brace up and be a man, and do my duty to the end.
>
> Among Zina's last instructions to me were these: that I put away her effects, letters, trinkets, etc., for her children when [until] old enough to appreciate them, and that I always allow them to come to me as to her, with their confidences, and that no one ever come between them and me. She told Horace, our eldest, to stay by me and help me and take my counsel and in due time go upon his mission. Said the sweet little mother and blessed Saint, "Race, if you are ever tempted to do wrong, stop and ask yourself, would this grieve my mother"? . . .
>
> Sunday morning at 8 or 8:30 I saw that a great change had taken place, that she was gradually sinking and passing under the influence of the opiates administered by the nurse in charge. I knelt beside her, put my arms around her and asked her if she knew me. She smiled, put her arm about my neck and replied "Why, of course, I love you." I had asked her if she loved me several times before and she had answered affectionately. This time she had mistaken "know" for "love." Do you know me, Zina, darling, I then asked. "Yes," she said. . . . From that time she failed [illegible] sad when I next spoke to her she could not answer. She died painlessly, the last six hours being simply a heavy sleep. Peace to her ashes, her spirit is with God.[17]

A few days after the funeral Orson took his children and put flowers on her grave.[18] He also baptized his second wife May's oldest son, Murray.[19] Then it was time to introduce the two families to each other. He had been forced to withhold knowledge of the arrangement from his children.

> This evening I took my daughters Emily, Helen, and Margaret and my little son Byron up to their "Aunt May's"—323 Second St. and made them acquainted with their little brothers Murray and Wendell, May's children. We spent a very pleasant evening with May and the folks, her half-brother, Pres. Rulon S. Wells also being present. I have prayed for years that my family might be united. I hope and believe this is the beginning of it.
>
> Before we went I told the girls, as I had previously told Horace (my eldest son), the facts of my marriage with May in 1888, their mother's consent, etc., and they all expressed a desire to become better acquainted with her and her children, of whom they had previously heard only by rumor; circumstances having prevented a full disclosure up to the present time. May gave Margaret a picture of her mother Zina, taken from Aunt Kate Wells's album. It is the photo of 1880.[20]

Orson combined his two households, and May became the mother of all his children, a task that he hints she did not relish, but which she bravely shouldered anyway.

In early June Orson's diary contains the first mention of a woman named Georgiana (no last name given), who would figure more prominently in his life at a later date.[21] He also received some recent photographs of himself with Zina: "They are very good, especially Zina's," he wrote.[22] His birthday brought him heartache, as he missed Zina deeply on that special occasion. "Tomorrow—July 1st, I will be 45 years old, having been born Sunday July 1st, 1853. For the first time in 20 years, barring the two birthdays of 1882 and 1883 passed while absent on my mission to Europe, Zina is not with me, to wish me joy and many happy returns. Ah, well! Others are left to do this, and some day I shall go to where she is and be happy with her forever."[23]

On his birthday Whitney wrote a letter, addressed to President Joseph F. Smith, the contents of which summed up months of meditation, prayer, humility, and introspection. It dealt with the statement and letter about reincarnation that he (with help from the Stayners) had prepared and submitted to President Smith some two years previously, as recounted in the last chapter. He wrote,

Joseph F. Smith (USHS)

> I am forty-five today, in good health, still working at the Church Historian's Office and still upon Volume 4 of the *History of Utah*. . . . I also wrote this day the following letter:
>
> Salt Lake City,
> Sunday July 1st, 1900
> To President Joseph F. Smith:
>
> Dear Brother Joseph:
>
> This is my birthday (I am forty-five years old); and I wish to signify it by turning over a new leaf in the book of my life. I have pondered and prayed much over the matter of the written statement that I made to you in May 1898, the subject of which need not now be mentioned. That statement I wish to withdraw. I have banished the subject [of reincarnation] from my mind. I no longer believe as I did, and I wish that nothing shall remain to perpetuate the matter either in my own memory or others.
>
> While I do not admit that my faith in the Gospel and my loyalty to the priesthood have ever wavered—for I know that they have not—I do acknowledge that I have been mistaken, honestly mistaken in certain things, and I desire to rectify that mistake. Will you help me?
>
> Believing you to be my friend, and one of my best friends I have on earth, I feel that you will do for me all that one dear brother would and should do for another.
>
> Yours Sincerely,
> O. F. Whitney[24]

Sending the letter to President Smith turned out to be one of the most important and life-altering steps Whitney would ever take, not because the letter itself had any great effect on President Smith, but because it signified Whitney's personal reformation. A few weeks later, he sought out President Smith to get feedback regarding his letter of contrition.

> Today I met Pres. Joseph F. Smith as he was driving away from the President's Office. He leaves for Mexico tonight. He apologized for not having answered my letter of July 1st regarding the written statement of May 1898. He said he felt well about it and glad to have me take that ground, and said he had read the statement [promoting reincarnation] as well as the letter [withdrawing the statement] to Pres. Cannon. When I asked him what Pres. Cannon thought he replied, "I wish you would have a talk with him about it." I asked if my sincerity was doubted by Pres. Cannon. "No; only he seems to think it will be difficult for you to overcome your impressions in relation to these things." I answered, "I think it will be difficult for Bro. Cannon to overcome his feelings about me." He half-smiled and I added, "This is my position. I have come to the conclusion that it was impossible for me to be right and all the Brethren (the Authorities) wrong upon any point, and this is the ground I surrender upon. If this doesn't satisfy Bro. Cannon I cannot help it; that's the best I can do." He gave me, "Good-bye and God bless you," and we parted. He said he had not seen Pres. Snow as he was sick.[25]

So ended Orson F. Whitney's nineteen-year obsession with reincarnation, theosophy, and the Stayners.[26] Nothing more is said about the subject in his diary, outside of a passing reference to old troubles at the time of his call to the apostleship, and mention of a few new codenames. Yet with Zina's death, and the deep grief and depression that came upon him,[27] other ideas found fertile ground in which to grow, ideas that had the potential to place him in great spiritual jeopardy.

For some years after the issuance of the (1890) manifesto that outlawed plural marriages in the United States, small numbers of such marriages had been performed secretly in Mexico and Canada, or on the high seas. One of the apostles that met with Orson's prayer circle knew of this and spoke to him about it: "Apostle George Teasdale, coming out of prayer circle this evening, made a certain suggestion to me upon which I may act."[28] Whitney was acquainted with a woman named Georgiana. He decided to court her with the intention of seeking another plural wife. "Got a buggy in the evening, about 6, and took the twins for a drive, May my wife with me. We drove up to Fort Douglas and beyond to mouth of Emigration Canyon and returned home, fine drive. Later in the evening took Georgiana for a drive, and made her a proposal, based upon Apostle Teasdale's suggestion and my wife May's remarks about V. P. at the lake last evening."[29] While this entry is not fully understandable, it becomes clear that Orson asked Georgiana to marry him, and he had his wife May's consent to do so. But the courtship did not last long. Georgiana had her own secret that she had withheld, enjoying Orson's company.

> This evening I took probably my last drive with Georgiana. She sent for me, asking me to come. I was not prepared for what she told me. It seems like a tragic dream. She is *married*; married and miserable; married and does not love her husband! It was a secret marriage. No one knows of it but myself, outside those immediately concerned. It took place only a short time ago. She shed bitter tears (the first I ever saw her weep), as she told me how mistaken she was, how she regretted this step she had taken, and how gladly she would retract it if it were possible. "I love you more than I ever did," said she, "and I have done nothing but weep since I took this step. I regretted it the moment I had taken it, and told him so; I don't know why I did it, except that I did not want to go back to work. I have lost the best and sweetest man that ever lived." This and much more she said. Her last words at parting were, "I love you with all my heart." ~~Why did God permit it?~~[30]

As far as is known, this was the only attempt Ort made at this time to obtain a plural wife. It is not known what he may or may not have done in the case of Maud May Babcock, except that he spent so much time with her it became noticeable to others. Furthermore, a decade later, Orson would find himself once more entertaining ideas of plural marriage, but again, as far as is known, he never took the actual step to get married to another plural wife.

Mindful of his troubles and grief, his brother and some friends gave him a present he sorely needed: "This afternoon my brother Horace G. with B. S. Young, John D. Spencer, and Rulon S. Wells walked into my office and presented me with a check for $700. This gift of friends who sympathize with me, in my recent sorrow and bereavement. The Lord be praised! It is His doing and it comes in answer to prayer."[31] His brother Horace, or "Bud," would come to his aid financially on more than one occasion.

Meanwhile, Orson wrote and published a poem about Zina and gave copies of it to friends and relatives, including President Snow: "Pres. Snow sent for me today and at 3 p.m. I had a very pleasant interview with him in his office (Presidents Cannon and Smith absent in Canada). The President gave me a recommend to Bishop John R. Winder at the temple, requesting him to administer [additional temple] blessings . . . to me and to my two wives, Zina (deceased) and May. He told me that my poem 'Zina' (a copy of which I sent him) had moved him deeply. He shed tears while reading it. He thought it very fine. Many have said the same."[32] President Snow, who would pass away but a year later, had loved Orson as a son and always sought to help and guide and counsel him as best he could.

A few weeks later, Whitney took May, now his only wife, to the temple.

> This day [October 11] I remarried at the Salt Lake Temple, my wife Mary Minerva Wells, whom I first married as a second and plural [wife] July 24, 1888 at Diaz, Mexico. She is now my legal wife. Bishop John R. Winder performed the ceremony, which took place about noon. Present, as witnesses: John Nicholson, Duncan McAllister, also May's mother, Lydia Ann Wells and Aunt Emmaline B. Wells.
>
> Immediately afterwards I received [additional temple blessings], May also receiving hers and then Zina's (deceased) by proxy. Aunt Em. received them for her daughter Emma (deceased) and for Fannie Adele McBride (deceased), other wives sealed to me soon after their deaths. They were sealed to me July 13, 1888, in the Manti Temple. . . .
>
> In the evening May and I took dinner at the [illegible] Café and then went to the theater, thus winding up a very happy and very memorable day.[33]

Orson later explained the reasons for the remarriage. "As soon as convenient we went to the temple and were sealed at the altar in the House of the Lord. This second ceremony was no more sacred and no more binding than the first, either to us or in the eyes of the Church. But it gave her the status of a legal wife and removed from her all disability imposed by the law of the land."[34] Two weeks later Orson noted, "My wife May and her two little boys, Murray and Wendell, took up their abode with me and the rest of the family at 45 E. 1st N. St. Horace is rooming on State St. and boarding with us; also our former boarder Mr. H. Lovey, the *Herald* artist. Little Margaret is spending the winter in Provo. All the rest of the family are at home."[35] Whitney now had his family as he wanted it, with the exception of Zina being gone. "Christmas Day, 1900: Walked up City Creek Canyon, then to Zina's grave in the city cemetery, called on Miss Babcock, and then returned home to dinner. Spent the evening with my family at May's mother's home."[36]

During the years of theosophy and reincarnation, along with all the rumors and deaths of friends and his wife, Bishop Whitney spoke at hundreds of funerals, blessed the sick, helped to feed the poor, gave many public discourses both in his ward as bishop and in the Salt Lake Tabernacle. He helped raise his children when at either home and did many other things that a man who is both a father and bishop did in his day. At the start of the new year (1901), he wrote, "I have [done] considerable preaching of late, principally at funerals, and the Lord has blessed me abundantly in comforting and instructing others. Pres. Snow and the Brethren treat me kindly; I am in good health, and begin the new century fully well spiritually and temporally."[37] Despite his difficulties, the overly-intriguing side of his life was not the major focus. Most of his time was spent with the routine duties of regular life.

Elders Orson F. Whitney's and B. H. Roberts's lives were similar in some fascinating ways that invite comparison. They were self-taught, unusually talented, believing and faithful, and giants of thought, oratory, and the printed word. Yet they also had to overcome serious personal issues that placed them at odds with the First Presidency and Quorum of the Twelve until they repented. Both men were so gifted and influential that their leaders viewed them as tremendous assets to the Church—not to be lost without a fight. Each was rescued after a soul-trying struggle. Each became powerful advocates for Gospel truth the rest of their lives. Neither Roberts's political views nor Whitney's reincarnation views defined them.[38] Instead, they were and are known as giants of their time and within their sphere, equal to any contemporary Church leader in their influence for good and reputations as faithful servants of God.

The new year began with time spent in the legislature: "Opening of the legislature, the senate, Democratic by one; the House largely Republican. I am one of the holdover Senators from last session. I nominated for president of the Senate Hon. A. J. Evans, of Lehi, Utah Co. who was elected by a vote of 10 to 8—a Democratic majority of 2, owing to the absence of one of the Republican Senators."[39] Then, "First day of balloting for United States Senator in the Legislature. Voting was done by the Senate and House separately. I was absent [at funerals]. Afterward attended a caucus of Democratic legislators at which I was determined that we cast our first complimentary vote in Joint Session for A. W. McCune."[40] And following that, "Voted for McCune accordingly. He received 25 votes on all Democrats present supporting him. Thomas Kearns, the Republican, won with 37."[41]

Whitney "accompanied the legislature to Logan to inspect the Agricultural College. Made a speech at the banquet given there, and in the evening attended a ball in our honor at the Thatcher Opera House."[42] Ort also pushed for passage of the "Evans" bill, designed as a measure to stop persecution of polygamists. It was vetoed by the governor, and since a two-thirds majority vote to override the veto could not be had, the bill was defeated.[43]

Then Whitney traveled to the west coast for an extended vacation, accompanied by his son Race. During this trip, he found his way to the bedside of President George Q. Cannon, who was convalescing at a home in Monterey, finally succumbing to a long bout of ill health. Orson's published autobiography does not acknowledge it, but he had developed a complicated relationship with President Cannon. On one hand, he deeply admired President Cannon's talent and abilities and leadership, seeing in him a pillar of wisdom and spiritual strength that had supported and steadied the Church for decades. But on the other hand, President Cannon had occasionally been a thorn in Orson's flesh, denouncing reincarnation and theosophical meetings, using his influence to effectively bar Whitney from ecclesiastical advancement for decades.[44] But all of that was a thing of the past—Orson had reformed. Cannon knew it, and knew what a tremendous and faithful asset Whitney had become.

Orson wrote of their final visit, "During the drive, or at its termination, I left Harry and Race to go on to Pacific Grove, while I got out at Monterey, to look up President George Q. Cannon who is there sick. Found him without much trouble, and at his request administered to him, assisted by Bro. Charles Wilcken and Dr. Clift. When Bro. Cannon was asked who should anoint and who [should] bless him, he said, 'Let Bro. Orson do both.' I blessed him that he might live to fully accomplish his mission and do all that he was sent forth to do. His wife Carlie and two or three children were with him. They were all very glad to see me. I left them in a few minutes to catch my train."[45] April found Whitney back at home in Salt Lake City. After general conference word came; "a bulletin at the *News* office reads as follows: 'President George Q. Cannon died at 1:20 this morning.'"[46]

The month of May was busy for Whitney. He was given the opportunity to speak in the Salt Lake Tabernacle for the first time in three years. He attended a birthday party for Bathsheba W. Smith, a prominent women's leader in Mormonism. He was able to pay off many of the bills related to his wife's illness and death. He wrote an article about President Brigham Young for the editor of the *Improvement Era*. Then, one year to the day of Zina's passing, the wife of Brigham "Bid" S. Young (Lottie) died, leaving Ort's dear friend filled with the same kind of grief he had been experiencing himself.[47] Orson himself seems to have been getting over the worst of his grief. "Went to Ephraim, Sanpete Co., where I addressed the alumni of the Snow Academy. Dr. J. M. Tanner also there. . . . Spoke also at a banquet in Opera House . . . and at Pres. Peterson's had some music. . . . I sang, whistled and recited for them. Had an excellent time throughout."[48] When he returned home, he "found letter from Georgiana and portrait from Miss Georgiana on my desk at the office. Georgiana, it seems, was at Lottie's funeral. Did not see her there."[49] He did not elaborate further.

In early June, Bishop Whitney officiated at the governor's wedding. "At seven this evening I performed the ceremony uniting in marriage my friend and brother Governor Heber M. Wells and Miss Emily Katz. She is not in the Church, but Pres. Snow sent word to me by Bishop H. B. Clawson that it would be all right for me to officiate if asked to do so. Prior to the wedding day I tried to convert her so that they might be married in the temple. But she said she could not be baptized unless she believed, but would ponder on what I said, and might join the Church later. It was a very pretty wedding. I received many compliments on the ceremony, which was partly [illegible]. It was said to be very impressive. Many wept."[50]

Soon thereafter, Orson's sister Gennie died.[51] This sad event was followed by Orson's attendance at the Heber C. Kimball family reunion, where he read an address written by Heber to those that showed up.[52]

Then another birthday found him, with his diary containing its usual summary of current events: "My forty-sixth [birthday] anniversary. I am still at the Historian's Office, very busy with my work. Am now preparing an article on 'Mormonism—What it has done, what it is doing, what it aims to do,' to be published in a California magazine *The Land of Sunshine* over the signature of President Lorenzo Snow. Am also still bishop of the 18th ward."[53]

Two weeks later he had finished the article. "Read to President Snow at the Beehive House this afternoon, Apostle Lund also being present. The article on 'Mormonism' prepared for the California magazine *Land of Sunshine* and to be published as from the pen of Pres. Snow. He was delighted with it, and complimented me over and over again, as did Bro. Lund. We all, however, felt to give God the glory."[54]

That July Orson met a Mrs. Sewall, a famous national women's leader and early feminist.[55] The day after hearing her speak at the Tabernacle, he was able to personally visit with her.

> Attended with May a reception for Mrs. Sewall at the home of Sister Emily S. Richards, and after Mrs. Sewall spoke, was called upon to respond and did so. In the evening May and I went to hear Mrs. Sewall lecture in the Assembly Hall, and she and her hostess, Sister

> Elizabeth McCune, then accompanied us home to my house, Mrs. Sewall having requested a private interview. We talked for about an hour and she said she had been helped by what I told her. One subject was Mormonism and spiritualism. I advocated the former and condemned the latter. "How may I obtain the spiritual gifts of which you speak?" the lady asked. "By embracing the Gospel," I answered, "and receiving the Holy Ghost." I walked home with Mrs. Sewall and Mrs. McCune to the Gardo [House]."[56]

Orson's firm rejection of spiritualism, as defined by practitioners of the world at large (with séances and occult influences) shows that he entertained no sympathy for such beliefs. Spiritualism was a popular pursuit among the educated and progressive socialites of the day.

At a cornerstone-laying ceremony for a new meetinghouse in his ward, the stake president took occasion to talk about their long-time bishop. "I will add that President [Angus M.] Cannon also remarked that I had been half my life a bishop and had made an honorable record, that I was wifeless and childless when I was ordained 23 years ago, and now I had ten living children, having buried one. Yes, I am now as old a bishop as I was a man when ordained to the bishopric at the age of 23."[57]

With most of the work finished on volume four of the *History of Utah*, Whitney was assigned to another project: "For several weeks I have been assisting Elder B. H. Roberts and Apostle A. H. Lund, upon the history of the Prophet Joseph, Andrew Jensen also assisting."[58] B. H. Roberts had been the original choice of the First Presidency and Church Historian to compile and write the seven-volume *History of the Church*, but Roberts's labor price was too high, and so President George Q. Cannon had been chosen instead. Cannon was considered a literary marvel at the time, but he had made little progress when his health declined and he died. Roberts was then reapproached and this time a workable deal was settled. Orson would spend many hours over several years reading Joseph Smith's history as part of Roberts's history committee.[59]

As autumn began, Orson was pleased when President Snow gave him a special favor. "Today President Snow gave me permission to have the temple work done for my brother Charles Spaulding

Whitney, born Nov. 21, 1964; died Aug. 4, 1886; and for my cousin Laurence Whitney Groo, born April 11, 1871; died Aug. 16, 1890."[60] Charles had committed suicide, so Orson was deeply grateful for the opportunity. "I was in the Temple at Salt Lake City officiating for Bro. Charles and Cousin Lawrence, receiving endowments for them—Charles on the 11th and Lawrence on the 12th. . . . A good work done, and I thank the Lord that I was privileged to do the same."[61] This may have been the last personal interaction Whitney had with the prophet.

That September, the nation, as well as Utah, was shocked to learn of the assassination of the President of the United States, William McKinley. Whitney wrote,

> Memorial Services for President McKinley: The portrait on the opposite page appears on the front page of the *Deseret News* of last evening—Thursday, September 19, 1901. The words beneath are a portion of an address delivered by me at the Tabernacle yesterday forenoon before a vast audience assembled to do honor to the memory of the martyred President, William McKinley. I was the appointed speaker for the occasion, the choice of the Stake President Angus M. Cannon, a choice sanctioned and endorsed by President Lorenzo Snow. I was notified but two days before, but I invoked divine aid and the Lord prepared me for the duty and brought me off triumphantly. I have been honored with compliments and congratulations from all sides, Mormons and Gentiles alike. Pres. A. M. Cannon told me he was going to send the [*Deseret*] *News,* containing the full address, to Mrs. McKinley.[62]

Then came the October general conference. Whitney noted an important development, "Attended most of the meetings of the general conference. Sunday p.m. Apostle Rudger Clawson was sustained as 2nd Counselor to President Snow in the First Presidency."[63] Clawson would only serve as a counselor for four days.

A few days later, Orson again felt the bitter taste that political involvement often meant for him.

> At the evening session [of the Convention] I was nominated for City Treasurer. Notes on the foregoing: I went before the City Convention with the 21st and 38th districts pledged to me by their own volition.

> My best workers were [friends names given]. W. J. Bateman hurt me all he could. A delegate named Hutchison offered to swing 19 votes my way if I would put up a support for him and his crowd. I declined. He then made Dick Morris a similar offer, and I heard the conversation between them. Dick said, "All right." I told him the fellow had made me the same offer but I had declined it. Gov. Blair told me that money won against me—money and the politicians.[64]

Afterward came the unexpected news that Ort's beloved father-figure and mentor President Lorenzo Snow had died. The news was surprising to all who heard, and especially sorrowful to Orson, who would miss him deeply: "Attended President Snow's funeral at the Tabernacle, and afterward went with the funeral party to Brigham City, by special train, to the burial. May went with me; also my counselors Bros. Patrick and Barton. We were assigned a place in the procession both at Salt Lake and Brigham [City]. . . . After returning I attended and spoke at the ward memorial service."[65]

President Snow's death meant that Whitney's friend Joseph F. Smith would become the President of the Church. "I wrote to President Joseph F. Smith, congratulating him on his ascension to the Presidency of the Church (yesterday, Thursday the 17th) and upon his choice of counselors—Bishop John R. Winder and Apostle Anthon H. Lund—a choice that seems to give general satisfaction. Prior to this, in the forenoon, had a call from and a long conversation in my office with Bro. John W. Young, just from New York."[66] Some thought that John W. Young, a long-inactive apostle and son of Brigham Young, arrived in Salt Lake City when he did with the idea of making a claim to the presidency of the Church. He had been an apostle longer than any other man, including Joseph F. Smith. However, under President Snow's administration, the First Presidency and Twelve had formally decided that the only criteria that mattered was length of years (seniority) as a member of the Quorum of the Twelve Apostles, and John had never been set apart as a member of that Quorum.[67] Orson did not record the substance of their conversation.

In late October, Orson was pleased to see one of his anonymous literary endeavors in print. "The November number of the

Land of Sunshine, a magazine published at Los Angeles, Cal., contains my article on 'Mormonism,' attributed, of course, to President Lorenzo Snow, at whose request I prepared it, some time since."[68] Whitney was pleased with the reach and influence this particular piece received: "The [*Deseret*] *News* this evening publishes in full the *Sunshine* article. . . . On the same date that the article was reproduced by the [*Deseret*] *News* (having originally appeared in the magazine *Land of Sunshine* of Los Angeles) the *Literary Digest*, published in New York City, reprinted a long extract from it."[69] A few weeks later he wrote, "Received a letter from Mr. Moody, of *Sunshine* [magazine] stating that the copies (2,000) of his magazine purchased by the Church containing the article aforesaid had been mailed to 104 prominent exchanges. [I] am now writing articles for the First Presidency for the holiday issues of local papers. Have had considerable of their correspondence to answer lately—inquiries about our faith and people."[70] He was trusted with the most sensitive and influential literary assignments: "Busy as ever, I wrote for various publications in and out of the Church, often preparing articles for others to sign, whose names were more widely known, more influential, and consequently more potent for good. Occasionally, articles to be signed by myself were solicited for histories, magazines, and other publications."[71]

The year closed with Bishop Whitney assigned to prepare and deliver a discourse in the Salt Lake Tabernacle on the Prophet Joseph Smith, commemorative of his birthday. "Delivered this afternoon at the Tabernacle my address on the Prophet Joseph, for which I was appointed by the presidency of the stake (the appointment sanctioned by the President of the Church) some few days ago. It was much appreciated. Among those present who congratulated me personally were President Joseph F. Smith, A. H. Lund, Apostle John Henry Smith, A. Owen Woodruff, the stake presidency, and others. . . . The *Herald* gave a very full synopsis of my Tabernacle address, and the *Deseret News* published it entirely with the remarks of Elder C. W. Penrose and Pres. Joseph F. Smith that followed."[72]

Then, after Christmas, "Spent these days preparing a biographical sketch of myself for Andrew Jensen's biographical dictionary [encyclopedia]. The nights were devoted to the settlement of the tithing of the 18th ward. As compensation for settling tithing for 1901 I received from the presiding bishop [the] authority to retain $250 out of tithing funds passing through my hands. This amount divided as follows: to O. F. Whitney, Bishop $75; to Robert Patrick, 1st Counselor $75; to William Barton, 2nd Counselor $75 (who also acted as clerk)."[73]

On New Year's Eve, he wrote, "And so ends the year 1901, a fairly prosperous year with me, though I am still without a home, living in rented quarters 45 E. 1st North, where I have dwelt since the summer of 1898. There our twins, Paul and Virginia, were born April 24, 1899, and there their dear mother died May 20, 1900. I am attached to the place for these reasons, though I fain would have a home of my own. I tried hard this year to get one, but found it impracticable. I feel grateful for my many blessings, however, for the good health of my family, for food and raiment, a roof over our heads, for employment and occupation, and above all for the blessings of the Gospel. The Lord has been very good and kind to me, and I praise His holy name, for all."[74]

Photograph taken in 1925. Standing, left to right: David O. McKay, Rudger Clawson, Orson F. Whitney, Anthony W. Ivins, Richard R. Lyman, Heber J. Grant, Reed Smoot, Charles W. Nibley, Sylvester Q. Cannon, George Albert Smith, and Joseph Fielding Smith. Kneeling, left to right: Hyrum G. Smith, Melvin J. Ballard, Stephen L. Richards, John A. Widtsoe, and George F. Richards (CHL).

Chapter 13

Elias: An Epic of the Ages and Other Events, 1900–1906

The death of Zina, with its accompanying intense grief and heartache, and the foiled attempt to obtain a plural wife sent Orson into a deep depression, serious enough for him to wish he were dead. He explained,

> This poem [*Elias*] was begun in the spring of 1900, not long after the death of my wife Zina, and while I was prostrate upon a bed of pain [grief], the inspiration was timely. I needed something of the kind to occupy my thoughts and dispel my gloomy feelings. While pondering upon the situation, and wondering whether my life's work was drawing to a close, I heard or seemed to hear a voice—inaudible to the outward ear, yet plain to the inward understanding—the same voice that had spoken to me on former occasions in hours of distress or deep anxiety. It now said,
>
> "Do you really wish to go?"
>
> "No," I replied; "I must not go until I have finished my work."
>
> "What would you like to do?"
>
> "Something that would live when I am dead, and go on teaching the Truth after my mortal tongue is still."
>
> "And what might that be?"
>
> I reflected, and my thoughts took this form. I would like to write a poem embodying all that I have learned, thought, or felt respecting the divine plan known as "The Everlasting Gospel." I would love to

> tell in heroic verse the sublime Story of God. "Mormonism," historically, doctrinally, prophetically—be that my theme, my task, with whatsoever else the Lord has for me to do.
>
> No sooner had I come to this conclusion, than the first lines of the poem formed in my mind, and weak as I was I sat up and wrote them down. Thus the work began.
>
> It took years to complete it, for I could not, of course, give all my time to poetry. I was still a ward bishop and an Assistant Church Historian. But I worked upon the great theme whenever I could, and found much delight in so doing. It burned like fire in my brain, and I felt that I must get it out or it would consume me. Day after day—sometimes twelve hours or more at a stretch—month after month, and year after year, I toiled on in the intervals of office work and outside engagements, till the poem, if not finished, was ready for a trial reading. This was toward the close of 1902.[1]

At the time Whitney wrote the above introduction to his epic poem, his memory failed him on certain specifics. His diary indicates he actually began writing it about late summer—"About this time I began my epic poem 'The Mormonead' . . ."—and it took just over two years for him to prepare a readable draft.[2] He was also unable to work on it as much as he remembered during those two years because of a heavy workload as an Assistant Church Historian: "I have re-named my epic poem 'The Voice in the Wilderness.' Have not written upon it much of late."[3]

Two months later a similar situation prevailed. "Have had a hard week; at the University every morning at half past eight; the rest of the day working like a beaver in the office. My poem 'The Voice in the Wilderness' I have had to lay aside. [Illegible] do the more pressing work, correspondence for the Presidency, etc., and my memorial address for Sunday."[4] But other times he could work on it feverishly: "In office all day at work on my poem 'Voice in the Wilderness' and other things."[5] And he often changed its name. "Have renamed my poem from 'The Message of Mormonism' to 'The Epic of Elias.'"[6] He was in the midst of what he and his friends considered his greatest literary contribution to Mormon literature.

In early January he enjoyed the accolades of his continuing rise in prominence as a bishop.

> A red letter day in the history of the 18th ward. This afternoon the regular fast meeting was held in the enlarged and improved Chapel and this evening a notable meeting of the conjoint M.I. Association took place. The house was packed with people from all parts, and we had a glorious time. President Joseph F. Smith, of the First Presidency . . . and other prominent brethren were our visitors and the priesthood and people of the ward were out en masse. . . . President Smith said he had been richly repaid for attending the meeting. "Bless you, my boy," he said at parting with a hearty grip of the hand. "I know the Good Spirit when I hear it, and I very much enjoyed your address." Many more congratulated me [illegible] feelingly. I spoke an hour and a half, and President Smith over half an hour, but people forgot all about the time and none looked or acted weary. It was an occasion to be long remembered.[7]

His friendship with President Joseph F. Smith also grew, with President Smith increasingly using and trusting him more at work. Orson's boss, President Anthon H. Lund, the Church Historian, also loaded him down with work. "Began a revision of the LDS Hymn Book by request of President Lund." And, "Am still on the Hymn Book revision. It's a hard job."[8] And further, "Have recently written an article for President John R. Winder to appear over his name in a national magazine. Theme: 'Mormonism not a Menace.'"[9]

Then, at the April 1902 general conference, Whitney was finally formally sustained.

> This is the closing day of the general conference of the Church. The 72nd Annual Conference. I attended all the meetings of Friday and Saturday but not those of today, being kept away by a funeral in the ward. This afternoon, when the General Authorities were presented, I was sustained as an Assistant Historian of the Church. The others chosen being Andrew Jensen, A. M. Musser and B. H. Roberts. This is the first general office I have ever held in the Church, though I have been doing the work of an Assistant Church Historian since January 1899. My appointment today came, as usual, as a complete surprise. I was not dreaming such a thing. I am thankful that the Authorities have this confidence in me, and I acknowledge the Lord's hand in the honor conferred.[10]

His speaking and writing, outside of his epic poem, continued unabated. He wrote a biographical sketch of his life for Andrew Jenson's *LDS Biographical Encyclopedia*, gave the Baccalaureate address at a state university, and wrote articles and answers to incoming doctrinal letters for President Joseph F. Smith.[11]

Yet even with the poem and all his other responsibilities, Ort could not forget his beloved Zina, missing her deeply. He wrote, "Two years this date since my dear Zina died. I am very sad and lonely at times without her, though my work prevents me from brooding. Sometimes at night I awake and get into a train of thought concerning her until my heart overflows. Just the other night, on retiring and feeling a little inconsolable, I prayed that she might come to me in a dream and comfort me. My prayer was answered. She appeared, bent over me, took my head between her hands, and kissed me tenderly. She looked beautiful and seemed very happy. I love her more than I ever did before."[12] This was not the last time Zina was permitted to visit Orson from beyond the veil.

September saw Whitney's epic poem finally reaching a presentable stage—too early still for publication, but far enough along to test before friendly audiences. "Am getting ready my poem 'The Messenger: an Epic of the Dispensations' for a first reading in the near future. Bro. D. F. Collett is typewriting it for me."[13]

That month also found Orson accepting a gift from his financially-wiser younger brother, the business manager of the *Deseret News*:

> Today my brother Horace G. ("Bud"), out of the bigness of his heart, offered me a house and lot . . . 18th ward as the [illegible] for a home. He learned yesterday that I was thinking of buying my mother's old home, 285 C. St., from the other heirs and thus seeks to forestall the venture. I have no words to express my appreciation of his brotherly kindness. God bless him! It is not the first time that he has shown me greatest kindness when I needed financial aid. More than money and property, for now, is the nobility that prompts such deeds of generosity and philanthropy.[14]

Then politics again intruded into Orson's life, much to his regret. "The Democratic County Convention meets today. . . . I have declined two or three times to be a candidate, but the leaders of the party insist upon it. They want me for county clerk. I shall submit the matter to Pres. Lund, and abide by his decision; being as I am his assistant in the Historian's Office."[15] Whitney obtained the necessary approval—"I received President Lund's permission to accept the nomination, which was made by acclamation last evening. . . ."—and ran for the office.[16]

President Lund confided his feelings in his own diary: "It is a day of suspense to those who are running for offices. Bro. Orson F. Whitney is running for the office of county clerk. I do not think he will get it and it will be worry, loss of time, and money to him."[17]

Lund was right. Orson was soundly defeated, explaining, "Election Day. Republicans overwhelmingly victorious. I was knifed by Gentile Democrats, and consequently ran behind my ticket. A prominent Mormon is doomed now in the Democratic Party, which is Anti-Mormon, so far as its Gentile members are concerned, speaking of course with some reservations. I attribute my defeat, or rather the knifing I received to the bitterness engendered against me when I placed in nomination, two years ago, Joseph Bingham (a Catholic) for the City Board of Education in lieu of Judge H. P. Henderson. He and others have never forgiven it."[18] Stunts like that by the Democrats eventually caused Whitney to switch to the Republican Party.

With political distractions behind him, Whitney was able to concentrate fully on his epic poem. He read it before a live audience of prominent and educated Latter-day Saints. The result was pleasing "The reading of the Poem at Col. Clayton's . . . last evening, was a most gratifying success. I had not dared to anticipate so much for it."[19] As he finished the first edition, he changed the title for the last time: "I have again changed the name of my poem from 'The Messenger' etc., to 'Elias, an Epic of the Ages by Orson F. Whitney' and I think that will stand as the title page. Am now typewriting the closing cantos, assisted by Bro. D. F. Collett."[20] Orson spent part of the Christmas holidays working on biographies for his volume four of *History of Utah*, and another part improving his poem.[21]

Emboldened by his success with the first reading, he approached President Smith about another, more prestigious reading. "Met

President Joseph F. Smith this afternoon and told him about the poem, and how proud and honored I would be to read it to him and a representative gathering in the Beehive [House] Parlor. He readily acquiesced and asked me to make out a list of those I would like invited. I consider it very kind of him. It will be an important event in my history."[22] His brother Bud helped him with publicity: "This evening's [*Deseret*] *News* contains the article on my poem with these headlines: 'A Mormon Epic, Bishop Whitney produces a great Poem—Eternal Truth—the Mighty Theme of the Dispensations told in Verse Sublime' . . . I consider this day a notable one in my life, from the publication of the foregoing article in the organ of the Church."[23] In two weeks Ort had the requested names ready. "Sent to President Smith the invitation list for the Beehive House readings for which he will set the time. Over 700 names are submitted, including all the General Authorities."[24] About a week later, plans solidified. "This evening I was sent for by President Joseph F. Smith, who acquiesced in all my suggestions relating to the proposed poetic readings at the Beehive House. Monday, Tuesday, and Wednesday, February 16, 17, and 18, inst, are the times set."[25] Invitation cards were mailed by a committee to three hundred guests, including all of the General Authorities.[26] The *Deseret News* ran an article announcing the reading, while the other (anti-Mormon) newspapers, the *Herald* and the *Tribune*, "ignored the whole business."[27]

The three designated days in February came and went, and Whitney basked in the glow of triumph.

> A red letter day in my life! This evening at about 10:45, I completed the reading of my poem in the Beehive Parlors and was the recipient of warm and enthusiastic applause, comment, and congratulations from such men as President Joseph F. Smith, President Lund, Bishop Preston, President Angus M. Cannon, C. W. Penrose, B. H. Roberts, J. H. Paul, H. G. Whitney, and many more, Governor Wells and wife included. It was a complete triumph, and I believe marks an epoch in my life. Nothing could be more hearty, soul-felt, and sincere than the compliments showered upon me from all sides. The three-nights readings constituted one of the most important events in my life. "Praise be to God, from whom all blessings flow."[28]

President Lund described the February 16 reading, "In the evening about four hundred people assembled to hear Orson F. Whitney recite his great poem *Elias*. It is a great theme. He deals first with his own spiritual awakening. Then a dream of meeting the Spirit of Song who gives him his harp. Then he describes the council in heaven, then the coming of Christ, the primitive Church, and the apostasy. He read four cantos only. Eight left. It took two hours to recite the four."[29] Two days later, he wrote, "In the evening I took Alvin Peterson with me to hear *Elias*. It was fine."[30]

Elder Rudger Clawson was also among those that attended. "Monday, Tuesday, and Wednesday evenings I attended a program meeting at the Beehive House, which was called for the purpose of giving Bishop Orson F. Whitney an opportunity of reading his last and greatest effort in poetry—his masterpiece—namely, *Elias, an Epic of the Ages*. The poem has great merit and will doubtless be issued from the press at an early day. It deals with the great plan of salvation as introduced and shown in the history of the Mormon Church."[31]

Orson enjoyed his success immensely, enough to push for the poem to be formally published.

> The recent readings of my poem at the Beehive continue to be "the talk of the town." Bro. John Nicholson called in today to tell me how much he enjoyed them and what he thought of the poem. "It is a great work and will make you famous," he said. I also received a note from the First Presidency, in answer to one I wrote to President Smith [the] night before last, asking him to appoint a committee to help me revise the poem and prepare it for publication. The Presidency express their pleasure and delight in having heard the poem, and named as a committee to aid me Elders Charles W. Penrose, John Nicholson and George Reynolds—a very good selection, I think, and one that suits me to a "T."[32]

Whitney's memory regarding the origination of the publication and committee request seemed to fail him in later years, for in his autobiography he wrote that he learned "that a project was on foot to publish the poem under the patronage of leading citizens." And, "These gentlemen [the committee], out of pure public spirit, took the initiative and launched the project, almost without my knowledge."[33]

The committee met three times during the first half of March to go over his work. During the third meeting "objection [was] made to my identifying Elias with the Holy Ghost. Will therefore have to change it."[34] Whitney's equation of Elias with the Holy Ghost in his first draft raises unanswerable questions regarding the evolution of his doctrinal views over the years. Since his poem received two major revisions and many minor edits before his death, he could have made any number of doctrinal changes. A few who have read *Elias* believe that Orson sought to camouflage his old reincarnation ideas in the lengthy text in such a way that they would not readily be noticed. Such a charge is difficult to refute, not only because the poem went through three revisions, but because Ort's poetic language was often capable of more than one interpretation or meaning. One reader might see reincarnation in a stanza whereas another might see reference to premortal existence. Such arguments, however, are best left to critics.

Mid-March saw Orson moving into the house that his brother Bud had given him, with some renovations to the front of the home having been completed. "St. Patrick's Day. Observed it by moving into my new home. . . . Worked awfully hard."[35] A few days later he met with the committee to receive approval for his doctrinal changes. "This same day—March 20—at 3 p.m. the Committee on Poem met at my office; Bro. Penrose offered prayer, and I then read to them my epilogue, 'The Angel Ascendant,' revised by me in accordance with certain suggestions made by them at our last meeting. They now approved it, and so ends the revision by the committee."[36]

In May, Orson was invited to attend a conference held at the Brigham Young College that was being held to explore Book of Mormon geographical theories: "At 7:30 a.m. today took . . . train for Provo to attend the Book of Mormon convention at the B. Y. Academy. Had a good time. . . . I referred to Mormon's words on faith, hope and charity—the test of faith—as the greatest internal evidence of the Book."[37] Soon thereafter in June, at the request of the First Presidency, Orson gave the oration commemorating President Brigham Young's birthday at a celebration held at the Saltair resort.[38] It was also during these years of working in the Historian's Office that Orson and B. H. Roberts became closer friends, often eating dinner at each other's homes or going fout or horseback rides together.[39]

For his birthday, Orson went to Logan, Utah, and read *Elias* to an assemblage at the Brigham Young College where he had once taught many years before. "I gave my first reading before the summer school and the general public. . . . Among notables present were Moses Thatcher, Charles W. Nibley, George C. Parkinson. . . . Bro. Nibley said, 'Thy name shall no more be Whitney, but Milton.'"[40]

Two days later Whitney reported, "Tried to sleep in the afternoon. Pored over my poem. Had a headache; B. S. [Young] blessed me. Gave my third reading at night and scored a triumph. . . . This evening witnessed a memorable incident, [illegible] direct answer to prayer."[41] What the memorable incident was, or the answer to prayer, is not known. During his visit to Logan, Whitney also renewed his friendship with Professor John A. Widstoe, a rising star in the Mormon firmament. "In the morning B. S. [Young] and I walked up to the Agricultural College and called at Prof. Widstoe's to see Susa Young Gates, lying very sick. Too sick to be seen, but Jacob, her husband, [and] Prof. Widstoe and wife were very glad of our visit."[42] The next day Orson rode the train back to Salt Lake City: "Returned to Salt Lake. Sat with Moses Thatcher most of the way and had a good talk. He is looking and feeling better than for years. . . . [I] am not very well. Have caught cold and feel a little worn down."[43] Thatcher, after being dropped from the Quorum of the Twelve Apostles, had overcome his morphine addiction, acquired during a fight to control stomach ulcer pain, and regained some measure of health. He and Whitney had maintained their friendship through all their personal trials and struggles.

In mid-July Ort wrote two puzzling diary entries in which he reverted to his use of codenames to disguise who he was talking about, the last two such to be found therein: "Mohammed today received a letter—the first one—from the Princess Irene, acknowledging the receipt of "Mr. Beaucaire" and photos of M. M. and Esther recently sent. About this time M. M. did a very foolish thing, which he much regrets. May the Lord forgive as F. does, and overrule it for good! Amen!" And then, "Mohammed wrote his first missive to ~~Irene~~ (E-re-nay)."[44] It is probable that these entries have nothing to do with reincarnation, but instead disguising attempts to flirt with plural marriage—a practice that, while slowly dying out, was still receiving limited secret authorization by President Joseph F. Smith in 1903.

Evidently, a woman, codenamed Irene, received from someone codenamed Mohammed a book and photographs of Orson and Zina, probably sent by him at the request of Whitney, and she, Irene, thanked Mohammed by letter for the gifts. The foolish thing that Whitney did is unknown, but it may have been a courtship or marriage proposal. Other diary entries at this time mention someone with the initials "M. A." with whom Whitney spent time on his trip to Logan. "F" is an unnamed woman that gave Orson her portrait for Christmas.[45] What Orson's wife May thought of all this is also unknown, if she knew anything at all. As his history has demonstrated and his future would as well, Orson had a deep and abiding belief in the principle of plural marriage, and his adherence to this conviction placed him in awkward, even "foolish" circumstances on occasion.

These years also saw Whitney being trained by the First Presidency for a greater work (than that of bishop) to come: "Was appointed today by the First Presidency to go to Boise, Idaho, for the 24th, and deliver an oration for the Saints there at their Pioneer Day celebration; also to attend meeting there on the following Sabbath."[46] On his way there, he "completed my preparation for the Boise trip, and left. . . . Spent the evening at M. A.'s and stayed at Lincoln House."[47] Once home he "made a written report to the First Presidency of my visit to Boise, by their appointment."[48]

But his time had not yet arrived. "General conference, which began Sunday the 4th closed today. George Albert Smith, son of John Henry Smith, and grandson to the late President George A. Smith, was chosen [as] an apostle to fill the vacancy left by the death of Brigham Young [Jr]. F. M. Lyman was sustained as President of the Twelve Apostles. I attended most of the meetings which were spirited and interesting."[49] A week later he spoke to those assembled in his own ward: "In the evening of Sunday the 15th (same day as I spoke in the Tabernacle) I spoke in the ward chapel on charity, defending Heber J. Grant, the Apostle, against his critics; and also showing the true mission of amusement and recreation. I had great power, and it was said that I never spoke better."[50]

By the end of the year, Orson's epic poem *Elias* was nearing readiness for printing. "Submitted ms of my poem *Elias* to *Deseret News* for estimate of publication."[51] He also managed to pay off an old debt, incurred at the time he was giving half his money to Charles Stayner: "This morning Bro. H. G. Park came to my house bringing a letter from Col. T. S. Webber, Superintendant Z.C.M.I., enclosing two notes given by me to that institution July 1, 1896, for $259 and Sept. 11, 1897, for $92.45 + $351.45 upon which I had paid $40, leaving $311.45 due with interest. Both notes were cancelled, upon my paying $175 check amt to Bro. Webber, a day or so since. Thank the Lord! This debt was contracted while I was out of employment in 1895 and a little later in Logan (1896) when I was struggling to support two families on a salary not large enough for one."[52]

Orson kept refining his poem: "Daily I am putting the finishing touches upon my poem *Elias*, which steadily improves as I work."[53]

No diary entries are available for 1904, so the details of the publication process for *Elias* during that year are unknown, except that a new committee with different members was formed to help the poem be issued. However, Orson's first entry of 1905 informs us that it took a year to be published—meaning copyedited, typeset, printed, bound, and shipped. "In the evening I presented my wife May with a copy of *Elias*—Autograph Edition de Luxe, which I intended as a Christmas gift had it arrived in time."[54]

The absence of a diary for 1904 means there is no recording of Ort's feelings about the so-called second manifesto issued by President Smith that April. Later happenings confirm that Orson was displeased with the crackdown on new plural marriages that it enjoined. Having been a loyal and practicing believer in the doctrine, Whitney found it contrary to his personal feelings and desires; however, he reluctantly sustained it with the other Brethren of the Twelve. But he was not alone in his reticence. Elder Rudger Clawson, a senior member of the Twelve, secretly married a plural wife after the second (1904) manifesto, his marriage representing the only one known (for that time) for which no formal Church discipline ever occurred.[55] Others of the Twelve who involved themselves in such marriages, such as Elders Matthias F. Cowley and John W. Taylor, were formally investigated and disciplined for their willful misbehavior. Two other members of the Twelve, Owen Woodruff and Marriner Merrill, died before their activities could bring formal discipline upon them. Several years later, Whitney saved himself from their fate by stopping short of a post-second manifesto marriage himself.

The First Presidency's confidence in and increased use of Orson kept him busy, silently acting as their amanuensis in many matters. He prayed at the dedication of LDS hospital and spoke at the Tabernacle. He wrote articles for Presidents Smith and Lund for publication in various magazines, and he wrote more articles for the *Millennial Star* (a long-running periodical published for the European Mission).[56] This trust, loyalty, and fidelity to duty in the extra assignments positioned Whitney close to the First Presidency, with weighty results. "At office, as usual, and in the evening May and I were at Sister Margaret C. Roberts, where we took dinner with other friends of Bro. and Sister Roberts. President Joseph F. Smith and his wives were among the guests. The President confided certain things to me, and during the conversation invited me to attend the fast meetings at the temple."[57] The probability is that President Smith used this occasion as an opportunity to confide in Whitney that he would be called to the apostleship at some future time, and that he should continue to prepare himself for it.

Orson had also given President Smith a copy of his newly published poem *Elias*, that Orson had dedicated to him. "Received today a beautiful letter from President Joseph F. Smith, dated yesterday, and acknowledging my [illegible] gift to him of *Elias*. He expressed his love for me, his confidence, and his thanks for my dedication to him of the poem."[58] Ort gave copies of the poem to as many friends and relatives as he could afford, noting their expressions of gratitude for his gift.[59]

With April came general conference and then the death of his sister. He wrote,

> Attended the opening meeting of the general conference at the Tabernacle. The speakers were President Joseph F. Smith, President John R. Winder, Elders Hugh J. Cannon, and Rulon S. Wells. Attended

> meetings that followed, including the Special Priesthood Meeting on Monday April 10. President Smith told me, after conference, that he looked for me once or twice, thinking to have me speak.
>
> My sister Lily's loan to me, of $300, borrowed in 1896, I believe, was paid by me on the 12th of this month by a check for that amount. The first regular returns from the sale of the poems *Elias*—Edition de Luxe. I still owe Lily some interest.
>
> A day or two after I paid her this check (or was it the same day?) she underwent an operation at the LDS hospital, for appendicitis. I have been up twice since to see her, and was at the hospital at the time of the operation, with my sisters Helen and Marian and brother-in-law Henry M. Dinwoody. I also blessed Lily previous to her going there.[60] [Then a month later] my sister Lily (Mrs. E. A. W. Paton) died yesterday morning. . . . [I] wrote a note to President Smith asking him to speak at Lily's funeral. Later in the day saw him, and he promised to do so if possible.[61]

Early sales of *Elias* were hopeful: "Received from H. G. Whitney [the] manager [of the] *Deseret News* a check for $109, payment for 45 copies of *Elias* cloth editions at $2.40. These have been sold at the News Book Store. . . . I am also revising *Elias* for some future edition."[62]

But as the year passed, the new *Elias* publication committee found themselves needing financial help.

> This forenoon, my friends Heber M. Wells and Richard W. Young, of the *Elias* committee, had an interview in my behalf with the First Presidency; Apostles John Henry Smith and Charles W. Penrose also being present. The result of the interview was a subscription by the Church for seventy copies of my epic poem *Elias*, at ten dollars a copy. This will take the bulk of my Jubilee edition off my hands. Added to the former subscription by the Presidency of 12 copies of the Edition de Luxe at $25, it will make an even $1,000 from the Trustee-in-Trust on account of the poem. I feel very glad and thankful.[63]

That summer, Orson enjoyed his first ride in a horseless carriage: "This evening (Thursday) May and I, with my daughter Helen, took our first automobile ride."[64] He also wrote further material at the request of President Smith, including a piece on the martyrdom of the Prophet Joseph Smith, finished at summer's end.[65] President Smith was contented. "Today (Monday 25th) I read to the First Presidency my pamphlet 'The Mormon Prophet's Tragedy,' and they were much pleased with it. President Smith will have it published in first class form, and he offered to pay me for the copyright, as he wishes to make the pamphlet one of the works of the Church. I told him I had written it as a servant of the Church, in time for which the Church paid me and I had no charge to make. Anything he saw fit to do would be perfectly satisfactory. 'All right,' said he, 'We'll fix that.'"[66]

Whitney also took time to reminisce: "Twenty-seven years ago on a Sunday evening, in the little school house inside Eagle Gate, the building owned by President Young, but used by the 18th ward for a meeting house, I was ordained a high priest (by Daniel H. Wells) and set apart as bishop of the 18th ward. I still hold that office and have the same counselors as then given me: Robert Patrick and William B. Barton. We celebrate the anniversary next Monday at Calder's Park."[67]

He also commented on criticism from his anti-Mormon acquaintances. "Judge Goodwin, in today's issue of his weekly, says, 'Bishop Whitney's address on Monday was a brilliant one, so brilliant that it will probably pass into Mormon history as inspired. But parts of its statements are open to criticism.' He then goes on to find fault with my story of the Mormon Battalion; that is the part of it which declares that the enlistment of the Battalion delayed the departure of the pioneers a year, which he calls "a [illegible] charge" against the government. Poor old Judge. The heated season is hard on him. He can't argue any too well under the best of conditions. In summer, he is completely inconsistent and irrational."[68]

That August Orson took a vacation, visiting his son Race in Portland, Oregon, and also spending time in Los Angeles, California, with old friends there. On his return, he finished his assignment from President Smith. "Completed the pamphlet article on 'The Mormon Prophet's Tragedy.' I began this before going to Portland, by request of President Joseph F. Smith."[69] Then October conference arrived, and with it a new literary project for Whitney.

> Closing day of the conference. I spoke in the Tabernacle by invitation of President Joseph F. Smith, who followed and gave the final

> address of the conference. This was the first time I had spoken at a general conference in 16 years. Since conference I have been busy getting out my pamphlet "The Mormon Prophet's Tragedy," and in preparing an article for the *Improvement Era* for December on "Joseph Smith in Literature." The following correspondence explains itself. It followed a proposal made to me by my brother H. G. Whitney, manager of the *Deseret News*, to write a *Student's History of Utah*, for use in the schools, a much needed work, and one that I have often contemplated writing. . . . I began writing the *Student's History* on the 27th of October, 1905."[70]

As the year waned, Whitney experienced a sudden and painful trial with his health, that almost cost him his arm.

> The accident . . . took place on Friday or Saturday the 10th or 11th of November. I was putting on a shirt and the cuff, starched and stiff, scratched my right wrist. I thought nothing of it, and let four days go by with consulting medical advice. On Wednesday the 15th, I went up to the L.D. hospital and [the doctor] told me what it was—an infection of blood poisoning, and a very serious matter. He took my case in hand and treated it skillfully and thoroughly; bound my arm in a splint, after wrapping it in clothes soaked with a solution of the chloride of mercury. I had to sleep with my arm aloft. I made daily visits to the doctor, and had my arm dressed and on Monday the 20th the swollen wrist was lanced—a very painful operation. I took no anesthetic. The wound was cauterized and poulticed, and several days later was opened and cleansed with [illegible] and other solutions. [Illegible] with caster oil was then applied, and the wound gradually healed. . . . I was away from my office about a month, and even now am hardly able to write, owing to the stiffness in my hand and wrist, resulting from inflammation. When I was taken sick I had just completed my pamphlet "The Mormon Prophet's Tragedy."[71]

The resultant illness left Orson too sick to join President Smith and others on a special trip to the east. "President Joseph F. Smith and a party left today in a special car for Vermont to be present at the unveiling of the monument erected in honor of the martyred Prophet at his birthplace, Sharon. I was invited to go, but did not have the money—$130—to pay the expenses of the trip, and also felt that while under treatment for my hurt arm and hand I ought to remain at home with easy access of my medical advisor. The President did not appoint me to go, or I should have gone. He left it to me to decide, saying he did not wish to work a hardship on anyone. I therefore thanked him and remained at home."[72]

With the new year, Ort "resumed work on the *Student's History of Utah*, and now have six chapters written."[73] But the effects of his previous infection were not all behind him: "About the first of February, I suffered terrible pains of a rheumatic nature in my left arm and especially under the left shoulder blade. At the same time a rash broke out under my left wrist and in other places along my left arm as far as the shoulder. [The doctor] who treated me, thinks it is the poison washing off, from my infection of last November."[74]

With the first edition of *Elias* having been issued and selling, Orson could not forget his poem, and continued working on it off and on for the rest of his life, giving it two further major revisions, one that was published in 1915 and a second that never moved beyond the manuscript stage. Whitney's call to the apostleship placed him in a position to give more time to the rewrites than he otherwise would have had. As an apostle, his main duties were to attend stake conferences, and he had few other duties during the weekdays, except those literary assignments given him by the First Presidency. That November he wrote, "Worked on *Elias—the Epic of the Ages*. Such is its new title."[75] Diary entries in 1907 and 1908 indicate time spent revising and improving the poem, having the new version retyped for publication, and having the first edition reprinted with five hundred copies.[76]

Chapter 14

Called as an Apostle of the Lord, 1906

Life changed again for Bishop Orson F. Whitney at the April 1906 general conference. He had been serving as a bishop for twenty-seven years, preaching, blessing, marrying, settling tithes and offerings, disciplining, and dealing with the numerous problems common to ward bishops. He had made it through an attempt to have him removed over his reincarnation views, and he withstood the occasional ill will of his first counselor. He remembered the many prophecies about him, given in his youth, that he would one day be called as an apostle, prophecies that remained unfulfilled until he humbled himself and forsook his reincarnation views. After several years of developing trust and proving his loyalty, he was in a position to receive the greater blessings of service in the Church that the Lord had for him. The call did not remove cares and trials from him, nor did it diminish his occasional forays into depression or "melancholy." Such would be his lot until his golden years.

Developments began as the first session of the April conference concluded.

> First day of the 76th Annual Conference of the Church. I attended and sat in the auditorium of the Tabernacle. President Joseph F. Smith was the first speaker, and made some very interesting and significant remarks. . . . I went home to lunch and was taking a bath when a phone message from the President's Office summoned me

> to meet with Bro. Francis M. Lyman, the President of the Twelve Apostles. I went down to the President's Office, on my way to the Tabernacle, and had a private interview with President Lyman and Apostle John Henry Smith in the rear office. I was asked about my health, my faith and feelings, and answered the questions satisfactorily, I suppose, and was then told that I might be wanted tomorrow.[1]

It is significant that President Lyman and Elder Smith interviewed Bishop Whitney prior to his new calling. These two apostles likely had more knowledge of his past history with reincarnation than others of the senior Brethren.[2] As far as what Ort wrote in his diary, he never mentioned reincarnation again after his letter to President Smith, and, taken at face value, must be viewed as having completely forsaken the offending doctrine. April 7th proved to be one of the most dramatic and eventful days of his life:

> Attended the morning conference meeting; after which, met by appointment at the Historian's Office, with President F. M. Lyman and Apostles John Henry Smith and George A. Smith (his son). Elders George F. Richards, of Tooele, and David O. McKay, of Ogden, were also there (in President Lund's room). We were told by President Lyman that we three—Elders Richards, McKay, and myself—had been chosen to fill three vacancies in the Quorum of the Twelve; the vacancy caused by Brother M. W. Merrill's death, and two others, caused by the resignations of Apostles John W. Taylor and Matthias F. Cowley, who had not been associated with the Council of the Twelve since last October. Judge of my astonishment! He went on to tell us what would be required of us, asked for and received from each of us our views and feelings, and then enjoined us to strict secrecy regarding the whole matter, until it should be made public in a proper way. I attended the afternoon meeting of conference, also the religion class meeting just after.[3]

Then came his sustaining; "I attended Conference all day, sitting in the bishop's stand. Just before the close of the afternoon meeting, I was called and sustained as a member of the Council of the Twelve Apostles. . . . In the evening a party of friends called in to congratulate me and spent the evening. My phone was kept busy with calls of congratulation. My ward people are both glad and sad; and so am I for obvious reasons."[4] Whitney was emotional and euphoric, yet also overcome with feelings of inadequacy common to all called to high Church office.

> A day of days to me. I attended the Special Priesthood Meeting at 10 a.m. in the Assembly Hall, and at 2 p.m. a meeting in the Salt Lake Temple (First Presidency's Room) where, at about 2:25, I was ordained to the apostleship and placed in the Quorum of the Twelve, under the hands of President Joseph F. Smith (who was mouth [voice]) and the following named Brethren: Presidents John R. Winder, Anthon H. Lund, Francis M. Lyman, Apostles John Henry Smith, Rudger Clawson, Hyrum M. Smith, George Albert Smith, Charles W. Penrose, Patriarch John Smith, Elders Seymore B. Young, Brigham H. Roberts, George Reynolds, J. Golden Kimball, Rulon S. Wells, and Joseph W. McMurrin, of the First Council of the Seventies.
>
> A copy of my ordination blessing, recorded by Secretary George F. Gibbs, will be found elsewhere ~~in this journal.~~ The same brethren laid hands upon Elder George F. Richards, and he was ordained (before me) an apostle, in like manner by President Joseph F. Smith. After me, Elder David O. McKay was ordained an apostle by President Smith, and Elder Charles H. Hart, as one of the First Council of Seventies; also by President Smith. In this last ordination Bros. Richards, McKay, and myself took part, by President Smith's invitation.
>
> In the priesthood meeting at the Assembly Hall we three—the new apostles—were in order introduced to the meeting, and each spoke briefly, accepting the call to the apostleship. Bro. Richards succeeds the late Apostle M. W. Merrill. I am put in the place of John W. Taylor, resigned; and Bro. McKay in place of Matthias F. Cowley, resigned.
>
> At 4 p.m. the First Presidency, the Apostles, and their wives were entertained at dinner by President and Sister John R. Winder at their home. . . . After dinner a most enjoyable time was spent until 11 p.m. The Presidents and all the Apostles (present) spoke. Among the good things said of me were from President Joseph F. Smith, who assured me and all present that the Lord accepted of me, that past clouds were all dispelled, and I was wanted in the position to which I had been called. (He had told the priesthood meeting that I was one of the staunchest and most faithful men in the Church, and

> had rendered the cause valiant service as poet, orator, and historian, as well as bishop.) He said at President Winder's, that he had for years wanted me in the Quorum of the Twelve, that in my veins ran the blood of Apostle Heber C. Kimball, etc., and at the Temple he referred to my relations with the Prophet Joseph, through my mother's sealing to him in wedlock and said that I represented the Prophet by virtue of that relation, as an apostle.
>
> President Winder said it was as clear to him that we three had been chosen by the Spirit as light was distinct from darkness. Bro. John Henry Smith said it had been a dream of his life that I would be called to the apostleship. Many other kind things were said. Bro. Penrose said the Saints would rejoice over the call of us brethren to these positions.
>
> Nineteen years ago this [coming?] summer Apostle John W. Taylor predicted that I would be an apostle. We were traveling together south and were on the train about opposite Murray. I little dreamed, nor did he, that I would succeed him in the Quorum. He was always very good to me.[5]

President Anthon H. Lund, of the First Presidency, who participated in the ordination, recorded his own impressions, "I had felt very sad about the resignation of Bros. Matthias Cowley and John W. Taylor, but while Pres. Smith ordained the brethren I felt it was the Lord's will and this feeling was so sanctifying that I was melted to tears."[6]

In his autobiography, Whitney cleared up a matter relating to his ordination that his diary does not clarify satisfactorily, but he personally felt it to be of enough importance to note:

> Except in one particular, my ordination blessing, stenographically reported by Secretary George F. Gibbs, did not differ materially from the blessings pronounced upon Brothers Richards and McKay. And that exceptional item was left out of the Secretary's report, through a misunderstanding. The President had said that I would represent the Prophet Joseph Smith in the Council of the Twelve, but Brother Gibbs omitted this promise, so precious to me, thinking, as he subsequently explained, that those words were uttered after the President had taken his hands from off my head—which was not the case. I was right under his hands when the words were spoken, while

the Secretary was writing at a table on the other side of the room.

I forbore to mention the matter upon first reading the written blessing, supposing the President had seen fit to eliminate that part; and it was not until after his death and then upon the suggestion of his successor, that I inquired of Brother Gibbs and learned from him that he alone was responsible in the premises. Of course, the mere omission of words from a sheet of paper would not invalidate an act done by divine authority. But it would have been gratifying to me to have had the blessing just as it was delivered, as a matter of record.[7]

A day later, Elder Whitney met with his new associates:

At 10 a.m. I sat in Council for the first time with my Quorum, the Twelve Apostles, (eight of whom were present) in the Apostles Council Room at the Salt Lake Temple. I opened the meeting with prayer at [the] request of President F. M. Lyman and spoke during the deliberations that followed. Those present were F. M. Lyman, John Henry Smith, Rudger Clawson, Hyrum M. Smith, Charles W. Penrose, George F. Richards, and Orson F. Whitney, Apostles. . . . The business discussed pertained to the missions and to the manifesto. At 2 p.m. I assisted my brethren, the Apostles and Seven Presidents, in setting apart missionaries at the temple annex. Went home very tired. . . . So ended my first day of active service as an apostle.[8]

The next day President Joseph F. Smith officiated at the temple wedding of Elder Whitney's daughter Helen.[9] The day after that, Elder Whitney found himself in another sacred meeting: "Sat for the first time with the Presidency and Apostles of the Church in the regular weekly Council meeting at the Salt Lake Temple. The Apostles (9) met at 10 a.m. and the First Presidency came in at 11. The manifesto and the Taylor-Cowley subject were the main ones under consideration. We adjourned about 2 p.m."[10]

The passing days quickly turned into a week: "A week since I was called to be an apostle. I have been overwhelmed with congratulations from all sides, Mormons and Gentiles; all seem pleased with my appointment. . . . This evening I spoke at the ward chapel and was followed by Elder B. H. Roberts, who paid me a glowing tribute for my work as a bishop during the past 28 years. Counselor Robert

Patrick presided [conducted], but it was at the request of Apostle Rudger Clawson and President Joseph S. Wells that I addressed my old congregation."[11]

Elder Whitney now encountered a life of both old and new, and he was asked to give an accounting of his personal economic position to the First Presidency.

> Made a statement of my financial and domestic circumstances to President Joseph F. Smith and Counselors. At 2 p.m. assisted my brethren, the Apostles and Seven Presidents, to set apart missionaries at the Temple. My little boys Wendell and Paul wandered off about 5 p.m., and gave us a great scare. May and I, with others, walked the streets until a late hour, in a pouring rain, searching for them. At last I found them, at 11 p.m., or thereabouts, in the 3rd circle of the Salt Lake Theater, enjoying the play. They had to be whipped.

> Salt Lake City, April 17, 1906
> President Joseph F. Smith, City
>
> Dear Brother:
>
> According to your suggestion, I herewith submit a statement of my financial and domestic circumstances.
>
> I am in debt $1500, $1200 to Zion's Benefit Building Society, and the remaining $300 to the State Bank of Utah. I am paying to the Building Society $18 a month, interest and dues; and my note at the Bank draws interest at the rate of seven per cent per annum. Originally I owed the Building Society $2500, which I borrowed several years ago to build a home. The money obtained from the Bank was to fit out my daughters, Emily and Helen, prior to their marriage. My sole income is my salary: $200 a month, out of which I pay tithes, offerings, donations, taxes, insurance, dues, interest, tuition, etc. And with what remains endeavor to support my family, now consisting of ten persons, mostly small and all dependent; virtually two families rolled into one.
>
> During 1905, with the proceeds from sales of my poem *Elias*, I was enabled to materially reduce my Building Society debt and pay a larger tithing than ever before. The entire edition of the poem is now sold out, and I do not expect to realize any more from that source.
>
> For years I have struggled under a burden of debt, and have succeeded [text missing] out of the financial slough in which I found myself, as the result of various misfortunes. I want to be a free man

and a follower of your counsel—to get out of debt, and keep out. In this hope, after obtaining your permission, I entered into a contract with the Deseret News Company, to write for them a *Student's History of Utah*; a work much needed, and I believe highly important to the interests of the rising generation. The amount I am to receive for this work will just lift me out of debt, and not a dollar more. Meantime I must go on living, paying interest, dues, etc., as before.

My daughter Helen, during the past year, has been my assistant (typist), and has drawn $40 a month for her services. With this amount she clothed herself and helped her sisters. Helen was married, as you know, on the 11th inst., and has moved to Idaho. Since April 1st her sister Margaret has been working in her place, and is now helping me to wind up the affairs of my department in the Historian's Office, which department I propose turning over to my successor on the 1st of May.

President Lund has kindly consented to give me the use of a desk at the Historian's Office for correspondence, mail delivery, etc., but for my regular work upon the *History*—which I understand it is your desire I should complete—I shall fit up an office at home and employ my daughter Margaret to assist me; paying her out of any allowance made to me henceforth by the Church. I expect to complete the *History* within a year, working intermittently between my duties as an apostle.

Your Brother,
Orson F. Whitney[12]

One of the first items considered at the next meeting of the First Presidency and Twelve was what to do about replacing Bishop Whitney, who had been serving in that regard for so long.

Attended the Council of the First Presidency and Apostles at 10 a.m. It was decided among other things to reorganize the 18th ward bishopric next Sunday evening. Bros. T. A. Clawson will be bishop, John A. Evans 1st, and Lafayette T. Whitney 2nd Counselor. My old counselors, Robert Patrick and William B. Barton, will be made patriarchs. . . . At 5 p.m., met with the Presidency and most of the Twelve at the President's Office to consider position and prospects of Senator Reed Smoot. Took supper with my friend B. H. Roberts, at my invitation, downtown.[13]

Regarding the fate of his former first counselor, Elder Whitney explained, "It was I that nominated Robert Patrick for the high council. I had previously named him in the Council of the Apostles for bishop but finding that the stake presidency and high council were unanimous for a younger man, I withdrew my nomination, and at the next meeting, when President Smith proposed that Elders Patrick and Barton be made patriarchs, I mentioned Bro. Patrick for the high council as well. I had previously recommended his selection as such to President Richard W. Young. . . . As for me, I am simply astonished at the love and [illegible] showered upon me by everybody. In the good feelings of the people of the ward and their deep regret at parting with me, I find ample compensation for my (nearly) 28 years service as a ward bishop."[14]

A few days later, the question of what to do about the two former Apostles that had resigned came up, and Elder Whitney's thoughts were solicited. "At 2 p.m. I was at the temple, setting apart missionaries, among them my nephew Horace B. Whitney. In this work I assisted President F. M. Lyman and other Apostles. At about 3 p.m. Bro. Rudger Clawson and I, at his suggestion, went up to the Historian's Office, and sat for half an hour or more, talking of Bros. John W. Taylor and M. F. Cowley, etc."[15]

At the next meeting of the Twelve and First Presidency, Elder Whitney received his first stake conference assignment: "At 10 a.m., met in Council with the Apostles and at 11 with them and the First Presidency. Was appointed to attend the Alpine Stake conference at American Fork Saturday and Sunday."[16]

Attendance at stake conferences, near and far, would consume most of Elder Whitney's weekends for the rest of his life. The stake visits varied little from each other, except for names and places. In fact, visiting stakes, touring missions, and meeting with the First Presidency and Twelve to counsel and conduct the business of the Church became so routine that Whitney chose to omit mention of most of it in his autobiography. He explained, "It is not my purpose to enter upon a detailed account of all my labors as an apostle. There is no room for it, nor any need of it. It would be both superfluous and tiresome." Elder Whitney's introspective statement is quite correct; the lengthy accounts of his visits to myriad stake conferences recorded in his diary are not reproduced here, unless something remarkable or exceptional happened. The lists of places, names, order of speakers, people ordained, train schedules, homes at which he stayed or ate, and like items are of limited worth. Only perhaps a third of Whitney's autobiography covers his tenure as an apostle; much of that consisted of travelogue, excerpts of speeches, and family matters.

However, his diaries do contain many items of great interest and mystery that he omitted when telling his own life story. These items added flavor and sometimes puzzling intrigue to his life as an apostle of the Lord.

The main assignments that never ceased for Whitney—mostly accomplished between stake conferences or while traveling—continued to be literary. More and more he wrote important letters and articles for President Joseph F. Smith: "Compiled an article on 'Woman's Work and Mormonism,' for the *Young Ladies Journal* and continued working on an article for President Joseph F. Smith, 'The Future of Mormonism,' for publication in an eastern magazine. He gave me the commission for it last Tuesday. Susa Young Gates prophesied to me today that I would yet be one of the counselors in the First Presidency. At 2 p.m., I assisted some of the Apostles in setting apart a class of trained nurses, at the temple annex."[17] Elder Whitney wrote the assigned articles, but Gates's prophecy went unfulfilled.

With his call to the Twelve, Whitney needed to vacate his office and make room for Joseph Fielding Smith Jr., the prophet's son and new Assistant Church Historian. "Moved my effects from the Historian's Office to my home and spent the forenoon writing on the article 'The Future of Mormonism.' In the afternoon, [I] assisted in setting apart missionaries at the temple. Afterward, called on Sister Mary Stayner, 19th ward."[18]

Then Elder Whitney gave his farewell address as bishop of the 18th ward.

> The program was carried out to the letter, and it was a red letter day in the history of the ward and in my own history as well. . . . In my address I spoke of the surprises that had come to me, such as my call to the mission field and to the bishopric and to the apostleship.

> Another surprise was that I had lived to see the day when a bishop could be accounted successful, without being distinctively a business man, a manager, and a dispenser [illegible]. I had tried to be a father and a friend to my flock and had endeavored to be kind and charitable to all. I had taught them true principles, and told them how to live. I might not have had the ability to do some things, but I always knew how things ought to be done. I was not an impractical dreamer that some people supposed. My dreams were my ideals and I thanked the Lord for them; but I was more wide awake, even as to temporal things, then some people imagined. I paid a tribute to my counselors and gave them full credit for all they had done."[19]

Knowing what many ward members thought they knew of parts of his past, Apostle Whitney may have used the farewell to justify his lengthy service and reputation as a poet and literary man. The irregularities of parts of his past caused him to take extra notice of words of approval and commendation.

If Whitney wasn't at a stake conference, he was usually a featured speaker for the Sunday services in the Salt Lake Tabernacle. "Addressed the congregation at the Tabernacle by request of President John R. Winder. Last Thursday at Council I offered to go to the South Sanpete Stake Conference, but President Smith was anxious that I should finish the magazine article 'Truth of Mormonism.' So I remained in Salt Lake. I had full freedom at the Tabernacle and all who spoke to me about it expressed themselves as highly pleased with my discourse."[20] A few days later it was almost done: "Worked on article 'Future of Mormonism' and read it to President Smith; having taken lunch with him at the Beehive just previously. He suggested one or two slight changes. . . . This morning I had a long talk with Bro. B. H. Roberts, relating to him a dream had by Sister Prescilla Murphy, which she told to me last Sunday morning. He also related one."[21] Later that same day Elder Whitney "completed the 'Future of Mormonism' article and delivered it to President Smith, who thanked me heartily for it."

Later that month, Whitney was pleased to hear a compliment from someone that did not know they were giving it:

> A peculiar incident happened to me today. I was on the Sixth St. car going up to see Bro. John A. Evans, when a lady, a stranger,

> engaged me in conversation. She said she and others were here from the east, on their way to California, and were so interested in the Mormon people, who had treated them kindly. "Some of my friends," said she, "were here last summer, or fall, and heard at the Tabernacle Bishop—Bishop—what was his name? Bishop Whitney I believe it was; and they told me to be sure and hear Bishop Whitney. But I am afraid we are not going to hear him." Said I, "I am Bishop Whitney." And she almost fainted. I spent most of the day upon a biographical sketch for the *Millennial Star*, it being sent for by President Heber J. Grant. Toward evening I received a notice from Secretary George F. Gibbs that I was expected to attend the Granite Stake Conference tomorrow.[22]

Busy as things were for the new Apostle, he found himself settling into enough routine that he could continue an interrupted project. "Resumed work this morning upon my *Student's History of Utah*, which I have not had time to touch since the April conference. In the afternoon, assisted my Brethren to set apart missionaries at the temple. Was left in charge of the meeting at which the missionaries were instructed, and Bro. Rulon S. Wells and I addressed them."[23]

Some of Elder Whitney's duties remained the same as bishopric work: "Worked on my *Student's History* most of the day. . . . Bro. John A. Evans, whom I have visited repeatedly since he was hurt, is gradually sinking. Elder George Albert Smith and I visited him the other night, by special request of President Smith, who could not go in person. We blessed him, Bro. Smith being mouth, and he seemed to know us, but is evidently losing his hold upon mortal life."[24] Less than a week later his friend was dead and Whitney spoke at his funeral. After that, he attended the marriage of his daughter;

> Emily's wedding day. She is my oldest daughter, and marries Winslow Farr Smith, son of Apostle John Henry Smith. . . . At 10 a.m. today I went to the Temple to attend the regular Council. Was appointed to attend the Box Elder Stake Conference on Saturday and Sunday. After Council, went below [the fourth floor] where, at about 3 p.m. the marriage of Emily and Winslow was solemnized, Apostle John Henry Smith officiating; myself and George Albert Smith signing

> as witnesses. A number of other relatives were present. . . . Race and Helen being home for the wedding, it was our first entire family reunion in several years.[25]

Elder John Henry Smith recorded his doings that day as well. "at 3 p.m. today I sealed Emily Whitney, daughter of Elder Orson F. Whitney and his wife Zina Smoot Whitney to my son Winslow Farr Smith at the Salt Lake Temple in the presence of a number of kinsfolk and friends. The witnesses were Elders Orson F. Whitney and George Albert Smith. We had a most agreeable time at the home of Bishop O. F. Whitney, receiving an army of friends and relatives."[26]

Orson could be proud of this wedding: a daughter marrying the son of an apostle in the holy temple; he had been given occasion to lament others of his children marrying otherwise.

As Elder Whitney settled into working from home, he mentioned a pleasant surprise, "Spent most of the day reading . . . and fitting up my home office and library. Moved most of my books into the new repository, formerly May's bedroom, where I have been working and shall continue to work upon my *Student's History*. I forgot to mention among yesterday's incidents, a letter signed by the First Presidency, Joseph F. Smith, John R. Winder, and Anthon H. Lund, enclosing my note for $300 and accrued interest, owing to the State Bank of Utah, and cancelled after payment by the Trustee-in-Trust [President Smith]. It was very kind of the Brethren, and an act much appreciated by myself."[27]

At this time in Church history, it was thought imprudent for the President of the Church to officiate in the marriage of a couple outside of the temple, where priesthood sealing keys were exercised. President Snow had once done it, and received some quiet grumbling from his Brethren. This abstinence meant Elder Whitney was given the privilege. "At 10 a.m., attended [the] Council of the Apostles in the Temple. Was appointed to attend the North Sanpete Conference on next Saturday and Sunday, to accompany President Joseph F. Smith. At 7 p.m. married, at the Beehive House, C. Earnest Richards . . . and Lila West, of Ogden, Utah. He is a Gentile and she a Mormon. President Smith had been asked to perform the ceremony, but he thought it wise to delegate it, and so sent for me."[28]

Elder Whitney was finding the work an apostle did to be exhausting. "Wrote some letters declining to deliver 4th of July orations at different points, and wrote during the forenoon on the [*Student's*] *History*. In the afternoon, wandered around aimlessly, trying to rest my mind. Went to bed at 8:30 p.m. very tired."[29] Overworked and tired as they were, some perks were given to the Twelve that helped them relax: "Wrote on *History*, and at night attended theatre . . . . May was with me. My tickets were obtained from Manager George D. Pyper, agreeable to an understanding that the Church allows the Twelve to occasionally have this privilege."[30]

As July of 1906 began, Whitney attended the special quarterly meeting of the Twelve Apostles. The meeting had been inaugurated by President Snow years before in his quest to bring a unifying spirit of brotherhood to a fragmented Quorum of the Twelve.[31] The tradition continued: "At 10 a.m. I met with my Quorum in quarterly conference—the first occasion of the kind for me. We had a glorious time, unbosoming ourselves to each other. Bro. Reed Smoot met with us, having just returned from Washington. The speakers were Francis M. Lyman, John Henry Smith, Rudger Clawson, Reed Smoot, Hyrum M. Smith, George Albert Smith, Charles W. Penrose, George F. Richards, Orson F. Whitney, [and] David O. McKay. We were in session until 4:15 p.m."[32] The Apostles used the meeting to confess their weaknesses and faults, to strengthen one another, and to bear solemn witness and testimony, occasionally sharing sacred personal spiritual experiences. Elder Whitney elaborated,

> During most of the time since my ordination, my duties have consisted of weekly visits to the stakes, with occasional tours of missions, and such other service as the presiding authorities have required of me. Once a week, at a regular Council meeting, the Apostles report their labors to the First Presidency and to one another, and join in prayer and the transaction of important Church business. There we receive our appointments from the President of the Twelve, sanctioned by the First Presidency, with general directions to govern us in the discharge of our sacred duties. On certain days we set apart and instruct missionaries, and on any and every day do whatever needs doing for the good of the Cause. Every three months, the Twelve, or as many of them as can assemble, come together in a quarterly meeting,

> and every six months they convene in joint session with the First Council of the Seventy and such of the mission presidents as are able to attend; the latter reporting conditions and prospects in their fields of labor and receiving such advice and instruction as the Apostles see fit to impart.[33]

Soon Elder Whitney encountered Angus Cannon, his former stake president and then patriarch, recently returned from a mission. "Met on the street in the afternoon Patriarch Angus M. Cannon, just home from Europe. He said, while shaking my hand, 'I heard of your call to the apostleship at Liverpool. I congratulate the Church.' I thanked him for the splendid compliment."[34]

Patriarch Cannon was by no means alone in his effusive congratulations. Within days of his sustaining, many letters poured in, and also many personal visits, that echoed similar feelings. From among the written communications, the new Apostle selected samplings for his diary. Of these, some refer to the trying spiritual struggles he had endured in preparation for his call and some came from members of his old theosophy group. One of them, John Donaldson, wrote:

> No man in Israel felt more gratified than I did, although it was no surprise, to hear of your being called to the apostleship. My soul was filled with humility. I knew it would come sooner or later. No man alive today has endured what you have, and no man knows it better than I do. I thank God I have known you so long; your example in many things has made me a better man. . . . I know God has been watching you. He could never forsake a man who has been so true, and patient in suffering and yet unwavering in his faith to God and his brethren. . . .[35]

Maude May Babcock wrote, "I must . . . tell you with what joy I voted for you yesterday and recognized that after your hard struggles the Lord would now place you where you belong. I, no doubt, can [illegible] as keenly as anyone, except yourself, what you have gone through. . . ." Further, "Your education in spiritual things, costing you such suffering, will be now of use to the people, and a work of preparation will begin."[36]

Josiah E. Hickman, a professor that Whitney had met years before at the Brigham Young College in Logan (Utah State University), and who in future years became one of Elder Whitney's closest friends and confidantes, wrote, "I have watched your course since I was 18 years of age and have said for years that, if I had the spirit of discernment, you would sometime be one of the Twelve. I now find that I have not been mistaken. I rejoice in your promotion."[37] Whitney even heard from an old flame, Georgiana, a member of his ward he had once pursued unsuccessfully with hopes of another plural wife: "Among the many friends delighted with your promotion, no one will realize your worthiness of the position more than [I], 'Georgiana.'"[38]

In his own autobiography, Elder Whitney only hinted at the depth of his tribulations. "There were other trials, too, which made these petty money troubles, annoying though they were, mere trifles by comparison. But no dissertation regarding them would be understood by anyone who has not been similarly placed. Suffice it, though hard to bear, those trials were beneficial, and I would not part with the priceless experience that came out of them."[39]

Soon Elder Whitney found himself in the role of defender of the Church, publicly refuting the uninformed claims of a local Presbyterian minister. He explained the circumstances,

> In the morning I was at the 18th ward Sabbath School, and in the afternoon at the Tabernacle, where I spoke as per the following reports of the city papers [several newspaper clippings follow of Whitney's discourse, reviewing the premortal existence, the godhead, and the doctrine of a Mother in Heaven as taught in the hymn "O My Father."] Many have expressed to me their great satisfaction with my reply to Dr. [William M.] Paden. It came about in this way. I went to the Tabernacle, not knowing that I would be called on to speak, though I had thought it probable, and the Paden incident had been on my mind since reading of it in Saturday evening's [*Deseret*] *News*. After I had gone into the stand, President John R. Winder said to me, "Why, I didn't know you were in town, or I would not have hunted for a preacher. I have asked Judge King to speak this afternoon." I answered, "I shall be glad to hear him." [Illegible] told Brother Winder that I thought Paden should be answered, and he immediately fell in with the idea, and forthwith proposed to excuse Brother King and let me speak instead. Judge King, on being consulted, was quite pleased with the change, and I then suggested that the hymn "O My Father" be sung by the choir just before I began. This was done, and the rest is told.[40]

At the next Council meeting of the First Presidency and Twelve, Elder Whitney was complimented for his defense of the Church: "At 10 a.m., was at the Temple, in council, as usual. . . . In the reports President John R. Winder stated that I had handled my subject on Sunday 'in good shape and to the satisfaction of every soul present'; [illegible] President Lund and Patriarch John Smith also spoke of the enjoyment it gave them. . . ."[41]

Elder Whitney also recorded a trip he made, along with two other Apostles, to the Utah Stake conference held in Provo, and noted a brief visit with an old friend and relative that he had discussed doctrine with on a few occasions in former years. "Conference continued at 10 a.m. Between meetings I had an interesting conversation with Patriarch Oliver B. Huntington. He showed me a little book in which he had recorded things said to him by the Prophet Joseph Smith. One was that the earth had been inhabited 3 times before Adam came upon it; the former races having been destroyed."[42] Huntington was known as one that loved to pass on supposed statements he was alleged to have heard from Joseph Smith, many of them of questionable worth and provenance.[43]

At the same stake conference, Josiah E. Hickman, one of those in attendance, recorded his opinion of the sermons he heard that day from the three visiting Apostles. "Provo: We held our quarterly conference last Sat. & Sun. Apostles John Henry Smith, Reed Smoot, and Orson Whitney were with us and spoke well. Whitney is a power. Now here comes a little side talk. I don't appreciate John Henry Smith's discourses for he speaks in too general terms. He is eloquent, but not persuasive. He is flowery in word and phrase but too vague. Smoot is too gushing, yet he holds an audience well. He will be more stable in time. Now, Mr. Journal, keep this quiet for the present. These brethren are prophets, but Whitney is a prophet, poet and orator."[44]

A few years later when their friendship truly blossomed, Josiah's opinion of Whitney would only improve.

Because of its recent prominence, one of the subjects that the First Presidency and Twelve were obliged by public sentiment to address was the situation and fate of former Elders Taylor and Cowley. Elder Whitney was no exception. "At the close of the meeting the priesthood convened and were addressed by Brother Penrose and myself upon the Taylor-Cowley matter."[45]

That August, Elder Whitney was attending a stake conference with Elder Francis M. Lyman, the President of the Quorum of the Twelve. A comment made by Lyman was particularly satisfying to him. "During the conference at Heber City, President Lyman said to me, 'Will it turn your head if I pay you a compliment?' 'I guess not' I replied. 'Well, one of the things that I like about your preaching is that you don't try to be eloquent.' I answered that I never knew a speaker to be truly eloquent when he tried to be; that all one needed to do was to be earnest, get inspiration, lose himself in his subject, and eloquency would take care of itself."[46]

In early September, Elder Whitney took charge of setting apart the outgoing crop of missionaries. "Was excused from my contemplated trip to the Big Horn Stake, on account of not having free railroad transportation from Denver to Cowley. Elder George Albert Smith went instead, with Bro. George F. Richards. At 2 p.m. I was at the temple, assisting in setting apart and instructing missionaries. Being the senior and indeed the only Apostle present, I presided, and was assisted in setting apart and instructing the missionaries by President Seymour B. Young and Charles H. Hart. I blessed nine in one company, and ordained Elder Carl W. Ross a Seventy while the other Brethren set apart a company of ten."[47] At that time Elder Whitney was rarely the senior Apostle for anything.

At a mid-September meeting, he found himself being assigned for a two-week visit to two stakes with little notice. "Attended regular Council meeting in the Temple, and was given a two weeks appointment to visit the St. George and Parowan Stake conferences, starting tonight. Made all preparations, bade my loved ones good-bye, and took the San Pedro midnight train. . . ."[48] In St. George, Elder Whitney found himself standing at the same pulpit in the Tabernacle where President Snow had seven years earlier received a revelation that all faithful Latter-day Saints were to pay a full and honest tithing. Whitney himself enjoyed no such marvelous vision. "During my remarks I accidentally tipped over a glass pitcher of water at my right hand, deluging two of the brethren in the stand below."[49]

The St. George scenery enraptured Elder Whitney, the stunning sight nearly making him late for a meeting:

> From the summit of Sugar Loaf, a huge red cliff half a mile above the town, I see St. George below me, nestling between two ranges of majestic bluffs, forming the narrow valley in which the town is situated. It is a pretty spot, in spite of the barren surroundings. The houses are embowered in trees, of sidewalk and orchard and the contrast between the green verdure and foliage dotted with white homes, and the red and gray of the sod surrounding the place, is marked. To my left is the Temple, white and stainless, shining in the sun, and beyond the shallow water and sand [illegible] of the Rio Virgin, which here meets the Santa Clara and flows off in a winding course among hills and mountains. It is a beautiful morning and all nature smiles. But I must return from my ramble and attend a meeting of the Relief Society of the stake.[50]

He also found himself reminiscing about his past in that locale. "A week since I left home. Have much enjoyed my trip thus far. It is 32 years since I passed through Cedar [City] on my way to St. George . . . and 33 years since I came as far south as Cedar [City] as a sewing machine agent for the Elias Howe Company. J. O. Young and I were then partners. The next autumn (1874) I made the trip with Bro. Clawson; my first trip to St. George, and the only one, thus far, except the one just made, from which I am now returning."[51] On his return, he found "all well with [his] family."[52]

He then got to enjoy another testimony meeting with his Quorum. "At 10 a.m., proceeded to the temple and opened with prayer, at President Lyman's request, the regular quarterly meeting of the Apostles. Present: all the Apostles, members of the Council of the Twelve, excepting Heber J. Grant, in Europe. I was the first speaker. We were in session until nearly 6 p.m., and had a most enjoyable time."[53]

Chapter 15

The Misadventures of Race Whitney

Two years before he died, Elder Whitney spoke in general conference and taught doctrine that has since become perhaps his most well-known and oft-quoted instruction, at least in modern times. In April of 1929, he taught,

> The Prophet Joseph Smith declared—and he never taught a more comforting doctrine—that the eternal sealings of faithful parents and the divine promises made to them for valiant service in the Cause of Truth would save not only themselves, but likewise their posterity. Though some of the sheep may wander, the eye of the Shepherd is upon them, and sooner or later they will feel the tentacles of Divine Providence reaching out after them and drawing them back to the fold. Either in this life or the life to come, they will return. They will have to pay their debt to justice; they will suffer for their sins and may tread a thorny path, but if it leads them at last, like the penitent Prodigal, to a loving and forgiving Father's heart and home, the painful experience will not have been in vain. Pray for your careless and disobedient children; hold on to them with your faith. Hope on, trust on, till you see the salvation of God.[1]

Others holding the same high office have since quoted these remarkable words, coming from Elder Whitney in the twilight of his apostleship.[2] The strong but comforting doctrine itself has been much discussed and debated, but little has been said or written about why Elder Whitney would ponder the subject, grapple with it, and then teach it so forcefully and with such conviction and surety to the Latter-day Saints. While a complete answer to such a question may be beyond recall, surely a partial one now stands.

Elder Whitney, mighty witness and apostle that he became, had some wayward children of his own who did not follow him in the path of righteousness he trod and the example he set; some did, but others did not. Prominent in the diaries among them is Horace, or "Race," Ort's favored eldest son and firstborn. This chapter, reviewing Race's short but eventful life, is not included to judge either him or his father in their successes and failures. Yet some lessons are still unmistakable. It is apparent from Whitney's diaries that as a busy bishop, reporter and editor, preacher, writer, and polygamist (along with other diversions), that Orson was often away from home. Naturally this would impact his effectiveness as a father and guide. Yet no matter the reasons or the fault, Race eventually wandered and went his own way, largely forsaking the teachings of his youth.

The diaries refer to Race as a baby and a child; but the first time he is spoken of prominently is when Bishop Whitney arranged for him, as a young and green reporter for the *Salt Lake Herald*, to accompany President Snow's traveling party to St. George and throughout southern and central Utah, at which time President Snow received the famous tithing revelation. As recounted in chapter eleven, Race was asked to speak in a large public meeting and did well, earning compliments from President Snow and others. It would seem that Race was on the straight and narrow path then, but in the years after, the diaries indicate that he drifted. Talented, witty, and intelligent as he was (or as his father thought he was), he made many poor choices. One of them was drinking. We do not know when he started, but the evidence indicates that Race became an alcoholic, a habit that would prove his undoing.

Good as he was at what he did—writer, reporter, dramatist—Race struggled to stay employed for very long. He also made a poor choice for a wife. It is with this decision that he again finds mention in Orson's diary: "Went this evening with my son Race to see Miss Rosemary Gloez, his young lady. She is not a Mormon but is a very charming girl, aged 20, finely educated, a native of Boston. . . . They are a Hungarian family and nice people. Race and Rose are madly in love with each other. They want to marry. While I hate to see him wed outside the Church, I prefer this to no marriage, or a life on the stage, which he says is the alternative."[3]

About two months later, the day of the wedding arrived.

> Race's Wedding Day. At a quarter to 3 p.m. my wife May and I proceeded to the residence of Mr. and Mrs. Gloez on Capitol Hill (where they have recently purchased a home) and where the wedding company was fast arriving. It was snowing, but inside all was beauty, comfort, and brilliance. . . . At a few minutes past three I pronounced the marriage ceremony uniting my oldest son and first-born child Horace Newel Whitney and Rosemary Matilday Gloez. Afterwards a banquet and toasts. . . .
>
> It was a superb affair throughout. My two regrets were Zina's absence (though she may have been hovering near) and the fact that my son's wife is not a Latter-day Saint. I pray, however, that she may yet become one, that Race's heart may also turn more to His Lord and to the religion of his fathers, and that God will bless this marriage for their [illegible] good and the happiness and prosperity of all concerned. Amen! The young couple are aged 21 and 20 respectively; are apparently well mated, and are very much in love with each other. . . . I gave them a set of my *History of Utah* (four volumes) and presented Race with the gold watch his mother gave me many years ago. I also made them a present of the marriage certificate. I could have done more had my means and circumstances permitted.[4]

Whitney's sorrow at his son's life course may have awakened within him a desire to be more watchful of his other children, who tested his fatherly patience. "Yesterday I whipped for the first time in my life one of my children: my little boy Bert, Zina's youngest, next to the twins. It hurt me awfully to do it, but I had to, for his sake. He is not the first of my children to deserve a whipping by my means, but the first one I ever punished in that way. I used a little switch upon his shoulders, and was not angry but sorrowful. I afterward reasoned with and was kind to him, and I think it all did him good."[5]

Meanwhile, Orson missed his absent son, whose marriage, little more than a year-and-a-half old, was falling apart without his knowledge. "On arriving at my office this morning [I] found Race with Rose awaiting me. He returned yesterday [from the east]. Had not received my letter, as he started for home immediately on getting the money I sent him. I was overjoyed to see him. Had him and wife up to the house to a turkey dinner. Have tried during the day to get a place for him on the *News*. . . . In the evening was told by my friend John E. Hansen, city editor of the *Deseret News*, that agreeable to my request they were going to offer Race a position on the *News* staff."[6]

It seemed the match of a rich Hungarian Bostonian with a poor, aimless, Mormon boy, was ill fated. (Later it would come out that Race's mother-in-law had interfered and poisoned her daughter against him.) Ten days later, on Christmas Eve, the axe fell. "Spent most of the day at home, took dinner with my family, and in the evening we all went up to May's mother's to the usual Christmas tree. Did not stay late. My day was saddened by the troubles of my son, Race, whose wife yesterday started proceedings for divorce; alleging non-support."[7] Rose had joined an eastern opera company as a singer, with Race becoming a promoter; but all for naught: "Race took dinner with us today and will begin living with us at home from this time."[8] And Ort got his son the job: "Race began working this morning for the *Deseret News*, as a reporter. He now lives with me."[9]

At first, things went well for the young journalist in his new position. "Race is doing fine work on the [*Deseret*] *News*. An article of his in this evening's issue . . . has been highly commended by the manager of the paper, and others."[10] But despite his best intentions, things did not go as Orson hoped. No diaries for 1904 are available, so the details are not known, but by early 1905, Race was no longer with the *Deseret News*; he had moved and remarried Rose.

> Received letter from Race, telling of his remarriage with Rose, a fact with which I was already acquainted through the following announcement in the *Salt Lake Herald* of Sunday the 15th inst: "Mr. and Mrs. Horace N. Whitney Remarry and Settle in Portland: Mrs. Rosemary Gloez-Whitney and Horace N. Whitney, both of Salt Lake, were married in Portland, Oregon, last week and are now at home to their friends in that city. This statement will cause surprise

> among the friends of the young people in this city. It will also recall a romance that was the talk of the town for a time three years ago. Three years ago, Miss Gloez and Mr. Whitney were married in this city. She was a singer with the prospects of a brilliant stage future; he was a member of the *Herald* staff. After the wedding the bride accepted a flattering offer from an opera company in the east and Mr. Whitney became the advertising man for the company. Relatives came between the young couple to cause trouble. The upshot of this was a suit for divorce filed by the bride in Salt Lake a year ago. The application was granted by the court and it was considered here that the romance was at an end forever. The last act puts a different face on the matter, and all Utah friends of both bride and groom will extend good wishes for the future. It is known that the reconciliation between the young people came about through the diplomacy of a chorus girl. Mrs. Whitney was with the Fields opera company in the east. The chorus girl made a discovery one day as to how Mrs. Whitney felt toward her former husband. She passed the tip to Race and the reunion is the outcome. The bride has surrendered her position in the opera company and she and her husband are settled in Portland."[11]

A surprised Whitney quickly responded. "Wrote to Race at Portland, giving him and Rose some fatherly advice."[12] But the reconciliation was not to last long, if the mother-in-law could help it: "This afternoon I intend going to a reception given by Race's wife, Rosemary Gloez Whitney, at her studio on Main St. She is here on a visit by her mother, who has forgiven her for remarrying Race without her knowledge. . . . Rosa has again left Race and gone east."[13]

With his wife absent with the opera company, Race went to San Francisco, hoping to drum up financial support for a play, or operetta, he had written, and to work as a reporter. This move placed him right in the middle of the great San Francisco earthquake of April 1906. Orson felt deep relief when he could finally contact his son. "God is good! Race escaped unhurt in the awful earthquake at San Francisco. . . ."[14] Further word came soon. "This morning's *Tribune* has correspondence from San Francisco, in which the following paragraph occurs, 'Escaped Sockless: Race Whitney, a son of one of the new apostles, was one of the newspaper men of San Francisco who suffered in the earthquake. He escaped, sockless and with but meager clothing, and late Sunday evening had not laid down to rest. Jokingly he said he believed he would see if he could not talk some fellow out of a pair of socks, as it was very inconvenient to be running around as he had since the first shock of the earthquake.'"[15] In a letter to his father, which was published for all to read in the *Deseret News*, Race wrote of his experience.

> I hardly know where to begin in relating this story. I do not want to picture all the horrors that we newspapermen have encountered, and yet I want to give you a clear idea of the terrible situation. . . .
>
> The people here are in a state of panic. The city is under martial law. Over 50,000 people are camping in the streets and public parks, weather cold, provisions dealt out by the government. . . .
>
> Meanwhile, Wally Young and I are sleeping in comparative luxury. We found a furnished flat that had been deserted by a terror-stricken family, and have the privilege of using it until they return from their place of refuge, wherever that may be. . . .
>
> Between all of us we eke out a fine existence—appointing daily committees on grub, on cooking, on housework, etc. Cooking all done in the street. No fires, nor lights allowed in the houses. We have had a dozen earthquake shocks since the [main] destroyer but none of them very dangerous. The great fear now is an epidemic as the result of [un]sanitary conditions. The sewer system was wrecked. . . . One of the most horrible features of the whole thing was the condition of over 100 women the second night of the disaster in Golden Gate Park and the Presidio, the common camping grounds. The mothers were without shelter or medical attention, and many of them died with their babes. Literally scores of men have been shot dead for stealing or for refusing to work when commanded. One offense is quite as grave as the other in these times. If a soldier tells you to do a thing and you hesitate, it is as much as your life is worth.
>
> I understand the first reports that went out placed the loss of life at 300. Absurd! That many were crushed in two hotels that I know of. The exact number may never be known, but it cannot possibly be under 3,500, and may run as high as 6,000. The streets are filled—or were until a couple of days ago—with women and children crying aloud for their loved ones, and men went through town half-crazed, searching for their families. . . .
>
> Millions of dollars were lost to dynamite in the effort to check the raging fire. The fire itself is beyond description. If you can

> imagine a mass of buildings extending from Fort Douglas to the Jordan river, and from Mill Creek to Anderson's tower, all burning, you have some idea of the fearful, yet inspiring, sight.
>
> Wally and myself had been working at the *Chronicle* office late on Tuesday night. . . . So it was about 5 o'clock [a.m.] when we started home. We were standing in front of the Auditorium Hotel when the crash came. Instinctively we started for the middle of the street, and, where we had stood less than one second before, there was a pile of bricks seven feet high. The whole top of the structure had fallen down. It had four stories to run and we had about 60 feet. We won. It was the first earthquake I had ever experienced, and believe me, they are very unpopular with your eldest son. . . .
>
> To return to the first crash. It was terribly spectacular to see houses crumbling and hear the crash of timbers as great wooden structures tottered from their foundations or were wrenched out of shape. In less time than it takes to tell it, the street we were on . . . was filled with men and women in nightgowns or blankets, or entirely naked, running back and forth like so many sheep. In running we had to spread our feet wide apart to keep from being hurled to the ground, so violent was the tremor.
>
> "They come in threes!" Wally shouted. "There will be two more. Get to the middle of the street." And away he rushed, me following. Suddenly—God only knows how—I saw that he was directly under a mass of electric wires and the danger suggested itself to me. I called to him to come away from the wires, and he started back. He had no sooner rejoined me on the sidewalk than the wires came down, sputtering and tearing up everything they touched. That we were not both electrocuted was the second miracle of the morning. Eventually, we moved cautiously up the street. Half the fear had left us, or probably the full fear had not yet come to us, for we began to congratulate ourselves; first, on our escape, and second, that we were probably the only reporters on the street at that hour and could therefore make thrilling stories of what we had seen. Laughable indeed, looking back on it. We little dreamed that a few hours later every newspaper office in town would be smoldering ruins, as well as half the town.[16]

Race concluded the letter with a brief note for his father, mentioning his call to the Twelve: "In conclusion, Father, accept my belated congratulations and fondest wishes upon the recognition which has recently been given you. Your loving son, Race."[17]

The next month Race returned home, out of work and money, the earthquake having destroyed his latest employment hopes. He spoke to the young people of the 18th ward about the earthquake, describing its tremendous devastation.[18] He also helped his father, who could not type. "Spent most of the day on the biographical sketch, assisted by Race, who managed the typewriter and composed parts of the article. Completed the sketch and sent it to Bro. [George] Reynolds."[19] When Elder Whitney's time allowed, he helped his son: "Called on my son Race at his room in the Orpheum Hotel and had a good long talk with him."[20]

But he did not remain long in Salt Lake. "Race came to dinner. He leaves tonight for Los Angeles. . . . I let Race have $100 as a loan. He and his wife Rose have again separated. Thank the Lord!"[21]

In 1907 and 1908, Race spent time in both Portland, Oregon, and Los Angeles. Even though he worked, he always seemed to need more money, and his father helped him with it as he could. "Wrote to Race, sending him [a] money order for $20 as a gift from myself and wife."[22] Race continued trying to find someone to underwrite his operetta, considering it the most important personal possession that he had saved in the earthquake. He thought he had found some interested parties in Los Angeles.

Having been divorced from Rose Gloez a second time, Race soon met and fell in love with one Margaret Gallagher (also not a Latter-day Saint), the proprietor of a boarding house, and they became engaged. It was then and there that Race's alcoholism finally caught up with him. As his illness worsened, he informed his ever-attentive father: "In the afternoon I was on my way to the Tabernacle, expecting to speak there, but having heard that an important telegram was at the Western Union Office relating to Race, I went there instead. Race is in the hospital at Los Angeles and needs money for expenses."[23] And, "Sent to Miss Margaret Gallagher at Los Angeles $100 for Race."[24] The amounts of money Orson sent Race were considerable for the times, and quickly drained his resources. Yet his son grew worse. "The Tabernacle was thronged with many standing, when the conference resumed this morning. . . . In the afternoon Tabernacle meeting, I was given the first hour, and David O.

McKay followed me. I was greatly blessed by the Spirit and received many congratulations. Telegraphed to Eugene Lewis at Los Angeles to call in the elders for Race, who is very sick, and telegraphed Margaret Gallagher . . . in answer to an urgent letter from her on Race's account, that I would leave for Los Angeles Monday night."[25]

With the urgent call coming as it did at general conference time, Elder Whitney was obliged to skip some sessions. "Completed my preparation for going to Los Angeles and had so much to do that I was unable to attend the meetings of the conference, which closed this afternoon. In the evening, after dinner, called my family together, gave them a good 'talking to,' had prayers with them, bid them good-bye and at 8:30 p.m. started for the . . . depot to take my train . . . for Los Angeles. Went to bed at 10:30, but did not sleep till after the train pulled out. It was raining when I took my train."[26] In two days he had reached his destination:

> [Much of this entry is illegible] At 8 a.m. . . . reached Los Angeles and was met by Eugene Lewis who [illegible] me to Race's. . . . My boy is very sick but was overjoyed to see me and wept with delight. Stayed with him most of the day . . . and had some good talks with him. Met his fiancée, Miss Margaret Gallagher, who with her sister Nellie keeps this rooming house. Margaret is a sensible, modest, sweet, good little woman, and entirely devoted to Race. He could not be in better hands. Met a Dr. [illegible] who attends Race. . . . He pronounces Race's ailment [meritritria?]—a nervous disease, resulting from excessive use of alcoholic stimulants. . . . He [illegible words] (and is now better than when I was sent for) and it will take a long time to build him up again. During the day I walked around the city a little, visiting [illegible] points of interest. . . . Wrote letters home and at 7 p.m. retired, occupying Race's room at Hotel Francis, he having another in the same building.[27]

Elder Whitney spent time visiting with his son, and deciding what to do next: "Arose at 7:30 refreshed, having slept soundly. . . . Spent most of the day with Race, reading and conversing. Dr. [illegible] advises me to take him home, and I shall do so, if he [illegible]."[28] Once Race could travel, they would leave. "Spent the forenoon with Race, and wrote to my brother Horace G. about his condition; also telegraphed him. Lost my glasses and ordered a new pair. . . . In the afternoon went to Long Beach, where I rambled over the old scene, with a sad sweet feeling tugging at my lonely heart. . . . I will return to Salt Lake next week."[29] While in Los Angeles, Elder Whitney (who found his glassed the next morning), proofread his *History* manuscripts and conference talk, walked around, and visited with Race and his fiancé. "Received letters from Salt Lake, and ms [manuscript] of my conference address. Began revising it. Telegram came from Horace G., informing me that money I had sent for—$200—was at First National Bank awaiting my call. . . . Margaret Gallagher, Gene Lewis, and I gathered up Race's effects at his office. . . ."[30]

Some money he sent for soon arrived: "Drew from the First National Bank $200, sent me by wire from Salt Lake. Purchased railroad ticket for Race, and engaged Pullman drawing room for next Friday night when we shall depart for home. Wired Horace G. to that effect and also wrote him, and wrote to May and the family. Paid Margaret Gallagher $121, Race's hotel and laundry bills. His R. R. ticket was $30 and the Pullman drawing room $20."[31] The drawing room made the return trip to Salt Lake City more comfortable for both father and son. "Race and I both slept well. We had the drawing room of the Pullman Sleeper. . . . Race stayed in bed all day and his meals were brought to him. Toward evening he suffered severely. I administered to him. . . . I wrote to Margaret Gallagher concerning him. Race is restless and is not sleeping very well. Neither am I."[32]

Upon reaching their destination, Elder Whitney took Race home and personally nursed him for a couple of days, with help from his daughter Emily.[33] It seems that with his father's attention and care, and the ordeal he was enduring, Race found a better feeling growing within him toward the gospel his father had taught him. He soon asked for a priesthood blessing. "Worked on *History* in the forenoon, and in the afternoon went up to see Race. Wrote to Margaret Gallagher about him. Met with the *History* committee. . . . Elders B. H. Roberts and John Henry Smith, at my request, and by Race's desire, came up and we prayed for and administered to him. He suffers terribly, but is slowly gaining ground."[34]

Orson procured a wheelchair for Race, and visited him often

during the next three weeks.[35] At first Race seemed to be improving, but then took a turn for the worse, and he again had to be hospitalized. "Visited Race. He is no better. God alone can help him it seems to me."[36] The next day, "Visited Race at the hospital. They have put him in a cooler room . . . on the north side. He is about the same—rational and irrational by turns—on a liquid diet, very weak and helpless."[37]

It became a daily watch: "Was at the hospital twice during the day. Took a bouquet of flowers to Race in the morning. . . . Wrote to my daughter Helen, Sister Margaret Dusenberry, and Margaret Gallagher, Race's fiancée, in Los Angeles. Dr. Paul, Race's physician, phoned me that the end might come tonight. That was my own impression."[38] The end was not long in coming.

> At 7 a.m. or a little before, was summoned to the hospital. Race was failing. Received a second call to come quickly. Had slept but little; [illegible line] could and walked up to the hospital. Race had died at about 10 minutes [illegible] 7. He failed rapidly and died peacefully. He was nervous and delirious as he has been for days until about 12:30 when they gave him some [hyacine?] to quiet him, and from that time he was peaceful to the end. Spent the rest of the day making preparations for the funeral on Thursday, assisted by my brother Horace G. and the family. Received many callers during the day and evening.[39]

The funeral was impressive in both those who were attending and speaking.

> Went with my folks and friends to see Race at undertakers, Joseph E. Taylor's establishment. He looked calm and peaceful—much better than while suffering at the hospital, and prior to that time. . . . [illegible line] my home to the 18th ward chapel where the funeral service was held from 5 to 6:30 p.m. Bishop H. A. Clawson and counselors presiding. The speakers were Elders B. H. Roberts, J. Golden Kimball, and John Henry Smith. Opening prayer, President Francis M. Lyman; Benediction, Elder George F. Richards.[40]

Elder Whitney grieved deeply for his son, whose life had been so full of promise, but had led to so much heartache and disappointment. When assigned to visit a stake conference three days later, he refused to go. "Stayed in all day, going over Race's effects. Received a phone message from Hugh J. Cannon, notifying me that the Liberty Stake Conference was in session today, and that I was expected to be there. I excused myself. I have no heart to open my mouth in public today."[41]

Elder Whitney's mind naturally turned to the spiritual condition of his other children, as he hoped for better from them. Some two months later he wrote, "Bert's birthday. God bless him and make him a good man!"[42] The feeling was so strong upon him that despite his busy schedule, he adopted something resembling family home evening and scripture study: "At night called my family, and especially my boys, around me, and read to them from the Bible. It is my purpose to keep it up and teach my children and the children of the neighbors the scriptures."[43]

A year later, Elder Whitney did all that was left that he could for Race. "Spoke at the temple meeting at 9 a.m. and handed in my son Race's name for rebaptism."[44]

And then, "Spent [illegible] of the day in the temple, where I ordained my son Charles Byron Whitney to the office of elder, and re-ordained my son to the office of elder for and in behalf of my dead son, Horace Newel Whitney, Elder William W. Riter being mouth in Race's ordination. Byron and I then passed through the temple, he to receive his own endowments, and I to be endowed for "Race." . . . Joseph S. Peery was baptized for Race [on] Tuesday."[45]

Such were the choices of Race Whitney, and such were a contributing reason to why Elder Whitney pondered and taught the powerful doctrine quoted at the beginning of this chapter. He was personally invested in its truth and the hope it brought him and other faithful parents.

The month that Elder Whitney helped perform the vicarious temple work for his son Race, he felt great joy in the decisions made by another son: "Spent the forenoon on the *History* work and at 2 p.m. went with my son Byron to the temple, where I set him and others apart for their missions. Pres. F. M. Lyman, John Henry Smith, George F. Richards, Hyrum M. Smith, and Seymour B. Young were also present."[46]

He had no need to mourn this second son's course. "Worked as usual, and helped Byron to complete his preparation for departure. . . . This is my first missionary boy, and I am proud and happy, though a little sad over his departure. It is a day I have long waited for. God bless him, give him success, and return him home in peace and safety!"[47] Elder Whitney's desire was eventually granted. "Letters from my son Byron, his Mission President Franklin J. Hewlett, and Dr. Guy Carleton Lee. Byron is honorably released from his mission in South Africa, and is probably now on the ocean, or about to sail from Capetown for Liverpool. His health dictated a change of climate. Pres. Hewlett speaks highly of him, said he was as 'humble as a child,' ready to stay or go, as the Lord willed."[48] The homecoming was sweet: "My son Byron returned today from his mission to South Africa. . . . Went immediately home to meet and greet my dear boy. We had a joyful family gathering. Byron is some down in health, but is in the best of spirits, and returns home with a testimony of the truth, after 2½ years of faithful service."[49] Elder Whitney took pride in his son's accomplishment. "Went calling, with my sons Byron and Bert, during the forenoon. We called [on] . . . the First Presidency, to whom Byron gave a brief account of his mission, answering every question promptly and intelligently. The President said to him at parting, 'Honor your father and your mother.'"[50] The admonition was telling. Just over a year later, Elder Whitney officiated at Byron's temple marriage.[51]

Of his other children, most did not serve missions. Some were married in the temple as Ort desired, while others were not.[52] Some did later. He eventually was able to marry, or seal, in the temple, to worthy spouses his daughter Virginia, son Murray, and (but three months before he died) his son Wendell.[53] These occasions made him very happy.

One day when visiting his daughter Emily, with the spiritual welfare of his family on his mind, Elder Whitney used the occasion to the best advantage: "Took dinner with my family at the home of my son-in-law, Winslow Farr Smith, and during the afternoon, dinner being over and all seated round, I bore to them my testimony and enjoined upon them stricter obedience to the gospel."[54]

Chapter 16

Elder Whitney Goes to Work, 1906–1909

As the October general conference convened, Elder Whitney found himself, for the first time, sitting in a new and very visible location. He also received his first major Church-related committee assignments. "General conference opened in the Tabernacle at 10 a.m. Sat with the Apostles in the stand. Met with the First Presidency and the Apostles in the President's Office 9 a.m. where I was sustained as a member of the General Church Board of Education and as a member of the General Board of the Church Religion Classes."[1] Along with the routine meetings, Elder Whitney enjoyed the social aspects of his new calling:

> At 10 a.m. a special priesthood meeting convened in the Assembly Hall. . . . At 2 p.m. the Apostles met with the Presidents of missions in the temple and heard reports. . . .
>
> At 5 p.m. May and I joined the First Presidency, the Apostles, and their wives at President Winder's, where we had dinner, and then a sociable evening. Speeches were made by President Smith, President Winder, President Lyman, and most of the Apostles present.
>
> This morning President Edward J. Wood, of Alberta Stake, delivered to me a fur coat (cowskin) ordered by me in Cardston, Canada, last August. It was made in Montreal, and sells usually at \$100. I got it through Bro. Wood at [the] cost [of] \$65. I paid him \$20 on account, for which he is to send me a receipt.

> President Winder said, as President Smith had said in the Conference, that no mistake was made when the new Apostles were chosen, referring to our conference discourses.[2]

Late autumn arrived and with it the cold weather incident to travel, but he also received some good financial news. "Snowy and cold, as was yesterday. Spent the day making calls, nursing my cold, and making preparations for a two weeks trip to Panguitch and Kanab Stakes, upon which I start Thursday. Received today from the First Presidency a check for $200, payment in full for the copyright of my pamphlet 'The Mormon Prophet's Tragedy.' I had offered to donate the copyright to the Church, but the Presidency preferred to pay for it."[3]

At a Council meeting held before Christmas, Elder Whitney passed on a memento given him for President Joseph F. Smith: "In Council at the temple 10 a.m. Was appointed to attend Tooele Stake conference Saturday and Sunday next. Gave to President Smith a silver dollar sent to him by Patriarch Nathan Adams of Kanab, to help pay his fine of $300 in the district court."[4] President Smith was dealing with continued government persecution for living with his plural wives.

That Christmas, Elder Whitney was assigned to speak at the Salt Lake Tabernacle. "Arose just in time to catch a hack that was passing the hotel, and which took me to the train. Did not get breakfast, but thought the fast would do me good. I am to speak at the Tabernacle in Salt Lake tomorrow and I feel the need of divine aid. God help me. Arrived home about 1 p.m. . . . Retired early, being very weary, while the folks loaded the Christmas tree."[5] The next (Christmas) day: "At 11 a.m., attended the special Christmas service at the Tabernacle and delivered the address, the only one given, the rest of the program being musical. The Lord did help me. My address was described by the city papers as timely, eloquent, and powerful, and I was the recipient of numerous complements and congratulations."[6]

As a member of the Twelve, Elder Whitney needed to have his portrait painted. "Last day of the year. In the forenoon posed before artist John Hafen for my portrait. It is for the Temple, cost $125, and is paid for by the Church. . . . Posed again from 3 to 5 p.m. for

Hafen, and spent the evening at home with my family."[7]

January 2nd was the quarterly meeting of the Twelve, at which "President Lyman, during his address, warmly commended my labors as an apostle, said I had 'done magnificently,' etc. and borne my full share of the burden [illegible]."[8] Such words were a great comfort.

Then a new assignment came Elder Whitney's way; others were involved, but because of his particular talents, the effort would temporarily consume him. "At 10 a.m. in Council at the temple. After the regular proceedings, partook of the sacrament, as usual, after the quarterly meeting. Was named one of a committee to frame an answer to Senators J. C. Burrows and Fred T. Dubois, against their charges on the Smoot case."[9] Burrows and Dubois were bitter anti-Mormon U.S. Senators determined to disallow duly-elected Senator Smoot his seat in the Senate. To do so, they spread the standard anti-Mormon charges around Congress and the press. The purpose of the address was to formally and publicly refute their libel and state the true doctrines of the Church. When finished and approved, it would carry the authority of the First Presidency and adoption by the Church with sustaining vote.

The committee moved forward: "At ten a.m., met at the President's Office with the other members of the committee. Received instructions from the First Presidency and organized for work. I was elected chairman and Joseph Fielding Smith Jr. [as] secretary. The other members of the committee are B. H. Roberts, F. S. Richards, David O. McKay, James E. Talmage, LeGrand Young, Richard W. Young, and Nephi Morris. We will hold our meetings in the Templeton Building at the office of the First Council of Seventy. Held our first meeting at 3 p.m. today."[10]

The committee met frequently throughout January, with some further organization.

> Spent most of the day at home, writing. . . . On Friday last the Committee on Address adopted my suggestion to treat the subject in three parts and to subdivide the Committee as follows: O. F. Whitney, R. W. Young, and Joseph Fielding Smith Jr., on History and Character of the Mormon People; David O. McKay, James E. Talmage, and

> Nephi L. Morris, Religion and Priesthood including Polygamy and the Manifesto; and B. H. Roberts, F. S. Richards, and LeGrande Young, the Political [illegible] and Commercialism.[11]

By the end of January, progress had been made;

> In Council at the temple with the other Apostles, considering the question of the Seventies meeting on Sabbath mornings throughout the Church. We were in session from 10 a.m. till 1 p.m. From 2 till 5:30 p.m., met with the general Committee on Address and heard the reports of the general subcommittees. A committee on revision—O. F. Whitney, B. H. Roberts, James E. Talmage, and Nephi L. Morris was appointed, to sift and sort the various manuscripts, etc.; and report something for the general Committee to work on. All the ms [manuscript] was ordered to be typewritten.[12]

February continued with feverish committee work putting the "Declaration" document together. Yet other matters still found consideration:

> At the temple, 10 a.m., in council with the Apostles and First Presidency. No appointment, owing to Committee work. I will here state that yesterday afternoon I attended a meeting of the First Presidency and Apostles, at which Elder B. H. Roberts read to us an article on the immortality of the soul. It involved the trinity of the soul—a doctrine that I preached many years ago, and which I believe was revealed to me at Liverpool 25 years ago. I told the brethren of this yesterday, and that I had set forth the same doctrine in my poem *Elias*. That is, that man is intelligence, spirit, and matter, and the intelligence, unlike the spirit and the body, never was created.[13]

On February 20, good news came. "Reed Smoot, her [Zina's] brother, retains his seat in the U.S. Senate. The vote was taken today, and is in his favor by a vote of 43 to 27. Today I met with the general Committee on Address at 10 a.m., or with some of them."[14] Reed Smoot's victory was cause for rejoicing, but came with a high price. The Church had been put on trial in his name before the country.[15] Meanwhile, the Committee work was wrapping up: "Gave final revision to the address, 'Declaration and Defense' and gave it to the printer. Bro. B. H. Roberts, Nephi Morris, and I put the finishing touches to it, and Morris and I read the proofs."[16] The next day: "Held 2 p.m. meeting with the Committee. After some slight amendments, we adopted the address, and I was authorized to report it to the First Presidency as the product of our labors. We have held more than 50 meetings while preparing the document. I gave a copy to each of the First Presidency, with accompanying documents."[17]

With the main work on the document finished, Elder Whitney could again take stake conference assignments, with one to Idaho, where his friend George C. Parkinson was the stake president. While there, they experienced a miracle: "Arose at 8 a.m. Had slept well. Dreamed of Zina. . . . In the evening Bro. Parkinson and I called at Bro. Sol. Hales and administered to his daughter, Hattie Vilate (Mrs. Milton Thatcher). She had La Grippe [flu], and had not slept for 60 hours. She went right to sleep while I was blessing her, and later was reported free from pain."[18] They learned further results the next day. "After breakfast I blessed Bro. Parkinson's daughter Vera, who is nervously afflicted. He assisted me. . . . Pres. Parkinson saw me to the [train] station. He says the stake conference just closed is the best one they ever had. . . . Bro. Hales said this morning that his daughter to whom we administered last evening was "a new girl." It was a remarkable case of healing. The family shed tears of joy over it. I have felt the power of God all during the conference."[19]

Back in Salt Lake City, Elder Whitney helped prepare for general conference. "At 3:30 p.m. met with the Committee, First Presidency, and Apostles and completed the address or declaration. I was authorized to have it printed—1,000 copies for free distribution at conference time."[20] The next day he "met with Pres. Lund and Bro. Roberts and decided on the title of the pamphlet. Then gave it to the printer."[21]

As March ended, Elder Whitney was invited to speak at the funeral of a daughter of Moses Thatcher, the deposed former Apostle. Elder Whitney would be invited, but unable, to speak at his funeral some two-and-a-half years later. After being dropped from the Quorum of the Twelve for insubordination, Moses Thatcher was unable to realize his political aspirations of becoming a congressman or senator, and his final years he saw a gradual decline in health. Elder Whitney's presence and kind words at his daughter's funeral helped smooth a difficult rift:

> A bright and beautiful day, in contrast, they say, with the weather for a week preceding. . . . At 2 p.m. proceeded to the [Logan] Tabernacle, which was thronged in every part. The congregation was mixed, all classes, creeds, and conditions attending. Sister Langton had been known and loved by all. The stand and casket was a perfect bank of flowers. Moses Thatcher, the father [of the deceased], sat among the mourners. Bishop Guy Thatcher conducted the service, which was beautiful, sad, and impressive throughout. George Thatcher and choir rendered the music. Elder Joseph Cardon of the stake presidency offered the opening prayer, and the speakers were George Barber, James Langton, George Albert Smith, and myself. I was given most of the time, (as it had been announced that I would deliver the funeral sermon); the other brethren speaking briefly. During my remarks I referred to my friendship for and interest in Bro. Moses Thatcher and his family. It had a good effect. The entire family and many others expressed their gratitude and great satisfaction with all that was spoken. Mormons and Gentiles voiced their appreciation.
>
> In the evening I called on Bro. Thatcher and family, all of who, as well as the Langtons, thanked me warmly and even tearfully for the kind expressions concerning them and the funeral sermon over their dear departed one. . . .
>
> Going home, President Isaac Smith [stake president] and I conversed about Bro. Moses Thatcher and what might be done for him, and I advised Isaac to lay the matter before Pres. Joseph F. Smith.[22]

Moses had lost the privilege of exercising the Priesthood, but kept his membership in the Church, and he had been an active member in some respects. Elder Whitney's long friendship with him had helped to stabilize him and heal old wounds. At the next meeting of the Twelve, Elder Whitney tried to arrange aid for Thatcher. "At 10 a.m., met with my Quorum in the temple in our regular quarterly meeting. Eleven of the Twelve present, C. W. Penrose (in England) being the absent one. In speaking I made mention of Moses Thatcher and expressed the wish that something might be done for him."[23] Also at this time, he felt particularly close to his deceased wife: "Dreamed of Zina repeatedly. She seemed very near to me."[24] As the years passed, other dreams of her would follow.

With the arrival of the April general conference, the work of Whitney and other members of the "Declaration" committee could finally find fruition:

> Opening day of the general annual conference. At 9:30 I was at the *Deseret News* Office, where I received from the supervisor (Bro. Tingey) of the Job Printing Dept. 25 copies of the Declaration, which I was appointed yesterday to read; also 3 reading copies. Took them to the Tabernacle and delivered them to President Joseph F. Smith.
>
> On the way I met President Baxter, of Woodruff Stake and his counselor McKinnon. The latter informed me that his daughter, who was shot, was made whole by the blessing I gave her while at Randolph last winter. "She never felt a pang after it," he said.
>
> The meeting opened at 10 a.m. with a splendid discourse from President Joseph F. Smith, who introduced the subject of the Address, which I then read to the congregation. It took me just about one hour. My voice held out well and I received many compliments on the reading. I closed at 12:30 p.m. President Lyman moved for the adoption of the Address. Elder John Henry Smith seconded it and by a rising vote the vast congregation passed the resolution unanimously.[25]

Besides reading the address, Elder Whitney spoke at the last session. "At 10 a.m. today the Tabernacle was thronged above and below, with many standing. . . . Just before the meeting dismissed, I received the following note from President Smith, 'My dear Bro. Orson: This afternoon will be divided between John Henry Smith, yourself, and President Lyman—[illegible] not to exceed [30?, 36?] mts. [minutes] each. Joseph F.' May went with me to the afternoon meeting. The speakers were those named in the note, and President Smith, who closed the conference with a characteristic address and benediction."[26] [The late April and early May diary entries are mostly illegible.]

Memorial, or Decoration Day, found Elder Whitney meeting with the Brethren to hear a doctrinal paper written by Elder B. H.

Roberts. "In Council at the temple 10 a.m. No appointment, owing to my engagements Saturday and Tuesday. It was an all day session, the latter half of it devoted to the consideration of a theory advanced by Bro. B. H. Roberts as to how the Book of Mormon was translated."[27] Then he attended the funeral of Elder George Teasdale:

> In Council at the temple, 11 a.m. Appointed to attend Salt Lake Stake Conference Sunday. . . . At 2 p.m., went to the Assembly Hall to attend the funeral of Apostle George Teasdale, who died at 7:15 last Sunday evening. Acted with my brethren of the Twelve, as one of the pallbearers, and carried the casket from the hearse into the building, and out again. The attendance was not large owing to the rainy weather. I offered, by request of President Smith, the opening prayer. . . . At 5 p.m., attended a meeting at the President's Office where Reed Smoot read to us his reply to Senator Burrows to be published in the *New York Independent*.[28]

With conference concluded, as well his work on the Address, Elder Whitney was again free to attend stake conferences. "Took the 7:10 a.m. train for Ogden; was met at the depot by President Shurtliff and taken to his home. . . . In the forenoon meeting of the conference, which convened at 10 o'clock, in the [Ogden] Tabernacle, President Shurtliff, Andrew Jenson, and I were the speakers. I spoke for an hour and had a rich flow of the Holy Spirit, everybody delighted with my discourse."[29]

With Elder Teasdale's death, Elder Whitney was given charge of his temple prayer circle: "In Council from 11 a.m. till [blank] p.m. Appointed to Bingham Stake Conference next Saturday and Sunday. At 6:30 p.m., met with my old prayer circle (President Teasdale's circle) and presented my letter of appointment from the First Presidency dated July 22, 1907, as his successor. The brethren received me joyfully and sustained me, unanimously. I offered the opening prayer. By a coincidence, I was mouth [voice] in the opening prayer in the circle, this morning also—the Apostolic Circle."[30]

With the mantle of the apostleship upon him, Whitney's discourses seemed to carry an even greater spirit and power. "At 2 p.m., spoke in the Tabernacle, using the 76th Section, Doctrine and

Covenants, as the basis of my hour's discourse. President Winder, Bro. H. J. Grant, R. W. Young, and many others expressed their interest and pleasure in what I had said. In the evening, [I] had another splendid time at the chapel, thanks to the Spirit of the Lord."[31]

While traveling to his next stake conference in Wyoming, some adventure befell him, and nature gave emphasis to the words of his sermon:

> Arose at 7 . . . and at 8:15 started for Thayne, to hold a 10 o'clock meeting. It threatened a storm (had been thundering during the night) and we had not been long on the way when down it came—the worst storm I was ever out in. The lightning and thunder were terrible—one shock so near that our horses shied out of the road. It rained, and hailed a deluge. I felt very solemn, and prayed fervently several times for driving protection. Just before the tempest subsided we took shelter in a house by the roadside, being invited in by a Brother William Moultree. In half-an-hour or more, we resumed our journey, and opened meeting on time. . . . The storm continued, the deep thunders bellowing and the vivid lightning flashing, while I was speaking. President Burton added a few words, closing a very interesting meeting.[32]

In September of 1907 Elder Whitney penned one of the more perplexing notations found in his diary since his call to the apostleship: "'A change came o'er the spirit of my dream.' Spent the day in reading and private business. . . . A momentous interview, which may change materially my course of life, closed the day."[33] No further explanation is ever given, nor is the identity of the person he spoke with. Whether he may have meant that an opportunity to improve his financial status might become available, or perhaps something related to an ecclesiastical matter, is not known. It's hard to imagine a greater change to his life than that entailed by his call to the Twelve a year and a half before, considering the constant stake conferences, travel, Quorum meetings, literary or speaking assignments, succeeding diary entries, and his own autobiographical writings. All this indicates that his course of life did not substantially change, materially or otherwise, after this date. He became neither extremely rich nor poor and spent his life in the harness of the apostleship. If this notation referred in some way to his forthcoming brash flirtations with plural marriage, no actual marriage occurred. It would seem that whatever it was that may have happened, it probably did not.[34]

At a meeting of the First Presidency and Twelve that month, Elder Whitney was able to show off and win accolades for a new poem. "In Council at the temple 10 a.m. until 1:50 p.m. Submitted my poem, 'The Fair Demon[?],' to President Smith, who praised it, and read it aloud to the Brethren present. I gave it to him for publication in the *Improvement Era*, of which he is the chief editor."[35] Then a signal honor came to Elder Whitney: "With May, attended fast meeting in the temple. Miss Babcock, lately returned from Europe, was the first speaker, and President Smith closed. . . . Spent the afternoon at home, looking over my poem *Elias*, which I am about to have copied and sent east, possibly for publication. I learned that in the 18th ward priesthood meeting this afternoon, it was unanimously decided to name the new ward [illegible] in my honor, 'Whitney Hall.'"[36]

With general conference quickly approaching, President Joseph F. Smith found himself obliged to choose a new apostle. "Quarterly meeting of the Apostles in the temple, 10 a.m. till 4 p.m. A splendid time. All present spoke, namely F. M. Lyman, J. H. Smith, H. J. Grant, Rudger Clawson, Hyrum M. Smith, George Albert Smith, George F. Richards, Orson F. Whitney, and D. O. McKay. Absent: Reed Smoot, in Washington, and C. W. Penrose in Europe. Each of us was requested to submit for consideration a few names, from which might be selected, if the Spirit so indicated, a man to fill the vacancy in our Quorum caused by the death of Bro. Teasdale."[37] But seeking to fill up the Quorum of the Twelve was not the only matter from the meetings that concerned Elder Whitney.

> Regular Council in the temple, 10 a.m. to about 2 p.m. Received from Brother Heber J. Grant my released Deed of Trust held by Zion's Benefit Building Society. The amount paid by Bro. Grant was [$446.50?]. It was a gift to me, prompted by the generous heart of the giver, who may God bless for his kindness! It is understood that I may repay it with literary work—[writing] the *Life of Sister Grant*, Heber's mother—at my convenience. The gift came as a complete surprise, and was accompanied by a letter worth more than gold to me. Heber, it seems, was touched by some reference made by me during my remarks of yesterday, in which I spoke of my own financial

> condition, my lack of ability as a businessman and financier, and my appreciation of his ability to acquire wealth and his generous disposition to wisely and generously use it as distinct from the Spirit and conduct of some men who worship money, seek it for its own [illegible] sake, and hoard it with stingy meanness, etc., unwilling that a dollar should pass through their hands to bless others. [Illegible] of this matter, I gave permission, the other day, to Bro. George W. [illegible], who is a poor man, to publish and sell for his own benefit, my poem "Truth the Immortal." This at his solicitation. At the close of our meeting (about 3 p.m., today) we partook of the sacrament.[38]

Having his home's mortgage (for remodeling) paid off certainly helped Elder Whitney, who struggled economically with a large, dependant family and had nothing but his Church living allowance and proceeds from literary works to remunerate him. The kindness and generosity of his brother Bud, Elder Grant, and President Joseph F. Smith had helped Elder Whitney where he seemed unable to help himself. "Laid before Pres. Smith and counselors my financial condition, and they granted me an extra appropriation of $150 to pay my taxes and other items. This sees me out of debt, thank the Lord! I am now square with the world for the first time in many years."[39]

Then conference began. "Opening day of the general conference. I was about starting for the Tabernacle when I was summoned to my sister Helen's, to administer to her little son . . . threatened with cerebra-spinal meningitis as the result of an accident. Reached the Tabernacle in time for the opening exercises. . . . President Joseph F. Smith made the usual introductory address, a splendid and powerful discourse of about 50 minutes. . . . Later, attended the Seventies conference in the Assembly Hall."[40] Elder Whitney spoke in the last session of the day:

> The speakers at the conference this forenoon were Rudger Clawson, Hyrum M. Smith, and George Albert Smith. President Smith informed me that I was expected to speak in the afternoon, and that he wished me to take most of the time and speak upon a subject previously assigned to me, namely, a reply to Bishop F. S. Spaulding of the Episcopal Church who in a sermon at St. Mark's Cathedral, Sunday a.m. Sept 22, attacked Mormonism.

> In the afternoon the Tabernacle was thronged above and below. George F. Richards was told to take thirty minutes, and did so. I was then given the time and spoke for an hour and seven minutes. The Lord helped me and I had great freedom. President Smith thanked me, "God blessed" me, and I was showered with cordial congratulations. After meeting went with May up to my sister Helen's, whose little son Eugene died at about 5:45 p.m.[41]

The final session of the conference saw Elder B. H. Roberts impress Elder Whitney by speaking in his finest form, as well as the selection of a new apostle.

> Closing day of the conference. The congregation at the Tabernacle was so vast that an overflow meeting was held in the Assembly Hall. The quiet throng in the Tabernacle was addressed by Elder Reed Smoot (just back from Washington), David O. McKay, and Rulon S. Wells. . . .
>
> At the Tabernacle in the afternoon an immense congregation assembled, and overflow meetings were held in the Assembly Hall and in Barratt Hall. The first speaker at the Tabernacle was President Samual O. Bennion, of the Central States Mission, the second B. H. Roberts, who gave a masterful arraignment of Missouri, and a splendid historical [illegible], showing how that state had [illegible] in blood and [illegible] crime against the people of God. He quoted repeatedly from my own remarks of yesterday, and spoke for an hour and 15 minutes, perhaps longer.
>
> While he was speaking, a note from President Joseph F. Smith was passed around to the members of the Quorum of the Twelve, asking each of us to write Yes or No opposite the question, "Will Anthony W. Ivins suit you as a member of the Quorum of the Twelve?" or something to that effect. I answered Yes, and believe the answers were all in the affirmative. Bro. Ivins was on a list of seven names that I handed in, as requested, to the President last Wednesday morning.
>
> At the close of Brother Roberts magnificent address, President Smith presented the General Authorities, including Anthony W. Ivins as one of the Twelve Apostles, succeeding, or rather filling the vacancy caused by the death of Bro. Teasdale.
>
> A cranky Welshman in the congregation voted against President Smith, with [illegible] insulting remark, and was shown to the door

> owing to the disturbance that he continued to create. Otherwise the voting was all unanimous.
>
> After the meeting closed (and the conference), the First Presidency and Twelve retired to the Beehive House where Pres. Smith, assisted by the rest of us, ordained Bro. Ivins an apostle and set him apart as a member of the Quorum of the Twelve.[42]

October ended with Elder Whitney attending the Weber Stake conference (in Ogden) with Elder Heber J. Grant, and writing an article about President Smith for the *Juvenile Instructor*.[43] He found it increasingly common to be asked to write items needed by the First Presidency. "Fasted during the forenoon, and at 3 p.m. [I] was summoned to the President's Office to confer with the Presidency on the preparation of an article for the Christmas [*Deseret*] *News*."[44] Elder Whitney was also able to attend a local stake conference with the prophet: "A few minutes after 10 found me at the Granite Stake Tabernacle, in the priesthood and officers meeting of that stake. President Joseph F. Smith and Elder Rudger Clawson also present, and a splendid congregation numbering 1,000 brethren and sisters. President Smith was the first speaker, and virtually the only one; and he delivered one of the grandest discourses I ever heard. He took all the time, and we were all glad that he did."[45]

In early December, Elder Whitney dealt with a miserable illness: "Indoors, suffering from the worst cold I ever had—a sort of influenza. . . . Walked out a few minutes on Saturday and Sunday. Friday, was summoned to a special meeting at the President's Office, but could not go. [Presiding] Bishop William B. Preston [illegible] of failing mentality, was honorably released from office."[46] A few days later he was recovering enough to get out and around. "Stayed indoors till late in the afternoon, and then walked downtown. Read proof at [*Deseret*] *News* Office of "At Bridal Veil Fall,". . . Read in the [*Deseret*] *News*, on my return home, that the Presiding Bishopric of the Church was reorganized, with Charles W. Nibley in the chief place, and Orrin P. Miller and David A. Smith as his Counselors."[47] Elder Whitney learned the details later: "In Council at the temple 10 a.m. to 2 p.m. Learned full of the reorganization of the Presiding Bishopric and the release of James Jack as Church Treasurer, and the appointment of Arthur Winter in his stead. I was appointed to the Ensign Stake Conference for Sunday next; also to speak in the 17th ward Sunday evening. This is my wedding day [anniversary]."[48] President Joseph F. Smith would later make a humbling point regarding Charles W. Nibley's call to be the Presiding Bishop of the Church, a story that involved Elder Whitney peripherally. Nibley wrote,

> There was a large gathering at the McCune home, all of the Presidency and most of the Twelve and many other prominent members of the Church were there. Elder Orson F. Whitney had been called on to offer the invocation and in his prayer he prayed for President Smith as prophet, seer, and revelator, etc. A little later in the evening President Smith was called on for some remarks and he stated that to be called President of the Church was all the official title that he cared for, not that he did not hold the office of prophet, seer, and revelator, as well as President of the Church. He did hold those offices by the right of his calling and ordination and through the providences of the Lord he had been brought to the office, but he never sought it. He said he believed he lived, truly he tried to live, so that the Lord could reveal Himself to him, so that he would have the spirit of prophecy and that he would be able to fill the office of a Seer. All these gifts were his because of the position that he held. But he rather deprecated the idea of using these titles, which were sacred, too loosely and on each and every occasion. But he said, "More than once or twice in my life I have heard the voice which has given revelation to me, and never in my life did I hear it more plainly or clearly than when this man (pointing to me as I was sitting near his feet) was called to be [Presiding] Bishop of the Church." It would be difficult to tell what my feelings were when he uttered those words.[49]

With the advent of 1908, Elder Whitney summed up his circumstances:

> Another New Year opens. It finds me in fairly good condition, every way. My health is not all that it might be, owing to a recent attack of "the grip" [flu] or something akin thereto, but I feel grateful that my family is all well. I am practically free from debt; own the humble home I dwell in—160 Fourth Ave—and am firm in the faith of the Gospel. My children are all at home, except the married girls, Emily

> (who with her husband and baby lives in Salt Lake) and Helen, who is still in Sugar [City]. She expects to be a mother soon. Her husband, Billy, is with us today. Race, my oldest son and firstborn child, is still in Los Angeles, and has recently been sick.[50]

The next day, Elder Whitney went and "saw . . . the barber about a toupee."[51] Apparently his attempts to stimulate hair growth had failed and the balding process was winning the day.

Later in the month, Elder Whitney found himself visiting again with an old theological opponent and friend. "At 2 p.m., helped to set apart missionaries at the temple annex. At 4 p.m., had a pleasant interview with Bishop F[ranklin]. S. Spaulding, of the Episcopal Church, who came to my home for the purpose. We discussed my reply of last October to his sermon of September 22, and he explained that he had been misunderstood—that he had not intended to mention 'the purity of the family' in Mormondom, and ought to have used the word 'integrity' instead of 'purity' in his sermon. We also discussed Mormonism and Episcopalianism in general, and parted with mutual expressions of good will."[52] Whitney then reported their conversation to the Brethren. "In Council at the temple 10 a.m. to [blank] p.m. Appointed to Pioneer Stake Conference for next Sunday. Reported to the Council my interview with Bishop Spaulding. President Smith and the Brethren were pleased, and felt that I had done a good thing. During the meeting the question of my completing the *Student's History of Utah* came up and was discussed, and it was decided that I should go ahead with it and be released from taking 'long trips' until after its completion."[53] Within a short time, Whitney would find Spaulding sitting on a two-man committee of approval for another history book. Along with the history work, Elder Whitney received another short-term committee assignment: "Met at 9 a.m. with President Lund, B. H. Roberts, and James E. Talmage at the Historian's Office as a committee appointed yesterday to consider certain matters, respecting 'celestial marriage' as the term is used in the Idaho Constitution."[54]

Through February and March, Elder Whitney worked on the *Student's History of Utah*. A new proposal was then made: "A proposition was made me today by the *Deseret News* to write another history of Utah, suitable for [students?] in the 6th, 7th, and 8th grades of the public schools. I am to get $1,000 for it; 300 pages."[55] The new project became an immediate priority. "Wrote on the new *History of Utah* [making of a state], and completed chapter one, "The Great American Desert." My assistant in the *History* work is Frances Thomasson, who is a good typewriter and an intelligent critic. I find her help very valuable."[56]

The work moved forward: "Worked on *History*. Last evening, I handed to H. G., my brother, chapter [one?] of the school *History*, ready for printing. Today, copied chapter two."[57] And, "Answered letters from Bishop F. S. Spaulding and Prof. George M. Marshall, two of the Committee of Supervision on my *History*. At 10 a.m., met in the temple with my Quorum and the mission presidents. Was in session until 3 p.m. Received from the *Deseret News* the first proofs of my *History*. Chapter one—'The Great American Desert.'"[58] Elder Whitney sought advice from James E. Talmage (not yet an apostle) during general conference. "Opening of the 78th Annual Conference of the Church. Was at the Tabernacle in my place at 10 a.m. An unusually large congregation for a weekday gathering. President Joseph F. Smith, the first speaker. . . . During intermission I read to Dr. James E. Talmage chapter one of my *History*, and adopted certain amendments proposed by him."[59]

By mid-May, enough was done for Elder Whitney to submit the work to the school textbook convention. "Worked on chapter nine. The Text Book Convention, which has been in session here for several days, adjourned this evening, after adopting text books for the county district schools for the next five years. My little *History—The Making of a State*, went through almost by acclamation, everybody commending it on the three sample chapters presented, with the dummy showing size, style, etc. The aim will be to complete the work for introduction in the schools next fall. The *Deseret News* owns the book, but I was paid for writing it. It is a school history of Utah, suitable for the grammar grades."[60] Throughout April, May, June, and July, Elder Whitney labored on the history: "Worked on *History* and visited Race twice. Completed chapter 21 today and brought the Utah history up to date. May add a chapter on 'The Character of the State.'"[61]

At about the same time he was wrapping up his history work, Elder Whitney's son Race died of causes incident to alcoholism. This tragedy delayed the work some, but by August, Ort was moving forward again. "The *Salt Lake Tribune* of this morning pours out over a column of coarse, brutal, and lying abuse upon me for my remarks on 'liars' at the Tabernacle last Sunday. My discourse at the 18th ward chapel Sunday evening gave much satisfaction to all right-thinking people. Read final proofs of the school *History of Utah* [illegible line]."[62] Then, "In Council at temple 10 a.m. to 2 p.m. I agreed to go to the [illegible] conference at Payson Saturday and Sunday. At 3 p.m., attended a Board of Education meeting at President's Office, and was summoned by phone to the *Deseret News* Office to give final glance at and OK the last forms of the *History* before it went to press. Today, therefore, I complete my labors upon the work began last April. Afterwards my appointment was changed from [illegible] to Box Elder."[63] The completed work was soon in print. "Saw the first books (*History*) from the Bindery, and took one with me to Brigham City."[64] As soon as he could, Elder Whitney passed the joy around: "In Council at the temple 10 a.m. to [blank] p.m. Presented to the First Presidency and the Twelve, for the *Deseret News*, each a copy of the school *History*."[65]

In early December, another enigmatic notation is present in the diary. "Worked on *History of Utah*. Talked with Lorenzo Snow."[66] This statement could have meant one of two things: that Elder Whitney had a sublime spiritual experience in which he was blessed to communicate with his deceased friend and mentor, or it could mean that he spoke with one of two sons of the late prophet, both bearing his name.

With April came general conference, where Elder Whitney spoke despite some illness. "I was the opening speaker in the Tabernacle this morning. . . . My text was taken from the Declaration of Independence. The Lord was with me. . . . At 6:30 p.m., attended a general priesthood meeting in the Tabernacle. Went home and retired, feeling quite unwell."[67] Then he took it easy. "Sick with influenza. Could not attend the closing day of conference, nor the special priesthood meeting that followed. Wednesday evening, with my wife, attended the usual dinner party at Pres. Winder's and recited, but was hardly able to be there."[68]

By May, Elder Whitney was well and back to work, though he found his latest work under attack from the enemy. "Worked as usual. My attention was called to an editorial article in the *Salt Lake Tribune* of Friday morning, making a mendacious assault upon my school *History of Utah—The Making of a State*."[69] He immediately replied, "Spent the day answering the scurrilous attack by the *Tribune* on my book."[70] And, "Worked on *History* and sent letter (written yesterday) to the *Tribune* editor, Col. Nelson."[71] Elder Whitney disliked leaving "scurrilous" public attacks unresolved.

Chapter 17

New Polygamy, Evolution, and Laura Hickman, 1909–1910

In 1909, the First Presidency decided to begin cracking down in earnest on cases of new polygamy that arose since President Joseph F. Smith issued his official statement on plural marriage, commonly called the second manifesto, in 1904.[1] Both Presidents Woodruff and Smith, as well as President Snow's counselors, had given authorization, on a limited basis, for some new plural marriages in Mexico, Canada, and on the high seas (outside the boundaries of the United States), since the first manifesto of 1890. But with his official declaration, President Smith determined to put a final end to all new polygamy, and he therefore assigned the Quorum of the Twelve to investigate and to impose disciplinary measures as warranted.[2]

Because Elder Whitney was a member of that Quorum, he found himself involved in the proceedings. However, this assignment was not one that he desired and his heart was not in it. He was a firm believer in the doctrine and practice, having been a polygamist himself for some years and having unsuccessfully attempted to become one again more than once since the death of his first wife.

During most of the years that he and his Quorum were investigating and disciplining men for new polygamy, Elder Whitney was actively courting a potential plural wife himself, one Laura Hickman, with whom he fell in love and carried on an intermittent platonic relationship for near eleven years. Elder Whitney lived in a different time than his modern apostolic counterparts; the reason he was able to court Laura in semi-secrecy was because her family, especially her brothers, also believed in plural marriage. But there was no physically immoral component to their relationship. From what we know, it seems to have existed in a purely intellectual and emotional realm. Somehow, while seeing Laura, Elder Whitney was able to carry on his many Apostolic duties and preach with the same vigor as ever. Yet all was not well, and some problems developed, as will. The drama and complexities of life did not desert Whitney upon his call to the Twelve.

Mary Laura Hickman

July found Elder Whitney and the Quorum of the Twelve beginning their disciplinary measures. "In Council most of the day, investigating rumors as to polygamy."[3] And, "In Council all day in the temple over the polygamy rumors."[4]

Then Elder Whitney's wife's mother passed. "May, my wife, who has been staying with her mother the past few nights, sent for me this morning, stating that the end was near. I went over at once, and found her mother gradually sinking. I have blessed her frequently of late and kept her name in the prayer circles at the temple. Wednesday, we prayed that she might be released and depart in peace. Mother passed away peacefully at 11:20 a.m., surrounded by her family at her home. . . . I wrote a notice of her death and took it to the *Deseret News*."[5]

With the funeral behind him, Elder Whitney was free to travel to Canada that August with President Francis M. Lyman of the Twelve.

Along with visiting the Canadian stakes, one of their main purposes was to visit a new polygamist. "Arose at 7 a.m., and after breakfast we started on our return to civilization. At Fish Creek Ranch, Pres. Lyman and I, as per prior arrangement, had an interview with Alpha J. Higgs, whose flight from Salt Lake with Elizabeth Badger, after a supposed plural marriage, has created a sensation. Pres. Lyman told him he was living in adultery. Bro. Higgs admitted nothing, declined constantly to make any statement, and we left him to return to Mountain View, 7 or 8 miles away, where he is temporarily employed. He felt bad. I pity him, and told him I wished I could help him out of his trouble."[6]

While in Canada, Elder Whitney learned that an old friend had died.

> Spent the forenoon at the office of the stake presidency, writing to Pres. Smith and council a report of the Alberta Stake conference. . . . Pres. Lyman and I had our pictures taken. . . . Pres. Lyman told me today that my discourse yesterday afternoon was superb. He said it was a remarkable manifestation of God's power, and that we had been blessed abundantly—remarkably—during this visit to Canada. I feel so too. . . .
>
> I forgot to state that this morning the following telegram was handed to me by Bro. L. A. Wilson. "Logan, Aug. 22, 1909. O. F. Whitney, Cardston. [Illegible] father [Moses Thatcher] died last night. Entire family wish you to speak at funeral, Thursday next. Answer. Moses Thatcher [Jr].
>
> I was answered thus: Cardston, Aug. 23, 1909. Moses Thatcher Jr. Logan.
>
> Much regret. Important engagements prevent. Love and blessings to all.
>
> Francis M. Lyman, Orson F. Whitney

President Lyman and Elder Whitney returned on September 1st.[7] The next day, Elder Whitney received perhaps his most important doctrinal writing assignment from the prophet. "President Smith commissioned me to prepare an article on 'The Origin of Man,' for the *Liahona* and *Elders Journal*."[8] Whitney moved forward as requested: "Took the 8:15 a.m. train for Salt Lake . . . and after lunch at home worked with Frances [his secretary] on the article for the First Presidency, 'The Origin of Man.'"[9] Over the next several days, he finished it. "Completed my article on man's origin and listened with others at [the] President's Office. James E. Talmage now reading on 'The Great Apostasy.'"[10]

Elder Whitney's task had been quite mentally taxing: "Ensign Stake Conference. Attended the morning meeting in the Assembly Hall. . . . In the afternoon, at the Tabernacle, I was the only speaker. My theme, the Book of Life. Had good freedom, though somewhat fatigued from a hard week's work on my literary task—'The Origin of Man.'"[11]

Then it was time for the prophet to hear it. "Today I read to the First Presidency the article on 'The Origin of Man.' They were pleased with it, and Pres. Smith thanked me. It will be read again to the Twelve (with the Presidency) and some of our Church school brethren."[12] President Smith wanted the piece to be thoroughly reviewed: "Read to the Presidency and others my article, 'The Origin of Man.'"[13] And three days later, "Worked on *History* and read ms [manuscript] of revised article 'Origin of Man' to Dr. Talmage, Dr. Widstoe, and President Brimhall."[14] On October 14, the First Presidency put some finishing touches on it. President Anthon H. Lund recorded, "The [First] Presidency read the article on the origin of man, written by Orson F. Whitney. It was much improved from the original. As it will go out under our names, the Presidency made a few changes."[15] A week later, the document went before the Twelve also. "Our meeting at the temple lasted five hours. The statement as to our position on the origin of man was read and sanctioned by the Twelve."[16]

This document was signed by the First Presidency and published in the November 1909 *Improvement Era*. Although Elder Whitney wrote it, its formal approval by the Twelve and the First Presidency places their authority upon it, and Elder Whitney became but one name among all his Brethren to approve it. The document has stood as the foundational statement of the doctrine of the Church for over a hundred years. It has been discounted, marginalized, misinterpreted, and attacked by those in and out of the Church who disagree with it, but remains safely above the fray as the approved position of the Church on the origin of man.[17] Perhaps the most pointed and powerful portion of the document states,

> It is held by some that Adam was not the first man upon this earth, and that the original human being was a development from lower orders of the animal creation. These, however, are the theories of men. The word of the Lord declares that Adam was "the first man of all men" (Moses 1:34), and we are therefore in duty bound to regard him as the primal parent of our race. It was shown to the brother of Jared that all men were created in the beginning after the image of God; and whether we take this to mean the spirit or the body, or both, it commits us to the same conclusion: Man began life as a human being, in the likeness of our Heavenly Father.
>
> True it is that the body of man enters upon its career as a tiny germ embryo, which becomes an infant, quickened at a certain stage by the spirit whose tabernacle it is, and the child, after being born, develops into a man. There is nothing in this, however, to indicate that the original man, the first of our race, began life as anything less than a man, or less than the human germ or embryo that becomes a man.
>
> Man, by searching, cannot find out God. Never, unaided, will he discover the truth about the beginning of human life. The Lord must reveal Himself, or remain unrevealed; and the same is true of the facts relating to the origin of Adam's race—God alone can reveal them. Some of these facts, however, are already known, and what has been made known it is our duty to receive and retain.[18]

During the time Elder Whitney was busily preparing "The Origin of Man" article for the First Presidency, another notable event took place. He was able to meet the President of the United States, who seemed to impress him favorably. "In Council at the temple from 10 a.m. to 2:15 p.m. No assignment owing to the visit of President [William Howard] Taft. From 3 p.m. to 5 p.m., met with the Council of the Twelve (7 members) and Bro. Matthias F. Cowley. Before separating, the Apostles present sanctioned the nomination (by the First Council of Seventies) of Elder Ben E. Rich to succeed President George Reynolds (deceased) in that council."[19] The nomination was later changed to Levi Edgar Young. Evidently Rich's late polygamous relations became an obstacle to unanimous selection.[20]

The next day Orson "went to Saltair on President Taft's special train at 9:60 a.m. Met and shook hands with the President on the floor of the Saltair Pavilion. At 11 a.m., attended a special organ recital at the Tabernacle, in honor of President Taft."[21] And the next day, "Heard President Taft at the Tabernacle (a good sensible talk). . . ."[22] The local Salt Lake anti-Mormon ministerial group became furious that President Taft associated with the Mormons.[23]

After Taft departed Utah, October general conference convened. This particular conference held a few dramatic moments. One of them was President Joseph F. Smith's sermon: "Eightieth Semi-Annual Conference of the Church opened in the Tabernacle at 10 a.m. A vast congregation. President Joseph F. Smith was the first speaker. His discourse was powerful and timely—the care of the youth being the principal theme and home industry second. False prophets was the concluding part of his discourse."[24] Another memorable talk involved an apostle that had been enduring severe mental and nervous issues for some time, keeping him from his regular duties in the Quorum. Those present listening little knew what he had been, and would again, endure. "Conference continued. . . . In the afternoon Elder George Albert Smith, who has been disabled for several months, spoke a few words."[25] Lastly, Elder B. H. Roberts gave a talk that did not sit well with the Brethren, including Elder Whitney, who counted Elder Roberts as a close friend. Whitney's private reaction says, "Conference continued. . . . The address of Bro. Roberts was eloquent, but was not imbued with the Spirit of the Lord. It caused sorrow to his friends, and doubtless gave aid and comfort to the enemy. . . . President Joseph F. Smith closed the conference with a few timely remarks, during which he read from the prayer uttered at the dedication of the Kirtland Temple. His closing words were a dignified and telling rebuke to the foolish remarks made by some of the brethren. God forbid that I should ever deserve such a reproof. I want to strike my blows on the right side of the fence, and use what strength the Lord has given me in building up, and not pulling down, His work. Amen!"[26]

A week later, a repentant Roberts discussed his error with the First Presidency. President Lund wrote, "Bro. Roberts came in and told the President that if his speech was radically wrong he would let it be left out of the conference pamphlet [report]. President Joseph F. Smith said to him to submit it to me, and what I suggested [to change] would meet his mind. I told Bro. Roberts to make what changes he desired and we would go over it together."[27]

That November, Elder Whitney renewed his association with Josiah E. Hickman. Consequently, these two men would spend many hours together over the rest of their lives and build a strong bond of friendship. Josiah Hickman wrote, "Apostle Orson F. Whitney was the speaker at our exercises. It was a very commendable address. He stayed with me. The next day I was closeted with him until nearly 3 p.m. I learned some things which I had not been fully informed on before. He, like myself, knows that authority has been given to perform plural marriages since the [1890] manifesto. He says the Twelve are united in putting it [polygamy since 1904] down. He has revised his poem—*Elias: An Epic of the Ages*. He is now writing a school history of Utah."[28] Whitney and Hickman related to each other on a spiritual and intellectual level of mutual trust and affinity, and he confided to Hickman matters that he withheld in plainness from his own diary or later removed.

The new year, 1910, started with the Quorum of the Twelve investigating cases of new polygamy. One sign that Elder Whitney did not enjoy being part of the inquiries was that he said (in his diary) very little about them. For instance, "In Council with my Quorum on the Israel Barlow Jr. case, suspected of polygamy. We sat from 10 a.m. till 12:30 p.m., and then took recess till 3:30. . . . The inquiry in the Barlow case was resumed at 3:30. He was disfellowshipped."[29] The Quorum returned to his case twice in February.[30] Often, if a "new" polygamist came before the Twelve and lied to them, for whatever reason, they were excommunicated.

During January, Elder Whitney was again given a rush literary assignment. "While at work, as usual, [I] was notified by Secretary Gibbs and subsequently by President Joseph F. Smith that an article on 'Mormonism' for the *Catholic Encyclopedia*, now being published in New York City, must be prepared at once, and that it was desired [that] I should write it. I answered the President that I would drop everything else and put the article right through. 'God bless you,' he said."[31] Within a week he had it ready: "Completed, this forenoon, the article for the *Catholic Encyclopedia*, and I delivered it to President Joseph F. Smith. . . ."[32] President Smith passed it on, hopeful it would do some good. "In Council, at the temple 10 a.m. to 3:30 p.m. Assigned to Summit Stake Conference. President Smith reported that my article for the *Catholic Encyclopedia* had been accepted by Dean Harris without an alteration, and forwarded to New York City."[33] Later it was learned that someone working with Dean Harris, the local Catholic prelate, altered part of the article negatively, before it was published in the *Catholic Encyclopedia*, causing irritation with all involved.[34]

By mid-March, the oldest counselor in the First Presidency neared the end of his days. "Later visited President John R. Winder and blessed him, Bishop Nibley having first offered family prayer. I read by Pres. Winder's request the hymn "Lord, We Come before Thee Now," and then we prayed. Heard a sweet voice say, 'You're my darling, aren't you,' in a dream."[35] One might suppose that Elder Whitney felt he heard his wife Zina's voice from beyond the veil, though he did not so indicate. He and May attended President Winder's funeral at the end of the month.[36] For a reason not given, Elder Whitney decided to sell some property that he had owned for a long time. The sale made him the richest he had ever been in his life. "Accepted an offer from Jesse Knight, of Provo, made through his agent, Rulon S. Wells, for the purchase of my 80 acres desert land over Jordan, opposite Sandy. I have held it and paid taxes on it since November 1887. Knight's offer is $1,250."[37] He then invested most of it. "Loaned $1,200 to the Consolidated Wagon and Machine Company, taking their note bearing interest at 6 percent, payable quarterly. Gave May $25 for a dress and invested a similar amount elsewhere."[38] It was unusual for Orson to have money to spare.

After his talk at the April general conference, Elder Whitney relished a compliment given him by one he admired: "Conference continued. . . . I spoke 20 minutes, the Lord was with me, and I was warmly congratulated by many. President [Joseph F.] Smith leaned over to our stand and said, 'Orson, I could have listened for an hour longer. It was altogether too short.'"[39] At the conference, President Smith called his cousin, Elder John Henry Smith, into the First Presidency as Second Counselor, and his son, Joseph Fielding Smith

Jr., as the newest member of the Quorum of the Twelve.[40] At the next meeting of the First Presidency and the Twelve, they were welcomed into their new positions: "In Council 10 a.m. to 2 p.m. No assignments. . . . Anthon H. Lund as First Counselor, John Henry Smith as Second Counselor, and Joseph F. Smith Jr. as an apostle and one of the Twelve were set apart (the last named ordained) all by President Joseph F. Smith; the remainder of the Council assisting. During the subsequent proceedings, Charles W. Penrose was released from presiding over the European Mission, and Rudger Clawson appointed to succeed him. Worked on *History* until 5 p.m. and then took May to the Beehive House, where we took dinner and spent the evening, with a select company, including the leading Brethren and their wives."[41]

Later that month, Elder Whitney spoke at the funeral of the wife of his old friend and Utah's first governor, Heber M. Wells.[42] Wells later remarried outside the Church, disappointing Elder Whitney. Then, while he was visiting some friends, their stovepipe fell over, "burying all beneath, including myself, in soul-sickening soot. Dug myself out and departed at an early hour. Spent the afternoon in bed and the dumps. . . ."[43] Elder Whitney, for a reason he did not give, also removed his beard, becoming clean-shaven for the first time in thirty years.[44] (He did not remain beardless; later photographs show a stubble or short beard.)

Then, Elder Whitney was able to participate in another miracle: "Administered again to little Waldemar Clayton, threatened with appendicitis, and took his name to the temple to be prayed for."[45] The next day he rejoiced, "Waldemar Clayton has been healed by the power of God. No operation necessary. Doctors all astonished."[46] Elder Whitney himself visited a doctor, a son of President Snow, to remedy one of his own ailments. "At 9:30 [I] kept an appointment with Dr. Lorenzo W. Snow, who cured me of partial deafness, by [suctioning?] out my right ear. I was instantly relieved."[47]

In early May the Quorum of the Twelve investigated Judson Tolman, a very elderly stake patriarch who had taken it upon himself to marry several women to men in plural marriages, under an assumed authority that he admitted he did not possess. "In regular Council until 3 p.m. Assigned to Juab Stake Conference at Nephi, to leave Saturday morning. From 3:45 to 6:30 p.m., sat with my Quorum on the Tolman case."[48] Tolman is one who was not excommunicated until it was learned that he lied to the Twelve by telling them that the plural marriages he had performed, and the plural wife he had married, were pre-1904.[49]

A major milestone arrived when Elder Whitney finally finished his history. "Completed my *Popular History of Utah*, so far as first draft is concerned."[50] He then did a proof on it and helped the publisher with illustration placement, and was paid the last installment owed him.[51]

Elder Whitney arrived late at a stake conference that summer, one of the few times he was happy not to speak: "Took the . . . train for Clearfield and entered the conference meeting at 11:15. Hyrum M. Smith was speaking and continued to the close, not knowing I had arrived. I was glad and he sorry, for the heat was intense and speaking difficult. He would fain have shared the time. Attendance about 700. Every tomato box occupied. . . . It was awfully hot but a good meeting. Everybody glad and gratified. Took the 4:49 motor line home."[52]

Then came the fateful days, whether for good or ill, that Orson Whitney became better acquainted with the younger (thirty-six-year-old, single sister of Josiah: Mary Laura Hickman. "My birthday again. I am 55. Spent the forenoon . . . working on footnotes for the *History*. . . . Met Laura Hickman at State Bank Corner, just getting on car for Union Station, returning to her house in Benjamin."[53]

Two days later Orson visited her at home; an occasion that would impact the next decade of his life. "Byron's Birthday—19. He is . . . filling a mission, and is doing well. At 10 a.m. I attended the temple fast meeting, and was one of the speakers. At 4:10 p.m., took the Salt Lake Route for the south and at Provo mailed on train a letter to Chicago written after leaving Salt Lake. About 7 p.m., got off at Benjamin (my first visit to the place) and Thomas Daniels drove me to Hickman's (the only hotel [boarding house] in the place) where I was kindly entertained. Spent the evening conversing on poetry, reciting, etc., with members of the household."[54] Orson Whitney had enjoyed himself socially before, often during stake conference visits, and was often the life of the party. But on this extended visit he became captivated by one member of the large family in particular: "Wrote to May, and spent the day revising *Elias*, assisted by Laura Hickman."[55] He spent the next day doing the same thing. The day after that, he was to go home. "Intended returning home today, but missed my train. Spent the day reading canto 10 and epilogue of *Elias*, and later in reading 'It Never Can Happen Again' and in recitations, singing, conversation, etc. Retired about midnight."[56] Orson enjoyed himself immensely: "Read to Laura 'It Never Can Happen Again.' She drove me to the station, where I caught the 3:20 train for Salt Lake."[57]

On arriving home, Orson wrote the first of many letters to make their way between them. "Wrote to Prof. Josiah Hickman and to his sister [Laura]."[58] The Hickman family was large, and some of them went by their middle names. Leslie and Francis (both men), Josiah, and Laura were those that Orson became the best acquainted with. All were very well educated, receiving more post-high school education than most people of their day did. They had been or were students at Brigham Young College in Provo (now BYU), or were schoolteachers and principals. Josiah earned a doctorate and became a well-known figure in Utah educational circles. They all loved poetry, music, recitation, oratory, and lofty, highbrow literature. Orson, who spent much of his life fighting depression, felt comfortable and happy with this family. To be with them was enthralling, especially when one of them was single, smart, and beautiful. Ort could not forget his holiday at their home.[59]

His next stake conference happened to be near where Josiah lived. "A bright and beautiful day, after yesterday's rain. . . . In the afternoon a . . . congregation assembled. Speakers: . . . myself and Elder Gibbs. He started for home at 5 p.m. and I went with Prof. Hickman up to the post (Old Fort Cameron), now Murdock Academy, where he lives. While awaiting supper, we walked to the new Academy building, now in course of construction, and I told him of my visit to Benjamin, etc. He is my friend."[60] Elder Whitney spent several days with Hickman, reading and talking: "At Prof. Hickman's reading to him *Elias*, over which he is enthusiastic, pronouncing it 'a wonderful poem.' So thought his sister Laura, at Benjamin. While at his home began and all but completed a humorous poem

'The Village Siren,' and left him a copy. He gave me pictures of his family 1907–8."[61] One of the subjects that Elder Whitney and Josiah discussed in-depth was the work of the Quorum of the Twelve regarding new polygamy. Hickman explained,

> Apostle Whitney came Sunday and stayed with me until Wednesday evening. We had an excellent time together. He read most of his *Elias: An Epic of the Ages*, to me. He is reviewing it and improving it for re-publication. It is truly a masterpiece of art. I feel it stands with Milton's *Paradise Lost.* He read to me part of three days. The rest of the time we discussed various subjects. He is a very intellectual man. He is truly a poet, orator, and prophet.
>
> He told me of his visit to Mother's home [in Benjamin]. He was there four days. He has written a very humorous poem of his visit there. He thinks the world of Laura. I find he has much the same opinion of our [Church's] situation [that abandoning plural marriage was wrong] as I have. . . . Though he acquiesces in the policies of the Twelve, yet he is not heart and soul with them. He feels that we are cowardly and are on the run; that when the scare [threats of persecutorial legislation] of Washington [D.C.] begins, we begin to buckle rather than do our duty and fear God only. He does not believe those who have gone into that principle of late [since 1904] are committing adultery. He says that they [the Twelve] are not cutting brethren off [excommunicating] for entering it [instead disfellowshipping them], but in one or two cases they did [excommunicate] because (as in Higgins' case) they would not answer their questions. He has some very advanced ideas on religious subjects. They are really embodied in his [poem] *Elias.*[62]

For whatever reason, Orson did not explain himself nearly so clearly in his own diary, and Josiah Hickman's record is needed for clarification. It also helps explain why Orson let himself associate with Laura to the extent he did.

After leaving Hickman, Orson started for Salt Lake City. "Arrived at 6:30 a.m. Went home, bathed, and breakfasted, and attended Council 10 a.m. to 1:30 p.m. No appointment. Sent copy of the '[Village] Siren' to the subject [Laura]."[63] We can only speculate at the comic content of the verse about Laura. Within a week, Whitney had written to Laura and bumped into one of her brothers.

"Met Francis Hickman on the street. He is principal of Emery Stake Academy at Castle Dale."[64] Laura always wrote back: "Communication from Laura Hickman asking information. In Council from 10 a.m. to 2 p.m. Assigned to Woodruff Stake."[65] Shortly thereafter, Whitney "recited, at [Francis] Hickman's 'The Village Siren,' much to the amusement of him and his wife and his sister, Eunice Richardson."[66] Then he sent Laura a gift: "In Council with the Apostles, in the temple 10 a.m. to 2 p.m. . . . Book to Laura Hickman."[67]

With the investigations by the Quorum of the Twelve going on, those, such as Josiah Hickman, who had taken plural wives since the 1890 manifesto occasionally found themselves the subject of unwanted publicity. Josiah wrote, "[There is] a very false rumor to the effect that I was cut off the Church for polygamous marriage of recent date or that I had married someone. This report has gotten such a hold that it is virtually all over Zion. Many are the various comments pro and con over it. Apostle Whitney wrote me to the effect that he had had to brand it as a lie in Salt Lake. The spirit of the lie is broadcast and is producing a great unrest amid the people. The *Tribune* is dishing me up in editorials in a most scandalous way."[68] Hickman was lucky he had Elder Whitney to run interference for him with the Twelve. He had married a plural wife in 1902, just two years before issuance of the second manifesto.

As August ended, Orson found himself headed south to Benjamin. "Took the 10:15 train for Provo, and spent today there. Met Winslow, my son-in-law, at the barber shop. Took the 6 p.m. train for Benjamin and spent the evening with the Hickman's. Thomas Richardson, husband to Eunice Hickman . . . drove me from the station to the hotel, and took supper with the family, as I did. Conversed with Laura and her mother until about 11 p.m. and then returned."[69] The next day, "Arose early, and after breakfast walked in the fields. Returning had some interesting conversations with Laura, her mother, and her married sister, Eunice Richardson. After dinner at about 3 p.m., Laura drove me to the train . . . and I returned to Salt Lake. . . ."[70] From later clues, the probability is that one of the subjects that Orson discussed with Laura and her family was science and philosophy, as contrasted with scriptural truths. While attending the University of Chicago, Laura became imbued with worldly theories of higher criticism (that the supernatural miracles as described in the Bible were really fictional accounts) and the theory of evolution. She eventually extricated herself from the atheistic notions that had ensnared her, and rekindled her testimony of God and Mormonism. For his part, the sources suggest that during the time he spent with her, Whitney fell in love. "Spent the afternoon going over and destroying old letters. Letter to Laura. (Sentimental)."[71] Elder Whitney does not explain either the content of the letters or his reasons for destroying them. If they related to reincarnation, Charles W. Stayner, or were love letters passed between a potential plural wife such as Georgiana, Maude May Babcock, M. A., or V., it would explain his desire to destroy them. "Attended and spoke at the fast meeting, in the temple, and spent the afternoon at the Historian's Office, continuing the literary slaughter of yesterday."[72]

That October, Elder Whitney began writing what he variously called a novel, a poem, and a romance, about Laura.[73] He had big ideas for it. "General conference. Pres. Joseph F. Smith was present (he has been ill for a month), and spoke with power. . . . Worked at the *News* Office and at home upon my story: a religious and philosophical romance, designed to present, in a way to enlist the attention of the youth of Israel and the world at large, the views of the Latter-day Saints regarding life—past, present, and future, and the relationship of each to each."[74] Whitney would later revise his thesis, and narrow the plot to a love story between a hero and a heroine, and her troubling encounter with higher criticism and atheism. The foreword states, "This poem has a definite purpose. To combat the influence of the so-called 'Higher Criticism,' which is indoctrinating with hurtful effect the minds and hearts of many of the youth—that is its paramount aim. The story form is chosen to make the theme more attractive and insure wider perusal, especially on the part of young people. The reader, while absorbing the romance, will partake necessarily of the instruction." In the synopsis he wrote, "The heroine is a Western girl, born and reared in the region of the Rocky Mountains, beautiful and accomplished, but tinged with atheism, imbibed at the college where she completed her education. The hero is a New Englander, a Harvard graduate, who, from an independent attitude toward creeds and churches, is won to the religion of Jesus

Christ, and endeavors to convert the lady of his love. His vocation, like hers, is that of teacher."

The semblance to Laura Hickman is unmistakable. Furthermore, "The New England youth and the fictitious narrator of the story were college chums, and it is through the latter that the former, while on a visit to the West, becomes acquainted with the young woman whom he recognizes as his fate. The mutual relations of the pair, with the pros and cons of the great problem dividing them—the problem of atheism versus religion—form the backbone of the narrative."

Elder Whitney named his poetic romance 'The Pledge Eternal,' a telling title he would later change.[75] Knowing what Orson was up to, Laura's brother Josiah Hickman wrote, "He is . . . starting a novel based up[on] his experience here a year [actually three months] ago."[76] Also, "I went to Heber to attend the Wasatch conference with Apostle Whitney & Elder Hart. I took my turn in speaking with the brethren. I spoke three times. Bro. Whitney and I spent all the time, going and coming, reading and criticizing a new poem which he has written, entitled 'The Pledge Eternal.' Outside of his *Elias* it is the best and lengthiest poem he has written. We spent three or four hours on it while at Heber. Of course I am not an accomplished critic when it comes to poetry. I am of most help in analyzing and criticizing the psychology and logic of it. I am of some worth when it comes to that. The poem is based upon Laura's life, etc."[77]

It is impossible to determine how much of the finished poetic novel reviewed Laura's life story, and Whitney's exact feelings for her, and how much of the work is fiction. He worked on it for years, giving it thorough revisions, and made sure the main characters were well disguised before its publication. But he made no secret of it with Laura, reading it to her and making use of her help to improve it. The Founder's Day celebration at the Brigham Young College gave Elder Whitney a new opportunity to see her, she having then moved from Benjamin to Provo:

> Took the 8 a.m. train for Provo and was met by President George H. Brimhall, who put me into an auto, and I proceeded uptown . . . I joined the BYU procession, then parading the streets. I was in an auto containing, besides myself, Pres. John Henry Smith, Senator

> Reed Smoot, Jesse Knight, and his son J. W. We headed the procession, in which I recognized various acquaintances, among them Laura Hickman, who is now a teacher (of English) and a student at the BYU. Arriving at the University, the students, faculty, and visitors filed into the building (College Hall) where, after music by the orchestra and the choir, prayer by Andrew Kimball, and an introductory address by Pres. Brimhall, I was introduced by him as the orator of the day. I spoke for an hour or more, and the Lord certainly was with me. Jesse Knight told me it was the best talk he ever heard. Pres. John H. Smith, in his speech referred to it as "a wonderful oration," and Reed Smoot called it a splendid speech. [~~Laura] said,~~ "You did wonderfully well," and many others offered compliments and congratulations. I called on ~~Laura and took supper with her and her brother Leslie. She had invited me~~ while at College Hall.[78]

He thoroughly enjoyed his visit. "Spent the day in Provo, resting. Read [illegible] ~~to Laura in the afternoon~~, and again took supper with her and Leslie. She helped me with chapter one of my romance '~~The Pledge Eternal,' which is my~~ [illegible] ~~my poem~~ [illegible] ~~here.~~"[79]

A troubling aspect of Whitney's visits with Laura was his concurrent work with the Twelve to investigate suspected new polygamists. That autumn, the Twelve interviewed a number of men to ascertain involvement. Whitney mentions "the Parkinson case"[80] and "the Tolman case"[81] and the "Cutler" and "Hart" cases.[82] All of these men were formally disciplined by the Quorum of the Twelve for plural marriage disobedience. Elder Whitney sat with them in Apostolic court—and then he saw Laura. He wrote her often and his visits to her affected his disposition: "Took train for Provo, called at 187 E. 3rd N. [Hickman's address] and went home unhappy. Slept but little."[83] But the next two days his visit went much better. "Returned to Provo. Happy evening. On Founder's Day I found myself—Laura."[84] His diary entries sometimes sounded similar to what he had written in his youth when courting Nerva and Zina: "Spent the forenoon rambling and resting. Read Mark Twain and Tolstoy on Shakespeare. Spent the afternoon 2 to 4 at 187. ~~Gave Laura a blessing; read to~~ her from Tolstoy's book. And at 4:34 took train for home."[85]

In September and October, Elder Whitney spoke at the funeral of Lorenzo Snow Jr.,[86] showed his deceased son Race's former fiancé around town for a few days,[87] and worked on his history as well as writing a number of times to Laura.[88] That year he also saw an article written about himself published in the *Improvement Era*, and he wrangled some misbehaving sons.[89]

LDS Church General Authorities outside Salt Lake Temple. Front row, left to right: Rudger Clawson, Reed Smoot, George Albert Smith, George F. Richards. Second row: Orson F. Whitney, David O. McKay, Joseph Fielding Smith, James E. Talmage. Third row: Stephen L. Richards, Richard R. Lyman, Melvin J. Ballard, and John A. Widtsoe, 1930 (USHS).

Chapter 18

Orson, Laura, and Dick, 1910–1912

The years 1910 through early 1912 were some of the strangest of Elder Whitney's often perplexing life, and in some ways the most unusual of his diary entries. Orson did not explain himself, his reasoning, or his motivations, or else he later removed such, leaving the reader bereft of satisfying conclusions to the plot. Instability caused by depression, or perhaps a midlife crisis, may have played a part and could explain much.

Along with continuing his platonic courtship of Laura Hickman, Orson began a friendship with a mystery man that he nicknamed "Dick" in his diary. He kept Dick's identity secret, leaving few clues. They passed many letters and postcards between them, sometimes multiple per day. Orson's friendship with Dick predominates his diary for about a year and a half, until Dick simply disappears for several years except for one brief reappearance. Dick probably lived in or around Provo, Utah, possibly had some connection to Brigham Young College, and was probably a Hickman relative, employee, or boarder. (None of Laura's brothers were named Dick or Rick or Richard.) He and Ort exchanged poetry, articles, books of fine literature and science, and birthday and Christmas gifts. If Orson felt their correspondence was going well, whatever its purpose was, he was happy, even delighted. If not, he became depressed, morose. He enjoyed visiting Dick and the visits were always in Provo. No mention is made of Laura or Dick visiting Orson at his own home.

To some modern readers observing the situation, using a "presentist" lens to view the mysterious association, Orson's friendship with Dick may perhaps hint of same-sex attraction.[1] However, such a conclusion is not supported in the diaries, nor by Whitney's abhorrence of sexual immorality of any kind. His strong and persuasive teachings of worthy personal behavior, his exercising of the gifts of the Spirit and powerful Apostolic ministry during these years and to the end of his life ably argues against such conclusions.

Orson continued visiting Laura Hickman as often as he could and wrote her regularly. His decade-long courtship with her, which never materialized into marriage, seemed to reach a comfortable intellectual and emotional plane and remained there. His visits to her home likewise filled him with happiness or misery, depending on how they went. Depression seems to evince itself in these inexplicable friendships. Whether any of the Brethren knew about Laura or Dick is doubtful. Through it all, Elder Whitney kept up his busy schedule of weekly stake conferences and public speaking. As usual, he spoke with convincing power and authority, often acknowledging the presence of the Holy Spirit and the prized compliments from his Brethren. He was becoming a great force and influence for good among them, with few peers.

September of 1910 seems to be the first hint of his friend Dick in his diary: "Completed and mailed to a friend ["Dick"] in Provo a poetic skit entitled 'My Silent Partner.'"[2] November found their correspondence taking off. "Took the 5 p.m. train. . . . While waiting, however, I went up to the Riverside Inn and wrote to 'Dick.'"[3]

Replies were often close at hand: "At my office found [a post]card ~~from 'Dick.'~~ (Edwin Booth). Spent the day writing, etc."[4] Edwin Booth was a famous Shakespearean actor contemporary with Whitney, and postcards often carried his picture. Their correspondence carried on alongside Elder Whitney's regular schedule and ministry. "Read 'The Conqueror.' Helped to set apart missionaries. Attended meeting of the Apostles and Presidency at President's Office. Copied letter ~~from Dick~~ and sent card and Conference Report."[5] While perusing his diaries for material to be used in his memoirs, Ort scribbled out many mentions of Dick and Laura. "~~Mailed letter to 'Dick.'~~ At 10 a.m. in Council at temple on Tanner case,[6] and remained so occupied until about 3:00 p.m. Read 'Chanticler' (Edmond Rostand's translated by Gertrude Hall) 1st Act to Frances. Sent 'Chanticler' to 'Dick.'"[7]

That November, in a highly unusual move, likely motivated by his morose mood, Orson skipped a stake conference assignment to see Laura. In the regular meeting of the Twelve, he was assigned to visit the Yellowstone Stake, but did not. "Read 2nd and 3rd acts of 'Chanticler.' Not feeling well, worn and worried. Decided not to go north to Yellowstone Stake."[8] Instead, he "spent the morning in the Canyon. At 4:10 took train for Provo, arriving about 6. Spent the evening at 187 [Laura Hickman's] reading 'Chanticler,' etc. Slept at the Roberts house [hotel]."[9]

The visit buoyed his spirits. "Spent the day in Provo. . . . Dinner with Reed and George Smoot at Dusenberry's; supper with Laura and Leslie—'Chanticler.'"[10] But soon he had to go home. "Returned to Salt Lake on the 8:25 San Pedro [train]. . . . Card from 'Dick' on my desk (Julia Marlowe [a famous actress]), also letter from Byron. Read 4th act of 'Chanticler' to Frances. Read to Senator Smoot and others at President's Office chapters of history on Smoot investigation and visits of Roosevelt and Taft. Met with my prayer circle. ~~Wrote to 'Dick' sending~~ [illegible] ~~literature.~~"[11] Elder Whitney did not mention what he told his Quorum president about the missed stake conference assignment.

New polygamy cases still occupied his time, as did work on his *History* and public speaking. "Walked up the Canyon, and returning called at my daughter Emily's, and wrote to my son Byron. In the afternoon spoke at the Tabernacle on 'education,' by appointment of the First Presidency and request of State School Supt. A. C. Nelson. It was considered one of my best efforts."[12]

Most diary entries during this period mention a letter or postcard, to or from Dick, and many to and from Laura as well. After the Thanksgiving holiday, he bumped into her. "Took the 9:50 a.m. [train] for Payson to attend, as a volunteer, the Nebo Conference. No one else there [of the Brethren] from Salt Lake. My presence much appreciated. . . . Took the 3:12 train for the north. At Benjamin, Laura Hickman came aboard, and as I had two seats, she sat with me as far as Provo, where [we] both got off. ~~I accepted an invitation~~

~~from her~~ [words illegible] ~~supper, 187~~ [E.] 3rd ~~North~~. Took a room at the Hotel Roberts, and then filled my appointment."[13] He lingered longer: "Spent the day in Provo, visiting old scenes, including the cemetery, and in the afternoon began a poem 'Dick Darling' in room 52, Roberts House. Supper at 187 [Laura's]. Read 'Solomy Jane' and act 4 of 'Chanticler.'"[14] That evening Orson returned home and a couple of days later met his new granddaughter, from his daughter Emily.[15]

He continued writing to Dick, along with other assignments, and worked on the new poem for Dick. "Completed revision of ms. 'Educational Ideals.' Worked on poem 'Dick Darling.'"[16] The content of the poem is not known.

Orson's censoring of his diary clouds any understanding of his actions: "On the train all night and all day speeding southward. . . . Reached Salt Lake at 6 p.m. Went to the Office. ~~Letter from 'Dick,'~~ [several illegible lines] ~~character~~ [illegible] ~~informing me~~ [illegible] ~~passage~~ [illegible] ~~to~~ [illegible]. Sent for same. Supper at home, and later, at President's Office. W~~rote a letter to 'Dick'~~"[17] Also, "Copied my ~~'Dick'~~ letter at Historian's Office, and mailed it."[18]

The fifteenth found him with Laura. "In Council during the forenoon. . . . ~~Letter from 'Dick'~~ [illegible]. Took the 4:10 for Provo, roomed at the Roberts [Hotel], and spent the evening at 187 [Laura's]. 'The Pledge Eternal.'"[19] Laura was an attentive and intelligent audience for Whitney's pieces, and he involved her in the revision process of his *The Pledge Eternal* poem, later renamed *The Love and the Light: An Idyl of the Westland*, as much as he could. The *Pledge Eternal* title, though later changed, seems to have carried great significance in personal meaning for them.

Only hints remain regarding much of his correspondence: "Beautiful letter from 'Dick'—best yet. Also a good letter from Byron. Worked as usual. Wrote to 'Dick.'"[20]

Elder Whitney had been assigned to a reading committee, reviewing Elder B. H. Roberts work that came to be known as the *Comprehensive History of the Church*, but at the time was prepared for inclusion in a magazine called the *Americana*. "In Council 10 a.m. to 2 p.m. Assigned to Ensign Conference. At 3 p.m., sat as a member of a committee to listen to the reading by B. H. Roberts of *History* ms [manuscript] for the *Americana* Magazine. Am suffering from a cold that has almost deprived me of the power of speech."[21] The Roberts history committee assignment would take much of his time between stake conferences.

Then Christmas neared. "Prophet Joseph's birthday. Stayed in, nursing my cold. Received ~~from 'Dick'~~ Christmas gifts—muffler, photo, book (Winston Churchill's *A Modern Chronicle*) and cards—one of them the 'affirmation' of 'Love is Risen.' ~~Answered 'Dick', sent confirmation~~."[22] Orson's "Love is Risen" poem eventually became part of the much larger *Love and the Light* about Laura.

Elder Whitney's illness almost prevented him from speaking on Christmas. "Copied poem 'Love is Risen,' and ~~[crossed out words]~~. Purchased various Christmas gifts. Owing to my cold, gave up hope of being able to speak in the chapel tomorrow evening and so informed the bishopric. Disagreement with F."[23] But Elder Whitney persevered. "Spent the forenoon writing at the office. Afternoon dinner with my family. Evening, having resolved to trust in God, went to the chapel and filled my appointment. The Lord blessed me wonderfully."[24]

Then Orson visited Laura. "With my little daughter Virginia, took the 8 a.m. train for Provo. Left her there with her Aunt Maggie and at 6 p.m. (having had an interview with Professor George H. Brimhall) went on to Spanish Fork and Benjamin. Met by Charlie [illegible] Hickman, who drove me to his grandma's, where I spent the evening with Laura and her mother. Read to them. . . ."[25] Orson enjoyed a four-day visit: "Arose well rested. Spent the day reading, mostly to Laura, from works of a psychological nature."[26] Soon it was time to go home again. "Same, except that at 3 p.m. Laura drove me to the station, where I took the 3:20 for Provo. Arriving there, joined my little daughter at Dusenberry's, and phoned home that I would be there tomorrow about noon."[27]

As 1911 began, Elder Whitney again briefly summed up his present circumstances: "The opening day of the New Year finds me in good health and in the enjoyment of peace and happiness. At 10 a.m., attended the temple fast meeting. At 2 p.m., was at the 18th ward fast meeting where I blessed and named my infant granddaughter: Dorothy Smith."[28] Letters continued to and from Dick unabated as the weeks passed. For example: "Quarterly meeting of the Twelve, 10 a.m. to 4 p.m. Letter from 'Dick,' a most delightful one, written Saturday last. Answered same."[29] New polygamy cases continued as well. "Sat with the Council of the Twelve on the case of Henry S. Tanner—new polygamy. He was disfellowshipped."[30]

One letter from Dick hints at a subject of discussion: "Worked at *News* Office. Letter from 'Dick,' enclosing notes on psychology of religion. Began an answer to same."[31] Such clues raise the possibility that Ort may have been helping Dick with personal issues regarding science, philosophy, and religion, as he had Laura.

Then Orson met a prominent educational leader of his day, who he would keep up a cordial friendship with for years. "Read to my history committee; worked at *News* Office; met Dr. Guy Carleton Lee and went to hear him lecture at night. . . . Lee's lecture was so crowded, could not get a seat. Went to the Orpheum."[32] The next night he was successful. "In Council from 10 a.m. to 1 p.m. Wrote to Byron. . . . Letter from 'Dick.'. . . Heard Dr. Lee lecture in the evening at the Elks Club Room on 'The Mind of a Man.'"[33] A mutually profitable acquaintance bega.: "Read to history committee in the forenoon. Took luncheon with Dr. Lee at the [illegible]. He offered me a place on his Advisory Board of the Rational Society for Broader Education. Wrote to 'Dick.'"[34] Orson was able to see Laura twice as January closed.[35]

As the days passed, Elder Whitney heard Elder Roberts read his historical manuscripts, and Elder Whitney read his own to his own little committee. Both worked through the vetting and approval processes of their day. Also near-daily letters continued to and from Dick.

February began with Elder Whitney being involved with investigating some BYU professors that had been too vigorous and uncompromising in their teaching of the theory of evolution as scientific fact to students.

> At 10 a.m., attended meeting General Church Board of Education. At the last meeting, Dec 28, Supt. Horace Cummings reported verbally in brief upon the BYU and the views and teachings of certain instructors regarding the origin of man (evolution). He was requested to submit a written report at the next (this) meeting, and

> now did so. Supt. Cummings was followed by Dr. Brimhall. After hearing them a committee was appointed (consisting of Pres. Lyman, Heber J. Grant, Hyrum M. Smith, C. W. Penrose, George F. Richards, George H. Brimhall, and Horace Cummings) to investigate the situation at the BYU and interview especially three of the professors—Henry and Joseph Peterson and Ralph Chamberlain—and report findings to the University Board of Trusties. At 4:10 took train for Provo, sitting in the special car of the Governor (Spry) and the legislators on their way to Nephi, to inspect dry farming in that section. I spent the evening at 187, conversing with and reading to Laura. Stayed at the Hotel Lamar.[36]

The controversy regarding the teaching issues at the church school created enough attention that some of the leading Brethren took occasional opportunity to speak about the matter at various stake conferences. "At the forenoon meeting, which was well attended (735) in spite of muddy roads, etc. . . Bishop David Smith then spoke, followed by Pres. Anthon H. Lund, whose discourse was instructive and impressive. Subject: faith and the word of God vs. higher criticism and false science."[37] The visit enabled Whitney to see Laura again. "Went with Pres. Anderson and the Smith brothers to administer to a sister who was ill and bedfast. Also visited the Manti Temple. Took the 1:05 train for the north and got off at Provo. Spent the evening at 187 [Laura's], reading 'An Affair of Dishonor,' etc. Slept at the Lamar."[38]

On Valentine's Day, Ort was not forgotten: "Valentine's Day. 'Dick' remembered me with a comic deluge. At night heard Prof. S. H. Clark, of Chicago University, read 'Chanticler' at the First Congregational Church. Splendid. Received today 'That Old Sweetheart of Mine' from Laura."[39]

Then Elder Whitney heard the report on the BYU biology teachers: "In Council from 10 a.m. to [blank] p.m. Pres. Lyman reported the findings of Board of Education Committee, on the BYU teachers, Henry and Joseph Peterson and Ralph Chamberlin. It was a written report recommending that the services of those teachers be dispensed with, unless they conformed their teachings to the instructions of the BYU Board of Trustees and the General Church Board of Education."[40]

As February passed, Orson worked further on his poetry, gave more readings, wrote Dick, and spent some evenings with Laura.[41] Elder Whitney also sat with the Council of the Twelve as they questioned former Apostle John W. Taylor regarding his continued involvement in new plural marriages. "In Council 10 a.m. to 2 p.m. on John W. Taylor case. Took 4:10 [train] for Provo. Spent the evening at 187 [Laura's]."[42] Having been a friend of Taylor since their younger years, and having taken Taylor's place in the Quorum of the Twelve, the trial and resulting excommunication of Taylor was hard on Whitney, who on leaving the meeting brazenly visited Laura. He found himself navigating a confusing state of affairs. Josiah Hickman recorded his own observations about Taylor.

> I had long talks with Supt. Cummings, Pres. Young, Apostle Whitney, J. Golden Kimball, and John W. Taylor. I learn with regret there is much commotion north [in Salt Lake City]. The Apostles are tracking down those who have entered plural marriage since 1904 and even earlier. Elder Henry S. Tanner has been disfellowshipped. Bro. John W. Taylor is to appear tomorrow before the Twelve for an investigation. I am apprehensive of results, for Jno. W. says he will not lie down and have indignities heaped on him. He had, last week, 3½ hrs. private interview with Pres. Smith. Bro. Taylor made some very severe charges against the work of the Apostles and their methods. He asked Pres. Smith if he believed his father's revelation. Bro. Smith said he did. He asked Pres. Smith why he did not carry out its behest, etc.[43]

What saved Elder Whitney from a similar fate to Taylor and Cowley is that he did not marry Laura, whether by his choice or hers. This fact kept him from the same fate as those he helped investigate. He also kept his relationship with her on an intellectual level, and always slept elsewhere when he visited her. "Took 8 a.m. train for the north, and at 4:34 p.m. got off at Provo. Roomed at the Roberts [Hotel], and spent the evening at 187, reading to Laura the poems to be rendered next Sunday evening. She helped me revise them."[44] Elder Whitney gave his reading: "Regular council at the temple. Assigned to North Sanpete. Pres. Lund reported 'a delightful evening' last Sunday, 'listening to Bro. Whitney's poetic readings.'"[45]

Such readings were a favorite pastime. "Took the 4:10 for Provo (Bro. Young to join me there) and stayed with the Dusenberrys. Spent most of the evening at 187, reading 'Napoleon' and 'Columbus' to Laura."[46] And, "On the train nearly all day between Moroni and Provo, where I called on Sister Josephine Hickman Finlayson, and arranged to give my program of Poetic Readings in the Provo 6th ward, Sunday eve, April 2, under the auspices of the MIA conjoint. Took supper at 187 and spent the evening there. Maeser Memorial Building beautiful by moonlight. Slept at the Lamar, as did Brigham S. Young, my comrade. Gave Laura 'Problem in Eve-olution' for 'White and Blue.'"[47] He also sent some of his work to Dick: "Worked on *History*, and composed comic poem 'The Germ Ubiquitous,' and sent it to 'Dick.' Also dialogue sketch, 'Heard on the Train.'"[48] These were humorous and satirical poems, some of which were later published.

Orson continued seeing Laura during March, reading poetry to her, eating with the family, and going out walking.[49] History committee work and speaking assignments, as well as the usual weekend stake conferences, occupied much of his time. He visited a sick friend, and was saddened at the death of his sister, Laura Whitney Rynders.[50] Another sad jolt: "In Council on the John W. Taylor case. He was excommunicated."[51] As usual, Elder Whitney commented little or nothing on new polygamy cases in his diary.

With the new month (April) Orson continued seeing Laura, but also hinted that perhaps his many visits were being noticed. "At 7 p.m. gave my program of Poetic Readings in the Sixth ward. . . . After the meeting walked up to 187 [Laura's] and stayed a while. Heard some scandal that annoyed me, but had a memorable and happy evening notwithstanding."[52]

At the next Quorum of the Twelve meeting, Whitney made a proposal: "[Line crossed out.] Spent the day in quarterly meeting with the Apostles. Presented to the Council my proposition that a portion of our time in these meetings be devoted to the reading and discussion of leading questions of the day, religious, scientific, [illegible], philosophical, etc., with a view to a common understanding and unanimity of view, concerning the same. The Brethren were pleased with the suggestion and it was adopted unanimously."[53]

Then April general conference arrived. "General Ccnference opened in the Tabernacle at 10 a.m. Pres. Joseph F. Smith delivered an interesting address, full of good things, and Pres. Anthon H. Lund followed. Pres. John Henry Smith was reported ill at home. I took Bro. J. E. Hickman to luncheon at my home. . . . Both meetings were spirited and edifying. Wrote to 'Dick.'"[54]

Mid-April found Elder Whitney writing a protest against the unapproved alteration of an article he had written previously for the *Catholic Encyclopedia*. "Assisted by Frances at her home, I began a letter to Dean Harris of the Catholic Church, protesting against [illegible] in article on 'Mormons' in their recently published *Encyclopedia*. I wrote the article, by request of the First Presidency, the Dean having solicited it and he approved it without changing a word, but it was garbled by the editors or censor in New York, and hence the [illegible]. Letter from 'Dick.' Answered."[55]

Elder Whitney was later deeply gratified by the compliments of President Smith:

> In Council at temple during the forenoon and till afternoon. The brethren all reported their intense enjoyment of the general conference and the reception of Monday evening. At the reception I responded to the toast "The First Presidency" and my remarks were much commended. Pres. Smith in his response said (after referring to me as "a poet, a philosopher, an orator, and a historian"), "Ever since he was a little boy, and I a young man, I have had a more than an ordinary appreciation for Orson F. Whitney. He possesses talent, and has seen fit to use it for the building up of Zion, and in making her name good and pleasant throughout the world. I appreciate his kind words concerning me and my counselors," etc. Many others congratulated me warmly, not only for the address at the reception, but for my remarks at the conference. Six months ago, at a special gathering in the Beehive House, Pres. Smith said of me, "I always felt that Orson ought to be prominent in the Church, on account of his ability. I love to hear him [illegible] upon and defending the truth, etc." At 6 p.m., May and I sat down, with others, at the Beehive House to a dinner given by Pres. Joseph F. Smith to the Twelve, et. al.[56]

Soon Easter neared. "Read to my history committee; prepared by reading, for my Easter Sermon in Logan. Sent Easter cards to Laura Hickman, Maude Babcock, and M. A. T."[57] Then came the Easter sermon. "Easter Day. Took the 8 a.m. train for Logan, arriving about 12:20 p.m. Stayed at Newel Kimball's and in the afternoon delivered the Easter Sermon in the Tabernacle before the mutuals of the stake. House packed. Felt fine, and the Lord blessed me. Spoke 45 minutes. Everybody delighted."[58] Between preparing the Easter sermon, and writing a letter about the *Catholic Encyclopedia* article to Dean Harris, Elder Whitney got a bad headache. After that, two of his teenage boys ran away from home, and he had to deal with the juvenile court on the matter.[59] Orson ran into Dick, taking the same train, on his way to Provo to visit Laura Hickman. Such clues in the diaries indicate that Dick knew the Hickman family well: "Took the 8 p.m. [train] (Owl) for Provo. ~~'Dick' was~~ on the same train and we sat together all the way, and walked up from the depot to 187. Stayed (I did) at Maggie's [his sister's]."[60] Elder Whitney then spoke at a stake conference in Provo.

> Utah Stake Conference. Provo Tabernacle well filled. Many BYU students present, also the leading spirits of the faculty, including Henry Peterson. President Joseph F. Smith preached a powerful discourse, aimed at the fallacies of so-called science and the Higher Criticism. He was the only speaker and was on his feet 1½ hours. Afternoon speakers: myself and J. Golden Kimball. Fine congregation; approximating 1,700 to 1,800. I spoke for an hour or more upon the destiny of the Latter-day Saints as the saviors of the nation, narrating my acquaintance with Dr. Guy Carleton Lee [and] my connection with the National Society for Broader Education, treating the current monthly topic suggested for discussion by Dr. Lee, the Managing Director—"How May the Fathers of the Nation Best Be Brought to Realize Their Duty in the Rearing of Children?" [Afterward,] "Good boy," said Pres. Smith, as I sat down. After meeting an auto drive with Jesse W. Knight et. al. up Provo Canyon. . . . ~~Later~~ [illegible] ~~"Dick~~."[61]

On his return home Orson sent Dick another poem he had written, intending to have it published in the BYU student newspaper.

"Copied 'Seen from Hamlet,' etc., and [I] sent it to 'Dick' for 'White & Blue.'"[62] Also, "In Council 10 a.m. to 2 p.m. Assigned to Yellowstone Stake Conference. Note from 'Dick,' enclosing ms to be corrected and returned for 'White & Blue.' Made the desired changes and re-mailed ms, with letter."[63] This seems to establish that Dick had some connection to BYU.

Soon, Elder Whitney heard feedback regarding his and the First Presidency's letter to Dean Harris, who denied knowledge that changes were made in the article on Mormonism in the *Catholic Encyclopedia*. "May 9, 1911: Sat with committee and heard part of B. H. Roberts *History of the Church*. Worked on my own *History of Utah* and wrote to 'Dick.' I was told today that Dean Harris wept on reading my letter written recently."[64] Harris felt saddened that someone had altered the encyclopedia article and betrayed his Mormon friends.

On May 10 and 11, Elder Whitney and the rest of the Twelve questioned Elder Matthias Cowley about his involvement in new polygamy, after being dropped from the Quorum and having been told not to involve himself with it in any way.[65] Elder Cowley was more apologetic and repentant than Elder Taylor had been, and was therefore treated more leniently.

Returning from a stake conference on the train, Orson spent some time with Dick in Provo: "Drove from Castle Dale to Huntington, took dinner . . . and continued on to Price. Caught train and reached Provo at 10:15 p.m. 'Dick' was waiting for me, and after a pleasant walk and talk I registered at the Lamar and retired."[66]

As May ended, Whitney turned again to his long poetic romance: "Decoration Day. Revised chapter one of my story 'The Pledge Eternal.'"[67]

That June, Laura graduated from BYU. "At the Provo Depot to meet 9:52 a.m. [train.] Saw Leslie and Laura Hickman, who are off for home in Benjamin, school having closed. Laura received her degree, B.A., yesterday in the BYU. . . . Remained in Provo today to attend funeral of Joseph Harris in 6th ward. Pres. Smith and some of his family were present. 'You hit the nail on the head, Orson,' was his comment. Rambled around Provo in the evening. 187 dark."[68] Orson stayed around to visit with the Hickman's: "Arose at 6 a.m.

and at 8:30 was on the road to Payson, with Leslie Hickman, behind a good horse 'Milton.' We had a fine talk, and on the way called at his mother's home in Benjamin, after which we continued on to Payson, reaching there at 11 a.m. . . . Rode with Leslie a mile or more toward Benjamin, and walked back to Payson for exercise. Supper at John H. Dixon's (Leslie's father-in-law)."[69] The next day, he "worked on *Elias*, sitting in the cool, on Dixon's lawn, and while there received a phone message. 'Wanted at Benjamin on Church matters.' Soon after Leslie arrived, and I drove his rig back to his mother's home where I was cordially welcomed. Had a very pleasant visit, including dinner, supper, and a heart-to-heart talk with Dick. LaPrele Daniels, Logan, arrived from Provo. Laura going to meet her at the station. I had Dick's room, and he the one next. Heard him say in a dream: 'I have [felt?] myself as much yours since Christmas, as if a [illegible words] are one.'"[70]

If Dick had a room at the Hickman's, he was likely living there. Orson offers no explanation of his talk with Dick, nor Dick's talking in his sleep, but described the next morning, "Awoke at 6 a.m. and heard Dick say, 'Go to sleep again.' Did so, and arose at 8, and after the usual greeting and breakfast, read to Laura, her mother, and Miss Daniels from Joseph Vance. After dinner bade good-bye and walked to the station 35 minutes. Train at 3:40. Reached Salt Lake about 6. Walked out in the evening and met Josiah E. Hickman. Had a talk with him."[71] No indication is given of subjects under discussion, but the probability is that some of the talk related to Laura. Josiah and Ort talked together often. "Roberts history committee. Luncheon with J. E. and Francis Hickman. Met Laura, their sister, most unexpectedly, at gate of BYU Memorial Building. . . . Afterward had a long ramble ~~with Dick~~ over 'The Primrose Path.'"[72]

Orson's allusion to the primrose path is not clear. This Shakespearean phrase usually means walking a path of ease and sin to destruction, a course abhorrent to Elder Whitney. Perhaps he enjoyed being at ease among friends, where he did not have to worry as much about protecting his Apostolic dignity. "In Council during forenoon. Met J. E. [Hickman] and Lamar Hickman at B.Y. Memorial Building. 'Perfect Way.' Spent the evening with Dick at [the] Constitution Building. Hotel Utah opened."[73] Then he said farewell to his friends: "Met Dick at Constitution Building at 3 p.m. and at 4 sent J. E. [Hickman] & Laura off to the Depot, en-route to Benjaman. Began to revise *Elias*, assisted by Miss May Carlisle. Worked from 7 to 9, then went with my wife through the Hotel Utah."[74] Then he composed another letter: "~~Wrote to Dick a long letter and did little else, though~~ I tried to write on chapter two of 'The Pledge Eternal,' my romance, but was too tired to make much headway. Retired early and slept well."[75]

Independence Day arrived: "Spent the day quietly at home, working on romance and *Elias*, and at office reading over old letters (Dick's). At night May and I called on Aunt Susan and Sister Kate Wells and had ice cream on the lawn."[76]

Soon Orson was back with Laura. "Regular Council day. In the temple from 10 a.m. till 2:15 p.m. Got excused to attend funeral service. . . . Took the 8 p.m. [train] and got off at Benjamin 10:30. Dick met me with rig, and drove me to Rest Haven [the name of Laura's family's home]. Happy evening."[77] Orson was spending more time, outside of his Apostolic ministry, with Laura and Dick than he was at home. This eventually caught up with him, but in the meantime he noted an anniversary: "Just a year ago, by today's date since I left Benjamin for Salt Lake, returning from my first visit here, which began on the evening of Sunday, July 3. Dick's present for my birthday reached me this morning. Scarf pin, opal, and pearls."[78]

As the Apostles investigated new polygamy, they received occasional oversight and direction from the First Presidency, especially President Joseph F. Smith. He counseled them to employ compassion with those who were unaware. "In Council. Assigned to Weber Stake conference for Sunday. Pres. Smith today made a magnificent speech, pleading for mercy and consideration for those led into polygamous relations, thinking they were doing right. It was in answer to a remark made by Elder George F. Richards on the Eldridge case. I went up to the President after the meeting, grasped his hand, and said, 'God bless you for what you said.' I would not have missed it for anything. Called on [illegible]. Cards to Dick."[79] Elder Whitney, perhaps because of his own feelings, interpreted President Smith's counsel as direction to the Twelve to scale back the intensity of their work. Josiah Hickman recorded a clue about matters in his own diary: "I had a long walk and talk with Apostle Whitney. I took dinner with him. He told me something new in the turn of affairs concerning those who have entered plural marriage since the manifesto. It was a comfort to me and just what I have been looking for. I pray our liberation shall continue."[80] While there may have been a temporary relaxation in the investigations and disciplinary actions, the issue grew over the years as the so-called "fundamentalist" movement of splinter polygamist groups took root and grew.

Evidently Dick was subject to depression like Orson. "Sad letter from Dick, written Wed, Thurs, and Friday, Answered it."[81] Then, "Letter from Dick. 'Normal' once more. Wrote to Dick."[82] But following that, "In Council starting forenoon. No appointment. Sad, sad letter from Dick, canceling hopeful one of yesterday. It much depressed me, but I resolved to be stoical."[83] Again, no hint of the problem or issue is given. "Started a letter to Dick, and did little else, I was so depressed."[84] Whitney was on an emotional rollercoaster. "Spent the morning and till 1 p.m. in City Creek Canyon, brooding, and composing letter to Dick, thinking it might be the last. After dinner and a nap at home went down to the office and there to my joy was a letter from Dick, making matters right and proclaiming once more: 'All is well. Pets leap at Master's touch.' Wrote at once in reply, sending parts, but not all, of melancholy epistle I was about to copy and mail when interrupted by Dick's change of heart."[85] So the soap opera correspondence continued, in conjunction with regular duties. "Wrote on romance and answered letter from Dick, received today. Again at hospital, administering to Sister Wells."[86]

August found Elder Whitney being forgotten or ignored by local leaders for a stake conference. "Spent the day in a futile attempt to get to the Summit Stake conference. Started by 7:10 train and by way of Ogden, Echo, and Coalville, reached Park City. No one meeting me, I returned to Salt Lake, arriving at 5 p.m. Sad letter from Dick. Began a reply."[87]

Then comes one of the more mysterious entries regarding Dick: "Letter and card from Dick. Answered. Daring scheme proposed"—but no mention of what the scheme was.[88] Nothing overly unusual occurred in Elder Whitney's life after that letter. Next, "In Council as usual. Assigned to San Luis Stake (Colorado) with Joseph W.

McMurrin. Card from Dick. 'All is well.' Wrote [Dick]."[89] Then, "Wrote to Dick, mailing at Helper, 2 p.m. No further impediments." And no further explanation.[90] During this time, Laura Hickman seemed to recede into the background of Orson's diary, with Dick moving forward as the main subject mentioned. "Had my picture taken, and sent to May and Dick."[91]

That August, Orson was part of some doctrinal discussions. "My daughter Margaret's birthday. Gave her five dollars. In Council at 10 a.m. Assigned to Jordan Stake. At 4 p.m., met with the First Presidency and Roberts history committee on 'Mormon Philosophy' or 'Eternalism.'"[92] And, "At 10 a.m., the session of yesterday was resumed; also at 3 p.m. Card from Dick. Took the 5:25 train. . . . Got off at Provo, roomed at the LaMar, spent the evening at 187 [Hickman's]."[93]

Two days later, after a stake conference: "Arose early after a good sound sleep (having retired early). . . At the close [of the meeting] we were driven by Bishop Bills to the station, where Bro. [George Albert] Smith took train for Salt Lake, and I for Provo. Visited the cemetery, had supper with Dick, and slept at the Lamar [hotel]."[94]

The unknown issues between Orson and Dick continued. "Purchased 'Creative Evolution' for Dick. Helped to set apart and instruct missionaries at temple annex. Note from Dick. Answered, both to Provo and Benjamin."[95] Furthermore, "Worked on *Elias*, with Frances, copying new ms. Note from Dick. 'Ask no more,' etc. At 2:30 p.m., answered for President [Joseph F.] Smith a letter of inquiry from Carl E. Johnson of Moscow, Idaho. At 3 p.m., meeting of Church Board Education. Sent cards to Dick, Provo."[96] Whether Whitney was helping Dick in a struggle over evolution or science or something else entirely is not given. Letters and cards continued daily between them as August passed into September.

Elder Whitney then received another literary assignment from President Smith. "Made a start, assisted by Frances Thomason as typewriter, on the *Oakland Tribune* article to be signed by the First Presidency, and published in October, the opening day of the Pacific Panama Exposition. The article, illustrated and dealing with Mormonism, historically and doctrinally, will fill a page of the *Tribune*, and will . . . cost the Church $1,000, that being the price fixed by the publishers. My work, of course, is free, barring $10 paid to my typewriter. At 4:10 p.m., took train for Provo, stopped off at Pleasant Grove for school meeting, and caught the 9:30 'Owl' reaching Provo at 10. Stayed at Dusenberry's. Enjoyed the evening immensely, especially the P. G. [?] part."[97] By month's end the article was ready. "Read to the Presidency the *Oakland Tribune* article. They liked it. Bro. Penrose also present. Thought it excellent. Had it copied and delivered it to the Presidency and it was sent off by mail."[98]

Elder Whitney also prepared a special talk to be given at the October general conference. "Assisted by Frances, I completed and copied the Orson Pratt Memorial Address for delivery during the coming general conference. At night wrote to Dick and mailed it."[99]

On October 4, Elder Whitney entered an intriguing note in his diary, perhaps in response to some criticism he had heard:

> In Council from 10 a.m. to 3 p.m. Took the sacrament.
>
> Note: I wish to state here, for the use, if need be, of anyone interested enough in me to speak or write about it hereafter, that I have never, in all my experience as a speaker and writer, asked from the Church one dollar for any sermon, lecture, or article spoken or written by me in its interests. For 35 years I have preached, lectured, and written for the Church—often for the First Presidency, whose signatures to the articles were necessary that they might have greater influence for good, and have also contributed frequently to papers and periodicals published in the Church; and have given my service free—glad to do it for the promotion of the cause of God. Only twice have I received from the Church patronage for anything I have published, and then it was not solicited by me, but came as a spontaneous offer from the First Presidency. The first instance was when President Joseph F. Smith and Counselors (or the Trustee-in-Trust) subscribed for certain copies of *Elias*, my epic poem, first editions; and the second instance was the purchase by the Church for $250 of the copyright of my little book, "The Mormon Prophet's Tragedy," a review of John Hay's article of the same title.
>
> Spent the latter part of the day in literary work.[100]

Orson F. Whitney (CA)

General conference began, with Elder Whitney filling a specified assignment: "A slight decrease in the attendance at conference. . . . Note from Dick on my desk at the office. . . . Pres. Smith came down from the uppermost stand to tell me that he would skip me this afternoon in order to have my address tomorrow morning at the Orson Pratt Memorial Service."[101] Elder Whitney gave the talk. "At 7 a.m., met the First Presidency at their Office and delivered to them the printed proofs of the *Oakland Tribune* article, which they received yesterday morning, and gave me to read last evening. At 10 a.m., was at the Tabernacle where, before a packed congregation, I delivered the Pratt Memorial Address, occupying about 40 minutes. Strict attention was paid, and it evidently made a profound impression. I was congratulated warmly by most of the Brethren on the stand, some of who said it was one of the greatest addresses they ever heard. The Lord's be the glory. In the congregation, in reserved seats, were many of the Pratt family, including Arthur Pratt, not a member of the Church. . . . In the evening I prepared my Memorial Address for the papers."[102]

Soon thereafter, Ort "wrote again to Dick, accepting invitation to speak at Pleasant Grove next Sunday evening on education."[103] Then Orson's son-in-law's father died, also Orson's mission president and mentor in the Twelve. "Wrote to Dick but did not send. Card from Dick prompted the letter. Worked on *Elias*. First thing this morning I visited the family of Pres. John Henry Smith, who died a little after midnight."[104] Then, "Funeral day of the late President John Henry Smith. At 11:30 a.m. I was at the home of the deceased on West Temple Street opposite Temple Block, and accompanied the casket as a pall-bearer to the Tabernacle, followed by the family and friends. The Tabernacle was thronged. I offered the opening prayer. . . . At 4 p.m. [I] assisted to set apart missionary's at the temple annex. Wrote to Dick, sending [illegible] card. Called on Smith family."[105]

For November 10, Orson's diary notes, "Dick's birthday (1870–1912). Letters from Dick. Wrote to Dick. Worked on *Elias*."[106] This entry indicates that November 10 was Dick's birthday, but the parenthetical dates do not reference his lifespan, as he was alive in 1916.

Later in November, Orson wrote a poem he titled "Undone Penance" and sent it to Dick, again without explanation of content or reason.[107] Then a further enigmatic notation: "Wrote Dick at R.R. station, 10:15. Expurgated P. G. letter for Dick."[108] Orson referenced expurgating (or censoring) a letter twice more, but with no explanation.[109]

In early December, President Joseph F. Smith called a new counselor, one that may not have been Orson's own first choice, according to later comments: "In Council. Assigned to Duchesne.

Pres. Smith announced Charles W. Penrose, Second Counselor and James E. Talmage as the new Apostle."[110] Talmage and Whitney became influential peers among their Brethren and in the Church.

The year 1912 began with Elder Whitney seeing an old friend. "At Freemont Stake conference, Rexburg. Spoke five times. Too much. And (on Sunday), witnessed the dedication of the stake tabernacle by Pres. Joseph F. Smith. By his direction I ordained my old friend John Donaldson a patriarch. This was also on Sunday, the 7th."[111]

Elder Whitney also relocated his office. "Transferring my effects from Historian's Office to Bishop's Building. About the middle of the month began to move my books and papers from the Historian's Office to the Bishop's Building, 40 North Main, where I have been given a new desk in the Committee Room."[112] A few days later, he visited with Dick: "With Dick at Brigham Young Memorial Building."[113] And he kept sending him books. "Council. Assigned to Alpine conference with Talmage. Wrote Dick and sent more books with [illegible] article."[114] Yet Dick's days in Orson's life were numbered.

That February, Orson had a serious conversation with his wife May. While the subject of their talk is not mentioned, with Orson's attention being directed toward Dick and Laura, and with him being gone from home visiting them so much, the prospect is that May had finally had enough. She wanted changes and got some: "May and I had a long talk at night, which resulted happily, though we had to miss a party. . . ."[115] Dick then abruptly disappears, and is only mentioned once by Orson in his diary thereafter, four-and-a-half years later (August, 1916): "At 6:15 took [the train] for Provo. Put up at Roberts house and spent the evening at 691 N. Academy Ave [Hickman's]. Found my friend 'Dick' in poor health, and worked half to death. Did what I could to comfort him."[116] But things remained otherwise with Laura. Ort continued to see her no matter what his wife may or may not have thought, said, or known.

Chapter 19

Writing and Speaking in the Ministry, 1912–1914

The years 1912 to 1914 proved to be calmer, more settled years for Elder Whitney, with further writing, speaking, and other projects occupying his time when not visiting stakes and missions. February 29th found him with other dignitaries at a special social function honoring Emmeline B. Wells, a prominent leader and advocate among the women of Utah. "At night, May my wife and I attended a reception at the Bishop's Building, in honor of Aunt Emmeline B. Wells, who is 84 today. It was quite a brilliant affair. I was her escort into the hall, where all present arose to greet her. Ex-Governor Wells was Master of Ceremonies. He and my brother H. G. Whitney ('Bud'), Pres. C. W. Penrose, Junius F. Wells, and Pres. Joseph F. Smith made addresses and I recited. . . ."[1] Elder Whitney had known, respected, and loved Wells his entire life.[2]

Roberts's History Committee

Elder Whitney continued working with the Church history review committee, organized for the purpose of hearing and approving Elder B. H. Roberts's historical pieces being published in the *Americana* magazine. He sat with the group listening to Roberts's readings at various times as the months passed. He made special note of readings on the Mountain Meadows Massacre and the Echo

Canyon War, but did not comment further.[3] Two years later he wrote, "In company with Elders B. H. Roberts and Joseph Fielding Smith Jr. I went to the home of Pres. C. W. Penrose, where Bro. Roberts read to us, as a committee of two, some chapters of his *Americana History of the Church.* We blessed Bro. Penrose at his request, I being mouth [voice]."[4] Elder Whitney's work on his own various Utah histories made him a particularly valuable committee member.

Writing for President Joseph F. Smith

President Smith continued using his gifted literary colleague. He, or the First Presidency, asked Elder Whitney to write an article for an Ohio historical publication, to answer general and doctrinal correspondence, to draft letters addressed to the incoming and outgoing presidents of the United States (Taft and Wilson), and to prepare a letter on the temporal affairs of the Church.[5] Soon the letter was turned into an officially approved pamphlet. "Read the Wooldridge letter to the First Presidency. They warmly approved my work and authorized the publication of 10,000 copies of the letter in pamphlet form to be distributed at the Bureau of Information and to other places. The pamphlet will be entitled, 'Mormon Activities. An answer to Questions Concerning the Practical Workings of the Church of Jesus Christ of Latter-day Saints.' By Orson F. Whitney, Salt Lake City, May, 1913."[6] Elder Whitney was also placed on a committee assigned to review and improve the accuracy of the Book of Mormon text in anticipation of a new edition. "Also assisted him and Elder A. W. Ivins in revising [proofreading] certain parts of the Book of Mormon, preliminary to a new edition to be published in Chicago."[7]

Other such projects included a doctrinal textbook to be studied in priesthood and other Church classes, entitled "Gospel Themes."[8] This work would occupy much of his time between conference visits and while traveling, becoming his largest non-poetic doctrinal effort.

Defending the Church

As an Assistant Church Historian and an apostle, one of Elder Whitney's duties—wherein he excelled as few others—was defending the Church against unceasing attacks. "At Council Thursday, I received no out-of-town appointment, so that I might speak in Forest Dale on 'The Redemption of Zion,' to counteract the efforts of one eastman, an apostate, who has been imposing upon some of the German Saints in Granite Stake, professing to be the 'one mighty and strong.'"[9] He felt his effort to be successful: "Filled my Forest Dale appointment, speaking on 'The Redemption of Zion.' A splendid congregation greeted me (608) and every seat was taken. . . . Received many congratulations."[10]

Elder Whitney also raised his voice in opposition to one of the more public and strategic anti-Mormon attacks of his day, instigated by a leading local prelate. "Addressed the faculty and student body of the BYU in College Hall at 11 a.m., making my contribution to the Spalding literature, in reply to Bp. F. S. Spaulding's recent attack on the Book of Abraham. After my hour's talk, which called forth loud applause, I met with the faculty in prayer meeting and addressed them."[11] Spaulding's efforts became a concern: "Met Bp. F. S Spaulding as I was coming down to my office this a.m. and had a talk with him about the controversy over the Book of Abraham. He asked why I had not answered, along with the others (Roberts, Widtsoe, Nelson, et al.) his criticism of Joseph Smith as a translator. I replied that I had answered him several times while preaching in different places, but it had not got into print. He then asked me what I had said, and I told him, in brief. 'Well,' said he, 'That is the way to answer me, instead of lugging in a lot of bitterness. You are right—internal evidences are the real test of anything that claims to be true.'"[12] Further narration of Whitney's defense is found in his autobiography. To Spaulding, he said,

> Truth is truth, where'er 'tis found, On Christian or on heathen ground.
>
> And whether it be taken from an ancient hill in North America, as was the Book of Mormon; or from the catacombs of Egypt, as was the Book of Abraham, if it's true, it's true, no matter who translated it or how many supposed flaws appear in the translation. The character of the content and the spirit accompanying it, determine better than all else the truth and authenticity of such a work. We know Shakespeare's writings by the very sound of them. They have the Shakespearean ring, and thereby literary experts can tell the difference between his writings and all others. We recognize Milton's

> poetry by the Miltonic ring, the poetry of Byron or Tennyson by the Byronic or Tennysonian ring. Then, if God speaks, why should it not have a Godlike ring, something that no man can counterfeit, nor any but a spiritual expert fully discern or appreciate?[13]

Josiah Hickman, probably Elder Whitney's best friend at that time, joined the fray: "I attended stake priesthood meeting last night and conference today. Bros. Whitney and Goddard were the visiting Brethren. They spoke well. After meeting I went auto riding with Brother Kimball, wife, and Bro. Whitney. Bro. Whitney tells me that he appreciated very much my reply to the Rev. Spalding. He said he went and asked the *Deseret News* to print it. He thinks it very strong. He says that Pres. Ballif has said very complimentary things of me and my work and deplored the fact that the Church schools could not pay me what I am worth, for I am a growing power, he said."[14] Whitney felt Josiah, like himself, excelled in speaking and literary skill.

Spaulding was not the only critic to inquire of Whitney;

> Another would-be censor of our sacred books once accosted me with the question, "Bishop Whitney, do you believe the Book of Mormon to be the Word of God?" "I certainly do," said I. "Well, can't God speak grammatically?" "Of course He can." "Then why was this grammatical error left in the Book of Mormon?"—and he quoted it. "Do you really wish to know?" "Yes." "Well, I believe that was left there just to keep you out of the Church!" He seemed surprised. "Doesn't God want me in His Church?" "No," I replied. "He only wants honest seekers after truth; and if you think more of a grammatical error than you do of your soul's salvation, you are not fit for the kingdom of heaven, and the Lord doesn't want you." It has been said that Goliath of Gath, when the stone sank into his forehead, was astonished, such a thing never having entered his head before. It was the same with this man.[15]

Courting Laura Hickman

Josiah's sister Laura remained a significant presence in Orson's life. He mentioned her often as she appeared in various settings. One of these occurred in a meeting of the Twelve: "In Council and was assigned to Cassia Stake. Hyrum M. Smith made a special report on religion class work in Pleasant Grove, speaking very appreciatively of Miss Laura Hickman, who has charge of it, and was a genius in that line. Since she took charge it had trebled in numbers and efficiency."[16] When making his report, Hyrum likely had no inkling of Orson's feelings for her.

Orson had become sufficiently close to the Hickman family that he felt right at home with them. "Spent the day in Provo. Called at J. E. Hickman's and at J. W. Nixon's. Wrote on a comic poem 'Leslie Hickman's Wooing,' which Francis Hickman will read at the wedding of his brother with Olive Nixon on the 5th of June."[17] Then, "In Council from 10:30 a.m. till 3 p.m. Mailed to Laura Hickman, Benjamin, the humorous poem on her brother's approaching marriage, June 5, 'Leslie Hickman's wooing.'"[18] Some two weeks later they met again. "Worked all day at the office, writing on my story 'The Pledge Eternal.' Met Laura Hickman on the street, about 7 p.m. She had just arrived from Benjamin, and I directed her to her brother Francis's place of staying. . . ."[19] Orson celebrated Independence Day, 1912, with supper at the Hickman's, and several days later sat near her on a date with his wife: "Attended the ceremonies of removing first ground for Main Building of University of Utah, and was asked to speak, but [I] declined. Afterward went with G. Francis Hickman through the gymnasium. At night took May to the Orpheum. . . . Laura Hickman and Carlos Palmer sat next to us; the Culmer's just back of us."[20] If May did not know about Laura before that date, she probably did after. Whitney spent time with her on three occasions over a mid-July week, going swimming, eating, and socializing.[21] But the good times soon ended. "Said good bye to the Hickman's (Francis & Laura) who went home today."[22]

Orson saw the Hickman's during general conferences. "Met J. E. and Laura Hickman at south gate of Temple Block at 4 p.m." He then ate with them. " Second day of conference. I was one of the speakers at the forenoon session. 'Good boy,' said President Smith appreciatively as I left the stand. Lunched with the Hickman's at the cafeteria."[23] Josiah explained Orson's attentions in his diary: "I have received a letter from Apostle Whitney. He is very friendly towards me—mostly for Laura's sake."[24]

Preaching with Power and Authority

Opportunities to speak and teach the Gospel throughout the Church continued for Elder Whitney, who rarely turned down an invitation or asked to be excused from such an assignment. He even complied when sick: "Suffering from a severe cold, but filled an afternoon appointment in Ogden, speaking to a fine congregation at 2 p.m. The Lord blessed me abundantly."[25] General conferences were his grandest stage. "In general conference at Salt Lake City. Great gathering. Splendid Spirit. My turn to address the vast congregation came on Saturday afternoon. I was the first speaker at that session. . . . I was blessed of the Lord. Pres. Joseph F. Smith grasped my hand and wrung it as I passed out of the stand, and many expressed fervently their appreciation. Leslie Hickman sang, and his brother Francis and his sister Laura were in the congregation."[26]

After conference, a major sea disaster gave Elder Whitney a theme to address: "Attended meetings of the Liberty Stake conference, the Assembly Hall in the forenoon, Tabernacle in the afternoon. Bro. Wells and I both spoke in the Tabernacle, main subject, the recent Titanic ocean disaster of a week ago."[27] The Apostle could not have succeeded as he did without Divine help. "Attended the Memorial Service for Patriarch Joseph E. Taylor, held in the Tabernacle at 2 p.m. There was quite a large attendance. Pres. Joseph F. Smith presided, and he and Pres. C. W. Penrose, in reverse order, were the speakers. . . . At night I was the speaker at the 18th ward chapel. Full house, closest attention. Theme: Washington. 'Never spoke better,' my friends said. I felt greatly blessed of the Lord. I know He was with me."[28]

Elder Whitney spoke at the fifty-year rededication of the Bountiful Tabernacle, March 16, 1913, and at the funeral of John Beck, a friend and member of his old theosophy group.[29] Then came another memorable occasion:

> Took the 7:15 train for Provo, and on the way read to Pres. Joseph F. Smith (who was going, with his son, Bishop David A. Smith, to Payson, to dedicate a meetinghouse) the first draft of the letter I have written to Mr. W. M. Wooldridge of Hinsdale, Montana, explaining

> temporal workings of the Church. The President was much pleased with my work, said it was "very fine," and proposed that it be published.
>
> At Provo, I attended the forenoon session of the Utah Stake conference and was the main speaker. George Albert Smith and David O. McKay, of the Twelve, were also there. My discourse gave great satisfaction. Theme: "The Salvation of Souls." Prof. A. C. Lund told me it was the strongest impulsion toward righteous living that he had received for a long time. David McKay was delighted with it as were the stake presidency and others. I rested during the afternoon (not having been appointed to attend the conference) and took a walk, meeting by chance Laura Hickman, her mother, and brother Leslie and wife.[30]

Elder Whitney took special note of his greatest successes instructing the people. "Quite a notable day in my personal history. I attended by appointment the Ensign Stake conference, the forenoon session of which was held in the 21st ward chapel. At the afternoon session (in the Tabernacle) I was the first speaker, Dr. James E. Talmage following. At night I lectured in the 18th ward on 'The Spirit World—Suggested by the Return of Peter Grimm.' It was a splendid audience from all parts of the city, and I felt extremely well in speaking."[31] Then Elder Whitney caught another cold at the wrong time: "General conference. I spoke Sunday forenoon, and though hampered by a cold, I was blessed of the Lord, and warmly congratulated by the Brethren upon the stand and many others."[32]

Writing Poetry

Despite his busy ministerial schedule and literary assignments, Elder Whitney found time to refine his epic poem, occasionally feeling inspired in his efforts. "In Council. Assigned to Union Stake, Oregon, and next day, at 2:45 p.m. left. . . . Worked busily on *Elias* en route, and during the journey discovered, I believe, and mended a defect in the tenth Canto that has always marred for me that section of the poem. I recognized the inspiration of the Spirit of God, and felt very grateful to Him for enabling me to see how to improve my work and to [illegible] the important changes that I feel are necessary and will strengthen the structure of this whole epic."[33] Even so, Elder

Whitney had to divide his precious spare time with his other enlarging piece: "May and I attended the pageant in honor of the Pioneers, at Liberty Park this forenoon, and the afternoon I spent in my office, working on and just about completing 'The Pledge Eternal,' my new poem. In the *Deseret News* next Saturday will appear an editorial on my poem, 'The Educator.' Pres. Smith has authorized a special edition in brochure for distribution among prominent school men in Utah and elsewhere."[34]

When opportunity arose, Orson ran it past Josiah Hickman, who wrote, "I had two nice talks with Apostle Whitney. He read me his new poem 'Pledge Eternal'"[35] Times of travel were beneficially used by Elder Whitney. "I returned from my long journey . . . today, over the Salt Lake Route from Los Angeles. . . . While on this journey worked upon a new poem entitled 'The Pledge Eternal,' begun two years ago and laid aside. At Los Angeles, Miss Josie Hinckley, formerly my typewriter in Salt Lake and now on a mission in Southern California, helped me to copy the poem as far as written."[36]

If unable to work on his personal poetry projects, Elder Whitney hammered away at his assigned literary work. "Today I completed, by writing the preface, my latest literary work, 'Gospel Themes,' for the use of the priesthood classes of the Church. I began it last August, and have worked hard to bring it forth, the labor having been much interrupted by other duties and engagements. Read my poem 'The Pledge Eternal' to a literary friend, Miss Laura Hickman, who pronounced it 'powerful and elegant.' She advised me to publish it in time for Christmas of next year."[37]

With the amount of work he had done on it, one surmises that *The Pledge Eternal* had grown larger than its initial design, loosely describing Laura's experience with science and religion and love. She must have felt flattered at such attentions from an apostle of the Lord. Whitney visited her New Year's Day, 1914, and found inspiration to improve his work: "Spent an hour or so at my office, reading over 'The Pledge Eternal' and adding some lines lately suggested by the Muse."[38] Then came the main name change: "I have renamed my new poem ('The Pledge Eternal') 'An Idyl of the Westland.'"[39]

As Elder Whitney's birthday made its annual appearance, his epic poem neared the conclusion of its first thorough revision, the only such revision to be published. "My birthday—59. Took my family to Saltair in the afternoon. Earlier in the day, Supt. Horace Cummings and I called on the First Presidency and secured from the Trustee-in-Trust the loan of $1,000, without interest, to finance the publication of *Elias*, revised and annotated as a text book for the Church schools."[40] All major reworking and rewriting that he did after the 1914 edition, a work that he continued for the rest of his life, never saw print.

Elder Whitney again sent Laura the poem about her: "Spent the day at my office, 2nd floor of Bishop's Building, finishing 'An Idyl of the Westland.' . . . Sent a copy of it to Miss Laura Hickman, Provo (691 N. Academy Ave), requesting a criticism. Am preparing to go east, and expect to start next Saturday, a week from tomorrow. Have been working on *Elias*, the text book, and on the Utah history condensation, until I am all worn down."[41] *Elias* arrived in time for the holidays. "*Elias*, the new edition (annotative) has arrived from Chicago, and sales have now begun. The December number of the *Improvement Era* contains my poem 'The Lamb of God'—a section of *Elias*; and the *Young Ladies Journal* 'Love is Risen,' a selection from my unpublished 'Idyl of the Westland.'"[42]

With *Elias*'s publication, Elder Whitney could again read it to audiences. "Attended regular Council at the temple, but got excused to take the . . . train for Logan, where at 8 p.m. I reviewed before a splendid audience in Nibley Hall, my poem *Elias*. It was rapturously received by what Pres. Jensen, of the B.Y.C. declared to be the finest gathering of intelligence and culture that he had ever seen in Logan."[43] Such occasions found Ort immersed in his element, basking in joy, far from his depression. After the success in Logan, he went to BYU. "Spent the day in Provo, guest of Pres. George H. Brimhall, and at 7 p.m., went to the Maeser Memorial to read *Elias*. Reading at 7:30. Splendid hearing."[44] Elder Whitney gave each member of the Quorum of the Twelve a copy of the new book.[45]

Whitney's friend Josiah was one who heard him read: "I heard Orson Whitney read his *Elias* twice during the holidays. I consider it a very excellent epic poem. I tell him he will have to be dead 100 years before it will be fully appreciated. I rode from here to Salt

Lake with him. He told me that Erastus Snow [once] said that the Prophet Joseph told him that this earth was peopled twice before Adam began the race."[46]

Polygamy Investigations Continue

January and June of 1914 found Elder Whitney meeting with his Quorum to investigate more cases of new polygamy. He notes the names of Joseph Silver (excommunicated for insubordination), Thomas G. Clark (same), and a Dr. McGregor (disfellowshipped). The insubordination cases meant the offenders refused to tell their true tale to the Quorum of the Twelve, who were not disposed to tolerate deceit and evasion in so important a matter.[47] Josiah Hickman explained, "I had a short visit with Apostle Whitney. We had a long walk. He says that Pres. Smith is determined to stop all plural marriages and that is why they are cutting off those who have recently gone into that principle [married a new plural wife]. They intend to handle [discipline] the one [officiator] who married [sealed] them."[48]

Again, Elder Whitney put himself in extremely tenuous and uncomfortable circumstances. During the very years he sat with the Twelve on the new polygamy cases, he continued seeing Laura Hickman whenever he could and it is unlikely the Twelve knew.

Whitney's School History—*The Making of a State*

Elder Whitney spent many days preparing a second edition of his school *History of Utah*. "Began the revision of my school history—*The Making of a State*, prior to the issuance of a new edition by the *Deseret News*. The *History* has just been readopted for the State Text Book Commission for supplemental use in the public schools during the next five years. The *Deseret News* owns the book, but my royalties on the sales of the new edition will bring me in several hundred dollars. The *Salt Lake Tribune* attacks the book, as it did when it was first published." Of course, Elder Whitney could not let the *Tribune* attack go unanswered: "Assisted Bro. Sjodahl, editor of the *Deseret News*, on a reply to another attack from the *Tribune* on *The Making of a State*."[49] But the damage was done, as he explained,

> Am writing a new poem "The Educator" for the N.E.A. event of next week.
>
> Apropos of this great convention, Supt. A. C. Nelson called on me requesting my assistance in the preparation of a paper to be read by him at the N.E.A. Convention. I had to decline owing to press of other work and I suggested Levi Edgar Young as a substitute. "Oh, you can do it so much better," said the Superintendant. And yet it was he with others of the State Text Book Convention who sidetracked my book *The Making of a State*, in deference as I believe to the attacks made upon it by the *Salt Lake Tribune*, and that same Convention gave preference to a book of Levi Edgar Young's, dealing with a similar theme. What I call sidetracking was dropping my book from the regular to the supplemental sphere or plane. Horace Cummings books "Nature Studies" were also adopted by the Convention.

In the same manner that Orson had once been invited to visit stake conferences by men such as John W. Taylor, Moses Thatcher, and Lorenzo Snow, long before his call to the apostleship, Elder Whitney occasionally invited Josiah Hickman to accompany him. Hickman wrote, "Apostle Whitney asked me to go with him & Hyrum Smith to attend Benson Stake conference, held at Lewiston. I went with him [and] was gone Sat. & Sun. We returned Mon. morning. He stopped off here until the 2:30 train for the purpose of administering to Edna D. Chambers. He gave her a good blessing but she is worse again today. We have again poured out our souls unto the Lord for her this afternoon. The pain left her before we took our hands off her head."[50] A few months later, Elder Whitney gave Josiah a fine gift: "Bro. Whitney made me a present of a volume of Joseph Smith's teachings."[51] Their friendship would continue until Whitney's death.

In July of 1913, Orson's work administering his mother's estate drew to a close. "Received my share of my Mother's estate ($3,706.35), proceeds from rentals and sale of her property 285 C. St., Salt Lake City. The amount received, $741.27, was one-fifth of the amount thus realized. The other heirs being my sisters, Helen Bourne and Florence Dinwoody, and Ed Talbot, my deceased sister Genevieve's husband, guardian of her children. My sister Helen received two-fifths, including the share that would have gone to my sister Lily, had she lived."[52]

The year previous, Orson had also transferred ownership to the Church of some precious and special items that had been held by the Whitneys for over a half-century. Orson felt the Church should have them. "Busy all day in my office. Wrote to President Joseph F. Smith, presenting to him or to the Church a number of Nauvoo relics, for many years heirlooms in the Whitney family. Among them was a lock of the Prophet Joseph's hair, a chip spotted with his blood, a revelation to Newel K. Whitney and a blessing upon his daughter, Sarah Ann, both by the Prophet Joseph."[53]

During mid-1914, Elder Whitney undertook a special short mission. "I am under appointment from the First Presidency to dedicate LDS meetinghouses at St. Paul and Winnepeg. But shall go by way of Independence, Nauvoo, and Carthage. After visiting St. Paul, Winnepeg, and Chicago, it is my purpose to go on east."[54] The lengthy trip became a chance for him to visit important Church history sites across the midwest. "July 11 to September 6, 1914. Between these dates I was absent from my home in Salt Lake City, filling a short mission in the eastern states. My letters to President Joseph F. Smith, descriptive of my travels and experiences, have been published in the *Deseret News*, and appear also in the semi-weekly issue of that paper."[55]

Whitney pasted the newspaper clipping descriptions of his travels and adventures into his diary. He also included a chapter summarizing his travels in the east in his autobiography.[56] On his return, one of the first things he did was visit Laura: "Left for Nebo Stake by the 4:20 train to attend conference. Got off at Provo, and made a call or two. Stayed at the Roberts house."[57]

Chapter 20

Reading, Writing, and Romancing, 1915–1921

By 1917, Orson's two main poems, *Elias: An Epic of the Ages*, and *Love and the Light: an Idyl of the Westland*" became finished enough for him to begin reading them to others. As noted in the introduction, poetic readings were a form of entertainment and education enjoyed by the cultured and refined of the day. It was a chance for Whitney to showcase both his poetry and his gifts of expression. "This evening I read my poem *Elias* in the Ogden Tabernacle, to a splendid audience, under the auspices of the Weber Academy. Had strict and sympathetic attention, and never delivered it better, if so well. Remained in Ogden overnight, guest of my friend, David O. McKay."[1] A few days later, his other poem received like treatment: "Gave the reading of the *Idyl*, as per arrangement, and scored, I think, a big success. . . . I began reading at 4 p.m. and was two hours and twelve minutes on my feet—not continuously or without rest, for there were musical numbers interposed. My audience was choice, select, appreciative, and even enthusiastic."[2]

As the weeks and months passed, he gave other readings: "In Provo all day, getting ready to read my poem the *Idyl* at the BYU this evening. The reading came off as arranged, over 100 present—a very choice and select gathering—lovers of poetry. Among those present were Supt. H. H. Cummings, Dr. G. H. Brimhall, Prof. J. E. Hickman . . . Laura [Hickman] . . . and other members of the faculty.

The affair came off in the Art Room specially decorated, lighted, and flowered for the occasion thanks to Miss Reynolds, who bore most of the burden of preparation. Pres. Brimhall presided, Prof. Hickman offered prayer, and Supt. Cummings pronounced benediction. It was quite a triumph for me. I never had read it so well, and the appreciation was unbounded. 'We were spellbound,' said Miss Hickman."[3]

As successful as the poetry readings were, all did not go as he hoped. Orson attempted to find a large, non-Latter-day Saint-oriented publisher for his *Idyl*, but because of being virtually unknown outside of Mormonism, it was politely rejected. "Special priesthood meeting at Assembly Hall. Just before conference I received the following letter, which was no surprise, though I did my best to anticipate a different outcome."[4] The publisher, Haughton-Mifflin of England, did not see Orson's poetry selling well, and were mitigating the extra financial risks caused by World War I. Over the ensuing decades, Haughton-Mifflin would find great success in publishing the imaginative fantasy novels of J. R. R. Tolkien (*The Hobbit* and *The Lord of the Rings*). Orson would find no such success with his own religiously-oriented prose.

With outside publishing houses passing on Elder Whitney's works, he still found ready acceptance among his friends. Regarding his *Idyl* he wrote, "President Smith, at Santa Monica, called the poem 'a masterpiece' and pledged financial aid for its publication. Senator Smoot, Bishop Nibley, and all present likewise praised it warmly."[5] President Smith attached a conditional string to his offer, evidently finding fault with something doctrinal in it: "Made an important change in my poem—the *Idyl*—out of deference to a suggestion from President Joseph F. Smith, who wrote me from Santa Monica, California, concerning it. My pamphlet 'The Strength of the Mormon Position' is just from the press. Received advance copies from Zion's Publishing Co., Independence, Jackson County, Mo., a day or two ago. Have given this pamphlet's copyright and all to the Church."[6] Of his reading before prominent brethren, Elder Whitney enjoyed positive results. "At Council today Pres. Charles W. Penrose commented in his report on the poem and its reading. Said he, 'We all agree who were there that it is the best thing we ever heard.'"[7]

The copyright for the *Idyl* was sold to the Church and later published by President Smith. "Received from Treasurer Arthur Winter a check for $1,800 purchase price of my poem, now owned by the Church and to be published by the *Deseret News* Company."[8] Some six months later the book was ready. "This day is fixed for the issuance and placing on sale of my poem, *Love and the Light* purchased by the Church and published through the *Deseret News* Company's establishment. I got the first copy from the press yesterday. Today the poem is in the show windows of the *Deseret News* and Sunday School Union Bookstores."[9]

Although the basic plot of the *Idyl* roughly followed Laura Hickman's experiences in former years, Whitney's main purpose in the novel-poem was to help young readers realize that Gospel truth trumped the theories and philosophies of men, to teach them that worldly wisdom and academic arrogance paled before God's word, given to men through prophets. The lesson was of eternal significance for all.

> Last night (July 1 or early this morning July 2) I had a rather remarkable dream. I thought I was climbing a hill or mountain slope, and ahead of me was some superior Being acting as my guide and encouraging my ascent. Over my right shoulder and extending back was a strong cable, which I grasped with both hands. Behind me the cable—which was not of rope or anything rough, but rather of silk or flax, soft to the touch—parted into innumerable ribbons, each one attached to an individual, and by this means I was drawing a great multitude up the mountain. I was quite happy in my task, and seemed to have a giant's strength; I pulled with ease, and at times ran rejoicing, in my strength. Presently I looked back to see who the people were that I was helping on and up, and all at once it flashed across my mind that they were the Mutual Improvement workers or young men and young women of the Church. I awoke feeling happy that I was helpful, or had been, or would be, in so good a cause. The interpretation suggested to my mind was that the cable symbolized my lately published poem, *Love and the Light: An Idyl of the Westland*, written purposely to strengthen the faith of the young people and draw them nearer to the truth.[10]

Others of the Brethren agreed with him. "Today, at the quarterly meetings of the Twelve, while addressing the Brethren, I related the dream, but not the interpretation, when [illegible] President Heber J. Grant said, 'It means your book.' Thus confirming my own thought in relation to it."[11]

Writing Articles for the First Presidency

Since his days in the Historian's Office, Orson had been tasked with preparing articles, letters, speeches, and other such materials for the First Presidency. The assignments did not end with his elevation to the apostleship, but continued, with some interruptions, until his passing. Many of his productions received some sort of publication, whether limited or wide. Elder Whitney rarely received credit for these productions, as they were meant to be ghost written in behalf of the First Presidency, whose signatures appeared on them. Other times they were simply writing assignments given him by the First Presidency, and his own name could be attached as author. He wrote pieces for magazines, encyclopedias, and stand-alone pamphlets.[12]

Occasionally feedback reached his ears: "About this time I read to the First Presidency my new Gospel pamphlet 'The Strength of the Mormon Position.' They approved it. Dr. Talmage afterwards told me that President Smith said it was the strongest 'arraignment' he had ever heard of the [blank]."[13] Whitney left off the identifier.

In March of 1917, Elder Whitney again moved to new offices: "Began to move my effects from my old office in the Bishop's Building (40 North Main) to my new quarters—Room 206, LDS Church Offices, 47 E. South Temple, Paul assisting me."[14] This building was later renamed the Church Administration Building. The move took two days. "Have a bad cold, but continued the work of moving into my new office—room 206 LDS Church Offices, 47 E. South Temple."[15]

Knowing he had a talented and knowledgeable aid, President Smith asked Elder Whitney to assist with reviewing a scripture commentary book that his son Hyrum had written:

> March 22, 1917.
> Elder Orson F. Whitney, City.
>
> Dear Brother Orson:
>
> I should be pleased to have you and Joseph F. Jr. act as a committee to hear the reading of a work on the Doctrine and Covenants by Hyrum M. You will please render your best assistance to see that no error in doctrine or inaccuracy in history, should there be any, escapes notice. Hyrum will confer with you as to the time that will be convenient for the reading.[16]

The review committee went right to work. "Spent the forenoon in my office, reading with Hyrum M. and Joseph F. Smith Jr. part of the ms of Hyrum's work referred to in his father's letter. We have had several previous sessions thereon."[17] The committee meetings continued into July.[18] The book contained the text of the Doctrine and Covenants, along with historical notes and explanations. The lengthy work was eventually published as *Doctrine and Covenants Commentary*. Many years later Hyrum's brother Elder Joseph Fielding Smith was assigned to a new committee of revision.[19]

Another time-consuming project was the preparation of over twenty biographical vignettes for the *National Cyclopedia of American Biography*. These reviewed the lives of prominent leaders such as Willard Richards, George A. Smith, Jedediah M. Grant, and George Q. Cannon.[20] Later, Heber J. Grant was added.[21]

On his 1914 trip to Church history sites such as Nauvoo, Illinois and Liberty, Missouri, Elder Whitney had picked up some items and relics of historical significance; these he passed to Church ownership. "Presented to President Smith a fragment of the old jail door at Liberty, Clay County, Mo., purchased by me in July 1914, while on a visit to that place. He presented it to the Deseret Museum."[22] Elder Whitney then received permission to move ahead with a new literary idea: "At a recent social function, I informed President Joseph F. Smith that I felt 'moved upon' to prepare another pamphlet to be entitled 'Latter-day Prophecies and Their Fulfillment' and asked him if he approved of it. He answered, 'Yes indeed; go ahead.' And I am going ahead, accordingly. Am also perfecting my other work 'The Strength of the Mormon Position,' which has been accepted as a Church work and will be published at Independence, Jackson County, Mo., the headquarters of the Central States Mission."[23]

With film technology available to them, Elder Whitney and many of the other Brethren were immortalized. "Saturday, Got out to special priesthood meeting, and posed for 'Movie' on Tabernacle grounds."[24] A year later, in 1917, they also had their pictures taken. "After regular Council, the Presidency and Twelve stood for their portraits in front of the temple, the Clawson Brothers having the camera."[25]

Then in 1920 another important reading committee assignment came. "For a few weeks past I have been one of a committee revising the Book of Mormon, preparatory to a new edition of that sacred record. There are six of us: George F. Richards, myself, A. W. Ivins, Joseph Fielding Smith, James E. Talmage, and Melvin J. Ballard. Our labors consist in comparing previous editions, correcting printer's mistakes, and re-punctuating, etc."[26] Elder Whitney did his share: "I am working hard on Book of Mormon Committee work putting headlines to the chapters for a new edition."[27] Then, "Completed the task assigned me by the Book of Mormon Committee (of which I am one) of putting headlines to the chapters of that volume."[28] With one task done, another arose: "Spent the morning in my office, working on Book of Mormon footnotes—that is, eliminating the footnotes now deemed unnecessary. Elder A. W. Ivins with me in the work."[29]

Preaching to the Latter-day Saints

Even with all his other duties, Elder Whitney did not neglect his stake conference assignments and speaking engagements. He was kept busy, sometimes encountering more difficulties than expected: "Left for Kamas Saturday morning to attend Summit Stake conference, Rulon Wells with me. After leaving Park City with Bp. Lewis, in bus auto, we got stuck in the mud, and I walked on over the mountains in a snowstorm, a distance of 7 miles, before I met relief coming to meet us. I quite enjoyed the tramp. Preached Sunday in Kamas and Sunday night in Coalville, returning home Monday."[30]

In June, 1915, Elder Whitney spoke at the funeral of his old stake president and friend, Angus M. Cannon.[31] The accolades for his orations continued as usual. "General conference opened at the Tabernacle, and continued until and including Sunday the 8th. I spoke on Saturday afternoon, and enjoyed great freedom. Many congratulations, from the First Presidency and other leaders. . . ."[32] Another talk was at the October 1916 funeral of the deposed John W. Taylor, the unrepentant post-manifesto polygamist, son of President John Taylor whom Elder Whitney had replaced in the Quorum of the Twelve.[33]

At the next general conference, Whitney gave two meaty talks. "General conference at the Tabernacle. My turn came to speak on Saturday afternoon. I was the first to address the congregation. My theme: Latter-day Prophets, etc. Sunday evening I spoke in the General S. S. Conference on the subject 'Faith—a Principle of Power.'"[34] He also held forth in the temple. "Lectured on 'The School of the Prophets' in the temple before Presidency and Twelve."[35]

In 1918 Whitney's spoke at the funeral of an old associate that had been both friend and foe to him in his early years as bishop. "Funeral of Elder Robert Patrick, my former first counselor in the 18th ward bishopric, was held at 1 p.m. today in the ward chapel. I was the principal speaker and my remarks seemed to give great satisfaction to the mourning family and to all assembled. . . . In the evening with my wife called at the Patrick home."[36]

A month later, after his October general conference talk, Elder Whitney received a notable compliment:

I was the first conference speaker this morning. My subject "America and Her Mission." The Lord was with me. I was showered with kind words of congratulation, Pres. Smith was again with us.

"My dear Bishop, it was a divinely inspired discourse. I hope it will be published and distributed and broadcast without the change of a word. Your brother, [James E.] Talmage."

The above card was handed to me in the stand a few minutes after I had returned to my seat at the conclusion of my discourse. Many similar expressions have come to me since conference closed."[37]

Being an apostle positioned Elder Whitney to occasionally meet some of the prominent men and women of his day, such as the

President of the United States: "President Wilson in Salt Lake, and it was my good fortune not only to see and hear him but also to shake hands with him and his wife in the Tabernacle, where he spoke this evening. Governor Bamberger introduced me to Mrs. Wilson, and President Heber J. Grant presented me and my wife to the President of the United States. He was very kind and cordial. . . . The President's speech was a great one, and much enjoyed by all."[38] Not long after his visit to Utah, the President suffered some illness. "General conference opened. At the close of this morning's session, I was completely taken by surprise when President Grant, who had addressed the great congregation, announced to them that I would offer a prayer for President Wilson, who had been reported as seriously ill in Washington. I did so and the Spirit of God gave me free and fervent utterance. Many wore the expressions of appreciation that followed. President Grant had the prayer and his reference to it telegraphed to Senator Reed Smoot in Washington D.C."[39]

Elder Whitney spoke in a morning session, and after conference attended other events. "Spoke at an overflow meeting in the Assembly Hall. . . . Conference was followed by the usual social functions such as a reception at the Bishop's Building to president's of stakes and others, and Bishop and Sister Nibley's annual banquet at the Hotel Utah. At both I was made prominent by requests to entertain with humorous stories the assembled guests. Note: President Woodrow Wilson has been getting better ever since we prayed for him in conference."[40]

That year, Elder Whitney gave major talks on Joseph Smith's First Vision, and the Fall and Redemption, all standard Gospel subjects.[41] He also spoke at the funeral of his old friend George C. Parkinson.[42]

As Elder Whitney continued to magnify his sacred calling, he progressed in power and respect among the Latter-day Saints. The mantle of the apostleship grew upon him and was respectfully recognized by the people. "Reached Rexburg at about 10:40, and repaired at once to the Tabernacle, where conference was in session. As I entered, the entire audience of about 1,500 people, at a signal from the Stake President (Mark Austin) arose and sang 'We Thank thee, O God, for a Prophet.' I was overwhelmed, it being the first time I was ever honored with an ovation of that kind. I felt my utter unworthiness of it. But it gave me a splendid text for a discourse of an hour during which I was blest abundantly in addressing the large and attentive congregation."[43]

He continued giving major doctrinal discourses. "Addressed the faculty and student body of the Brigham Young University at Provo today at 11 a.m. My theme: 'The Life Before.' It was a splendid gathering, attentive and appreciative throughout. . . . After the lecture, took lunch in the university cafeteria with President Brimhall and some of the teachers, Alice Reynolds, Zina Y. Card, and Laura Hickman."[44]

Health Issues

As he aged, Elder Whitney dealt with various health issues common to many, especially older men: "General conference began. Could not attend on account of a sore throat and bad cold which has kept me indoors most of the past week."[45] Then he had a bad fall. "At my daughter Helen's most of the night. Childbirth, difficult. A boy. Dr. Lund gave me (there) an examination to ascertain the extent of an accidental fall two weeks ago. It was Sunday night (last day of conference) and I was going into a neighbor's house (Bro. Clive's) to get my daughter Virginia, when I tripped over an iron bar across the entrance to a lane, and was thrown heavily to the ground, breaking one or more of my left ribs. Very painful through services. Dr. Lund bandaged the hurt and I felt much better."[46]

The diaries contain many mentions of one ailment in particular: "In conference all day. Headache returned but the Lord blessed me with relief and I spoke freely and at length in the afternoon, much to the satisfaction of all."[47] Two years later, in 1920, another misfortune came along. "Have been laid up several days with a lame leg (a touch of rheumatics, my doctor says), but was able to keep an appointment in Provo this evening."[48] Elder Whitney fought his way through the health problems as he encountered them, rarely being interrupted significantly.

The Inexplicable

As has been seen, Orson F. Whitney's diary presents some unsolvable mysteries. Reasons vary, from missing pages to scribbled out portions to usage of initials, leaving some people unidentifiable.

Some entries are simply so brief they do no more than to dangle the proverbial carrot before curious eyes, leaving the reader unsatisfied. June 1916 offers some examples: "June 22, 1916. A bitter experience." The next day, "June 23, 1916. Joy, success, sorrow." The next month, Whitney mentions the maddening alteration of his diaries. "Spent the day at my desk, revising [editing] my journals."[49] And more over two more days. "Continued revising [editing] my old journals and putting labels on them."[50] On these days Orson did irreparable harm to all hope of complete understanding of why he did some of the things he did in his long, complex life. He even removed some pages after noting his alteration work.

It was a time of reflection: "Somewhat wakeful, thinking over many things."[51] If only he had explained more of what those things were, or if he had identified those he dealt with. "Explanation from, and reconciliation with, a dear friend, from whom I had been more or less estranged."[52] It can only be speculated who the unnamed friend was—perhaps Francis Hickman, whom Orson had helped investigate and excommunicate for new polygamy. But whom it was for certain is unknown.[53]

Changes in Church Leadership

Francis M. Lyman died in November 1916, having been Elder Whitney's Quorum President for ten years. Lyman, the son of Amasa Lyman and father of Richard R., was a spiritual giant and firm Quorum President that kept a handle on things.[54] In former years he had opposed Whitney's reincarnation views, speaking publicly against them. But with Whitney's reformation, he and Lyman had become good friends and worked well together. It was a sad day when Elder Whitney learned the news: "Called up early to answer phone message from the *Herald Republican*. President F. M. Lyman died about 2 a.m. and they desired an expression from me concerning him."[55] Two days later, "Went with the funeral train to Tooele, and there attended the funeral service and burial of Pres. Lyman. In the evening was at Heber J. Grant's birthday party—he is 60 years old. Presented him with a copy of my new *History of Utah*."[56]

With the death of the President of the Quorum of the Twelve, an adjustment became necessary. "In regular Council. Elder Heber J. Grant succeeded to the Presidency of the Twelve Apostles and was set apart by President Joseph F. Smith; the rest of the Council assisting."[57] Matters remained as constituted for two years, though President Smith's health began to deteriorate.

> Attended regular Council in the temple, and, with Elder David O. McKay, administered the sacrament. After dispensing it to the Brethren present, we retired to the Beehive House and took the bread and water to our beloved President Joseph F. Smith, who has been confined more or less with illness since April last. He was very glad to see us, and when I said, "We would like to bless you, President Smith," he at once replied, "I would like to have you"—with deep feeling. Brother McKay then anointed him with the oil, and I blessed him. We were assisted by Presiding Bishop C. W. Nibley and his Counselor David M. Smith. It was the first time I had seen the President since the dedication of the Hyrum Smith Monument.[58]

October general conference convened the next day, with President Smith able to speak twice in the early session. "All were overjoyed to see him when he entered."[59] It was during his illness around conference time that President Smith received great revelations, one of which later became section 138 of the Doctrine and Covenants. "A communication from President Joseph F. Smith, embodying a revelation, was read to the Council while in regular session today. It was interestingly discussed and we all united in accepting it as the word of the Lord through our beloved President and leader, now in retirement. It is to be published."[60]

Elder Whitney's ready acceptance of the content of the revelation confirms his rejection of his old views on reincarnation. Verse seventeen contains wording about the resurrection incompatible with multiple probations: "Their sleeping dust was to be restored unto its perfect frame, bone to his bone, and the sinews and the flesh upon them, the spirit and the body to be *united never again to be divided*, that they might receive a fulness of joy."[61] Elder Whitney now fully sustained this doctrine.

President Smith's health continued a steep decline. "The Council met fasting and prayed for President Smith—that God's will might be done."[62] Two days later the end came: "I did not learn of the President's death until between 10 and 11 a.m., when, walking from my home to the office, I saw flags at half-mast on the Church buildings and later read the announcement on the bulletin space of the [*Deseret*] *News* window."[63] Elder Whitney then paid his respects. "Called on President Smith's family, at the Beehive House, and tendered my sympathy and condolences. Am working on an article for the *Juvenile Instructor* to be headed 'President Joseph F. Smith as I Knew Him.'"[64] At the next meeting of the Twelve, President Smith was the subject: "At today's Council no business was transacted. Instead we all expressed ourselves regarding President Smith."[65] Elder Whitney served as a pallbearer at the funeral.[66]

On November 23, 1918, a meeting was held for the reorganization of the First Presidency, where President Heber J. Grant became the President of the Church. Elder Whitney made a major precedent-setting contribution to the office of "acting" president of the Twelve: "I was requested by President Grant to set apart Elder Clawson because I had made the motion that he be set apart as Acting President of the Twelve. It was the first time that one *acting* as president, in place of the president of the Twelve, had ever been set apart as such, and it met unanimous approval of all present."[67] Previous to this occasion, it was generally understood that a man could serve as a counselor in the First Presidency, or as President of the Twelve, but not both at the same time. This action changed that.[68]

Elder Whitney soon dreamed of his departed prophet and friend: "Thursday or Friday night I dreamed of President Joseph F. Smith. He was very kind and genial, and put his arms around me, asking me to bless him. I awoke feeling happy."[69]

At the next general conference, President Heber J. Grant was sustained. "The general conference of the Church, postponed from April on account of the influenza epidemic, opened at the Tabernacle at 10 o'clock this morning. The Authorities were sustained—voted upon by sections of the priesthood, according to [illegible] when a new Presidency is installed—and President Heber J. Grant then delivered an [illegible] and interesting discourse, followed by a shorter one from his First Counselor, President Anthon H. Lund, and the conference then took recess till 2 p.m. The speakers in the afternoon session were Pres. Charles W. Penrose, George Albert

Smith, and myself."[70] Nine months later, President Lund died. "On the way home from Provo yesterday, I learned of the death of President Anthon H. Lund, who passed away Wednesday the 2nd inst., at 10:30 a.m. Thursday 3rd, in Council. Appointed one of a committee of four on arrangements for Pres. Lund's funeral, next Sunday."[71]

Lund's passing necessitated the calling of a new counselor in the First Presidency. "Today, at the temple, the vacancy left by President Lund was filled by the advancement of President Charles W. Penrose to be First Counselor, and Apostle A. W. Ivins to be Second Counselor in the First Presidency. Rudger Clawson succeeding to the Presidency of the Twelve. Apostle George F. Richards takes Pres. Lund's place as President of the Salt Lake Temple."[72] A new apostle was also needed: "At Council in the temple today, John A. Widtsoe was sustained, ordained, and set apart as an apostle and a member of the Twelve, thus filling the vacancy caused by the advancement of Anthony W. Ivins to the position of Second Counselor in the First Presidency. Joseph Fielding Smith succeeds to the office of Church Historian (vacated by Pres. Lund), and Junius F. Wells to the position of an Assistant to the Church Historian."[73] Such were the changes in Church administrative leadership during these years.

Giving Blessings

In early February of 1917, Elder Whitney administered to a teenage girl named Laura Butler who had been suffering from some kind of heart ailment.[74] The blessing was successful, though later events showed she still needed further care. "Dot Smith (Hendrickson that was) phoned this morning from Sandy that Laura Butler, the sick girl whom I blessed last night, is wonderfully better, and the family [members] are overjoyed and grateful. The doctors had said they could do nothing to help her (heart trouble) but God has helped her through the prayer and power of faith."[75] Elder Whitney explained further,

> Attended, in company with Elder Joseph Fielding Smith Jr., the Jordan Stake conference, held at Draper. Saturday we went down on the [train], Sunday in Bro. Smith's automobile. I spoke at both Saturday meetings and Sunday forenoon. My address in the latter session ("Prophecy and its Fulfillment") seems to be greatly appreciated.

> Among those present was Laura Butler, the 16-year-old girl to whom I administered in Sandy (her home) last winter, after she had been given up by the doctors, and who was healed by the power of God. A beautiful girl, whose goodness shows in her face, as pure and innocent as an angel. No wonder God healed her. She was overjoyed to see me. Her mother told me that next morning after I blessed Laura (Feb. 4, 1917) the doctor came and was astonished to find so great a change in her. He had given her up (it was heart trouble) and had said that she might die any moment (as had her other physicians), but on seeing her, morning of the 5th, he said, "Why, something has happened here, your daughter is normal." "And she has remained normal," said Sister Butler, "ever since."[76]

Elder Whitney later officiated at the young lady's temple marriage.[77] Such miracles sprinkled Elder Whitney's ministry. "Recently I received a letter from Mae Nelson . . . of Preston, Idaho, stating that God had healed and restored her through my administration as recorded June 3 in this journal. Heard also from Monroe a similar case of healing under my hands—Magleby boy."[78]

Elder Whitney also assisted with administering to his friend and Apostolic associate, Hyrum M. Smith, son of President Joseph F. Smith and younger member of his Quorum:

> At about 1 a.m., was summoned to the bedside of Elder Hyrum M. Smith, who was seriously ill at his home. . . . Dr. James E. Talmage was with me. We hired a taxi from the Hotel Utah, the electric cars having stopped running for the night, and were soon at Bro. Smith's residence. The family were much agitated and Bro. Hyrum was suffering great agony. We blessed him repeatedly, and he went to sleep. We stayed till 6:30 a.m. and then took car for home. I was intending to join Patriarch Hyrum G. Smith at Richmond, Benson Stake conference, but this incident prevented. I went back to bed and slept till noon, and after eating went to the LDS hospital to see Bro. Smith who had been taken there. He was in the operating room just about to be operated on for appendicitis. I called on the Patriarch's folks and administered to his sick child. . . . Returning, went again to hospital and administered to Hyrum M. [Smith].[79]

This time the results were different. "A sad day for Israel. Elder

Hyrum M. Smith died last night at the LDS hospital. I did not learn of it until this morning."[80]

A Sacred Dream

In April of 1918, Elder Whitney experienced a dream to which he attached great significance and gratitude: "Early this morning while I was yet in bed and asleep, dreaming, a pair of hands were laid softly on my head. I thought, still dreaming, there must be burglars in the house. I must keep quiet, or they might attack me. The touch was so gentle that I soon lost all fear and presently put up my hands and took hold of those on my head. They were a woman's hands and I held them unresisting. Pretty soon I saw my deceased wife, Zina, mother to the twins, Paul and Virginia, and we embraced. It was her hands that I had been holding.

"I awoke comforted and happy. It was all so vivid; I would have sworn it was real. Perhaps it was." Elder Whitney treasured these rare reunions with his beloved Zina, extending as they did through the veil. The same day he wrote of work progressing on his novel-romance. "I am busy getting my poem, the *Idyl*, through the press. President Smith has consented to its being illustrated, and I have got Alfred Lambourne and J. T. Harwood to work on the pictures, a frontispiece and 7 headpieces, with one tailpiece, to cost approximately $230."[81]

The Flu Epidemic of 1918 and Whitney's *Saturday Night Thoughts*

In 1918, a great flu epidemic spread through the country, with Utah receiving no mercy as it swept along. "Had a call from Mr. J. N. Dolph, who knew my son Race in Portland. Mr. Dolph is the Red Cross Field Director and is doing expert work to stamp out Spanish Influenza, a scourge that has lately come to Utah after ravaging the east. All our public meetings and places of assembly are closed in consequence of this terrible epidemic—temples, Tabernacle included. Margaret writes from Chicago that she and Lester have had the 'flu.' Many are dying of it all over the land."[82]

With regular Church services cancelled and people's faith being tried by illness, Elder Whitney moved forward with a proposition to keep the local Latter-day Saints spiritually fed: "Have begun writing some special articles for the *Deseret News*, at the suggestion of the First Presidency. I volunteered, however, for this work; it being thought advisable that the *News*, now that all religious gatherings are suspended, should publish some articles of a religious cast and character."[83] Elder Whitney prepared a number of articles of a doctrinal and theological nature for printing in the *Deseret News*. These gave the people some spiritual food in the absence of Church meetings.[84]

On November 11, 1918, some marvelous news swept away the gloom of sickness. "The Great War ends with Germany's surrender. Armistice signed at 5 a.m., today, Paris time. All Utah rejoices with the nation and its Allies. Salt Lake takes a holiday and indulges in a pandemonium of delight. . . . My articles in the Saturday *News* are much and favorably commented upon, as far as reports to me are reliable."[85] World War I was finally over, and the world celebrated.

Having received positive feedback on his doctrinal articles, Elder Whitney's mind naturally leaned toward further literary ideas. "On this date I wrote to President Heber J, Grant, at Santa Monica, California, suggesting the re-publication of the *Saturday Night Thoughts* in book form for use in the Sabbath Schools, mutuals and priesthood classes. My article for the *Juvenile Instructor*—'President Joseph F. Smith as I Knew Him'—appears in the December number of that magazine, the front pages being devoted to it."[86] The idea met with approval. "About this time I received a letter from President Heber J. Grant, warmly approving of my proposition to republish *Saturday Night Thoughts* in book form, and promising financial aid."[87]

April general conference was postponed until June, due to the flu epidemic.

> In conference all day and in general Priesthood meeting at night. . . . Conference lasted until and including Tuesday the 3rd, and was followed by the usual special priesthood meeting on Wednesday. In the afternoon of that day I attended a reception at the Beehive House, given by President Grant and his wife. There I bade farewell to Elder George Albert Smith, one of the Twelve, who left at 5:15 p.m. for Europe to preside, succeeding Elder George F. Richards. During the

> conference, I wrote a letter to the First Presidency, asking permission to compile for publication in book form my *Saturday Night Thoughts*, according to a proposition previously made to Pres. Heber J. Grant, and by him cordially endorsed.[88]

Though it took two years to finalize, Elder Whitney's proposition was accepted and he rejoiced, "A red letter day for me. The First Presidency decided to publish, for the Church schools, my book *Saturday Night Thoughts*, which the school commissioners David O. McKay, Stephen L. Richards, and Richard R. Lyman with Supt. Adam Bennion, had warmly recommended to the Church Board of Education. I went to work at once to prepare the ms for the printers—the *Deseret News*."[89]

Elder Whitney Meets William Jennings Bryan

In 1920, the great statesman and orator, William Jennings Bryan, visited Salt Lake City. As fate would have it, he attended general conference and heard another great orator speak of things he had not previously recognized:

> My turn to speak came this afternoon—the second day and fourth session of the conference. Elder David O. McKay and Bishop Charles W. Nibley being the other speakers. It was one of the most spirited sessions and was much commented upon. I received many compliments and congratulations. In the congregation, close to the stand, sat Hon. William Jennings Bryan, the "great commoner," and Senator Robert L. Owen, of Oklahoma. They paid strict attention and were much impressed by what they saw and heard. . . .
>
> Colonel Bryan and Senator Owen afterward expressed their warm appreciation for what they had heard and witnessed, and I was told by several parties that Bryan was very pronounced in his commending of my address, which dealt largely with the doctrine of the personality of God, in which he is much interested. He went so far as to say that he intended using some of my ideas and arguments in a book that he is writing, namely *Back to God*. Elder Nephi Jensen, President of the Canadian Mission, sat right next to Bryan, and heard him say to Owen, as I got the story, "That is the soundest doctrine I ever heard." Elder Stephen L. Richards of my Quorum said

> that Bryan was full of the subject of my address, and referred to it repeatedly not only at the recital following the session where I spoke, but also at the Democratic banquet next evening, where Stephen L. was toastmaster. President Heber J. Grant said to me, as I met him in the Tabernacle next day, "Well, you've converted Bryan."[90]

Elder Whitney's friend Josiah Hickman shared his perspective of the occasion. "I came home last Fri. night and have been to S. L. conference. A good spirit prevailed & many good things were said. I took Apostle Whitney to dinner & the day following I went home to dinner with him. William Jennings Bryan, the great statesman, was in attendance at our conference one session. Bro. Whitney spoke at that session and gave our views on the character and image of God. Bryan was much impressed and said that he had always held that idea. He made most flattering comments on what he had heard and said that it was one of the greatest inspirations of his life."[91] Bryan died five years after his visit to Utah, where he encountered his equal in public speaking and his superior in spiritual matters.

Shortly after this, Elder Whitney left for a lengthy visit to a mission, and while gone received the news that his brother, Horace G. "Bud" Whitney, had died. Elder Whitney felt it best to remain on his mission tour, rather than return home for the funeral. He felt his brother would want it that way.

The Hickmans

As mentioned in earlier chapters, in 1910 Orson had become good friends with the highly educated Hickman family. He found them to be impressive, thinking much like he did on many issues, including plural marriage. Of the siblings, he writes the most about Josiah, Laura, Francis, and Leslie. Over many years he spent considerable time visiting the main family home in Provo, where Laura and her mother lived and the grown children often visited. These friends served as Whitney's intellectual sympathizers and supports for years. Josiah and Laura became perhaps Orson's best friends for a ten-year period.

As the months and years passed, Orson saw a great deal of Laura and her brothers. "Eighty-fifth Annual Conference of the Church opened at the Tabernacle at 10 a.m.; President Joseph F. Smith and Anthon H. Lund the speakers at the forenoon session. At noon met Josiah E., G. Francis, Leslie, and Laura Hickman on the grounds and took G. Francis to lunch."[92] For a time in 1915, when Francis went to California for graduate studies and Laura went with him for a time, Ort found a way to visit during his travels. "Reached Oakland [California] at 3:50 p.m. Got off and took Jitney bus to 2218 Union St. Berkley, where my friends the Hickmans, G. Francis and wife and his sister Laura were staying. I took a room in the same house, kept by a Mrs. Harriet F. Torrey, paying rent at the rate of five dollars a week."[93] Orson stayed long enough to see the main event of the day. "Saw the Fair at San Francisco—the great Panama Pacific Exposition. Wonderful architecture. Splendid exhibits. . . . Returned each night to Berkley by ferry boat."[94] Berkley held a new interest: "Visited the University of California at Berkley. Registration day for summer school. Met many Utah teachers and students. Was there much of the time during the week, attending classes, hearing lectures, or rambling over the beautiful grounds, sometimes alone, and at other times with others. Read my poem *An Idyl of the Westland* to Laura Hickman—an excellent critic."[95]

Evidently, over the summer of 1915, Orson had time to seriously reflect on his communications with Laura, and possibly Dick (mentioned in an earlier chapter). He seemed to realize that for someone in his position, he had written some things that would not be wise to have known outside his inner circle, so he took steps to remove the potential problems: "Went to Provo by the 4:35 p.m. train and was met at Station by my friend Josiah E. Hickman. I took a room at the Lamar, and went with him to his mother's home . . . to get certain papers, etc."[96] Having retrieved the evidence, he looked it over. "Returned to Salt Lake. Spent the day in my office sorting old letters and papers."[97] Then he knew what to do: "Busy sorting old papers, and tearing up many of them."[98] And, "Continued sorting and destroying of old papers. . . . At 2 p.m., had a call from Miss Laura Hickman, just from California (J. E.'s sister) and assisted her with her luggage to the [train] for Provo."[99] Whitney seems to have done his work of destruction well, for no letters to or from Laura Hickman or Dick found their way into the main archival repositories in Utah, if any survived at all.

The extent to which Orson became involved with the Hickmans regarding plural marriage is not clear, but available evidence suggests that it was a common topic of conversation with them. Josiah had taken a plural wife after the first manifesto (1890), but before the second manifesto (1904), so he was safe. Josiah's brother G.F., or George Francis Hickman, took a plural wife on January 24, 1915, some eleven years after the second manifesto, a move that Elder Whitney would likely have known about and perhaps been in sympathy with, but one that was completely unacceptable nonetheless. Within a few months, word was out, and the Quorum of the Twelve became involved. "Hickman case before Council of the Twelve," wrote Orson.[100]

Elder Whitney found himself in the untenable position of inwardly favoring the continuation of plural marriage and sitting with his Quorum on the investigation of his friend George Francis, whom he may well have discussed the matter with, and having no choice but to vote with his Quorum to excommunicate. This incident is one of the more ineffable quandaries of Elder Whitney's Apostolic tenure. Without knowing more, further conclusions on the matter would be speculative.

Yet the visits to Laura continued. "Took the [train] for the south. Got off at Provo about 6 p.m. and put up at the Roberts house and spent the evening at Hickman's—69 North Academy Avenue."[101] So did the letters: "Wrote to V. [?] and Laura."[102] V.'s Identity remains unknown, except that she had been a romantic interest of Orson's. He only ever wrote her initial in his diary. September found Orson at Hickman's at least twice.[103]

With 1916, Josiah wrote, "I attended conference here last Sunday evening. Apostle Whitney gave a fine sermon. After meeting he and I walked for an hour and talked over many things."[104] The subjects may have been the excommunication of George Francis Hickman, issues of plural marriage, Laura, and other subjects of mutual concern. That both Ort and Josiah omitted the substance of their visits from their diaries indicates that their visits were likely about sensitive matters.

That August, Orson records his last note about his old friend "Dick," still residing at the Hickman home: "At 6:15 took Orem Car for Provo. Put up at Roberts House, and spent the evening at 691 N.

Academy Ave [Hickman's]. Found my friend 'Dick' in poor health, and worked half to death. Did what I could to comfort him."[105] Dick remains one of the many mysteries within Whitney's censored diary. Late summer saw Whitney either visiting or writing Laura several times.[106]

Then an unexplained wrinkle developed and another man, perhaps a suitor, showed up: "In Council as usual. Letter from Laura Hickman at Provo to H. R.[?] at Salt Lake. Gave it to him, and he answered it. I could see by his manner that it was an unhappy communication, in fact he admitted as much but assured me, in confidence, that his reply was kind and conciliatory."[107] As fast as the episode arises, it disappears and no more is heard of the mysterious H. R.

Then Orson bumped into Laura again. "Ordained and set apart the bishopric of a new ward . . . administered to several sick persons; and took train . . . for the north. Got off at Springville to transact a little business, and at 5:40 went in by Orem car to Provo. Met Laura Hickman at Springville Depot and sat with her as far as Provo, where we parted, she to her home, I to Dusenberry's, where I had supper prior to taking [the train] to Salt Lake."[108] Orson's correspondence continued, "Wrote two important letters—one to Lester C. Essig, Kansas City, Mo., answering one from him, dated September 11, asking my consent to his proposed marriage with my daughter Margaret. I gave my consent, believing it to be the best course to pursue under the circumstances. He is not of our faith, but Margaret has chosen him, and from all reports he is a fine young man: clean, moral, honest, and respectable. He wants to investigate our religion and I shall hope for his conversion, and pray for it. My other letter was to Miss Laura Hickman, a high school teacher at Springville, Utah, and had reference to 'Blue Bird' and 'Chanticler' [poems]."[109]

If little else is known of what they talked about over the decade, poetry and fine literature were constants. Letters and visits continued. "Wrote to Laura Hickman, at Springville, concerning Founder's Day."[110] Then, "Went to Provo and spoke at the funeral of Ella Smoot Robinson, my sister-in-law. Again, I was greatly blessed in speaking. Put up at the Roberts House. Went to supper with Leslie Hickman, and afterward had interesting talks with his sisters Josephine and Laura."[111] Then an entry included a comment from Ort that seems to recall past times: "Whitney's *Popular History of Utah* just from the press of the *Deseret News*. No. 1 copy presented to me by Horace G. Whitney, manager of the *News*, who publish and own the work. No. 2 I presented to Frances [Thomasson], my assistant as typist in the compilation. Sent no. 3 to Laura Hickman, Springville, 'fulfilling a promise of long ago.'"[112] Here, "long ago" must have meant about five years, since that is how long Orson had known Laura then.

In early December, Orson and Josiah visited further. "We had conference Saturday and Sunday. Bros. Whitney and Nephi Jensen were the visiting Brethren. An exceedingly good spirit prevailed. I was called to speak for a short time Sunday afternoon. I had several walks and talks with Bro. Whitney. He took supper with us last night."[113]

Just before Christmas, Laura visited Orson, but not at home. "Attended opening session, Utah Teachers Association, held in the Salt Lake Tabernacle. . . . At 4 p.m. or a little later Laura Hickman called at my office for information about her brother. . . . President Joseph F. Smith, I am informed, purchased about two dozen copies of my *Popular History* for Christmas gifts."[114]

Orson visited Josiah in mid-April, but did not record the subject of their conversation. "Ran down to Provo on a little business and after transacting it, called on Prof. Hickman and spent the evening." However, Josiah did. It seems Josiah, who was selling insurance at the time but wanted to teach again, had asked Orson to intervene for him with the Brethren and the BYU administration to have him hired as a professor. Elder Whitney tried to help him but was unsuccessful. They also talked a little doctrine and scripture, with Orson confiding more in Hickman than may have been wise. "I find that Bro. Whitney does not agree with some of [Charles W.] Penrose's interpretations of the scriptures."[115] Orson had argued doctrine with Penrose before, and had his own ideas on some subjects. But now Charles W. Penrose was a counselor in the First Presidency, and Elder Whitney could do little about their differing ideas but complain in private.

Elder Whitney often started a day early for stake conferences held to the south of Provo so that he could stop at the Hickman's and see Laura; then he often arrived home from those stake conferences a day late, so he could visit her again.[116] For example, "Left for Tintic Stake on the [train]. . . . Stopped off at Provo and called on the Hickmans."[117]

The year 1917 drifted into 1918, with occasional visits and letters between Ort and Josiah as well as and Orson and Laura.[118] Josiah recorded, "While in Salt Lake I had a nice walk and talk with Apostle Whitney. He desires me to write him often so he can keep in touch with me."[119] With the passing of 1919 into 1920, the visits to Laura seemed to decrease, or fewer were recorded.[120] In July of 1920, Elder Whitney met the Hickmans at the National Education Association meetings held in Salt Lake City. "Met my friends, the Hickmans, from Logan and Provo, who are attending the NEA."[121]

In July of 1920, the Reed Smoot senatorial investigations in Washington D.C. were well underway and one of the sticks used by the federal government to beat the Church was plural marriage issues. Smoot was trying to put pressure on the First Presidency and Twelve to more rigorously discipline post-manifesto polygamists, and the situation was unsettling. Josiah explained, "Apostle Orson F. Whitney told me he was afraid other [more polygamous] brethren would be handled [disciplined], for Reed Smoot felt they would have to make a clean breast of it [polygamy] and excommunicate everybody who had gone in since 1890. . . . He also said that he feared that the brethren who had been cut off might testify against them (the Twelve) and the Church and its policies. He hardly knew what would come but he, with others, feared something of trouble would develop."[122] While post-manifesto polygamy issues continued to annoy the Brethren, Reed Smoot was eventually seated as a United States senator, without the need for the discipline he recommended.

Elder Whitney also began using Josiah Hickman as an occasional companion for stake visits. "At Preston, Idaho, attending the Franklin Stake conference, Elder Seymore B. Young, my companion. Elder J. E. Hickman also there. We three did most of the speaking."[123] Josiah provided greater detail.

> Apostle Whitney had written me to meet him here last Sat. and go to Franklin Stake conference at Preston. I did not get the letter but we met accidentally in Preston, but he insisted that I be with him

> Saturday afternoon and Sunday, so I did. He and I spoke in the afternoon, and Pres. Seymour B. Young and I spoke Sun. forenoon. I spoke on the psychological and physiological effects of "love."Love your neighbor, your God, your enemy. . . . Apostle Whitney declared that it was the finest speech he ever heard. I learn that he so reported before the Quorum [of the Twelve]. He declared that it was a new revelation to him and was very much impressed. I was reverentially grateful to know that the Lord had blessed me so and gave the audience understanding hearts. Apostle Whitney occupied the time in the afternoon. His speech was a brilliant review of our history: drivings, triumphs, etc. He and Pres. Young went home at 5 p.m. and I was asked to remain for the evening meeting. . . . Apostle Whitney is to be called to go to Europe to preside over the European Conference [mission].[124]

For Elder Whitney, 1921 proved an eventful year. He had been informed by his Quorum president in 1920 that the next year he would be called to travel back to Liverpool, England, to preside as president of the European Mission. Just before the April 1921 general conference, this news was announced in the *Deseret News*. About the same time that Elder Whitney left for England, Laura Hickman moved to Arizona. She remained there for some years, and then moved back to Utah, taking an apartment in Salt Lake City. On his departure for Europe, Whitney's diary does not mention her again. In May of 1921, he said his last farewells: "Ran down to Provo and bade my friends good-bye. Spent the evening, or part of it, at Hickman's—691."[125]

But the strange story of Orson F. Whitney and Mary Laura Hickman was not quite over. The years of correspondence and personal visits had their effect. Because Orson could not marry her without being excommunicated (as with his friend John W. Taylor), he could do nothing about his love for her, at least in mortality. Yet, it would seem he hoped to work it out another way. As will be seen in chapter 23, Orson and Josiah had become bosom friends, confiding many personal things in one another. After disclosing the extent of their trusting brotherly friendship, Josiah wrote, "I made him a promise (to him) which I will fulfill if the Lord is willing."[126]

While absolute certainty eludes, little doubt exists that Josiah's promise to Ort was that, on Orson's death, Josiah was to arrange to have him posthumously sealed to Laura. This conclusion fits well with Orson's earlier actions and desires, having had other deceased women that he had loved sealed to him in the Manti Temple. Orson's status as an apostle would have allowed for this to be done. Further, the original working title for Orson's work based on Laura's life, *Love and the Light: an Idyl of the Westland*, was "The Pledge Eternal," a title filled with personal meaning for them. Orson Whitney's online church genealogical records do not indicate a temple sealing of the two, but that is not unusual for such posthumous marriages. For now, no one knows if Orson and Laura were ever sealed together.

In her later years, Laura assisted her brother Josiah with his own writing projects and books just as she had Orson. She was a gifted teacher, literary critic, copyeditor, and poetry lover, being cultured, refined, and intelligent. She died in 1970 at age ninety-five, having lived a long and useful life of service.

Called as the European Mission President

With the public announcement that Elder Whitney had been called to preside over the mission in Europe, his stake conference assignments were curtailed as he made preparations to leave.

> I was at American Fork attending, with Elder Levi Edgar Young, the Alpine Stake conference. In the afternoon I addressed an immense congregation (1,665) in the stake tabernacle. The people were much impressed, and many came forward at the close to shake hands, bless me, and say good-bye. After the meeting, Pres. Stephen L. Chipman took me in his car to Provo, where I called on the Hickmans and bade them farewell. . . .
>
> I am so busy with the printer and with the preparations for my mission to Europe that President Grant has excused me from further stake conference appointments. So many of our friends are entertaining in our honor, that we (my wife and I) can hardly find time to do all that must be done before our departure.[127]

Elder Whitney also put his financial affairs in order: "Handed over my affairs to my son Murray W. Whitney, to act as my agent during my absence abroad. Drew out of the Consolidated Wagon Company $2,200, upon which I have been drawing interest for several years. In the evening [I] attended, with my wife, a very pleasant gathering of my friends at the hospitable home of Bro. and Sister Stephen L. Richards. President Grant and several of the Twelve were present and spoke. I responded. There was music and recitations, refreshments, etc., and altogether it was a most delightful affair."[128]

A few days later, "Met in regular Council at the temple, and was duly set apart as President of the European Mission, President Heber J. Grant officiating, assisted by his Counselors and several of the Twelve."[129] His wife received a like blessing: "This evening President Heber J. Grant called at my residence . . . and blessed and set apart my wife, May Wells Whitney, for her mission to Europe."[130]

Then the time for departure arrived: "Purchased railroad transportation to St. Louis for May and myself and made other preparations for departure tomorrow 5:15 p.m. Sold my home . . . to Anne L. Butler, wife of Bishop A. J. Butler, the papers passing today. The sum of $500 was paid down and $25 a month is to be paid during the next three years, with interest at 7 percent on unpaid portions till all is liquidated. President Grant, in whose name my new book is copyrighted, advanced me $300 on account of same. A full settlement will come later."[131]

President Whitney departed for his European Mission on May 24, 1921. "The day of my departure for the European Mission, over which I have been called to preside. My wife accompanies me, and at this writing, 6:15 p.m., we have just said farewell to our children and other dear ones, all who could come to see us off, and are on our way from the Union Depot . . . to Ogden and the east."[132]

Chapter 21

European Mission President, 1921–1922

President Whitney spent the first half of June crossing the Atlantic Ocean, arriving June 12. He did not get seasick, but his wife did. The boat captain, learning that Ort was something of a dignitary, showed them some special favors such as a tour of the vessel and dining with himself and his officers.

Upon landing, President Whitney and their traveling company preceded immediately to the mission home where Elder George Albert Smith briefed him on mission affairs. Whitney quickly integrated himself into routine mission life, writing editorials for the *Millennial Star*, getting acquainted with old scenes. "After returning, May and I walked down to old '42 Islington,' the former mission home, where I lived and worked on the *Millennial Star* as assistant editor in 1882–83.

After being in Liverpool for a week, the first letters from home arrived: "Received first mail from Utah. A letter from George F. Gibbs, Secretary, enclosing power of attorney from President Heber J. Grant, and a few other communications, the principal one from Thomas W. Brooks, accompanying an article for the *Star*. The Salt Lake papers . . . announce the death, or rather the funeral, of Sister Lucy Hickman, mother of [Laura and] Prof. Josiah Hickman."[1]

A week later, "In company with Pres. George Albert Smith and several of the elders of the London conference, attended an open air meeting in Hyde Park, near the Marble Arch. I was the second speaker, and for fifteen minutes [I] held the close attention of about 200 people, who faced us in a semicircle, and manifested much interest in what was said. An agitator named Palmer held a meeting nearby,and abused us, but we paid no attention to him. I enjoyed the meeting very much."[2]

Much of President Whitney's first weeks were spent sightseeing and touring the major landmarks in London. Then it was time to go to work. "This is my birthday. I am 66. The event was celebrated in a quiet but cordial and altogether charming way . . . where Pres. Smith formally announced the turning over to me, this day, the presidency of the European Mission. Later he introduced me to Mr. Green at the bank where mission funds are deposited. . . ."[3] Thereafter Whitney moved forward: "Spent the day mostly in my office, discharging the duties of President of the European Mission and editor of the *Millennial Star*. The June 30th number of this periodical contains President George Albert Smith's valedictory [message] and his welcome to me as his successor. The next number, to be issued July 7th, will present my greeting to the elders and Saints of the European Mission."[4]

President Whitney's main duties were to prepare mission correspondence; write editorials; visit with prominent government officials, editors, and police; oversee mission finances; decide where missionaries should serve and preside; and preach constantly.

A month after his arrival, President Smith left.

> Sailing day for President George Albert Smith and family, who are returning to Utah after an absence of about two years. Since my arrival on June 12, Bro. Smith has been diligently initiating me into the duties and requirements of my new position, that of President of the European Mission, and has spared no pains to instruct and qualify me for my labors in this land, for all of which I am duly grateful; and hope to profit by his counsels.
>
> At 12:30 p.m. he and his party left . . . for [their boat]. May and I, with the office force, accompanied them and took lunch on the boat, after which bade them good-bye and went ashore and back. . . . The departure of President Smith leaves me in full and sole charge of the European Mission. May the Lord strengthen and inspire me for the great responsibility.[5]

As with his first mission to England, his second would also result in a life-changing ordeal, further refining and humbling him.

Because President Whitney would be traveling extensively to visit the various countries encompassed by the European Mission, he had to make various travel arrangements. As he prepared to visit "the continent," he also busied himself writing editorials in advance for printing in the *Millennial Star* while he was absent. A new company of missionaries arrived and were assigned and sent to the various fields of labor throughout Europe.

Then President Whitney, with his wife and a few others, began their journey, visiting many locations in France, Switzerland, Germany, Belgium, and the Netherlands. They held conferences with missionaries and members in each major country, and also saw the sights. One stop was special: "At the morning meeting in Rotterdam, I related my dream (or vision) of the Savior, had while on my first mission in 1877. It created a profound impression. One of the brethren said, 'Rather than to have missed that meeting, I would have given five years of my life.'"[6]

The party continued on to Holland and then back to England. President Whitney had seen much, spoken much, and had a much better understanding of affairs and geography in the large mission he now presided over. As the excursion ended, he caught a miserable cold. "Six weeks since I started on my continental trip, with my wife and Elders Wheeler and Taylor. At 7 a.m. our boat reached Harwick, England. We passed the customs all right, but received a rather sharp reproof from the immigration officer for having failed to have our passports [stamped] by the British Consul at Rotterdam. It was an oversight, of course, and we were at fault, but I had trusted to others and been misinformed as I told him—being a comparative stranger in the country. This seemed to soften him a little and he finally decided to admit us, instead of returning us to Holland. . . . May and I went on to Liverpool, arriving about 4 p.m. Met a glad welcome from the brethren in the office, all of whom came to the station to greet us."[7] On his return, Elder Whitney had to nurse his cold, believing that he had "narrowly escaped pneumonia."[8] The cold and cough continued, so he did little speaking or exercising. "Still indoors, gradually getting better, though still coughing. Letter from

First Presidency, answering mine of August 1st—already answered—a fact evidently overlooked by the one who dictated the letter, probably President Penrose, who has been away."[9]

As soon as President Whitney recovered his health sufficiently he went to Scotland, again sightseeing and holding meetings with the members and missionaries. By the end of the month, he was back at mission headquarters, writing more editorials and letters, and taking care of mission business. Whitney's life was becoming a routine of travel to and from conferences throughout the mission, directing mission affairs from the office, overseeing the arrival and departure of missionaries, and writing a steady stream of editorials for the *Star*. President Whitney also regularly corresponded with the First Presidency: "Wrote a long letter to President Heber J. Grant, acknowledging his latest communications, and giving him up-to-date information regarding the European Mission. I asked permission to publish my proposed Gospel pamphlet, upon which I did some work during the day."[10]

Then a local difficulty arose, requiring the Mission President's personal attention: "Went to Sheffield, accompanied by Brother Morton, to adjust a difference between the Conference President, Elder Dan C. Smedley, and the Branch President, Bro. Shaw, who with others of the local priesthood, had made a charge of indiscreet conduct against Smedley and the conference clerk, Leigh Clark. Morton and I first met with the 8 missionaries laboring in the Sheffield Conference and instructed them; and in the evening we heard the cases of Smedley and Clark and decided that they had given cause for complaint. They apologized and were forgiven."[11]

President Whitney also made mention of a rare material purchase: "The only notable incidents of the day were the arrival of the American mail and my purchase at a sale of a new pair of shoes. . . . The shoes cost me [205?] shillings, or a little less than five dollars. In Utah or anywhere in America I would have had to pay 10 or 12 [dollars] for the same grade [quality]."[12] He also noted receiving copies of his freshly published book *Saturday Night Thoughts*, and gave copies to those he felt would appreciate it.

And he kept tabs as best he could on those at home. "Wrote to Sister Amy Brown Lyman [General Relief Society President] about

May's Relief Society position, and sent copies of the *Star* to the Hickman's in Provo."[13]

Mission affairs continued, with correspondence and speaking occupying most of President Whitney's time. With November came an important remembrance. "Armistice Day. At 11 a.m., all Liverpool stood still, for two minutes, in silent reverence, to commemorate the day when the Great War ceased. It was a solemn and impressive sight."[14] Elder Whitney's next conference was at Nottingham, where he "visited Robin Hood's caves and Nottingham Castle. . . ."[15] He went to more conferences and spoke over and again at numerous meetings, everything running together. "There being so little to record outside of my daily routine, I have decided to abandon my daily journal and mention from hereon only such things as are most important in my experience, which was my practice at home."[16] Despite stating his intent as such, Whitney seemed unable to stop making his usual entries.

As December moved ahead, President Whitney received a visit from Elder David O. McKay, then on the last leg of a special year-long assignment to travel around the world and visit all the missions of the Church and report conditions to the First Presidency. "My dear friend and brother, David O. McKay, of the Council of the Twelve, arrived in Liverpool at 6 o'clock this morning. Later in the day, Elder Hugh J. Cannon, David's traveling companion in his world-tour of the LDS missions, arrived from London . . . They remained with us at Durham House [the mission home] pending their departure for home."[17] The next day Whitney saw Elder McKay to his boat for America.

That Christmas, President Whitney spent the day quietly writing letters. Then, "In the evening spoke at the chapel service, Durham House, and told my dream about the Savior. It was listened to with rapt attention."[18] Sharing this sacred vision seemed to have become a way that Whitney could bear his Apostolic witness of Jesus Christ.

As the new year began, Whitney noted a rise in England of opposition to the work. "A new anti-Mormon assault has begun, the notorious 'Winefred Graham' leading the van. Many of the British papers are attacking us, mostly in London. Last Friday a reporter for the Liverpool *Echo* called at Durham House. . . ."[19] President

Whitney found himself in a battle: "This morning I was interviewed by a representative of the Liverpool *Courier* and *Evening Express* . . ."[20] In the interviews, he denied the usual anti-Mormon nonsense of new polygamy and other charges. "The storm continues. The most villainous assaults are being made against us through the venal and blackguard press. But it is resulting in good to our cause, just as such things always do. Every day brings letters of inquiry and requests for our literature from strangers who wish to know more about Mormonism."[21]

President Whitney still had to look after his family at home: "The Whitney family's fast and prayer day for my daughter Virginia, who is in poor health at her home in Salt Lake City. May and I fasted and offered up prayers for Virginia."[22]

Meanwhile, the British anti-Mormon propaganda onslaught continued. "A reporter for the London *Daily Mail* solicited an interview and came to Durham House for that purpose. The *Stunt* press (yellow journalism) continues to flood the country with falsehoods about Utah and the Mormons. Now and then a paper such as the London *Outlook* speaks out for us, but most of the decent journals are silent."[23]

President Whitney reported the situation. "Wrote to the First Presidency, giving a full and [illegible] account of the vicious raid now being made against the Church and its missionaries in this land."[24] The same day, Whitney received an inquiry from a newspaper, asking if he would meet an anti-Mormon's debate challenge. He declined and published his reasons in the *Star*. The jilted newspaper immediately responded. "The London *Express* has an article headed 'Mormons on the Run,' based on my telegram of yesterday."[25]

President Whitney issued a formal complaint to the police against a local Church of England pastor that was inciting his followers to attack the mission home. The police promised to protect the Mormons.

Then Whitney turned his attention to his health. "Called in Dr. Harrison Clarke . . . and underwent an examination for an ailment that has afflicted me more or less for years. He stated that there was a considerable enlargement of the prostate gland and advised an operation. I replied that I would think it over."[26]

Meanwhile, the crusade against the Church went on. "Another busy week. The persecution continues and my correspondence increases daily. Have sent out many copies of the *Star*, with letters setting forth our true position, in contrast to the slanders preached and published against us. Friday last, a small party of missionaries arrived, some of who (bound for Germany) were detained on board on a technicality, but next day were allowed to land and proceed on their way. . . . Yesterday brought a fine letter from Brother Ralph J. Pugh, London, advising me as to my operation, if I decide to have one."[27]

Whitney kept on the offensive against slander when he could. "During the past week 100 copies of the *Star* of Feb. 9 containing my editorial 'Certainly Not,' and 100 copies of the tract 'Anti-Mormon Slanders Denied,' were sent by my direction to London, to be mailed to members of Parliament and other leading men of the nation."[28] More missionaries were detained onboard ship, and President Whitney used his government connections to help clear the red tape so they could land and go on to their fields of labor. He also continued mailing copies of the *Millennial Star* to prominent people in Great Britain, hoping to slow the tide of anti-Mormonism.

That March Ort wrote, "Time is flying. Spent the day fasting and reading and at night preaching."[29] Although he caught another cold from the chilly, damp weather, it was again time to tour the branches and mission conferences. His cold kept him from visiting some, but he was able to attend others. While crossing the English Channel on the way to Ireland, he got seasick, which did not help his ill health. After an excellent conference, he commented, "The Irish Saints are a superior lot of folks, and I very much enjoyed their society." Afterward he recrossed a much calmer Channel.[30]

The First Presidency recognized Whitney's labors: "A letter from President Charles W. Penrose, dated March 27, 1922, says, 'I am greatly pleased with the work you are doing in every part of your mission, and especially with the course you are taking in regards to the uproar which Satan and his imps are now making in different parts of the world."[31] The next day President Whitney responded. "Wrote to the First Presidency, answering letters from them, and held a meeting with the departing missionaries. My new pamphlet 'The

Way, the Truth, and the Life' is out, and presents a neat appearance. Have sent copies to the First Presidency and the other General Authorities and all the mission presidents. I am now compiling my poems—such as have not yet appeared in book form—for publication here in Liverpool. Brother Morton is very kindly and generously assisting me by setting up the type, free of charge."[32]

Then it was time to hold more conferences in various locations, speaking and organizing the work in each area. He let the local press know that the Mormons were not targeting young women for conversion. He also received letters warning of mass demonstrations against the Church, and also notices from the yellow journalism papers threatening to petition the British government to deport all Latter-day Saints.[33]

As his first year of mission service passed, Elder Whitney referred readers of his diary to accounts of his mission activities as found in the pages of the *Millennial Star*, and also to letters he had sent to the First Presidency and Twelve and to members of his family. "I have worked hard—too hard at times—and I believe I am better satisfied with this year's service in the ministry than with any like period of my life. Besides the presidential and editorial [illegible] at Liverpool, I have twice visited the conferences of the British Mission; have traversed the Swiss, German, and the Netherlands Missions; have put forth a new gospel pamphlet—'The Way, the Truth, and the Life'; have started to publish a new volume of poems, 'Voices from the Mountains'; and have preached and written and studied almost incessantly. My health is only fair. I have suffered considerably the past six months with an infection of the bladder—enlarged prostate, cystitis, and gravel—and am now contemplating an operation at a London hospital, hoping for effectual treatment and permanent relief. I cannot go on without it, and [I] must stay and fill my mission. God grant me the help I need! And let me live to serve Thee!"[34]

President Whitney encountered some adventure on his next conference visit. "May and I, with Elders Pingree and Goddard, took train for Sheffield to attend conference. We arrived duly about 6:30 p.m. and put up at [illegible], a temperance hotel, so called. It had been recommended to Pres. Tomlinson, who secured us rooms there, as a desirable place. We found it very undesirable; a horde of roughs having rooms there. Their noisy conduct was very disgusting. They were 'special police,' we were told, held in reserve in case of trouble over the engineers strike then on. We attended a social at the LDS Chapel and then tried to get a night's rest as a preparation for the conference tomorrow, but were only in part successful, owing to the rowdy 'police.'"[35] As soon as possible, Whitney's group changed hotels.

The travel to and from conferences continued. President Whitney strove to help where he could. "Met with the President and elders of the London conference and had a plain, pointed, heart-to-heart talk with them. We poured out our souls, and I believe a better feeling will exist from henceforth among them. It is needed, for strained relations have been manifested for some time between the President and some of the elders." The same day, Orson had another physical examination: "We called on Dr. Leonard Dobson . . . who gave me a brief examination, and pronounced my heart in good condition, my blood pressure 140. This was confirmed later by Sir Charles Ryall, a specialist . . . to whom Dobson (Bro. Pugh's family dr.) referred me. They are both 'jolly good fellows,' and have very winning ways. Dr. Ryall examined me for bladder (prostatic) trouble and said that while there was nothing malignant there, I ought to enter the nursing home, where he could give me a more thorough examination. I decided to follow his advice."[36] Before proceeding, Orson received a blessing: "Brother's Morton and Pugh called at our hotel at 11 a.m. and blessed me and my wife. . . . May and I remained in the hotel until evening, when I entered the Forde Nursing Home next door, and was comfortably quartered in room no. 8. My nurse, Miss Jessie Alison Machritahie, is a Scotch lassie, who ~~is kindness itself and~~ thoroughly understands her profess, but, as I afterward learned, has more of the instinct of a housekeeper than a nurse."[37]

President Whitney's convalescence began. "Had a sound, refreshing sleep, and a good breakfast. Remained in bed by nurse's orders, and at noon my wife came in and spent an hour with me. . . . The dr. told me that he and Sir Charles Ryall were about convinced that my trouble is a stone in the bladder, but they will know positively before an operation is performed."[38] Whitney had to wait a week. "Dr. Dobson came in about noon and proceeded to put me under a process of preparation for tomorrow's operation. Later, my nurse added the finishing touches. It was all new to me, though quite familiar to them. May, faithful as ever, was with me as usual during visiting hours and read to me from the *Daily Telegraph*, and from 'Seekers after God.'"[39]

The operation would be the start of the greatest physical and mental trial Whitney would suffer during his life:

> It is this day, also, for my operation, here in a London hospital (nursing home). May the Lord grant me, His lowly servant, peace, safety, [and] protection! All being ready, shortly after the noon hour, I was escorted to the floor below and to the operating room, where I underwent the ordeal of surgery for which I had come. Sir Charles Ryall performed the operation, assisted by Dr. Dobson. I knew nothing, after passing under the anesthetic, until I found myself back in my room and on my back in bed, bandaged and helpless, and waited upon my nurse. I learned from my wife that I had been on the operating table an hour and a quarter, or from 12:15 to 1:30 p.m., and that not only my prostate gland had been removed, but also quite a number of stones had been taken out of the bladder, and the cavity thoroughly cleansed, with draining apparatus inserted through the wound made in the abdomen.
>
> I expected, on entering the "home" to remain there about a month, but I was doomed to a sad disappointment, being "a slow healer," as they say, and, besides, having to undergo a second operation for the removal of an obstruction in the urethra. I healed rapidly up to that time, but after that my progress was indeed slow. I spent 13 weeks and five days there—days and nights of mental agony, many of them; though I felt the sustaining power of the Comforter through it all, in answer to the prayers of not only myself and wife and children (far away), but those of the elders and Saints of the mission and elsewhere, who fasted and prayed for me repeatedly. My wife was a daily, ministering angel, and Bro. and Sister Pugh and Pres. and Sister Savage (Conference President and wife) were very kind and attentive. They administered to me often, brought me fruit and other delicacies, and as soon as practicable Bro. Pugh took me out in his car.
>
> These drives and daily short walks with my wife were a great help to me. I began to mend more rapidly, and finally, on Saturday, September 16, was able to leave the "home" and exchange for it the more

congenial atmosphere of the Pugh residence, where my wife and I were guests for the next ten days. It was there that I received word from the First Presidency that I was honorably released from the Presidency of the European Mission—an act of kindness prompted by a desire to relieve me of care and labor to render my convalescence more speedy. My successor will be Elder David O. McKay.

Notes: Sir Charles Ryall, my surgeon, died suddenly, early in September, while I was still an inmate of the Forde Nursing Home. My wife and I are still at Bro. Pugh's (September 25) but are planning to return to Liverpool day after tomorrow."[40]

A conscientious Elder Orson F. Whitney tried to return to duty until his successor could arrive. "The day of my return to Liverpool, after an absence of three months and seventeen days, the most of which time I spent as a patient in the Forde Nursing Home. . . . The last ten days or so my wife and I were guests at the home of Pres. Ralph Pugh. . . . Pres. Pugh took us in his car to Euston Station where we boarded the 2:30 p.m. through train for Liverpool. Arrived at Lime Street Station at 6:45 and were joyfully welcomed. . . . We taxied home to Durham House and after a splendid dinner had a long talk with the brethren, who gave me their blessing before retiring."[41] Soon thereafter: "At my desk again. Did considerable work, in spite of my weak condition. I am now preparing my new book of poems, *Voices from the Mountains*, resuming where I left off last June when I went to London for my operation. In an editorial article published today, entitled 'At My Post,' I announce to the readers of the *Star* my release and the appointment of my successor, Elder David O. McKay. The *Deseret News* of the 14th inst. makes the same announcement." Then a note:

For a fuller account of my life, labors, and experiences during the period of this my second European Mission, I refer the reader of these annals to the *Millennial Star* for the years 1921 and 1922. I was much gratified to receive this morning (October 10, 1922) a letter from the Presiding Bishopric—Charles W. Nibley, David A. Smith, and John Wells—in which the following passage occurred: "We learn of your release, and the appointment of our dear friend, Elder David O. McKay, to preside over the mission. You have done a wonderful work. You have been there at a time when it needed a man like you to stand up for the right and defend the Saints. Your mission has been full of problems which you have nobly and splendidly solved." In a former letter dated Sept. 28, 1922, Bp. Nibley says, "The *Millennial Star* comes regularly, and we read it and appreciate your editorials. Its fearless aggressiveness and the high ideals it conveys to the Saints are inspiring." The letters of the First Presidency and Twelve and others that I have preserved and filed contain many similar sentiments of appreciation.[42]

Elder Whitney recorded further health details, including the circumstances leading to his severe and extended nervous breakdown.

My wound closed today, and I was happy in the thought that my troubles were over. But alas! I found that I had gone [back] to work too soon for my best good, not having the strength necessary for the strain I was under, and the result was most disheartening.

One day I nearly fainted and, staggering into Bro. Morton's rooms, had him administer to me. I was at once relieved, but a day or two later, while walking with him in the park near Durham House, grew faint again and had to go in. Gradually I became weaker until I had to give up outdoor exercise and stay in. Called in Dr. Clarke who told me my trouble was "the difficulty experienced by the blood vessels in adjusting themselves to changed conditions"—those resulting from my operation and long detention in the "home." He proscribed for me and helped me to a degree, but still I remained disabled. I had to cease all mental activity and suffered agony with my nerves. Insomnia nearly drove me wild and I began to be fearful of a complete collapse. I was only waiting to get well enough to travel safely, before sailing for home (that being President Grant's advice) and also the advice of my doctor, who said that nothing would help me like my native air.

Finally I resolved to go, without waiting for the arrival of my successor (that being the privilege accorded me) and so, on the 10th of November, my wife and I, with a small party of elders and Saints, sailed from Liverpool on the S. S. Montclair, a Canadian liner bound for Montreal. It was the last boat of the season for that port, the freezing of the St. Lawrence preventing later landing there. On the ocean my health began to improve, though I was still very weak and had to be assisted in dressing and was virtually carried up on deck by two of the elders—Clyde Romney and Claude Hinckley—who I had released specially (their missions being practically at an end) for the purpose of accompanying me home. They were a great help, and faithful in every respect. Nobody could be kinder than these young brethren were to me, and my equally faithful companion.

All went well until within a day's distance from Montreal, when a sharp disappointment was experienced. A case of smallpox on board necessitated a quarantine and prevented the landing anticipated. The boat could not go to Montreal but had to land (240 passengers) on a bleak island (Grascil) in the St. Laurence, not far from Quebec. It was night, snow was falling, and everything was bleak, cold, and forbidding. But it had to be done, and so, on a tug boat that drew up alongside, we were taken over to the island, and after fumigating and [illegible] bathing, were quartered in barracks on that cold bleak rocky island, where we were detained eight days, pretty well cared for, considering all things, and yet suffering many inconveniences. It was no place for a sick man. We all underwent vaccination (some of us twice over) and would have been kept there 14 days (the legal limit) but for the influence exerted by Senator Reed Smoot (my brother-in-law) with the Canadian authorities, who sent a doctor (a prominent physician) down from Ottawa, who put an end to the petty tyranny of the island doctor (one [Aylan?]) and shortened the period of our detention. As fast as the vaccination "took," the passengers were liberated, and we among them.

We were "tagged" over to Quebec . . . and next day took [a] train for Montreal, arriving there about 9 or 10 p.m. Our party was now limited to four—my wife and I, and my assistants, Elders Romney and Hinckley (the others having gone on or been detained a day or so longer on Grascil. We received every courtesy from the railroad and other officials and at 11 p.m. or later were in a drawing room car and off for Chicago. Arriving there next evening, we were met by our children. . . . We remained in Chicago eight days, spending Thanksgiving there, and about the 3rd or 4th of December started for Salt Lake, leaving Chicago by the night train. I was gaining gradually, but it was slow work, and I had to be very careful not to overtax myself. The children saw us off and I parted from them with a heavy heart.

The next three days and nights we were cooped up in a drawing room car and could take no exercise. It was a severe experience for me in my invalid condition, but I survived, and on the 7th of December at 7 a.m. or thereabout our train pulled into Salt Lake. President

> Grant and a large party of relatives and friends met and welcomed us at the depot, and in due time we were under the roof of our daughter Virginia . . . she and her husband having invited us there. . . . It was a cold morning and the snow was deep, but we were mighty glad to be home once more, surrounded by kindred and friends who flocked to welcome us.[43]

Elder Whitney's mission ended, but his ordeal did not.

Orson F. Whitney (USHS)

Chapter 22

Recovery, 1922–1924

Upon reaching home, even with his family and friends around him, Elder Whitney found that he still had a long way to go before he would fully recover his mental and emotional normalcy:

> May and I remained with Don and Virginia about 2½ months (paying our way, of course), and there I slowly convalesced, learning to walk again and use my faculties. I could neither read nor write, nor even think clearly and vigorously, but this condition gradually improved, and I found the fresh mountain air very helpful and invigorating. But oh! How lonesome it was at times. We were so far away from the center of town and our old home in the 18th ward and saw so few people, that we felt (or I did) almost separated from mankind. While we had many visitors at first, they gradually thinned out and most of them came no more. Pres. Grant and wife called several times and he and other leading Brethren blessed me and showed me every kindness. Pres. Frank Y. Taylor, of Granite Stake, was also very kind, and it was he and a Bro. Anderson who took me on my first trip to the President's Office, where I was joyfully welcomed by the Presidency and the Office force. I made one or two trips to town on the electric cars and attended Council meetings in the temple, but the noise and jolting of the cars were so rasping on my nerves that I gave up going regularly. Automobile rides were much more agreeable and we felt much indebted to Henry and Floddy and other friends for courtesies of this character.

On invitation of Bishop Stayner Richards, I attended ward meeting one Sunday night and spoke a few minutes, but it took every ounce of strength to utter a few weak words—my first attempt at speaking in public since my long illness began. I did not try it again. Among little visits made from time to time were at Florence Talbot Williams's (my niece), and a Sunday dinner at sister Floddy's. . . . Bishop Butler, the purchaser of my home on 4th Ave., invited us to dinner and came for us with his car, also taking us back again. This was another pleasant experience. We had our children together—all that we could have—on Christmas and New Year, and observed those holidays appropriately. But as a general thing it was lonesome, and so far away from my former haunts that I longed to get away from the neighborhood where we were staying; and eventually the way opened for us to do so. Emily and Winslow, released from their mission, returned to Salt Lake sometime in February, and we made arrangements to board with them at their old home . . . until we could permanently locate. Accordingly, we moved up into the city, and as soon as we got settled, I began to attend more regularly the Council meetings in the temple. April came, and I was able to be at the regular quarterly meeting of the Twelve, where I spoke, giving an account of my experiences in Europe and since returning home. But I did not feel equal to the general conference meetings, and was excused from attending them. May and I were present at a party given by Brother and Sister Ballard at their new home on Federal Heights, in honor of Elder Reed Smoot and myself. I spoke there, and also at a reception given at the home of Patriarch Hyrum G. Smith, on Yale Ave., and attended by the members of my prayer circle.

I received many calls from old time friends while boarding with Winslow and Emily, and was frequently taken out for drives around the city. I walked out for exercise, but not as much as I needed to, in order to overcome the heaviness that weighed me down.[1] I gradually improved, however, though walking was no longer the delight that it used to be when I was in full command of myself. Pres. Grant frequently placed his car at our disposal and Dr. Lund, Pres. Ballif, Brother Ballard, and others were equally kind. I could walk down to the Temple on Thursdays, and as a rule one of the brethren would bring me back in a car. I read a great deal and almost wore my eyes out at it, after which my good wife read to me till my eyesight strengthened. I also began to write, composing several little poems—one for Mother's Day in the 18th ward, another entitled, "To His Memory," a tribute to the Prophet Joseph. This latter I read to the

Council of the Twelve, whereupon Pres. A. W. Ivins asked for a copy of it, to embody in an address given the following Sunday in the Tabernacle. It was published in the *Deseret News*, in the *Millennial Star*, and in the *Young Woman's Journal*. . . .

My birthday, July 1st, was duly celebrated, children and grandchildren assembling for that purpose. And as the summer wore away, and autumn came again, I was invited, with my wife, by Pres. Grant, to go with the party that attended the dedication of the Alberta Temple, at Cardston, Canada, but did not feel equal to the journey. The same is true of the Hill Cumorah celebration which followed. My inscription for the Temple was read at the dedication by Elder Richard R. Lyman, and also printed on the program of the proceedings. Subsequently the *Improvement Era* published it beneath a beautiful picture of the new edifice. My tribute to the Prophet was written Sept. 21st, the day of the celebration at Cumorah.

Meanwhile, we were continually looking out for a permanent home, and were debating whether to purchase a place or rent apartments. Finally we decided on the former action and bought a beautiful little bungalow on Fourth Ave., no 764, between L and M Streets and close to the dividing line between the 21st and 27th wards. We paid or agreed to pay for it $6,300, about a third down and the rest in monthly installments. . . . The house was handsomely furnished and equipped with all modern conveniences, and we just moved in and took possession of things just as they were, the former occupants leaving for California. We are very comfortable, more so than we have ever been and everybody who has seen our new home congratulates us on the excellent "buy." Pres. Grant called and was delighted with it— thought it "charming." Bert was with us when we moved in and assisted us to get settled. This was on Saturday, Sept. 29. A few days later he left for Idaho Falls. . . . He intends to return and live with us, he and his wife having parted, much to my regret. . . .

During the general conference week I attended the regular quarterly meeting of the Twelve, the joint meeting of the Apostles, Seventies Council and Mission Presidents, and the regular Council of the First Presidency and Twelve, all held in the temple, and was again excused from the general conference sessions. On the 27th of October I was at the birthday celebration in honor of General Daniel H. Wells, held in the primary rooms of the Bishop's Building, where the usual host of his descendants assembled and passed a very pleasant evening. Yesterday, Friday, Nov. 9th, we were honored by the presence in our new home of dear Aunt Susan, now 93, the last

> remaining widow of the grand old hero whose 109th anniversary was so recently celebrated [Daniel H. Wells]. . . . This, I believe, brings my diary up to date.[2]

Elder Whitney's lengthy and trying recovery continued:

> In the 21st ward chapel this evening, I made my fist talk in public since the beginning of my long illness. I spoke twenty minutes, and was followed by Pres. Heber J. Grant, who remarked to the congregation that I had spoken with my "old-time fire and spirit," which much pleased him. The occasion was the installation of a new bishop. . . . After the meeting, which seemed to be greatly enjoyed by all, I assisted President Grant and the stake presidency to set apart the new bishopric and the ward clerk. My son-in-law Winslow F. Smith is the new Stake President. May and I went with him and his wife to the meeting. I was not expected, and my appearance was a genuine surprise—a pleasant one, I believe, for many came to the stand to shake my hand and congratulate me on my recovery and upon my discourse. Winslow said it was "wonderful," as did Emily and my wife and many more. President Grant virtually prophesied that I would live many years to magnify my calling as an apostle—God grant it! It is the one desire of my heart. On the following Thursday, President Grant in our regular Council meeting in the temple referred to the occasion again and repeated what he had said in the 21st ward regarding the quality of my remarks. He was genuinely pleased. On the Saturday evening ensuing, May and I took dinner with President Grant and wife (Augusta) at the Hotel Utah cafeteria and afterward went with them to the theater, sharing their box. . . . A week later we dined again with Pres. and Sister Grant and from their box witnessed the light opera "Blossom Time."[3]

Slowly but surely Elder Whitney progressed, with invigorated oratory and literary output as sure signs of improvement.

> This date [Feb 17, 1924] was made memorable to me by my appearance, for the first time in almost three years, at a Sabbath evening service in the 18th ward—the ward where I was born, and over which I presided for nearly 28 years. I had been repeatedly invited by Bishop Clawson to speak in the chapel, but had not felt well enough

to accept. . . . The house was filled to its capacity, and I was given a splendid reception. My theme was the Sacrament of the Lord's Supper, dealing incidentally with Adam's original offering of sacrifice and the Jewish Passover. I also discoursed on the letter and the spirit, etc. I enjoyed great freedom, spoke for 55 minutes, and was listened to with almost breathless attention from first to last. It was more than a repetition of my former successes. I felt borne up as on angel's wings, and at the close a host of old-time friends flocked around me to offer congratulations . . . [many] commenting on my improved condition and the vigor with which I had spoken, and contrasting it with my weak and seeming-helpless mental and physical state of a year ago. Bro. Richards said he could only think of the scripture: "What hath God wrought." Bro. Richards has been very good to me during my illness and has spoken encouragingly on more than one occasion, predicting my recovery and restoration. Clyde Romney . . . (one of the elders who came home with me from England) was present in the meeting and coming forward at the close urgently invited me to address the YMMIA in his ward (he is the President of the YM) two weeks hence. I have also accepted an invitation to speak again in the 21st ward on Sunday, Feb. 24th. So much for my recent preaching, to which I will add that at the last quarterly meeting of the Twelve I spoke in such a way as to cause Elder Stephen L. Richards to remark that it "thrilled" him, and nearly all present also referred to it in commendatory terms. I have also administered to the sick in two or three instances of late. . . .

In a literary way also, I have been pretty busy since early in December (1923) when I undertook the work of revising and editing a manuscript of 22 chapters covering the *Life of President Franklin D. Richards*, this at the earnest solicitation of my friend Hon. F. S. Richards, his eldest son. The work, initiated by F. S., is written by Frank L. West, the deceased's grandson. I have given it a complete overhauling—have virtually rewritten it and have thus earned [$1,500?]. I have also written for the *Relief Society Magazine*, on solicitation of Associate Editor Aline L. Reynolds, an article "Two Great Educators," a reminiscent parallel on Dr. Karl G. Maeser and Dr. John R. Park, suggested by reading the epitaphs on their monuments in the City Cemetery. An article on "Why We Pray," for the Children's *Friend*, and a new poem, "On the Heights," for the *Improvement Era*, completes the list of my latest literary productions. . . .

On New Year's, President Grant called as usual, and Pres. Penrose came by in a car and saluted us. Among my callers on other days

> was James A. Langton, of the *Deseret News* editorial staff, who wrote a nice little piece for the *News*, informing my friends of my condition and prospects.[4]

That February Elder Whitney administered to more sick people, and kept his speaking commitments, feeling blessed in his work and noting the congratulations and compliments he received. He was then visited by the members of his prayer circle, who gave him "2 dozen cans of grape fruit and a long box of fine fresh figs."[5]

Soon thereafter, Elder Whitney fulfilled a promise to speak to a high priests' group and then gave a talk "in the Tabernacle, for the first time since the April conference of 1921." Whitney explained, "My talk to the high priests fulfilled a promise made many weeks ago to their President Franklin S. Richards, who at the close warmly congratulated me, as did Elders James H. Moyle, V. L. Haliday, and many others. It made a decided impression. My success was repeated at the Tabernacle. The Lord was with me there also. I spoke an hour at Whitney Hall and about 40 minutes at the Tabernacle."[6]

At about this time Elder Whitney wrote, "It is recognized now that I have 'come back,' and am speaking as well as, if not better, than ever. Thank the Lord for it!"[7] With his recovery, it seems that Elder Whitney was again able to accept stake conference appointments. "Attended the forenoon and afternoon sessions of the Ensign Stake conference, pursuant to appointment. In the afternoon, spoke at the Tabernacle, and was followed by Elder Richard R. Lyman. In the evening, spoke in the 11th ward chapel by invitation of Bishop McAllister. May and I walked through a blizzard from our home to the chapel, not expecting much in the way of a congregation, but to our surprise and delight the house was well filled. After the meeting, on invitation of Miss Maude May Babcock, who lives in that ward, we went to her home for supper. Both my talks of today gave great satisfaction."[8]

Then April general conference arrived:

> I was in my seat at the Tabernacle (first time in three years) when at 10 a.m. Pres. Heber J. Grant called the vast congregation to order and gave out the opening hymn. I was the first speaker in the afternoon.

> Took about 25 minutes; reported my mission to Europe and related my experiences in the nursing home and since leaving it. I was in good voice, felt well, and everybody seemed delighted to hear me and see me. I attended every subsequent meeting of the conference and thoroughly enjoyed the three days. Never was there such an outpouring of Saints. Even on the weekdays the Tabernacle was filled to overflowing, and the same might be said of the grounds outside. It was a great feast for me, after my long period of fasting. My passing through the crowd was almost an ovation, so many people stopping me to shake hands and congratulate me on my recovery. If I had risen from the grave, I could not have been greeted more joyously.[9]

Elder Whitney filled his part in all his meetings. "It fell to my lot to pronounce the benediction at the close of conference this afternoon."[10] Then, "Attended the special Priesthood meeting at 10 a.m. in the Assembly Hall. Pres. Grant asked me if I felt any the worse for the strenuous series of meetings I had attended. I replied that I felt the better for it, as indeed I do."[11] Elder Whitney felt the drama and solemnity of the occasion: "The general conference of the Church, just over, was the greatest in point of numbers that I have ever attended, and one of the greatest in the matter of the instructions given to the Saints. The Lord was certainly with His servants and His people. It was glorious. Monday evening, April 7, the day after conference, a reception was given by the First Presidency and Twelve to presidencies of stakes and bishoprics of wards, with their wives. We stood in line at the door (4th floor, Bishop's Building) and shook hands with the hundreds of guests who flocked in. Nearly all of them had something kind to say to me, and I was fairly showered with good wishes and congratulations on my recovery and upon the address I gave at conference."[12]

Elder Whitney felt honored. "In Council, as usual. Reported my experience during conference as a great feast, after a prolonged period of fasting."[13] His positive experiences continued: "In meetings all day—Liberty Stake conference. Assembly Hall 10 a.m., Tabernacle 2 p.m. Spoke in the Tabernacle on 'Joseph the Seer.' Enjoyed much freedom, and was warmly congratulated by all. 'A very splendid discourse,' said Pres. Hugh J. Cannon. 'A great sermon,' said Joseph H. Peery; and these were samples of the kind and generous expressions poured out upon me. Nearly all whom I meet rejoice over my recovery and in my teachings. The Lord is certainly blessing me in every way! To Him be all the praise!"[14]

Elder Whitney also kept up with his literary work. "Worked all day in my office, reading proofs of *Life of Franklin D. Richards*, now being printed. This is the work which I have been engaged in revising since early last December. I have put a great deal of work upon it, practically rewriting much of it and polishing it up generally for the author, Franklin L. West, at the instance of his uncle, my friend, F. S. Richards. I paused long enough in my literary labor to meet with others of the Twelve to set apart and instruct a party of sixteen missionaries. Being the senior Apostle present, I presided. Stephen L. Richards and I instructed them. My first service of the kind since returning from Europe."[15]

Chapter 23

A Marvelous Ministry Is Renewed and Concludes, 1924–1931

Having fully recovered his mental and nervous faculties, Elder Whitney progressively undertook more of the routine work of the apostleship. This meant he was again traveling to stake conferences, administering to the sick, marrying young couples, speaking, and writing. At one meeting, where a large number of investigators were present, eight of them requested to be baptized after hearing Elder Whitney preach.[1]

Another visit fulfilled a prophecy: "In the afternoon of this day I attended the Cottonwood Stake conference, held in the Granite Stake Tabernacle, Elder William A. Morton being my companion. Our presence together at a stake conference fulfilled a prediction made by him in Liverpool, when I was so weak and ill that it seemed to me very improbable that I would ever speak in public again. He said that I would and that we would yet attend a stake conference together. I made mention of his prophecy in my remarks this morning. After lunch at the Granite Tabernacle, I excused myself, leaving Bro. Morton and Andrew Jenson to represent me during the remainder of the conference. I started for Ogden, with my wife, in a car driven by a Bro. Goates. We arrived at Murray's home. . . . After dinner and a refreshing nap, the four of us, Murray, Dorothy, May and I—chaperoned by Pres. Thomas E. McKay—proceeded in his car to the Weber Normal College, where, before a brilliant audience of graduates with their parents and friends, I delivered the Baccalaureate sermon. . . ."[2] Shortly thereafter, Whitney delivered two more such academic sermons.[3]

Elder Whitney was speaking as much or more than ever—funerals, schools, stake conferences—and being magnified in his calling. "Was a speaker at the funeral of Bro. Lewis M. Cannon held at 2 p.m. in the Pioneer Stake Hall. A large attendance, including the families of President George Q. Cannon and Angus M. Cannon. . . . I felt the power of God upon me, and spoke with force and freedom. Many commented upon it. Pres. Hugh J. Cannon said it gave him a deeper insight into life's purposes. Others said it greatly comforted them. The Lord be praised."[4]

He also blessed the sick frequently, sometimes finding that they were "nigh unto death" (thereafter speaking at their funerals) and other times he enjoyed success. "During the past week I have administered several times to Sister Phebe Scholes Saville, at the home of Bro. John Sears, nearby. She had an infection in her foot. She received early and substantial help through the prayer of faith and is now convalescent."[5] Elder Whitney was also asked to review a literary work by his friend Elder Roberts: "Reviewed, by request of Pres. Grant, B. H. Roberts's work *Joseph Smith, the Prophet-Teacher*, in prospect of a new edition."[6] He also gave a blessing to Andrew Kimball (father of Spencer W. Kimball), then ill and near death. Returning at a later date, Ort found Andrew no better. "In company with Elder James E. Talmage called on Andrew Kimball, who is in a dying condition. We blessed him and bid him good-bye, asking the Lord to release him, this being his desire, he having suffered so long."[7] The funeral occurred only a few days later: "Was one of the speakers at the funeral of President Andrew Kimball, who died last Sunday night. The other speakers were President Grant and Dr. Talmage. The funeral was held in the 27th ward chapel at 2 p.m."[8]

Both Elder Whitney and his wife attended a social function that had extra meaning for her. "In the evening at 6 p.m. a dinner was given by the wives of the Twelve to their husbands at the Hotel Utah. It was also a sort of farewell to Brother and Sister Talmage, who intend leaving for Europe October 17, he to preside over the European Mission, Elder David O. McKay having been released."[9]

May spoke to those assembled. "May's address, 'The Ins and Outs of Durham House,' at the banquet last evening seems to have made quite an impression. Stephen L. Richards told me it was splendid—I had left before it was given."[10]

He scored his usual success with his talk at general conference, and also later in an address about Columbus. "A few days ago I received a kind note from Pres. Heber J. Grant, warmly commending my America address, delivered at the Tabernacle, on Sunday the 12th and published in full in the *Deseret News* Saturday the 18th. He referred to it as a 'very splendid address,' and stated that he had instructed the *News* manager (his brother, B. F. Grant) to reproduce it in the Christmas *News*. In the same note, the President requested me to write the Christmas greeting for the First Presidency. Wrote the greeting and read it to Pres. Ivins (Pres. Grant away and Pres. Penrose at home, ill). He approved it."[11]

Then Whitney ghostwrote a piece for his brother-in-law: "About this time wrote an article for my friend and brother, Senator Reed Smoot, entitled, "Why I Am a Mormon,' to be published in the *Forum* magazine. The Senator had suggested my name to the editor as one well qualified to furnish such an article and sign it, but the *Forum* man told him my name was not in the 'Who's Who' book and urged him (Smoot) to write it. He, being overworked and worn down, came to me, by suggestion from Pres. Grant, and I cheerfully undertook the task, completing it and sending the article to Washington."[12]

The stake conferences continued in rapid succession, with Elder Whitney having proved his health sufficiently solid to be entrusted with visits to locations beyond the environs of the Salt Lake Valley.

On Christmas Eve, 1924, Elder Whitney spoke at a funeral: "I occupied about 20 minutes, and if I am the judge, never spoke with greater freedom. Many told me so. My neighbor, John Sears, said it was my masterpiece. I felt the power of the Spirit upon me, and to God give all the glory."[13] A few days later, after preaching in a local Salt Lake ward, Whitney suffered a minor accident. "On alighting from the auto that brought me home, I fell heavily to the ground and had quite a jolt, but a blanket of snow prevented serious injury."[14]

January of 1925 found Elder Whitney in a new venue for his speaking. "Utah's inauguration anniversary. Spent it at home until

8 p.m., when I proceeded to the radio station [KSL], top of *Deseret News* building, and there delivered my address. . . . My subject: The Everlasting Gospel. Time of delivery: 25 minutes. It was my first experience of the kind. 'Magnificent!' exclaimed Earl Jay Glade, the director, as I closed. Almost immediately I was called up by phone by Edward H. Anderson, at his home, and asked for the address to publish in the *Improvement Era* for February. I have since received many compliments and congratulations on what my friends are pleased to term 'a wonderful sermon.'"[15] This would be the beginning of a number of radio addresses given by Elder Whitney.

More visits to stake conferences followed, including one to the Provo stake. "While in Provo, I met several old-time friends, whom I had not seen for years. Called on the Day family whom I knew in Wales, at the Hickman and Hansen homes; took lunch and returned . . . to Salt Lake."[16] This would be the second-to-last mention of the Hickmans in Orson's diary. Laura had moved to Arizona at about the same time that Elder Whitney left for his European Mission, and therefore was not present for this visit. She would appear but one more time in the diaries, simply to be mentioned as the author of an announcement in the newspaper.

A few days later, Elder Whitney was in Idaho, dedicating a new schoolhouse built in the small community of Whitney, decades earlier named after him.[17] At the April general conference, he spoke about miracles and then gave a special Easter address at a local ward. That summer he attended the commencement exercises of Brigham Young University.[18] After that he rode in an MIA Jubilee parade, and being very impressed by the proceedings, he noted, "I was proud of my religion and my people."[19] A week later Elder Whitney finished an article reviewing scenes from his youth. "Completed today an article on 'The Wasatch Literary Association,' to appear in the September *Improvement Era*."[20]

Then came a milestone birthday. "I am 70, but I don't feel more than 60, and scarcely that. Everybody tells me how young I look and how well I speak."[21] The work continued: "Addressed the high priests of Ensign Stake in the 20th ward chapel. . . . My address made a profound impression. The Lord is certainly with me in my ministrations among His people and wherever I go."[22]

General conference came and went, as did more mission tours and stake conference visits. Then Elder Whitney attended another important social function: "Attended with my wife a very pleasant party at President Anthony W. Ivins's home on B Street. The guests were the First Presidency and Twelve, the patriarch, the Presiding Bishop, and their wives; also Elder Rulon S. Wells, who is soon to leave, with Elder Melvin J. Ballard, and Elder Rey L. Pratt, for South America, to open a mission at Buenos Aires. Elders Ballard and Wells were the chief guests of honor, Elder Pratt having already gone. There was a program of readings, songs, speeches, and a splendid dinner. I read an original poem, humorously describing the opening of the South American Mission."[23]

During the years of his mission presidency, his recovery from his breakdown, and afterward, the constant diary references to revising either *Elias* or *Love and the Light: An Idyll of the Westland* cease. Elder Whitney seems to have largely put those works behind him, though his long and steady efforts at giving *Elias* a final revision never saw print.

He produced more poetry, occasionally mentioning it. One of the more well-known pieces appeared in January, 1926. "Began a new poem and on Thursday 14th finished it. Think I shall give it to the *Young Woman's Journal*. It is entitled 'The Soul's Captain'—a reply to Henley's 'Invictus.'"[24]

Another round of stake visits followed. "At Bear River Stake conference and priesthood convention. Spoke Saturday afternoon and forenoon and afternoon of Sunday. Ex-Congressman Milton Welling is President of that stake. Just before I arose Sunday afternoon he arose and said, 'If Orson F. Whitney had not been a great bishop, nor a great Apostle, nor a great orator, he would still be a great poet.' He then read to the congregation Henley's poem 'Invictus,' and my reply to it, a copy of which I had presented to him. Apropos of this poem, I have given it to the *Young Women's Journal* and it will be out in a few days, but meanwhile have had 150 printed slips run off for my private use. President Grant, to whom I gave a typewritten copy, also had 100 printed for his own use. My poem is entitled 'The Soul's Captain.' I have received many compliments, verbal and written, regarding this poem."[25]

With March came another radio address. "Was the appointed speaker over Radio KSL this evening. Subject: Poesy and Prophecy. It is regarded as one of the best things I have ever done."[26] As Elder Whitney entered the last five years of his life, his diary entries become more sporadic, with stake conferences, public speeches, and poetry becoming the main items noted.

The April 1926 general conference arrived, and with it the first mention of Elder Whitney's last major literary work, a narrative covering his own life that would be published with the title *Through Memory's Halls*. "Some weeks ago I began to write *Memoirs of Orson F. Whitney, Bishop and Apostle in The Church of Jesus Christ of Latter-day Saints*, and have now completed 15 chapters, Miss Vella Hart and Miss Rosalind Grant assisting as typists. I am much interested in the work, which I hope to be able to publish for the benefit of my children at least. It is not only the record of my life. It is my testimony to the truth."[27]

May and June found Elder Whitney touring missions in Canada and in the east, spending his birthday in Chicago with his children living there and giving an oration on Independence Day. "Returning from the east, I found all well at home. Everybody glad to see me, and telling me how much they had enjoyed my letters to the [*Deseret*] *News*. I had to decline invitations to speak in various places, needing a little season of rest after my seven weeks of travel and preaching. One invitation was to go up on the Weber [a river] with the D. P. Howells, Pres. and Sister Grant with the party. May's lameness would not permit her to go, and I would not go and leave her."[28] This is one of a few mentions in Whitney's diary about his wife May having some issue with a foot or leg, making it so that she could not participate in some physical activities he enjoyed.

Stake conference visits and public speeches kept Elder Whitney busy until October general conference.

> Second day of the conference. I was next to the last speaker at the forenoon session. After sitting down I was handed a note reading thus: 'Dear Bro. Whitney, I regard it as most fortunate for the Church that to one of our number is given the propriety, the capacity, and the inspiration to correlate the occasionally momentous events

> of the world with the eternal progress of God's work. I pronounce your address a masterpiece, and I heartily congratulate you. Your Bro. Stephen L. [Richards].' Many similar expressions, given verbally, came to me from such men as B. H. Roberts, David O. McKay, Melvin J. Ballard, Richard R. Lyman, et. al. Attended all the general sessions of the conference, which closed Tuesday p.m. At the mission presidents meeting held on Friday before conference, President Quinney, of the Canadian Mission, spoke most appreciatively of my visit to that part last summer; said it was 'the outstanding event of the year,' and had done them a world of good. Pres. [B. H.] Roberts, of the Eastern States Mission, also spoke in a similar strain regarding my visit to New York. He praised highly the article by Senator Smoot, in the *Forum*, headed 'Why I am a Mormon,' and said they intended making a tract of it for use in the mission and would print 30,000 copies. I asked him to send me one, saying that I had a special interest in it; and he replied, 'I know it; I recognized the authorship. It is masterly.' I also wrote for the Senator another article for an English paper. 'The Religion of the Latter-day Saints,' which has been reprinted in the *Millennial Star*, in the *Liahona*, and in the *Deseret News*. I have done lots of this kind of work for my brethren, including the Presidents of the Church, past and present."[29]

After conference, Elder Whitney was sent again to Canada, visiting other stakes around Alberta, and then back to Salt Lake. For one of the visits, Elder Whitney went with the prophet. "I accompanied President Heber J. Grant to the Cottonwood Stake conference, held in the Granite Stake Tabernacle. The attendance—2,200—was the largest I had ever seen there at the opening of a stake conference or any other meeting. It was accounted for by the fact that the Sunday School of the stake had all adjourned to permit the children to see and hear the President of the Church. Between forenoon and afternoon sessions, President Grant and I stood in line while 2,000 men, women, and children passed by and shook hands with us. After the 4 p.m. dismissed, the President and I called on Brother William A. Morton and administered to him. He is a very sick man."[30] Then Orson attended the prophet's birthday social. "President Grant's birthday—70. In the evening my wife and I attended a dinner party given in his honor by his ten daughters, at the home of his daughter. . . . I made a speech on 'When we were 21,' and several others spoke or sang. The guests were the General Authorities and their wives; also the widows of former Presidents of the Church. It was a very pleasant affair. Pres. Grant made the closing address."[31]

With December, Christmas neared. "Addressed the Bishops Club, of Liberty Stake, in the Belvedere reception hall, President Bryant S. Hinckley [father of Gordon B. Hinckley] presiding. Gave them, by request, a talk on Christmas and the Christ. Had a delightful evening. This club is made up of the bishops, stake presidency, high counselors, and their wives, a very nice lot of people. My address was the first of the current season's series. President [Bryant S.] Hinckley, who is a wit, was requested by Bishop Ashton, the program director, to introduce me, and this is how he did it: 'Brethren and Sisters, we promised you the best. Well, he is here, and will now speak to you.' He afterwards told me that he regarded me as 'the most eloquent expounder of the Gospel in the Church.' I replied that I did not aspire to that distinction, but liked to be in the front rank. Many congratulations followed."[32]

A few days later Elder Whitney again found himself in front of the microphone. "Was the appointed speaker at the KSL radio station, Vermont Building, this evening at 9 o'clock. My subject: 'A Marvelous Work and a Wonder,' published in full in the following Saturday's *Deseret News*. It was highly spoken of by many—by all, so far as heard from."[33] On December 23, Elder Whitney and other Church leaders visited the temple. "Passed through the temple, to refresh my memory on the ritual. President Grant and others went through. It was in honor of the Prophet Joseph's birthday."[34]

As he often did, Elder Whitney summed up the year as it ended: "I close the old year and begin the new, with grateful acknowledgments to the Great and Good Provider, for the many blessings showered upon me and mine. My wife and I are in good health, happy and contented in our little home. . . . We have good neighbors and many kind friends and are accounted faithful members of the Church and of the ward in which we live. We are out of debt, which is a great comfort, and have a little laid by 'for a rainy day.' Our children are too much scattered to suit us, but we cannot help it—they have to live where they can find employment."[35]

January of 1827 saw Elder Whitney briefly entering the fray of an argument started in Washington D.C., in the U.S. Senate. A dozen senators were asked their opinion on whether animals have souls (spirits), including Utah's Mormon senator. Elder Whitney wrote a letter to the *Deseret News*, establishing that Latter-day Saints knew that animals did indeed have spirits. He also noted the question in his diary. "Senator William H. King, a 'Mormon' boy, and an experienced missionary (we were in England together 40 odd years ago) surprised his friends in Utah by voting that animals do not have souls. Dr. Caleb Plummer, the bird man, phone me the same evening that my letter came out in the [*Deseret*] *News*, expressing his satisfaction at my attitude, and saying of King, 'He knows better than that, someone ought to teach him the first principles of Mormonism.'"[36]

On the heels of that little question, another minor controversy arose, pertaining to who might be the oldest, longest-running contributor to the *Deseret News*. Whitney made sure his voice was politely and respectfully heard in protest of someone else who antedated his own pieces written and printed during his first mission.[37] When others proved an earlier claim to his, he was quick to humorously step aside.

As February began, Ort learned of the death of his sister Helen. His generation was well underway in crossing the veil.[38]

Orson went to the dentist and had his last eleven teeth pulled, and lost ten pounds, taking no solid food while waiting for his false teeth to be made. He found it more difficult to speak clearly without them. He noted progress on his life story: "Have been busy upon my memoirs for some months, and they begin to take the shape I desire—quite readable, I think."[39]

April general conference came and went as usual, and Elder Whitney spoke there and at several funerals that month. His age began to show: "Spoke at the funeral of Sister Burton, in the Burton ward. Gave a talk over the Radio (KSL) at night. Worked too hard for my condition and have not been feeling normal since. Saturday I had a chill and fever, followed by a bilious spell after attending the matinee with my wife and a dear friend. Was better by night, but rather weak, and Sunday's work was a little too much for me."[40]

During one stake visit, Elder Whitney had his attention called to a miraculous incident from many years before. "While I was at Loa,

Wayne Stake on Sunday, May 8, a Sister Hanks reminded me of an incident connected to my first visit to Wayne Stake about 20 years ago. She had lost her sight, and while I was blessing her, she said, her sight was restored. I had forgotten all about it, and was glad of this reminder."[41]

Elder Whitney then helped prepare his grandson to serve a mission. "Set apart my grandson, Winslow Whitney Smith, for a mission to Switzerland and Germany. His father [Winslow Farr Smith] assisted me."[42] As the summer passed, Elder Whitney turned seventy-two but again mentioned he did not feel his age. He wrote a poem in honor of Charles Lindberg, the famous pilot who first flew across the Atlantic Ocean from the United States to France. He had Senator Reed Smoot deliver it to Lindberg. Then Elder Whitney gave another talk on KSL, this time speaking about baptism. Lindberg flew *The Spirit of St. Louis* to Salt Lake City and gave a speech in the Tabernacle, after which Elder Whitney shook hands with him, saying, "I feel it an honor, Colonel, to shake your hand."[43]

At general conference, Elder Whitney was almost the last speaker. "Immediately after conference I began a revision of my book *Saturday Night Thoughts*, in preparation for a new edition, the old one having been exhausted, since the senior classes of the MIA took up the study of it."[44] Then Elder Whitney had to miss another special occasion: "Upon this day the . . . Arizona Temple was dedicated by President Heber J. Grant. A large party went with him. I and my wife were invited, but her lameness prevented our going, and besides, I had a book in the press—my *Saturday Night Thoughts* (second edition), upon which I have been working for the past months."[45] Soon thereafter the book was printed and bound. "Received from the Deseret Book Store first two copies of revised second edition *Saturday Night Thoughts*, just from the press."[46]

A year previously, Elder Whitney had been notified by Quorum of the Twelve President Rudger Clawson that he was appointed to visit the Southern States Mission, which he did during November and into December. As was often the case, Elder Whitney wrote up lengthy accounts of his travels throughout the missions and sent them to the *Deseret News* for publication. He used these accounts, with some revisions, in the autobiographical memoirs he was preparing.[47]

The tour of the Southern States Mission ended before Christmas, and Whitney visited his children in Chicago before coming home to find his sister "Floddy" very ill. He administered to her first thing on his arrival.[48]

After Christmas, Elder Whitney stayed active. "The rest of the week I was busy at my office, and on my memoirs."[49] He was also given a new literary assignment: "I have received a commission from the First Presidency to prepare, conjointly with Elder B. H. Roberts, an article on Mormons for the *Encyclopedia Britannica*."[50] The article was completed by late February, with a number of stake conference visits intervening.

Afterward, Elder Whitney decided to write another poem. "Have completed my article for the *Britannica*; and [now] written a poem, 'A Call to Israel,' intended for use two years hence at the 100th anniversary of the Church (April 6, 1930)."[51]

Elder Whitney then recorded an unusual incident told him by a friend:

> Last evening, at my prayer circle in the temple, a member thereof, Elder Henry Clark, related the following: In conversation with Father Hunt, a local Catholic Monsignor, the latter told him of his recent visit to Rome and the Pope. His Holiness, it seems, is much interested in Western America, and especially Utah and the adjacent region. He asked Hunt who were the most pronounced opponents of Catholicism in this part of the country and Hunt replied, "Orson F. Whitney and two others" (whom he likewise named to the Pope). The other two were non-Mormons. "Whitney represents the Mormon attitude toward the Catholic Church," Hunt said to the Pope, adding: "Whenever they have anything to publish on Catholicism, Whitney prepares it." He gave the Pope some of my writings that he had taken with him from Salt Lake, and at a subsequent interview in the Vatican, His Holiness, who had read the writings, remarked, "Well, he is at least a gentleman—he has been a gentleman all the way through." "Yes," said Hunt, "he always maintains the standards of a gentleman." "Is there any hope of winning him from the error of his way?" asked the Pope. "Not the slightest," answered Monsignor Hunt. I related this to Presidents Grant and Ivins this morning, in the President's Office, where Brother B. H. Roberts and I were reading to them our joint article on the history,

> doctrine, and government of the Church, to be published, we hope, in a new edition of the *Encyclopedia Britannica*. Elder James E. Talmage was also present.

That Elder Whitney's theological thinking would impress the Pope in a respectful manner was gratifying to him. When he defended the Church or contrasted it with other faiths, he always tried to do so respectfully.

With a major Church milestone coming down the road, Elder Whitney put his mind to his poem that was meant to commemorate the event. "Today, in the temple, I read to the First Presidency and Twelve, such of them as could be present, my latest poem, 'A Call to Israel,' written for use, two years hence, at the proposed celebration of the 100th anniversary of the Church. It seemed to please everybody there. 'A lofty theme loftily presented,' said President Nibley, and all agreed with him. A round of hearty applause greeted the reading."[52] Though the diary does not mention it, Orson's published autobiography notes that in preparing this poem, he "received valued advice from Miss Laura Hickman, sister to Professor J. E. Hickman and teacher of English in some of the leading schools of the state. None of my scholastic friends have been more helpful to me than these twain. Miss Hickman has a high sense of literary values, and her intelligent, incisive criticisms have more than once put me on my mettle and prodded me into doing my best."[53] The last appearance of Laura Hickman in Orson's diary also came about this time, on May 5, 1928, accompanying a note about an announcement in the newspaper.

Orson also read the new poem to Josiah, desiring his feedback: "I went and visited with Apostle Whitney for nearly 2 hrs. Monday. He read me, for the second time, his thoughts in the form of a dialogue between Ephraim & Judah of the coming forth of the Gospel. He is preparing this for the 100th Anniversary of the Advent [restoration] of the Gospel. It is a beautiful poetic portrayal of Ephraim's part and his urging of Judah to awaken and do his part in the restoring of the Gospel. I took him and Zina Hickman, my brother's (George Francis's) wife to dinner."[54] (George Francis had been excommunicated for marrying Zina long after the second manifesto.)

At the April general conference, Elder Whitney gave his usual powerful message. "Spoke in the general conference, and the Lord blessed me signally. Subject: The Marvelous Work and Wonder. Pres. Ivins said it was 'a powerful and well-organized discourse,' and many others uttered similar sentiments. 'Beyond anything you have done yet,' said David O. McKay."[55]

That month Orson noted that his son Paul was married, with the ceremony being performed by John H. Taylor, President of the Northern States Mission, at the bride's parent's home.[56] He also spoke to new missionaries preparing to depart. "Addressed for the first time a class of prospective missionaries, at the missionary home."[57] In May, when the General Authorities held a meeting to begin preparations for the centennial celebration of the Restoration of the Church, Elder Whitney was ready to offer his poem for the program.[58] He then spent most of July on vacation, working on his autobiography.[59] As autumn began, he toured some stakes and missions in the east, reporting his travels and labors to the *Deseret News* as usual.

With October came general conference, and a missed opportunity to speak to some Catholics: "Second day of the general conference. I was the concluding speaker in the forenoon session. Enjoyed much of the Good Spirit and felt greatly blessed. As usual, was showered with congratulations. Before rising to speak, I was handed the following note: 'Orson—Levi Edgar [Young] tells me that a party of Catholic bishops will be here at 11 a.m. and he has been asked to bring the party to our conference. Shall be pleased to have you speak after their arrival. Yours, H. J. Grant.' But the Catholics did not come, and regret was expressed on the stand, for, said Pres. Ivins, 'It was just what they needed to hear.'"[60]

October and November were filled with more stake conference visits and poetry readings. One of them was to Josiah Hickman's stake, where he recorded his talks and friendship with Elder Whitney in greater detail than Whitney himself did.

> Today we had the first day of our quarterly [stake] conference. I was one of five speakers who spoke on some phase of the High Priesthood. Apostle Whitney was the visiting [authority]. He walked home with me after the afternoon meeting. Then Sunday morning he and I

> walked through the town until we were late for the 10 a.m. meeting. We were giving our views on great religious truths—thoughts and truths far flung, that it would be unwise to talk [about] in public or even promiscuously [indiscreetly]. I again met Bro. Whitney Monday morning before he took the Interurban [train] for Salt Lake. I still plied him with more questions, and in turn gave my views. Our spirits are quite kindred in our thoughts and judgments. He has a revealing mind to that degree that few ever possess. . . .[61]
>
> It is this revealing mind that makes the scientist, the discoverer of new mathematical truths, the inventor, the poet, the seer. Such minds are God-given. They add new light to this benighted world. They gladden the hearts of men and bring the earth a little nearer heaven's plain.[62]

For Josiah to be reticent enough to not record the content of their conversations was unusual and meant that lofty subjects indeed were spoken of. From Josiah's later notes it is evident that they spoke of profound and sacred matters, confidential outside the spiritual sphere of the moment.

Over the Christmas holiday, Elder Whitney applied his mind to his memoirs, moving the work forward, and feeling grateful for time away from routine business to work on them.[63] That winter, hiss schedule was filled with more stake visits and constant speaking. Conference passed, and then more stake and mission visits over the summer. 1929 was a busy year for the aging Apostle. After Christmas, Elder Whitney gave his final radio address:

> This evening, at about nine o'clock, I delivered over the KSL radio station, my 12th and closing lecture of the series 5 and 6, dealing with "The Apocalypse," or "What John Saw and Heard on Patmos," and "Latter-day Developments." This labor has occupied me every Sunday since October 13. I have been greatly blessed in it, and have reaped a rich crop of appreciative comment, verbal and by letter, from the Saints and from many strangers in various parts of the land. Five million listeners, KSL claims. Never have I had such an audience or such an opportunity, though the task was arduous. I published a revised edition of my radio talks, making a little booklet that sells at 50 cents. I don't expect to make anything out of it, but only to partly pay my debt to the printer.[64]

The Council of the Twelve outside the Salt Lake Temple, 1930. Rear left to right: Joseph Fielding Smith, James E. Talmage, Stephen L. Richards, Richard R. Lyman, Melvin J. Ballard, John A. Widtsoe; Front, Rudger Clawson, Reed Smoot, George Albert Smith, George F. Richards, Orson F. Whitney, and David O. McKay (USHS).

As Whitney entered the last full year of his life, he kept busy editing and polishing his life story, perhaps feeling a premonition that he needed to finish the work—the last major project of his life. "Am revising my memoirs, prior to publishing them, if I can afford it."[65] The crash of the stock market and the beginning of the Great Depression were staring Elder Whitney and the Church in the face.

During April, Elder Whitney's sister, nicknamed "Floddy," died, as did also May's brother, Junius F. Wells, one of the General Authorities.[66] During May, Orson toured the Central Stakes Mission, again writing reports to be published in the newspaper. During a stake conference visit with Elder McKay as his companion, their close friendship was manifest: "Attended the Salt Lake Stake conference and spoke in the Tabernacle and the Assembly Hall; also at a priesthood meeting Monday night in the 22nd ward chapel. My friend David O. McKay spoke Sunday morning, and in the quarterly meeting of the Twelve that followed, I praised his address. This explains the card. . . . 'My Beloved Jonathan: I prize your commendation because I honor your lofty soul and clear judgment, but more because I treasure your friendship. Appreciatively, your friend and brother, David.'"[67] For their friendship to be likened to that of the Old Testament David and Jonathan held great sentimental meaning for Elder Whitney, who equally prized his friendship with Elder David O. McKay.

With summer's end, Orson's hard work on his memoirs neared completion. "Have recently finished my life story upon which I have been working at intervals during the past 4 years or so, and am now reading the printer's proofs. The book is being published at Independence, Mo., by Zion's Printing and Publishing Co."[68] He was thrilled with the final product: "Received this day the from Zion's Printing and Publishing Co., Independence, Mo., 60 copies of my new book [*Through Memory's Halls*]: *The Life Story of Orson F. Whitney*, a work of 420 pages, written in spare moments during the past four or five years. I am very pleased with the appearance of the book and hope it will prove, as designed, a blessing to my children and kindred and friends."[69] He quickly gave it to friends and associates. "Presented to Presidents Grant, Ivins, and Nibley, and to others, each, a copy of my life story."[70]

Christmastime proved well suited for disseminating his new book with special pleasure. "Spent the forenoon, as usual, calling on friends; and worked a while, in my office, room 206, Church Office Building. Have been busy for many days sending out Christmas greetings and gifts. To each of my children and to dear friends, I have sent a copy of *Through Memory's Halls*. All who read it pronounce it most interesting. My regular work of visiting the stakes and sitting in Council with my Brethren continues, as in the past."[71]

That January, Elder Whitney's lifelong friend, John Q. Cannon, the talented but troubled son of George Q. Cannon, died. He took it hard, perhaps feeling his own mortality and age. "John Q. Cannon died today at his room in the Hotel Utah, about 3 p.m. On reaching home in the early evening, I walked the porch, as is my wont after dinner, and began [a] poem [about John Q. Cannon]."[72] Elder Whitney administered what comfort he could to John's widow, Annie, and spoke at his funeral.[73]

Then commendations began to come in about his autobiography. "I have many letters, warmly appreciative of my book *Through*

Memory's Halls, from various parts to which it has been sent in response to orders verbally or by mail. Everybody who reads it seems to be delighted with my life story, and I have placed it in many homes either by gift or purchase."[74]

Josiah Hickman quickly perused his copy. "I finished *Through Memory's Halls—An Autobiography of Apostle Whitney*. It is an excellent review of his life. He has dwelt on the high spots of his life. I see that my name was mentioned twice in it (p. 402 the last time). He says that none of his friends had been more helpful to him than my sister Laura and I had been."[75] The full true story of Whitney's dealings with the Hickman family may remain forever a mystery. Elder Whitney's diary entries became very few and sporadic during his last months, with few entries explaining his daily life. One of them mentioned attendance at a social with his Brethren: "Spent a very pleasant and profitable evening at the home of Elder Stephen L. Richards of the Council of the Twelve. The guests were the First Presidency, the Twelve Apostles, the patriarch, and our wives. After a fine banquet we reassembled in the parlors where a program was rendered. My talk on 'Friendship' seemed to make a decided impression. The family [members] were delighted, and I received many compliments from them and others."[76]

April 1931 general conference was the last time that Elder Whitney would be seen and heard in public:

> Conference continued. I was the closing speaker at the forenoon session. My subject, "The Spirit of the Lord." Though weak physically from the effects of a recent severe cold, I was strong mentally and spiritually and the Lord was with me. My friends were enthusiastic over it. . . . "God bless O. F. W.—I have not heard, nor have I ever read a greater address—I am thrilled with the power and inspiration of it. I am yours, R. R. L." The above note from Apostle Richard R. Lyman was handed to me just after I had spoken. Many others pronounced it a gem, a masterpiece, beautiful, [even] sublime.[77]

These words of personal praise (something he relished and cherished) were the last words Elder Whitney would write in his diary. His cold became worse, turned into pneumonia, and after being hospitalized, he died on May 16, 1931. As one might expect with Orson F. Whitney, he was working on a revision of his autobiography, making "corrections, changes, inserts, etc." up until the day he entered the hospital, when he gave the copy with the revisions to his wife May.

Josiah Hickman recorded his feelings at Whitney's passing,

> My heart has been made very heavy over the death of my great friend Apostle O. F. Whitney. . . . He died Sat. 5:59 a.m. and was buried today, Sunday (May 17). I did not go to the funeral as I could not find anyone who was going, but the funeral services were broadcast from the Tabernacle so I heard everything said or sung. Wonderful things were said of him. My heart has been most sad for he had been my beloved friend for years. But my sadness is for myself, for he has gone to a well-earned reward. He has finished a great life filled with usefulness and great deeds. He had even finished his memoirs—*Through Memory's Halls*. We all mourn and yet rejoice at his great life. He and I have confided many sacred things to each other. I made him a promise (to him), which I will fulfill if the Lord is willing.[78]

So ended the life of a great bishop, historian, poet, and Apostle of the Lord.

Appendix 1

Elder Whitney's Dream-Vision of the Savior

Elder Whitney shared what he referred to as his "dream-vision of the Savior" on many occasions, two of which are included in the main text of this biography. The first account is in chapter 2, as part of his autobiographical sketch, and the second is in chapter 5, when he first decided to record it in his diary. The two accounts given below are others related by Whitney that are not found in the text, but were published during Elder Whitney's lifetime.

My discourse, reported by the [*Salt Lake*] *Herald* was as follows: Testimony of dream of the Savior given.

I do bear my testimony that God has shown to me as well as to my brethren who have spoken, that this is the work of God and that testimony I hope to live by and, if needed, to die by.

I did not always feel as I do now in relation to this great work. Quite a number of the years of my life were passed without my having this testimony. It was not until the fall of 1876, thirteen years ago, that I was placed in a position to know for myself that this is indeed the work of God. True, I had been taught from my mother's knee that Mormonism was the gospel of Christ. I had been taught to revere the name and the memory of Joseph Smith as a prophet of the Most High; and in my mind he stood next, in my reverence for the Holy Priesthood, to the Lord Jesus Christ Himself. But it was not until I attained my majority that I knew this for myself.

At the October conference of the year 1870 I was called upon to perform a mission to the United States. I had hardly enough faith to go upon that mission. I was will to go, but I did not feel that responsibility of the soul which I would feel today, if I were called to go to the nations of the earth upon a similar errand, but it was not long before I became imbued with the testimony of which I speak. I was laboring in the state of Pennsylvania, and with my limited knowledge, my ignorance and the weakness of my faith, I did not feel that I was accomplishing very much. I remember that I became interested in writing for the press, in writing home to the papers here an account of the sights and scenes that I witnessed, and this, to a measure engrossed my mind so that I did not engage in my spiritual labors with that zest that I should have manifested. But right here God gave me the testimony which I have since held; and which to me now is beyond all price.

I dreamed one night while in that state, that I was in the Garden of Gethsemane. I saw the Savior and three of His Apostles through a little gate at my right into the garden. I stood, as it were, in the background, or the foreground of the picture, which I beheld as plainly as I now see your faces and the interior of the tabernacle. They did not see me, but I saw them. The Savior stationed those three Apostles in a little group and asked them to pray without ceasing while He went to the left and bowed Himself down to pray also. Presently He arose, and walking to where Peter, James, and John were kneeling, fast asleep, He shook them to wake them up, and again asked them to pray. He retired to His place and prayed again. He returned again and found them sleeping. Awaking them once more, He exhorted them to pray, to keep their eyes open, and not to sleep upon their watch. He returned to His place again until this had passed three times, and as He kneeled there praying to God to give Him strength to perform His mission to pass through the ordeal that was before Him—to drink of the bitter cup prepared for Him by His Father; and as He called upon God, the agony of His soul, and asked Him if it were possible to [text missing]. The tears streamed down His face; and gazing upon His mental agony I was constrained to weep in unison with Him. Presently He arose and beckoned His apostles to Him and the circumstances seemed to change.

The scene remained as it was, but instead of being in time before the Crucifixion, it now seemed to be after that event. I thought He was about leaving the earth and He was taking these Apostles with Him. My heart was so drawn out to Him with love, with sympathy for His great suffering that I ran out from behind the tree where I had stood gazing and fell down at His feet, clasped his knees and asked Him to take me with Him. I shall never forget the look of indescribable tenderness, affection, and compassion with which He gazed down upon me as I knelt before Him. He lifted me up and embraced me. I could feel the very warmth of His bosom against which I rested; and as He took me in His arms with all the tenderness of a father or an elder brother, He shook His head and said, "No, my son. Your work is not finished. You must remain and perform your mission. These (pointing to His apostles) have finished their work, and they can go with me, but you must remain." I was so anxious to go, I felt such a love for Him and a desire to be with Him that I clung to Him and plead with Him that He would let me go; but He continued to shake His head. "Then," said I, "promise me that when I have finished my work I will come to You at last." Again He gazed at me with tenderness and compassion, and He uttered these words in tones which pierced my very soul, "That will depend entirely upon yourself." I awoke and it was morning, but I knew that I had been gazing upon a vision, that God had indeed spoken to me and that He had told me the truth in plainness and simplicity. I saw that I, too, must be awake, that I must not sleep, that I must not consider any of the things of this world of paramount import to the mission which I was sent to perform as a servant of the Lord Jesus Christ; and I have often reflected upon the wisdom of the answer which He gave me when He told me that it would depend entirely upon myself (*OFWJ*, October 5, 1889).

From *Through Memory's Halls*, pages 81–83:

My communications to the *Herald*, the first one dated March 14, 1877, leaped at once into popular favor. This gratified me, of course, but I became so absorbed in the correspondence that it encroached upon hours that should have been given to religious study. Elder Musser chided me for it. "You ought to be studying the books of the Church," said he. "You were sent out to preach the Gospel, not to write for the newspapers." I knew he was right, but still kept on, fascinated by the discovery that I could wield a pen, and preferring that to any other pursuit except the drama, my ambition for which had been laid aside.

Then came a marvelous manifestation, an admonition from a Higher Source, one impossible to ignore. It was a dream, or a vision in a dream, as I lay upon my bed in the little town of Columbia, Lancaster County, Pennsylvania. I seemed to be in the Garden of Gethsemane, a witness of the Savior's agony. I saw Him as plainly as ever I have seen anyone. Standing behind a tree in the foreground, I beheld Jesus, with Peter, James and John, as they came through a little wicket gate at my right. Leaving the three Apostles there, after telling them to kneel and pray, the Son of God passed over to the other side, where He also knelt and prayed. It was the same prayer with which all Bible readers are familiar: "Oh my Father, if it be possible, let this cup pass from me; nevertheless not as I will, but as thou wilt." As He prayed the tears streamed down his face, which was toward me. I was so moved at the sight that I also wept, out of pure sympathy. My whole heart went out to Him; I loved Him with all my soul, and longed to be with Him as I longed for nothing else.

Presently He arose and walked to where those Apostles were kneeling—fast asleep! He shook them gently, awoke them, and in a tone of tender reproach, untinctured by the least show of anger or impatience, asked them plaintively if they could not watch with Him one hour. There He was, with the awful weight of the world's sin upon his shoulders, with the pangs of every man, woman, and child shooting through his sensitive soul—and they could not watch with Him one poor hour!

Returning to His place, He offered up the same prayer as before; then went back and again found them sleeping. Again He awoke them, re-admonished them, and once more returned and prayed. Three times this occurred, until I was perfectly familiar with his appearance—face, form and movements. He was of noble stature and majestic mien—not at all the weak, effeminate being that some painters have portrayed; but the very God that He was and is, as meek and humble as a little child.

All at once the circumstances seemed to change, the scene remaining just the same. Instead of before, it was after the Crucifixion, and the Savior, with the three Apostles, now stood together in a group at my left. They were about to depart and ascend into Heaven. I could endure it no longer. I ran from behind the tree, fell at His feet, clasped Him around the knees, and begged Him to take me with Him

I shall never forget the kind and gentle manner in which He stooped, raised me up, and embraced me. It was so vivid, so real. I felt the very warmth of His body, as He held me in his arms and said in tenderest tones, "No, my son; these have finished their work; they can go with me, but you must stay and finish yours." Still I clung to Him. Gazing up into His face—for He was taller than I—I besought Him fervently: "Well, promise me that I will come to You at the last." Smiling sweetly, He said, "That will depend entirely upon yourself." I awoke with a sob in my throat, and it was morning.

"That's from God," said Elder Musser, when I related to him what I had seen and heard. "I do not need to be told that," was my reply. I saw the moral clearly. I had never thought of being an apostle, nor of holding any other office in the Church, and it did not occur to me even then. Yet I knew that those sleeping Apostles meant me. I was asleep at my post—as any man is who, having been divinely appointed to do one thing, does another.

But from that hour all was changed. I was never the same man again. I did not give up writing; for President Young, having noticed some of my contributions to the home papers, advised me to cultivate what he called my "gift for writing." "So that you can use it," said he, "for the establishment of truth and righteousness." I therefore continued to write, but not to the neglect of the Lord's Work. I held that first and foremost; all else was secondary.

Appendix 2

Reincarnated Name Ledger

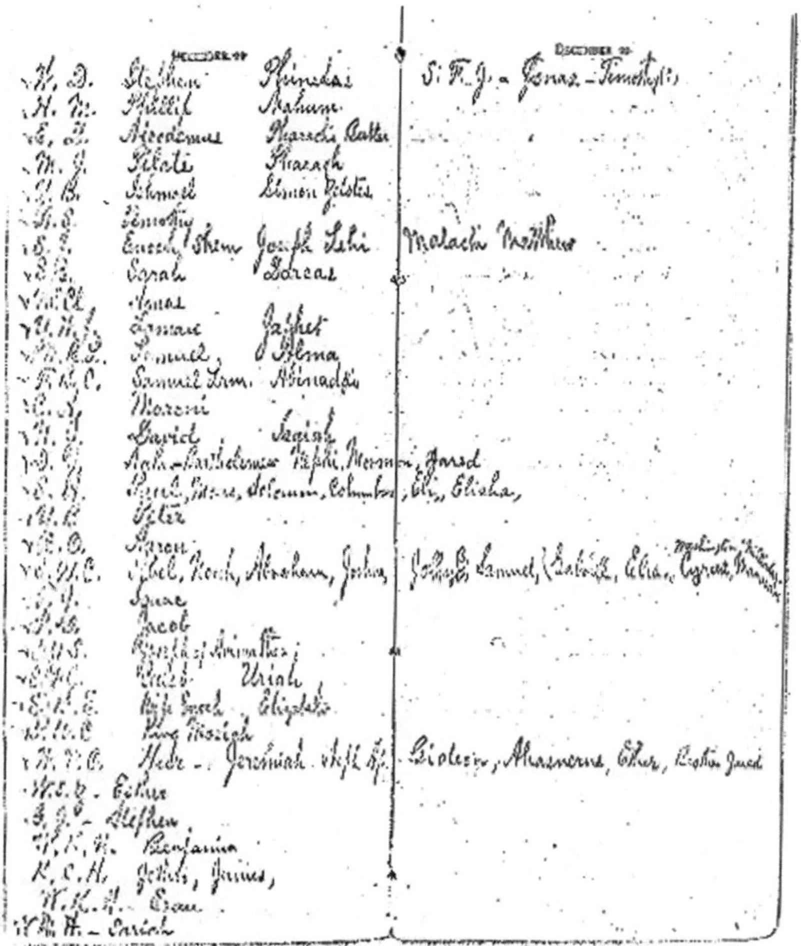

Proposed Key

W. D. – Stephen, Phineas
H. M. – Phillip, Nahum
E. D. – Nicodemus, Pharaoh's Butler
M. J. – Pilate, Pharoah

D. B. – Ishmael, Simon Zelotes
A. S. – Timothy
S. A. / Arthur Stayner[?] – Enoch, Shem, Joseph, Lehi, Malachi, Matthew
S. R. – Sarah, Dorcas
M. U[?].– Amos
Y. W. J. / John W. Young[?]– Laman, Japhet
W[?]. R. L. – Lemuel, Alma
F. B. C. – Samuel the Lamanite, Abinadi
C. A. – Moroni
N. J. – David, Isaiah
D. J. / John Donaldson – [?], Bartholomew, Nephi, Mormon, Jared
S. A. / Arthur Stayner [repeated?] – Paul, Moses, Solomon, Columbus, Eli, Elisha
Y. B. / Brigham Young – Peter
[?]. O. – Aaron
S. W. C. / Charles W. Stayner – Abel, Noah, Abraham, Joshua, [Jo?], Samuel, Gabriel, Elias, Cyrus, Washington, Manasseh
[?]. J. – Isaac
S. V. – Jacob
G. U. S.[?] – Joseph of Arimathea
S. C. – Caleb, Uriah
S. K. E. / Arthur Stayner's wife – Wife of Enoch, Elizabeth
P. W. C. / Charles W. Penrose – King Mosiah
W. [?]. C. – Hur, Jeremiah, [illegible], Gideon, [illegible], Ether, Brother of Jared
W. S. Z. / Zina Smoot Whitney – Esther
G. J. – Stephen
W. K. H. / Horace K. Whitney – Benjamin
K. C. H. – Jethro, James
W. K. H. – Esau
W. M. H. / Helen Mar Whitney – Sariah
S. F. J. / Joseph F. Smith – Jonas, Timothy[?]

Appendix 3

Letters from President Brigham Young to Orson F. Whitney

These letters were written to Orson F. Whitney while serving his first mission in Ohio:

Salt Lake City
June 28th 1977
Elder Orson F. Whitney
Elyria, Ohio

Dear Brother:

We were much pleased with the spirit and tenor of your communication of the 19th inst, as well as with the news it contains of brightening prospects for doing good in the field of missionary labor in which you are now travelling. You have our constant prayers that you may be enabled to do much good and bring many honest souls to a knowledge of the truth. Seek the Lord continually that you may be guided by him to the honest in heart; trust in Him at all times, that you may never be confounded by the corrupt or the worldly-wise, be patient under all circumstances, remembering that those who may attack you do so because of the Gospel message which you bear, which inculcates long suffering and patience to all men; never descend to argue with the wicked; the principles of the Gospel are too sacred to be quarreled over; bear your testimony in humility and leave the results with God. If they will not hear you in one place go to another, and He in whom we trust will open up the way before you.

We should be pleased to have you cultivate the gifts with which you are endowed, of writing for the public eye, so that you may be prepared to rightly use it for the spread of the truth and the establishment of righteousness upon the earth. We should be glad to have you communicate freely with the *Deseret News*. Your father, mother and the family generally are well.

May God abundantly bless you, preserve you from every evil, guide you in all your ways, and when you have fully accomplished the purposes of your mission bring you home in peace, purity, and safety to your family and friends in Zion, is the prayer of Your Brother in the Gospel,

Brigham Young

Salt Lake City, U. T.
June 19, 1877.
Elder O. F. Whitney,
Elyria, Lorain Co., Ohio.

Dear Brother:

We have read with considerable interest your letters to the *Herald* of this City, and from them as well as from other sources, we are pleased to learn that you are energetically proclaiming the word of Truth where opportunity offers. As you have found an opening for the spread of the Gospel in Ohio, and there are but few, if any, Elders in that State, we have thought it wise to have you continue your labors there, you will therefore in future report to Elder David M. Stuart (whose address is 1114 Cass avenue, St. Louis) who is the presiding Elder in the missionary district in which Ohio is situated, and he will direct you in your labors and travels. As soon as we can find a suitable Elder we will send him to your help. Of course this appointment releases you from laboring in the Pennsylvania district to which you were formerly called.

May the Lord abundantly bless you with His Holy Spirit that you may be able to do much good is the prayer of your brother in the Gospel,

Brigham Young

Appendix 4
Children of Orson F. Whitney

Orson F. Whitney and Zina Beal Smoot

1. Horace Newell Whitney (1880–1908), died at age 28
2. Heber Kimball Whitney (1882–1883), died young
3. Emily Whitney (1885–1973), married Winslow Farr Smith
4. Helen Margaret Whitney (1887–1962), married John Timpson
5. Margaret Whitney (1889–1968), married Lester Essig
6. Charles Byron Whitney (1891–1943), married Lillian Russell
7. Albert Owen Whitney (1893–1963), married Eva Ransom
8. Virginia Clayton Whitney (1899–1984), twin, married Donald James
9. Paul Van Cott Whitney (1899–1942), twin, married Evelyn Ganschow

Orson F. Whitney and Mary Minerva Wells

1. Murray Wells Whitney (1892–1972), married Martha Savage
2. Wendell Webb Whitney (1895–1971), married Mary Christensen

Key to Note Abbreviations

TMH: *Through Memory's Halls: The Life Story of Orson F. Whitney, as told by himself* (Independence, MO: Zion's Printing and Publishing Company, 1930).

HMWJ: Helen Mar Whitney Journal, as found in Whitney, H. M., Hatch, C. M., & Compton, T. (2003). *A Widow's Tale: The 1884–1896 Diary of Helen Mar Kimball Whitney*. Logan, Utah: Utah State University Press.

OFWJ: Orson F. Whitney Journal, as found at Orson F. Whitney Diaries, USU, COLL MSS 188, Special Collections and Archives. Utah State University Merrill-Cazier Library. Logan, Utah. Originals located at LDS Church History Library, Salt Lake City, Utah.

AHCJ: Abraham H. Cannon Journal, as found in *An Apostle's Record: The Journals of Abraham H. Cannon*, ed., Dennis B. Horne (Clearfield, Utah: Gnolaum Books, 2003).

JEHJ: Josiah E. Hickman Journal, online, accessed during 2013; http://hickmansfamily.homestead.com/JEHdiaries.html.

AHLJ: Anthon H. Lund Journal, as found in *Danish Apostle: The Diaries of Anthon H. Lund 1899–1921*, ed., John Hatch (Salt Lake City: Signature Books, 2006).

Notes

Introduction

1. Some few enemies of the LDS Church, carping on their anti-Mormon websites, have fumbled with a few out-of-context diary entries in order to press their case of aberrant doctrinal beliefs. But outside of such stray notice, there seems to have existed an enduring lack of attention regarding Elder Whitney's life as found in his diaries. As of this writing (2014), it would seem that very few researchers have closely read Whitney's diaries since copies were donated to public university libraries. One researcher that evidences some familiarity with the diaries is Michael Quinn. In his book *The Mormon Hierarchy: Extensions of Power*, he gives a summary of Whitney's life and church experience. Almost every sentence of it contains an error, inaccuracy, misinterpretation or misunderstanding of the source material. One of the more obvious is his mistaken conflation of "promise" with "prophecy."

2. *OFWJ*, December 1, 1921.

3. Matthias F. Cowley, at University of Chicago, Oct. 4, 1925, Church History Library Archives (MS F 559).

4. Often Whitney's handwriting is very poor and difficult to read. This opens up the possibility of some error in my transcriptions. Those wishing to check my work can always read the originals for themselves.

5. Correspondence, Bruce R. McConkie to Eugene England, February 19, 1981, 6–7; copy in author's possession. In my opinion, although Orson F. Whitney believed and privately taught some false doctrine within a small group of intimate friends, he meant no malicious harm; he committed no grievous sin during their meetings; he was seeking greater light and knowledge in the wrong places, not practicing deceit. He was also being misled by another through flattery. For an extensive review of prophets, scripture, and determining doctrinal authority, see Horne, *Determining Doctrine*.

6. One way to assure comfort with the teachings of past prophets of this dispensation is to recognize that collections of their words such as those found in the *Teachings of Presidents of the Church* series of manuals, as studied in priesthood and Relief Society classes, have been approved by the Correlation Committee of the Church, which consists of the First Presidency and Quorum of the Twelve.

7. "Shall We Record Testimony," *Improvement Era* 1:5 [March 1898], 372. The Prophet Joseph Smith declared reincarnation, or the transmigration of souls, to be a doctrine of the devil. See *History of the Church* 2:304–07. It is not known whether Whitney knew of this incident in Church history. Some have suggested that later in his life, Joseph changed his mind and taught the doctrine of reincarnation to his plural wives. This conclusion is based on the very kind of shaky and uncertain evidence that President Joseph F. Smith warned about in his editorial.

8. There may be some who claim that Whitney hid reincarnation doctrine in his poetry, such as Elias. Such is always a possibility, but would be hard to argue with certainty, since his poetic discourse was often subject to varying interpretation; people may find what they like therein, whether it really said it or not. His annotated edition of *Elias* explained and defined a number of terms from the text.

9. Woodruff C. Thompson, a student at the University of Utah, wrote a master's thesis in 1949 titled, *Orson F. Whitney: Mormon Writer*, which attempts to make an examination of much of Whitney's writings of all genres. While undoubtedly a worthwhile effort, Thompson seemed to be unaware of certain issues bearing on Orson's work, such as some of his early doctrinal beliefs, and therefore his work lacks analysis of Whitney's literary output from that perspective. Having said that, as of this writing, it is one of the more comprehensive examinations of Orson's poetry and historical output. Some few other stray articles about Whitney's literary accomplishments have appeared in various scholarly journals and church magazines over the years. See also Douglas, "A Survey of Mormon Literary Criticism," 4–11.

10. Lisa Tait, as quoted in a review of Jill Mulvey Derr and Karen Lynn Davidson, eds., *Eliza R. Snow: The Complete Poetry*; Lisa Olsen Tait in *Journal of Mormon History*, Vol. 37, No. 4, Fall, 2011, 264.

11. See http://uda-db.orbiscascade.org/findaid/ark:/80444/xv04257 (accessed September 2013).

Chapter 1

1. See Jenson, *LDS Biographical Encyclopedia* 1:674–81; 3:793–95; and John Nicholson, "The Author and His Work," in *History of Utah* 4:703–07.

2. Jenson's *LDS Biographical Encyclopedia* 4:722 contains the following short biographical blurb about Orson's father Horace: "Whitney, Horace Kimball, one of the original pioneers of Utah, was born July 25, 1823, at Kirtland, Ohio, a son of Newel K. and Elizabeth Ann Whitney. His father, later presiding Bishop of the Church, gave him the best opportunity that the times and educational facilities could command, and being very intelligent, and possessed of a retentive memory, the boy acquired a taste for learning and a love of literature which remained with him all his life. He was also an expert mathematician and an accomplished musician. In a word, he possessed gifts which in a less diffident man, would have brought him into great prominence. He learned the printer's trade in Nauvoo and set type for the first issue of the *Deseret News*, June 15, 1850. He performed military service with the territorial militia, was a member of the Deseret Dramatic Association, treading with recognized ability the boards of the Social Hall and Salt Lake Theater in the early sixties, and was for years a member of the theatre orchestra. Bro. Whitney died Nov. 22, 1884, in Salt Lake City, Utah, survived by his wives, Helen Mar Kimball, and Mary Cravath Whitney, and several children, among whom was the late Apostle Orson F. Whitney." See also Orson F. Whitney, "Newel K. Whitney." *The Contributor* 6 (1885): 125–29, and Poulson, "The Life and Contributions of Newel Kimball Whitney."

3. Further information about Helen Mar Whitney is found in Hatch and Compton, *A Widow's Tale: The 1884–1896 Diary of Helen Mar Kimball Whitney*; Holzapfel and Holzapfel, *A Woman's View: Helen Mar Whitney's Reminiscences of Early Church History*; and Compton, *In Sacred Loneliness: The Plural Wives of Joseph Smith.*

4. In his autobiographical sketch written for Andrew Jenson's *LDS Biographical Encyclopedia*, Orson noted that, "I had a horror of unchastity, which I had been taught to believe was next in heinousness to murder" (1:675).

5. For further information about the Wasatch Literary Association, see Whitney, "The Wasatch Literary Association," *Improvement Era* 28 (September 1925): 1017–19; *TMH*, 55–64; and, "Growing Up in Early Utah: The Wasatch Literary Association, 1874–78," in Walker, *Qualities that Count*, 61–79.

Chapter 2

1. *OFWJ*: "April 8, 1877: On the 24th, in the evening, was called to administer to Mrs. Margaret Frink who was sick with the Neuralgia, Br. Truman Frink assisting. We witnessed a miraculous manifestation of the Spirit of God in her being immediately better—almost entirely well. Next morning she came over to Bro. Frink's, where I was stopping, and am still, and requested a second operation [administration], after which given she pronounced herself entirely free and well, and to my certain knowledge from her own life, has remained so ever since. June 28, 1977."
2. For example, *OFWJ*: "July 2, 1877: Administered to John Jay Kirkbride for sickness and he was healed by the power of God." Also, *OFWJ*: "July 8, 1877: Administered to Emma Hamlin Kirkbride for sickness. The Spirit came so strongly upon her that she was very weak for several minutes, hardly able to raise her arms, though not so before the ordinance was performed. After a few minutes she announced herself feeling well. All glory to the great and good Ruler of the universe, who favors those who have faith in his power." Further: "December 29, 1877: Administered the ordinance of laying on hands to Sister Margaret Frink for headache. The spirit rested upon us powerfully. She was healed." And "January 14, 1878: Administered to Johnnie Sharp; bruised limb. Healed by the power of God."
3. *OFWJ*: "June 18, 1877: Received letter from Pres. Brigham Young releasing me from the Penn[sylvani]a district and appointing me to labor in Ohio."
4. *OFWJ*: "July 3, 1877: Received letter from Pres. B[righam]. Young requesting me to communicate with the *Deseret News*, and containing much valuable advice." See Appendix 3 for the text of this letter.
5. *OFWJ*: "July 9, 1877: Sent an article for publication in the [*Deseret*] *News*, on the 'United Order,' to Pres. Young for his supervision and approval. I have been a regular correspondent of the *Salt Lake Herald* since March 14, 1877, under the soubriquet of 'Iago.'
6. *OFWJ*: "August 6, 1877: . . . The feeling is very bitter against me here, on account of my success."
7. *OFWJ*: "August 30, 1877: Mrs. Dr. Chester Norton, an interested seeker after truth with whom I have been communicating by letter for some time, arrived here by invitation and brought with her the paper containing the sad news of the death of President Brigham Young at Salt Lake, Aug. 29, 1877, 4:01 p.m."

8. *FWJ*: "September 6, 1877: Mrs. Norton (Chester) brought with her a paper announcing the death of Pres. Brigham Young, which sad news was confirmed by reports from home a few days later. The Lord in his wisdom has seen fit to take Bro. Brigham home and we bow in resignation to his Almighty will . . . but we know that we shall meet him again in the spirit world where he has gone to continue his work as a friend and benefactor to his kind. Farewell, Brother Brigham, the heavens are weeping today as though in sympathy with Israel in this affliction. But while we weep and miss you, angels and the spirits of just men gone before are rejoicing to welcome you where your enemies never more can molest you. The Lord's will be done, Amen. Pres. Young died at Salt Lake, Utah, Aug. 29, 1877, 4:01 p.m."

9. *OFWJ*: "September 5, 1877: Mrs. Chester is an intelligent lady and a skillful physician and surgeon. Her ideas of marital relations corresponding with ours, she had some time before addressed a letter to Pres. Young asking him what chances there were in the midst of the 'Mormon' people for her *professionally*, as her sympathy with our peculiar doctrine of polygamy had rendered her very unpopular . . . where she resides. The letter was sent to me to answer. I did so and the result was her arrival here out of curiosity to talk with me, though at the time no thought of *religion* had entered her mind. Six days have wrought a great change; she is now a sincere penitent, an earnest believer, and if the Lord wills will be baptized tomorrow, at the same time with Brother and Sister Frink who wish to renew their covenants [be rebaptized]."

10. *OFWJ*: "December 24, 1877: Mr. John Good came in and desired me to lay hands on him for the healing of his head, which has troubled him for a long time with an agony of pain rapidly growing worse. I anointed him with oil and, in the name of the Lord Jesus Christ rebuked the disease and asked God to heal him. The effect was instantaneous and he went away free from pain. God is ever good to those who ask in faith. This is the fifth time His power has attended my administering in behalf of the sick, to their recovery. All praise and honor is due to Him, the great Giver of every good."

11. *OFWJ*: "January 16, 1878: My left arm was severely rheumatic after the baptism [in frigid water]. Used some liniment, at night, worse next day. At night anointed it with consecrated oil in the name of the Lord Jesus Christ and the pain left on the instant. It has not troubled me since."

12. *OFWJ*: "March 16, 1878: Received a letter from Bro. John Taylor,

President of the Church, informing me that I was honorably released from my mission and at liberty to return home to Zion."

13. *OFWJ*: "April 1, 1878: Reached Ogden at 6:15. Took supper with Willard Young and Rob Sloan. Reached Salt Lake at 8:20. Met Bud, Charlie, Sophie and Uncle Josh at the depot. A few minutes more and I was at home with father, mother, brothers, sisters and friends, from whom I have been absent seventeen months lacking 5 days. So ends my first mission as a servant of the Lord Jesus Christ, a period of time in which I have learned more useful knowledge than during any other of my life ten times as long. The Lord has been very kind and merciful to me and blessed me beyond all my expectations."

Chapter 3

1. *OFWJ*: "April 15, 1878, Salt Lake City: Since my return I have been elected Secretary and Treasurer of the Central Committee of Y.M.M.I.A. Also a home missionary and preached first in that capacity last night, Sunday 14, at the 20th ward. Have an offer from the *Salt Lake Herald* to become local editor, but I am trying to get on the *Deseret News* instead."
2. *OFWJ*: "April 16, 1878: Through the influence of Bro. B[righam]. Young [Jr.], I obtained a situation on the [*Deseret*] *News*. Thank the Lord for it."
3. *OFWJ*: "July 14, Sunday, 1878: At a meeting held in the 18th Ward school house at 6:30 pm., for the purpose of reorganizing the ward, I was ordained a High Priest and set apart to preside as Bishop over this ward. Counselor D. H. Wells was mouth, George Q. Cannon, Brigham Young Jr. present."
4. *TMH*, 106–07.
5. *OFWJ*: "August 10, 1878: Assumed the duties of local editor of the *Deseret News*, Succeeding Brother John Nicholson, who was called to go on a mission to Europe."
6. *OFWJ*: "January 2, 1879: Returned to Salt Lake, and my duties as local editor of the *Deseret News*. Was asked by Brigham Young [Jr.] to go east as business manager and correspondent for the [*Deseret*] *News*. He gave me time to reflect.

   "January 3, 1879: Accepted the office of business agent and correspondent for the [*Deseret*] *News* in the east, and intend leaving on the 20th inst. John Q. Cannon is to succeed me as local [editor]. Today, therefore, is my last as the local editor of the [*Deseret*] *News* an office which I assumed Aug. 10, 1878.

   "January 4, 1879: Initiated my successor into his new duties, and rendered him some assistance in writing. Wrote to M. E. R. Prepared some of the preliminaries of my departure.

   "January 6, 1879: Spent this day in Farmington. Went to surprise party in the evening, with M. Took her home. Bade her good bye. I like her more and more.

   "January 8, 1879: Wrote letters of introduction to eastern firms. Bought clothing etc. for my trip. Wrote to M. and then destroyed it.

   "January 21, 1879: Learned that my going east may be postponed indefinitely. . . . In the evening went to the birthday party of Sister Eliza R. Snow at the Lion House. She is 75 years of age. One of the best times I ever had.

"January 23, 1879: learned for a certainty—at least a probable one—that I will not go east. The 12 have decided, in view of existing complications with the Gentile world, to begin to draw the line of demarcation. I will probably go through the Territory, instead, as agent.

"January 27, 1879: Learned that a report is current to the effect that M and I are engaged. Wrote to her, informing her of the fact. June Wells started the rumor."

7. *OFWJ*: "February 5, 1879: Received orders to start Friday for Cache Valley. . . . Wrote short note to M. In the evening, attended a lecture in the 11th ward, by Elder Joseph F. Smith, on the Early History of the Church."

8. *OFWJ*: "February 12, 1879: A proposition was made to me to become editor of the *Ogden Junction*. My duties as Bishop prevents my accepting. February 13, 1879: Made a few calls. Assisted Frank [J. Cannon] on the [Ogden] *Junction*. He wants me to accept the editorial chair, but I cannot."

9. *OFWJ*: "February 25, 1879: Called on Bishop Liljenquist. Had a long conversation on general matters. . . . After dinner, visited a sick sister and administered to her. Was asked by the Bishop to attend a Sunday School Teacher's Meeting. Thought I would, but afterward changed my mind and spent the evening in writing to M."

10. *OFWJ*: "February 26, 1879, Hyrum: Wrote to the office. Went down to the Bishop's and made preparation for going to Millville. After dinner started away. Called at Bishop Liljenquist's and he gave me a patriarchal blessing. Went on to Millville and put up at Bishop Pitkin's.

    "March 1, 1879, Logan: First day of Spring. Came in like a lamb. Rambled on the hills. . . . Met Bishop Liljenquist who gave me my patriarchal blessing written out."

11. *OFWJ*: "March 25, 1879: Brigham Young [Jr.] told me he could not willingly permit me to leave the [*Deseret*] *News* for the [Ogden] *Junction*. I will probably resume the local side of the paper."

12. *OFWJ*: "March 21, 1879: Decided to go on to Farmington this afternoon. Wrote some for the [*Ogden*] *Junction*. Was again asked to become its editor. Took the 3:30 pm train for Farmington. Arrived . . . and after putting up at Bro. Clark's went up to Nerva's and passed a very [illegible] evening.

    March 27, 1879: Was again asked by the manager of the [Ogden] *Junction* to edit that paper—I again declined."

13. See *OFWJ*, April 8, 1879.

14. *OFWJ*: "May 1, 1879: After work went to Farmington. Spent the evening at Nerva's. Spoke of Emma [Wells]—her priority, etc."

15. For further information about and exploration of Abraham O. Smoot, see Berlin, "Abraham Owen Smoot: Pioneer Mormon Leader," 1955.

16. See *OFWJ*, May 22, 1879.

17. *OFWJ*: "May 26, 1879: Received a letter from Nerva—the last.
June 2, 1879: Opened a correspondence with Miss Zina Smoot, Provo."

18. *OFWJ*: "December 18, 1879: Married Zina B. Smoot, daughter of Pres. A. O. Smoot, of Provo; ceremony by Pres. D. H. Wells at the Endowment House, Salt Lake City, at 7:30 p.m."

Chapter 4

1. Bertha (Dolly) was born January 22, 1866, and would have turned sixteen during her acquaintance with Orson.

2. See *TMH*, 139.

3. *OFWJ*: "February 1, 1882: Brother Cross came in. Conversed upon preachers. He complimented me highly. Said it seemed like 'angel talking' to listen to me. My Patriarchal blessing says 'Your voice shall sound like the voice of an angel unto them' etc.
"February 2, 1882: Farr says everybody praises my sermon of Sunday night. One says I am a second Orson Pratt, another that I am the best preacher that ever came to London. These things are very flattering, but I must not get lifted up. What I am I owe entirely to my Father in Heaven and to Him I freely ascribe all the praise so lavishly bestowed upon me. He has been good and merciful to me always, and I hope I may live to deserve His care and kindness.
"February 21, 1882: After a testimony meeting I occupied the rest of the time. Farr walked back . . . with me. On the way he told me that Elder Hyrum Evans, after my remarks last Sunday evening, turned to him and said I was 'the most powerful speaker in the British Mission.'"

4. That night Orson had a dream that he recorded in his diary; see *OFWJ*, "January 30, 1882." The dream had to do with family issues at home, and Orson could not satisfactorily interpret it.

5. See *OFWJ*, April 18, 1882.

6. For example, *OFWJ*: "April 30, 1882: Bro. West spoke a few minutes and I followed. Felt very free and the power of God rested upon me. Spoke an hour and ten minutes. In the evening Pres. Carrington occupied the time. Staid with O[rmsby]. Confided to West matters pertaining to Donaldson. He goes to London to labor."

7. As summarized and quoted in letter, Joseph F. Smith to Orson F. Whitney, May 21, 1882; "Orson F. Whitney Papers," L. Tom Perry Special Collections, Harold B. Lee Library, Brigham Young University.

8. *OFWJ*: "May 21, 1882: In the evening attended meeting at No. 4 Oldham St. and spoke about 20 minutes—after four others had preached—about as freely and with as much of the Spirit and power of God as I ever enjoyed; I felt wrought up by what we had experienced in the afternoon. The audience shed tears while I was speaking and I realized myself, that a superior power had taken possession of and was speaking through me."

9. See *OFWJ*, May 10, 1882.

10. See *OFWJ*, June 4, 1882.

11. See *OFWJ*, October 16, 1882.

12. See *OFWJ*, November 3, 1882.

13. *OFWJ*: "November 14, 1882: Did not make much headway. In this afternoon felt very bad in the head and discouraged over my writing. Called at Anderson's. Returned to tea. Prayed and went to work, the Lord blessing me richly. Administered to Mary J. She was immediately healed."

14. *OFWJ*: "November 19, 1882: Attended morning meeting. Spoke a short time. After dinner went with Brothers R. R. Anderson, George C. [Parkinson] and Charles Lambert to meet President John H. Smith. . . . Happy greeting with Bros Smith, W. Groesback and James Urie."

15. *OFWJ*: "December 7, 1882: Worked on index & at night conversed till late with President Smith and R. R. A[nderson]."

16. See *OFWJ*, January 6, 7, 10, and 11, 1883.

17. See *OFWJ*, January 31 & February 3, 1883.

18. See *Journal of Discourses* 4:164, 247, 271; 6:3.

19. See *OFWJ*, February 21, 1883.

20. *OFWJ*: "March 4, 1883: Fast day. And here I am in London, to preside over the Conference for a season, during Bro. West's absence on the Continent. About a year ago I dreamed I was President of this Conference, but did not then see how it was coming to pass. But here it is."

21. See also *TMH*, 155–165.

22. See *OFWJ*, May 7–9, 1883.

23. An undated page in Orson's missionary diary notes that Rose Jane Hawkes was born December 30, 1862, making her twenty-one years old when Orson left for home.

24. I was unable to find any further references to Bertha/Dolly in the remaining diaries, including during the time Orson spent in England as European Mission President in his later years.

25. See *TMH*, 139.

26. I am indebted to Sylvia Blight and Julia Naylor, sisters, both of Great Britain, for the supplemental genealogical information about Bertha Atkinson-Tomlin and her family.

27. See *OFWJ* entries for June and early July, 1883.

Chapter 5

1. *OFWJ*, July 7, 1883.
2. For further information about John Nicholson, see Jenson, *LDS Biographical Encyclopedia* 4:684.
3. *OFWJ*, July 8, 1883.
4. *OFWJ*, July 11, 1883.
5. Very little is known about Charles W. Stayner. Jenson's *LDS Biographical Encyclopedia* 4:363, contains a very short blurb. *A Widow's Tale: The 1884–1896 diary of Helen Mar Kimball Whitney* contains a note by the editors (Hatch and Compton) regarding Orson's and Stayner's relationship: "Stayner was involved in spiritualism with Orson Whitney, who accepted him as a spiritualist prophet" (756 n.52). While perhaps broadly true, both Orson and Charles may have taken exception to the term "spiritualist" since they preferred to view their spiritual "theosophy" exercises as within the circle of Mormonism—even if others disagreed. In later years Orson would write that he rejected the spiritualism of the world.

   Michael Quinn has written that Whitney and the Stayners were partners in "séances." That word is not found in Whitney's diaries as describing his activities and is Quinn's own label (see Quinn, *The Mormon Hierarchy: Extensions of Power*, 714). The picture—of people holding hands around a table and using occult apparatus or language to summon spirits from the dead—that such a term often conjures in the mind's eye is inaccurate and misleading. From what Quinn wrote in his summary, it seems likely that he was somewhat familiar with Whitney's diaries, but only partially understood the story. It may be that the Stayner's were influenced by the same spiritualist movement in the 1870s that ensnared Amasa M. Lyman; such might be an interesting avenue for further research. See Lyman, *Amasa Mason Lyman: Mormon Apostle and Apostate; A Study in Dedication,* ("spiritualism" in the index); Hefner, "From Apostle to Apostate: The Personal Struggle of Amasa Mason Lyman," in *Dialogue: A Journal of Mormon Thought*, 90–104; and Walker, *Wayward Saints: The Social and Religious Protests of the Godbeites against Brigham Young.* This latter publication names a "T. J. Stayner" as leader of a spiritualist group that met in Ogden, Utah, in the early 1870s (see page 270). These apostate spiritualist groups did hold séances at their meetings. Amasa M. Lyman, a great orator-apostle before his apostasy and excommunication, faded in influence (and died in 1877) just a few years before Orson F. Whitney began to rise. The author of the present work is unable to make a determination of the truth or error of Whitney's spiritual exercises, and therefore withholds judgment. The Salt Lake Stake High Council did not withhold judgment on Charles W. Stayner, and threatened him with excommunication unless he renounced his revelations and self-proclaimed prophetic status; this he agreed to do, but instead went underground and took Whitney with him. As later events would demonstrate, Whitney would not be called to the apostleship until he had formally rejected his belief in reincarnation and had proven his spiritual stability for six years. For a detailed review of guidance and direction from prophets and apostles regarding how to determine the truth of any doctrine, principle, movement, fad, or cause, see Horne, *Determining Doctrine.*

6. For a review of Arthur Stayner's involvement with the sugar beet industry in Utah, see the *Deseret Evening News*, April 4, 1903; and the Wikipedia articles on Arthur Stayner and the Utah-Idaho Sugar Company. See also Arrington, *Beet Sugar in the West: A History of the Utah-Idaho Sugar Company, 1891–1066*, 6–11; and Taylor, *A Saga of Sugar*, 62–89.

7. For further information about *theosophy*, see the Wikipedia article: http://en.wikipedia.org/wiki/Theosophy (accessed 9/19/2013). This was a "Mormonized" form of theosophy, meaning they tried to mesh the general concepts with LDS doctrine.

8. *OFWJ*: "August 11, 1883: While I was conversing with Ma the other day she told me that [sentence illegible] Orson Hyde fell way from the Church in early days. He met with the mishap of falling into some water and being drowned. While out of his body his spirit very much desired. After he had been miraculously—for he was really dead—restored to life, he said that he had been where he was conversing with beings of another sphere. He saw, by the spirit, his dead body and loathed it, not desiring to return, but was told that he had his choice, either to return to that body, and finish his earthly life in it or else let it die and his spirit go back and take up a black body—the tabernacle of a negro. He chose the former and so came back to life a white man."

9. See crossed out *OFWJ*, July 10, 1883 diary entry.

10. *OFWJ*, August 10, 1883: "She told me a dream she had last night. She thought she saw a great moving crowd which seemed to be the Church, going towards a wall beneath which was a low culvert to pass under which necessitated bowing low and even creeping. On the other side were boats and a stream, which could only be attained by passing

through the culvert. Some came forward to go through but got frightened and turned back, for additional to the humiliation required there stood a man near the opening with a lash whose office it was to strike as many times as he could while they were going under, all who passed through. Zina saw herself come up and stand in terror before the culvert's mouth, hesitating as to whether she should go in or not. Just then she looked through the culvert and saw her father and mother in a boat and quick as a flash the conviction settled upon her that all who succeeded in getting to the boats were polygamists and their wives. She took the dream as a testimony."

11. *OFWJ*, August 30, 1883. For the accepted doctrine of the Church regarding Elias, see the entry for *Elias* in the LDS Bible Dictionary, where the name's use in the scriptures as a title is emphasized.

12. *OFWJ*, September 30, 1883.

13. Other accounts of this dream are found in Appendix 1.

14. *OFWJ*, December 3, 1884.

15. *TMH*, 177.

16. *OFWJ*, November 26, 1883. For an account of this event, see *Helpful Visions*, 9–22.

17. *OFWJ*, November 25, 1883.

18. *TMH*, 176.

19. See *OFWJ*, March 8, 1886.

20. *OFWJ*, November 22, 1884.

21. *HMWJ*, November 24, 1884.

22. *OFWJ*, December 26, 1884.

23. Helen Mar also noted Zina's baby delivery, see *HMWJ*, February 29, 1885.

24. *HMWJ*, March 6, 1885. According to his mother's diary, Orson experienced trouble with depression at this time. See *HMWJ*, January 22, 1885. Often one of the reasons had to do with financial struggles: "Just as I was going to retire Orson came into my room. We talked till about eleven o'clock—first upon our pecuniary affairs, then on heavenly matters, which were more agreeable to both of us" (*HMWJ*, February 28, 1885).

25. *OFWJ*, April 26, 1885. For more details about the circumstances and climate at the time this document was read, see Clark, *Messages of the First Presidency* 3:1–22. This same month, Orson met and visited with a "spiritualist" named Anna Kimball, a distant relative in S.L.C. conducting séances (see *HMWJ*, April 20, 21, 26, 1885).

26. See *HMWJ*, June 1-4, 1885.

27. See *OFWJ*, entries for October and November 1, 1885.

28. *HMWJ*, September 6, 1885.

29. *OFWJ*, November 1, 1885. For a complete review of these proceedings, see Gary James Bergera, "Transgression in the LDS Community: The Cases of Albert Carrington, Richard R. Lyman, and Joseph F. Smith, Part 1," in *Journal of Mormon History* 37: 3 (Summer 2011), 119–60.

30. *OFWJ*, November 8, 1885.

31. See *HMWJ*, October 11, 1885.

32. *OFWJ*, November 23, 1885. Whitney's call to the Twelve came in the aftermath of the Reed Smoot Senate Hearings, where the Church had been put on trial before the world in the name of Smoot.

33. See *OFWJ*, January 19 & 20, 1886.

34. *OFWJ*, March 28, 1886. It may be this dream that Orson read to John Donaldson and some Whitney family members. Helen Mar wrote: "Orson and family came to breakfast accompanied by Bro. Donaldson. They found us rather unprepared, as far as eatables, but were glad to see them, and had a good time after breakfast conversing upon the spiritual and prevailing topics of the day, and coming events, which are casting their shadows before. Orson read the two visions to Bro. Donaldson" (*HMWJ*, April 8, 1886).

35. *OFWJ*, April 6, 1886. For the text of the epistle Whitney and Talmage read, see Clark, *Messages of the First Presidency* 3:4–12.

36. *HMWJ*, March 28, 1886.

37. *OFWJ*, May 16 & June 10, 1886.

38. See chapter four, March 22, 1883.

39. For the list, see Appendix 2, "Reincarnated Name Ledger and Proposed Key."

40. *OFWJ*, June 12, 1886.

41. *OFWJ*, June 23, 1886.

42. *OFWJ*, June 27, 1886.

43. *OFWJ*, July 4, 1886.

44. For Bishop Whitney's account of his visit with Lorenzo Snow, and the proceedings of the Supreme Court, see Horne, *Latter Leaves in the Life of Lorenzo Snow*, 34, 162–64, 176–93.

45. See *OFWJ*, July 17, 1886. Orson's diary notes that Charles' death was "written of elsewhere," but what or where that meant is unclear. Abraham H. Cannon wrote in his diary that "Charles Whitney, a younger brother of Orson's committed suicide day before yesterday by shooting himself through the head. The coroner's jury state that it was done during a fit of temporary aberration of the mind. . . ." (See Horne, *An Apostle's Record: The Journals of Abraham H. Cannon*, 81 [August 6, 1886]).

46. *HMWJ*, August 11, 1886. For further information about Charley Whitney, see Godfrey, "Charles S. Whitney's Diary: A Nineteenth-century Salt Lake City Teenager," 215–51. Charley's girlfriend told Helen Mar that she thought the shooting accidental; this point will likely remain unresolved.

47. *HMWJ*, various days in August, 1886.

48. *HMWJ*, August 19, 1886.

49. *OFWJ*, August 23, 1886.

50. *OFWJ*, August 23, 1886. For more information about "Bud" see [Whitney, Orson F.] *In Memoriam; Horace G. Whitney: Biographical Sketch, Funeral Ceremonies, Resolutions of Respect, Editorials, Personal Tributes.*

51. *OFWJ*, September 8, 1886.

52. *OFWJ*, September 9, 1886.

53. See for example, the entry in *OFWJ*, October 4, 1886. We have very little information about what took place in the prayer or blessing meetings; however, Orson's mother Helen Mar left this account of a meeting she attended: "During the evening I was also blessed under the hands of Bro. Donaldson, Orson and Bro. Stayner—the latter being mouth. There were great and glorious promises made me, very similar to what had previously been, by Bro. Donaldson, and Bro Stayner did not know this till I told him of it. Although I felt sick I was rewarded richly in spiritual things, both in blessings, and conversation upon the work of

the Almighty, and the speedy coming of our Savior, etc." (*HMWJ*, April 11, 1886).

54. *HMWJ*, August 27, 1886.

55. *OFWJ*, October 6, 1886.

56. *OFWJ*, September 29, 1886.

57. *OFWJ*, October 8, 1886.

Chapter 6

1. See *OFWJ*, January 7 and 24, 1887. See also *HMWJ*, January 7, 1887: "Orson called and bid us good-bye. Going up to Bear Lake on a preaching tour, to be gone two weeks. His baby is sick with croup which makes him loth to leave home."
2. *OFWJ*, February 13, 1887. See also Horne, *Latter Leaves in the Life of Lorenzo Snow*, 163.
3. For the text of this epistle, see Clark, *Messages of the First Presidency* 3:108–29.
4. The reason: "This, I suppose, was because I had a voice and knew how to use it—thanks to my early training in elocution and my subsequent experience upon the stage and in the mission field" (*TMH*, 189).
5. *OFWJ*, April 20, 1887.
6. *OFWJ*, May 31, 1887.
7. *HMWJ*, March 27, 1887.
8. *OFWJ*, April 6, 1887.
9. *OFWJ*, April 20, 1887.
10. Correspondence, Orson F. Whitney to Joseph F. Smith, May 18, 1887, Church History Library.
11. *HMWJ*, March 24, 1887. Helen's diary also indicates that the Kimball family sold part of a graveyard they owned in order to help pay for Orson's work writing *Life of Heber C. Kimball* (see *HMWJ*, April 9, 1887).
12. *OFWJ*, April 30, 1887.
13. See *OFWJ*, May 15, 1887.
14. *OFWJ*, May 26, 1887.
15. See *OFWJ*, June 14, 1887.
16. *OFWJ*, June 28, 1887.
17. *OFWJ*, August 15, 1887.
18. *TMH*, 189.
19. *OFWJ*, June 28, 1887; see also January 5, 1888: "Attended fast meeting.

Elder Abinadi Pratt prophesied. Counselor Patrick took him to task for it rather sharply. I spoke to modify the latter's harshness and showed that men have a right to prophecy but, should use wisdom and be humble. Bro. Pratt asked forgiveness."

20. *OFWJ*, July 24, 1887.

21. *OFWJ*, July 26, 1887. Whitney's comment about the deliverer of Zion probably meant Charles W. Stayner.

22. *OFWJ*, August 1, 1887.

23. "Received from S. F. Kimball $50 on acct History H. C. K. making $300 in all, so far paid to me. Receipted for $300 to S. F. K. as agent of Kimball family, and he to return my receipt for $250 issued to him as a private individual" (August 6, 1887). Later in September Orson wrote: "I have received in all from the Kimball family Committee for writing the history of H. C. K. $950. They still owe me $50" (*OFWJ*, September 27, 1887).

24. *OFWJ*, included with entry for August 8, 1887. Orson explained further in a letter to Joseph F. Smith, then in exile on the underground: "Taking the test oath, registering and preparing to vote, is the all-absorbing topic. Our people generally are registering, all who can. No one likes to oath, it's a bitter pill, but they swallow it for the sake of being obedient to counsel and doing their duty. The redistricting of the territory will probably give the Gentiles quite a showing in the next legislature. Our best available men should be sent there to meet them" (Correspondence, Orson F. Whitney to Joseph F. Smith, May 18, 1887; Church History Library Archives).

25. *OFWJ*, September 7, 1887.

26. *OFWJ*, October 8, 1887. For the epistle read by Orson at the conference, see Clark, *Messages of the First Presidency* 3:132–57.

27. "Last night dreamed of seeing Apostle Joseph F. Smith at the head of a great body of Priesthood coming towards me. I was in Aunt Mary Whitney's yard and seemed to be living at the old homestead, my mother's. Joseph F., seeing me, called in tones of power and authority: 'Home! Home! And prepare!' I thought it was something in connection with the next conference of the Church or a future one at least—and that it was to be held on my premises or in some way affect me. If I remember aright my loins were 'ungirded' at the time. I went home but found the way barred. A new gate stretched across City Creek from the Whitney

corner to Harriet Kimball's corner—and all the street east of it appeared a finely laid out park and ground. I got in though and reached home" (*OFWJ*, October 20, 1887).

28. *OFWJ*, November 5 & 6, 1887.

29. *OFWJ*, November 15, 1887.

30. Correspondence, Orson F. Whitney to Joseph F. Smith, May 18, 1887; Church History Library.

31. *OFWJ*, 1887. Dating of this entry is unclear because the page with the date has been removed from the diary; the writing itself is positioned in the November time period, but Orson mentions Pres. Snow referring to his sister as "late" meaning she had passed away by then. She died on December 5, 1887, and Orson spoke at her funeral. It is possible that Orson was making his diary entries weeks or even months after events had occurred and therefore wrote as he did. Regarding her death, he wrote: "Aunt Eliza R. Snow Smith died at 5 minutes past 1 am in the Lion House, this City. I was in to see her a few days ago and blessed her at her request, and the power of the Spirit was upon me. . . . Sister Eliza was a great and noble spirit, a poet and a prophetess. She predicted to me several months ago that my History of H. C. Kimball would be a standard work of the Church, and a blessing to the Saints and his posterity" (*OFWJ*, December 5, 1887; see also December 7, 1887). Whitney's biography of Heber would indeed become a standard work of the Church for some years, until around 1900 when the term "standard works" was redefined to refer only to the Mormon canon of scripture.

    Pertaining to the notion that a person would need to be crucified in order to become exalted like the Son of God, President Snow taught: "Why is [a] man called to act as president over a people? Is it in order to acquire an influence and then to use that influence directly for his own aggrandizement? No, but on the contrary, he is called to act in such a position on the same principle as the priesthood was given to the Son of God, that he should make sacrifices. For himself? No, but in the interests of the people over whom he presides. *Would he be required to offer himself up on the cross as did the Saviour? No*, but to become the servant of his brethren, not their master, and to work in their interest and welfare" (see *Teachings of Presidents of the Church: Lorenzo Snow*, 219, emphasis added).

32. *OFWJ*, December 23, 1887.

33. *OFWJ*, December 26, 1887.

Chapter 7

1. *OFWJ*, January 17, 1888.
2. *OFWJ*, February 9, 1888.
3. *OFWJ*, February 6, 1888.
4. *HMWJ*, January 6, 1888.
5. *OFWJ*, February 9, 1888.
6. *OFWJ*, March 4, 1888. The next time Orson spoke there, he related that "Arthur Stayner said it was the grandest thing ever delivered in the Tabernacle" (March 25, 1888).
7. *HMWJ*, January 17, 1888.
8. *OFWJ*, March 25, 1888.
9. *OFWJ*, April 7, 1888. For the epistle Bishop Whitney read at the conference, see Clark, *Messages of the First Presidency* 3:156–63.
10. *OFWJ*, April 7, 1888. According to Helen Mar's diary, Orson was feeling quite stressed at this time about both his financial and living arrangements: "Orson came here in a disconsolate mood to see it there was any chance of getting a part of my house for him and the family as he'd rented his house, and the folks were to take it the first of next week, and he'd tried in vain to find another. I offered him my west parlor, and he offered $10.00 or more if I'd do him this favor" (*HMWJ*, April 3, 1888). However, Orson soon found another place that he was able to rent instead of having to move in with his mother.
11. *HMWJ*, April 18, 1888.
12. Helen Mar also wrote of the history: "My Father died 20 years ago tomorrow. His history, which Orson is writing, will be finished in a few days" (*HMWJ*, June 21, 1888).
13. *OFWJ*, May 19, 1888.
14. *OFWJ*, May 21, 1888.
15. For an account of the dedication of the Manti Temple, including Lorenzo Snow's contributions, see Horne, *Latter Leaves in the Life of Lorenzo Snow*, 207–08.
16. *OFWJ*, June 3, 1888.

17. *HMWJ*, June 3, 1888.

18. For a narration of this event, see *TMH*, 193–94.

19. *OFWJ*, July 1, 1888.

20. *OFWJ*, July 1, 1888.

21. *OFWJ*, May 22, 1889.

22. *OFWJ*, June 3, 1889.

23. As quoted in *Spencer W. Kimball*, 223. Eighty years later, a great-great-grandson of Heber's, Stanley B. Kimball, wrote the biography *Heber C. Kimball: Mormon Patriarch and Pioneer* (Urbana: University of Illinois Press, 1981). More academically oriented and wary of the spiritual, one wonders what Orson would have thought of it.

24. *OFWJ*, July 13, 1888. For further information about Whitney's father-in-law, Daniel H. Wells, see Hinckley, *Daniel Hammer Wells and Events of His Time*.

25. The editors of Helen Mar Whitney's diaries believe it likely that Orson kept knowledge of the plural marriage from his own mother. See *A Widow's Tale: 1884–1896 Diary of Helen Mar Kimball Whitney*, 29.

26. For Whitney's narration of this trip and marriage, see *OFWJ*, July 18-31, 1888; and *TMH*, 194–95.

27. *OFWJ*, October 11, 1888. See also entries related to Orson in *HMWJ*, August 21, 26, 27, 29, 30, and September 5, 6, 7, 9, 14, and 20, 1888.

28. See *OFWJ*, November 10, 1888.

29. *OFWJ*, November 24, 1888.

30. *OFWJ*, November 25, 1888.

31. *OFWJ*, November 26, 1888.

32. *OFWJ*, December 27, 1888.

33. See *OFWJ*, January 8 & 16, 1889.

34. *OFWJ*, January 17, 1889.

35. *OFWJ*, February 4, 1889.

36. *OFWJ*, February 8, 1889.

37. *OFWJ*, February 20, 1889; see also entry of March 12, 1888, and story given in *TMH*, 196–97.

38. *OFWJ*, February 21, 1889.

39. *OFWJ*, February 21 & 24, 1889.

40. *OFWJ*, March 1, 1889.

41. *OFWJ*, March 3, 1889.

42. *OFWJ*, March 7, 1889.

43. *OFWJ*, March 8, 1889.

44. *OFWJ*, March 8, 1889.

45. *OFWJ*, March 9 or 10, 1889. Precise date was removed from the diary.

46. *OFWJ*, March 9 or 10, 1889. Precise date was removed from the diary.

47. *OFWJ*, March 13, 1889.

48. See for example Horne, *Latter Leaves in the Life of Lorenzo Snow*, 346–47, where President George Q. Cannon teaches in a Salt Lake Temple Solemn Assembly that some of those present were literal descendants of Jesus.

49. *OFWJ*, March 17, 1889.

50. *OFWJ*, March 25, 1889. Whitney was spending time in the offices of the *Deseret News* to prepare a statement on the condition of the newspaper, desired by the Quorum of the Twelve. He finished it on the 17th (See *OFWJ*, March 22, 1889).

51. *OFWJ*, March 26, 1889. For the statement on the Holy Ghost as a personage waiting to take a body, see Ehat and Cook, *The Words of Joseph Smith*, 305 n26.

Chapter 8

1. For a review of these reorganization issues, see Horne, *Latter Leaves in the Life of Lorenzo Snow*, 211–59.
2. *OFWJ*, April 6, 1889.
3. *OFWJ*, April 9, 1889.
4. For further information, see Horne, *An Apostle's Record: The Journals of Abraham H. Cannon*, 33–34, 98–99.
5. *OFWJ*, May 5, 1889.
6. *OFWJ*, April 22, 1889.
7. *OFWJ*, April 24, 1889.
8. See *OFWJ*, April 29 & 30, 1889.
9. *OFWJ*, May 13, 1889.
10. *OFWJ*, no date given, but likely mid-May, 1889. Charles Stayner's name has been inserted into those brackets where it fits, although the space is empty in the diaries.
11. *OFWJ*, May 27, 1889.
12. *OFWJ*, June 3, 1889; see also June 15, 1889.
13. *OFWJ*, June 8, 1889. I have inserted in the brackets my best guess for the missing text, but that could be wrong. With the pages removed, it will never be known what was said between these two men, and whether Orson brought up his reincarnation beliefs at that time. See also *TMH*, 192–93, where Orson mistakes the timing of his work preparing the publication of the proceedings of Eliza R. Snow's funeral with that of Pres. Snow setting him apart to write his *Latter Leaves* history.
14. *OFWJ*, June 19, 1889.
15. Of his passing, Orson wrote: "My friend, Bishop James Watson, of the 18th ward, died this evening at half past 8 o'clock. His disease was inflammation of the bowels terminating in a fatal attack of typhoid fever. His death is a sudden and unexpected shock to the community. But few knew of his illness, and none of his danger. I feel much grieved over the event but am resigned to the will of Providence. He was a worthy, upright, kind-hearted and intelligent man. I loved him and he loved me. We were congenial in our thoughts and conversation. James Watson was no bigot, nor

hater of an idea merely because it was new. He dared to think above and beyond the plane of common places and traditions and was not afraid to express his thoughts whenever it was wise and proper to do so. He was no politician, no trickster, no coward, no fawning sycophant, but a brave, good and noble-minded, straightforward man, tender-hearted and sensitive as a child, a lover of poetry and sublime and exalted thought, and a faithful, big-hearted, broad-minded, philanthropic son of God. Peace to his ashes, and honored be his name and memory" (*OFWJ*, June 27, 1889).

16. *OFWJ*, July 1, 1889.
17. *OFWJ*, July 3, 1889.
18. *OFWJ*, September 15, 1889.
19. *OFWJ*, September 15, 1889.
20. See Appendix 1 for this account.
21. *OFWJ*, October 7, 1889.
22. *OFWJ*, December 7, 1889.
23. See *OFWJ*, October 7 and December 7, 1889 and January 2, 1890. Orson's literary agent for the book was Solomon F. Kimball, an uncle.
24. *OFWJ*, February 11, 1890.
25. See *OFWJ*, February 15 & 19, 1890.
26. *OFWJ*, March 7, 1890.
27. *OFWJ*, March 27, 1890.
28. See Appendix 3 for the full text of the letter. If Orson was taking the wording of the letter from memory to write in his diary, he did a remarkable job for so many years later.
29. *OFWJ*, April 3, 1890.
30. See *OFWJ*, April 12, 1890.
31. *OFWJ*, May 21, 1890.
32. *OFWJ*, October 6, 7, & 8, 1890. In his 1930 autobiography, Whitney added this explanation: "In the general conference I was called upon to read it to the congregation. I also read, by request, the Articles of Faith, to remind the people of the Church's attitude in honoring, obeying and sustaining the law. The vote was then taken and the manifesto accepted as the word and will of the Lord. The Church, out of deference to statutes

declared constitutional by the Court of Last Resort, withdrew further sanction from all marriages forbidden by the law of the Land" (203–04).

33. See *OFWJ*, October 13-18, 1890.

34. *OFWJ*, ca. December, 1892.

35. See *OFWJ*, December 30 & 31, 1892.

36. *OFWJ*, December 31, 1892.

37. For further information about Babcock, see Black and Woodger, *Women of Character: Profiles of 100 Prominent LDS Women*, 11–14. See also chapter 10 for further information about the concerns of the Quorum of the Twelve regarding Whitney becoming too "intimate" with Babcock.

38. *OFWJ*, April 6, 1893.

39. *OFWJ*, April 13, 1893.

40. *OFWJ*, April 13, 1893.

41. B. H. Roberts diary entry May 8, 1893; as found in *History's Apprentice: The Diaries of B. H. Roberts, 1880–1898*, 290.

42. *OFWJ*, June 10, 1893. It is apparent that Whitney was catching up by entering info into days from past months.

43. *OFWJ*, August 16, 1893. Orson's comment regarding the Church living the United Order (law of consecration) never materialized, but the Church placed a strong renewed emphasis on the law of tithing to relieve its crushing debt problems. For a detailed narrative of this period of Church history, see Horne, *Latter Leaves in the Life of Lorenzo Snow*, 284–362.

44. *OFWJ*, September 8, 1893.

45. *OFWJ*, October 8, 1893.

46. *OFWJ*, October 9, 1893.

47. *OFWJ*, March 12, 1894.

48. *OFWJ*, March 14, 1894.

49. *OFWJ*, March 18, 1894.

50. *OFWJ*, August 26, 1894.

Chapter 9

1. *OFWJ*, May 17, 1890.

2. *OFWJ*, May 20, 1890.

3. *OFWJ*, May 21, 1890.

4. *OFWJ*, June 20, 1890.

5. See "The History of Utah," in *Deseret Evening News*, July 12, 1890.

6. The "bitterly anti-Mormon" *Salt Lake Tribune* editorialized: "Of course it will be a history from the Mormon standpoint. It would not be otherwise very well, being written by Bishop Whitney. He is a sincere fanatic, and it would not be fair to expect that he would not color his writings, even as his mind is now colored, in favor of the faith he believes in and the people who are his personal associates and friends. He has better facilities for writing a history than any man not a member of the Mormon Church could have. He is a man of real ability. Perhaps he is better fitted to undertake a work of this kind than almost any other man in the Mormon Church" (*OFWJ*, ca. July 12 or 13, 1890).

7. *OFWJ*, July 14, 1890.

8. See *OFWJ*, July 22 & 23, 1890.

9. The prospectus stated: "A prominent feature will be the biographies of notable men and women, with fine portraits accompanying. It is the almost universal custom, in a work of this character, to take pay from those whose histories are inserted. The author proposes to express his own views, and accept no perquisites; not a line of reading matter will be paid for—not a cent accepted for biographical notice. The characters chosen to illustrate the work will be placed in the order where they belong, irrespective of considerations which should have no weight in the preparation of a just and impartial record of men and events." The prospectus is dated Salt Lake City, July 1st, 1890, and signed by Whitney.

10. See promotional item in Orson F. Whitney Collection, Church History Library Archives.

11. For a copy of the contract, see Orson F. Whitney Collection, Church History Library Archives.

12. "Preface," *History of Utah*, Vol. 4.

13. *OFWJ*, April 20, 1891.

14. *OFWJ*, June 1, 1891.

15. *AHCJ*, June 8, 1891. Elder Abraham H. Cannon's participation in the project is documented herein as found in Horne, *An Apostle's Record: The Journals of Abraham H. Cannon*, under dates given.

16. *AHCJ*, June 9, 1891

17. As quoted in a collection of documents related to Whitney's *History of Utah*, found in Orson F. Whitney Collection, Church History Library Archives.

18. *TMH*, 202.

19. *AHCJ*, June 12, 1891

20. *AHCJ*, June 15, 1891

21. *AHCJ*, June 16, 1891.

22. *AHCJ*, June 19, 1891.

23. *AHCJ*, June 24, 1891.

24. *AHCJ*, June 25, 1891.

25. *AHCJ*, June 27, 1891.

26. *AHCJ*, June 29, 1891.

27. *OFWJ*, June, 1891, no exact date given.

28. *OFWJ*, September 26, 1891.

29. *AHCJ*, December 3, 1891.

30. *OFWJ*, April 21, 1892.

31. *OFWJ*, ca, July 1, 1892.

32. *OFWJ*, January 31, 1893.

33. *OFWJ*, August 25, 1893.

34. George Q. Cannon diary, August 25, 1893; as found in Orson F. Whitney Collection, Church History Library Archives.

35. *OFWJ*, August 28, 1893.

36. George Q. Cannon diary, August 3, 1894; as found in Orson F. Whitney Collection, Church History Library Archives.

37. *AHCJ*, October 19, 1894.

38. *OFWJ*, July 9, 1897.

39. *OFWJ*, September 27, 1897.

40. *OFWJ*, August 21, 1899.

41. *OFWJ*, October 12, 1897.

42. *OFWJ*, October 19, 1897.

43. *OFWJ*, November 13, 1897.

44. *OFWJ*, November 15, 1897.

45. In a note concluding volume four, Whitney wrote: "In explanation of the placing here of the biography of William Jex, whose steel plate portrait will be found on page 525 of this volume, it is but necessary to say that the materials for the sketch did not reach the historian in time for its insertion elsewhere. The reader will probably notice other portraits, scattered through the four volumes, for which there are no corresponding biographies. The reason for their non-appearance is that the persons interested have failed to supply the necessary data, though urgently and in most cases repeatedly requested to do so, in order that the work might be completed to the satisfaction of all concerned" (as found in "Notes," last page).

46. *OFWJ*, November 18, 1898.

47. *OFWJ*, August 30, 1899.

48. *OFWJ*, January 1, 1900.

49. *OFWJ*, January 1, New Year's, 1901. This refers to the beginning of the work on volume one of *History of the Church*, which began under President Cannon's direction but was largely compiled and completed by B. H. Roberts. For further information on this project, see Horne, *Latter Leaves in the Life of Lorenzo Snow*, 293, 386, 398, 406, 408, 410. See also Searle, *Early Mormon Historiography: Writing the History of the Mormons, 1830–1858*. Various volumes of the Joseph Smith Papers being published by the Church Historian's Press of the LDS Church History Department also contain information about this project.

50. *OFWJ*, July 14, 1902.

51. *TMH*, 203.

52. For example, Elder Rudger Clawson's diary, speaking of a meeting of the Twelve, noted, "Apostle Clawson said he had made an investigation relative to the fourth volume of the *History of Utah* and found that the church is in no wise obligated to bear any part of the expense of its

publication; that the manuscript is now ready for the printer and bids are being sought by the Geo. Q. Cannon Co., who are prepared to meet the expense, with an idea of delivering the book at the next Oct. conference" (Rudger Clawson journal, June 12, 1902; as quoted in Rudger Clawson, *A Ministry of Meetings: The Apostolic Diaries of Rudger Clawson*, Stan Larson, ed., [Salt Lake City, 1993], under date given.

53. As quoted in Orson F. Whitney Collection, Church History Library Archives.

54. "Preface," in *History of Utah*, Vol. 4.

55. "Preface," in *History of Utah*, Vol. 4.

56. "Preface," in *History of Utah*, Vol. 4.

57. *Deseret News*, October 28, 1908; p. 10. This advertisement also mentioned that "several thousand sets" were sold in previous years. This is likely an incorrect figure, since all other sources point to but one edition of 2,000 copies having been manufactured.

58. For an effort to review and compare and contrast Whitney's *History of Utah* with that of a prominent anti-Mormon of his day, see Brigham D. Madsen's "Foreword" in Robert N. Baskin, *Reminiscences of Early Utah* (Salt Lake City: Signature Books, 2006).

Chapter 10

1. For an overview of Thatcher's issues, see Godfrey, "Moses Thatcher in the Dock: His Trials, The Aftermath, and His Last Days," 54–88.

2. *OFWJ*, January 15, 1895.

3. For further information on Moses Thatcher's difficulties, see Horne, *Latter Leaves in the Life of Lorenzo Snow*, 240–54 and Horne, *An Apostle's Record: The Journals of Abraham H. Cannon*, 5, 83, 172, 175n2, 266, 359–60, 364–65, 453. See also note 1 above.

4. *OFWJ*, ca. February 1895.

5. For further information about President Snow's service as president of the Salt Lake Temple, see Horne, *Latter Leaves in the Life of Lorenzo Snow*, 228–32.

6. See *OFWJ*, March 6 & 10, 1895.

7. Whitney provides no detailed description of these birthday celebrations held in the temple for President Woodruff, but Arthur Winter, a clerk and sermon reporter in the President's Office, described the previous two years' celebrations: "I forgot to mention that on Monday last I attended a social gathering in the annex of the temple, to which I had been invited by President Woodruff. The object of the gathering was to celebrate the birthdays of President Woodruff and his wife Emma." Also, "Today (March 1st) he is 87 years old and she is 56. There were about 300 of his friends there and we had a very nice time. The company first assembled in the 'Garden' room, where speeches were made, poems read and singing. Afterwards lunch was served in the Annex, of which all partook while in their seats with a plate on their knees. Then more speeches were made and more singing was had in the 'Garden.' We were together from 1 o'clock to 5 o'clock" (Arthur Winter diary, March 1, 1894; Church History Library Archives; transcription of holograph made by the author). The *Deseret Weekly*, February 24, 1894, pages 333–34 contains a very detailed description of the party program that year.

8. *OFWJ*, ca. March, 1895.

9. *TMH*, 211. Supporting Whitney's opinion of Roberts' lofty skill as orator is Davis Bitton, "A Masterwork of Mormon Theology?" in B. H. Roberts, *The Truth, the Way, the Life: An Elementary Treatise on Theology*, xl.

10. *OFWJ*, April 6, 1895.

11. *TMH*, 212, 213. For Roberts' side of the story, see Truman G. Madsen, *Defender of the Faith: The B. H. Roberts Story*, 219–20.

12. See *OFWJ*, May 13 & 14, 1895.

13. *OFWJ*, October 4, 1895.

14. See, for example, *OFWJ*, June 2, 1895.

15. *OFWJ*, November 1, 1895.

16. See *OFWJ*, November 4, 1895.

17. See *AHCJ*, September 5, 1895.

18. *AHCJ*, October 24, 1895.

19. *AHCJ*, October 27, 1895. Some believe that alcohol consumption was Whitney's Word of Wisdom problem. Nothing of this nature is mentioned in his diaries, but his mother's (Helen Mar's) diaries do occasionally mention alcoholic beverages being served at some social functions attended by Mormons. Strict word of wisdom adherence did not become a requirement for faithful and temple worthy Latter-day Saints until the 1930s.

20. *OFWJ*, ca. July 1896. For a review of the life of Abraham H. Cannon, see Horne, *An Apostle's Record: The Journals of Abraham H. Cannon*, 25–60.

21. See *TMH*, 215–17.

22. See *OFWJ*, January 16 and February 19, 1896.

23. *OFWJ*, March 7, 1896.

24. As Elder Bruce R. McConkie of the Quorum of the Twelve Apostles once counseled an erring individual, "One of the side effects of preaching contrary to what the Brethren preach is to get a spirit of rebellion growing up in your heart. . . . All of us need all of the faith and strength and spiritual stability we can get to maintain our positions in the Church and to work out our salvation" (Correspondence, Bruce R. McConkie to Eugene England, February 19, 1981, 9; copy in author's possession). Orson's stubbornness and rebellion about reincarnation notions caused him to pay a high price spiritually later in his life.

25. *OFWJ*, June 8, 1896.

26. *OFWJ*, ca., 1896.

27. *JEHJ*, January 12, 1896.

28. *JEHJ*, January 19, 1896.

29. *JEHJ*, February 16, 1896.

30. See *OFWJ*, November 15 and December 23, 1896.

31. *OFWJ*, January 1, 1897.

32. *OFWJ*, January 14, 1897.

33. *OFWJ*, March 1, 1897.

34. *OFWJ*, March 3, 1897.

35. *OFWJ*, March 23, 1897.

36. See "Pioneers of the Sugar Industry in Utah," *Deseret Evening News*, April 4, 1903.

37. *OFWJ*, April 6, 1897.

38. *OFWJ*, July 5, 1897.

39. *OFWJ*, July 24, 1897.

40. *OFWJ*, July 25, 1897.

41. *OFWJ*, July 27, 1897.

42. *OFWJ*, July 31, 1897.

43. *OFWJ*, August 22, 1897.

44. *OFWJ*, September 24, 1897.

45. *OFWJ*, ca. September 24, 1897.

46. See "Moses Thatcher in the Dock: His Trials, The Aftermath, and His Last Days," 54–88. See also *The Thatcher Episode; A Concise Statement of the Facts of the Case; Interesting Letters and Documents; a Review of M. Thatcher's Claims, Pleas and Admissions.*

47. *OFWJ*, September 27, 1897.

48. *OFWJ*, October 10, 1897. As usual, Whitney relished the compliments.

49. *OFWJ*, October 16, 1897.

50. *FWJ*, November 25, 1897.

51. For further information about John Beck's bankruptcy, see "John Beck may go to the Wall," *Salt Lake Herald*, December 1, 1898; see also other *Herald* articles, "John Beck's Bankruptcy," March 1, 1899; "John Beck's Ill Luck," April 30, 1899; and "John Beck Failed to Report," Aug. 2, 1899.

52. *OFWJ*, January 1, 1898.

53. *OFWJ*, January 3, 4, and 5, 1898.

54. *OFWJ*, January 5, 1898.

55. *OFWJ*, January 24, 1898.

56. *OFWJ*, January 31, 1898.

57. For further info, see *The Thatcher Episode; A Concise Statement of the Facts of the Case; Interesting Letters and Documents; a Review of M. Thatcher's Claims, Pleas and Admissions*.

58. *OFWJ*, January 6, 1898.

59. *TMH*, 260–61.

60. *OFWJ*, January 18, 1898. For the text of Reiner's speech in the Tabernacle, see Stuy, *Collected Discourses* 5:357–63 (January 16, 1898).

61. *TMH*, 222–23.

62. *OFWJ*, February 8, 1898.

63. *OFWJ*, March 6, 1898. Such is my best interpretation of this perplexing situation. In his talk to members of the ward, who sustained the motion to excommunicate, Whitney informed them that the woman had denied Joseph Smith's divine calling as a prophet, and asked to have her name removed from the rolls of the Church. Whitney's own views of theosophy did not entail such rejection of testimony; instead he sought by faith and fasting and prayer for greater revelations of the mysteries. See the *Salt Lake Herald*, March 7, 1898.

Chapter 11

1. See "Grant's Watershed: Succession in the Presidency, 1887–89," in Walker, *Qualities that Count*, 195–229.

2. See *OFWJ*, March 16, 1898. The Utah State Department of Administrative Services, Division of Archives and Records Services, describes the work, "The *Book of the Pioneers* was created as a record of those who arrived in the Valley of the Great Salt Lake during 1847, including the names, ages, autographs, and places of residence of all known survivors on 24 July 1897, the year of the jubilee. Separated into two volumes, pioneers with surnames beginning with A through L are grouped in volume 1 and those starting with M through Z are found in volume 2. Included are lists of members and survivors of the Brigham Young Company, the general emigration, the Mormon Battalion, and the Mississippi Company, as well as a table of the states and nationalities of the survivors. Reproduced in volume 1 is an early photograph of Utah pioneers taken on Temple Square 24 July 1897, by Springville, Utah, photographer Geo. Ed Andersen. A brief history of the commission appears in volume 1. Some of the jubilee activities covered in volume 2 include: history and dedication of the Pioneer Monument (Brigham Young Monument), the pioneer badge, the pioneer poem, the pioneer ode, the Hall of Relics (including a photograph of the exterior), and the Historians' Finale, a brief description of more prominent phases of the festival." http://archives.utah.gov/research/inventories/14107.html (accessed 6/21/2013).

3. *OFWJ*, March 20, 1898

4. *OFWJ*, April 11, 1898.

5. *OFWJ*, April 11, 1898.

6. *OFWJ*, April 27, 1898

7. *OFWJ*, April 29, 1898. I have been unable to locate Orson's reincarnation statement. In 2011, an anonymous compiler self-published a collection of quotations (many alleged to refer to reincarnation), culled from (mostly older) LDS literature. Entitled, *Teachings of the Doctrine of Eternal Lives*, the book may have covered some of the same theoretical ground as Whitney's letter. The meanings the anonymous compiler places upon the assembled quotations constitute a massive exercise in misunderstanding and misinterpretation of scripture and prophetic teachings, unpersuasive to spiritually mature and grounded gospel scholars. When one seeks to find a pet theory in a text, one can often find it, whether it is really there

or not. Proponents of reincarnation often interpret the scriptural term "eternal lives" as referring to one spirit eternally being reborn into a new mortal or immortal body—instead of the settled doctrine of the Church that the term means "eternal increase" or never-ending spirit progeny.

8. *OFWJ*, April 29, 1911.
9. *OFWJ*, May 5, 1898.
10. *OFWJ*, May 5, 1898.
11. *OFWJ*, May 8, 1898
12. *OFWJ*, May 8, 1898.
13. *OFWJ*, May 11, 1898; see also *OFWJ*, May 10, 1898.
14. *OFWJ*, June 3, 1898.
15. *OFWJ*, June 3, 1898. The identity of the J. N. mentioned is not given, but may have been John Nicholson.
16. See *OFWJ*, June 11, 1898.
17. *OFWJ*, June 19, 1898.
18. *OFWJ*, August 31, 1898; see also *OFWJ*, August 30, 1898.
19. *OFWJ*, September 2, 1898.
20. J. Golden Kimball Journal, Sept 8, 1898, Church History Library Archives.
21. *OFWJ*, September 4, 1898.
22. J. Golden Kimball Journal, September 9, 1898.
23. *OFWJ*, September 9, 1898.
24. *OFWJ*, September 9, 1898.
25. *OFWJ*, September 11, 1898.
26. *OFWJ*, September 23, 1898.
27. *OFWJ*, September 26, 1898. What Orson meant by the three priesthoods note is not clear.
28. *OFWJ*, October 1, 1898. Again, what Orson meant by the cryptic note in not clear. Possibly he was referring to Mahonri Moriancumer (the brother of Jared of the book of Ether) as being the Holy Ghost for another planet, a strange notion that could have easily come out of the many secret prayer meetings.

29. *OFWJ*, October 4, 1898

30. *OFWJ*, October 6, 1898.

31. *OFWJ*, October 22, 1898.

32. *OFWJ*, October 26, 1898. Whitney's figures in this entry are somewhat confusing.

33. *OFWJ*, November 9, 1898. As to B. H. Roberts, Orson wrote, "Received this day a very handsome edition of *Les Meserables* from my friend B. H. Roberts, as a memento of the late campaign. It was accompanied by a very nice letter in which he expresses the highest appreciation of my 'bravery and manliness' in defending him during the campaign" (*OFWJ*, December 7, 1898). See also Madsen, *Defender of the Faith*, 243.

34. *OFWJ*, November 10, 1898.

35. See *OFWJ*, December 16, 1898. He also wrote, "This morning saw Pres. Snow and suggested to him the organization of a 'spiritual mission.'" No further explanation given.

36. *OFWJ*, December 24, (Christmas Eve), 1898.

37. See *OFWJ*, January 1, 1899.

38. *OFWJ*, January 3, 1899.

39. See *OFWJ*, January 9, 1899. Senator Whitney noted that he was "chairman of the Committee on Education and of the Committee on [illegible] and Enrolled Bills, in the Senate. Also a member of seven other Committees" (*OFWJ*, January 11, 1899).

40. *OFWJ*, January 19, 1899; see also *OFWJ*, January 17, 1899.

41. *OFWJ*, February 11, 1899.

42. See *OFWJ*, January 11 & 16, 1899.

43. See *OFWJ*, April 6 and May 13, 1899.

44. *OFWJ*, April 6, 1899.

45. *OFWJ*, April 23, 1899.

46. *OFWJ*, May 14, 1899. For a detailed review of President Snow's trip to St. George and his renewed emphasis on full tithing payment, see Horne, *Latter Leaves in the Life of Lorenzo Snow*, 302–62.

47. *OFWJ*, May 27, 1899.

48. *OFWJ*, May 28, 1899.

49. Orson explained: "Mr. Noble Warrum, editor of the *Salt Lake Herald*, spoke to me today about my son Race and his work on that paper. He said 'Race' was doing fine. Mr. Hart, head of the reportorial force, had told Warrum that he (Race) was one of the best reporters in the city. He has risen steadily since he was correspondent of the *Tribune* (while in Provo) a year ago. He now commands $15 a week with prospects of an early raise. It was under Mr. Warrum, once editor of the *Logan Journal*, that Race got his first experience in newspaper work" (*OFWJ*, April 30, 1899). Race's job with the *Salt Lake Tribune* must have given his father heartburn. Orson could rarely mention the *Tribune* without editorial comment on their hate and bitterness toward the Church he loved. For example: "*The Salt Lake Tribune*, in its Anti-[B. H.] Roberts, Anti-Church fight, is doing some fearfully reckless lying nowadays" (*OFWJ*, July 12, 1899).

50. See *OFWJ*, April 24, and May 2 and 21, 1899.

51. *OFWJ*, June 9, 1899.

52. *OFWJ*, July 1, 1899.

53. *OFWJ*, July 2, 1899. The most detailed account available of this tithing solemn assembly is found in Horne, *Latter Leaves in the Life of Lorenzo Snow*, 342–48.

Chapter 12

1. *OFWJ*, September 4, 1899.
2. See *OFWJ*, September 7, 1899. Arthur died of lead poisoning.
3. *OFWJ*, December 3, 1899.
4. *OFWJ*, December 4, 1899.
5. *OFWJ*, December 18, 1899.
6. *OFWJ*, December 25, 1899.
7. *OFWJ*, December 26, 1899.
8. *OFWJ*, December 27 and 28, 1899.
9. *OFWJ*, December 29, 1899.
10. John Henry Smith diary, January 5, 1900; as found in *Church State and Politics: The Diaries of John Henry Smith*, 442.
11. *OFWJ*, December 31, 1899. Such amounts as described, if adjusted for inflation, would likely be in the hundreds of thousands of dollars that Orson gave to Charles over the years.
12. Orson's diary indicates that the social activities of what had become known as "the Stayner crowd" did not immediately cease; they still held parties and met for dinner and other occasions, but internal diary evidence suggests the secret prayer meetings gradually ended, likely sooner than later, and the group went their separate ways. Orson considered them friends and visited when occasion allowed.
13. *OFWJ*, February 14, 1900. At this time, prayer circles were organized, with presidents, independent of temple endowment sessions.
14. *OFWJ*, March 1, 1900.
15. *OFWJ*, May 23, 1900.
16. *TMH*, 231.
17. *OFWJ*, May 24, 25, 26, 1900.
18. *OFWJ*, May 30, 1900.
19. See *OFWJ*, June 2 and 3, 1900.
20. *OFWJ*, June 6, 1900.
21. *OFWJ*, June 7, 1900.

22. *OFWJ*, June 8, 1900.

23. *OFWJ*, June 30, 1900.

24. *OFWJ*, July 1, 1900.

25. *OFWJ*, July 27, 1900. For a review of what the First Presidency was doing at the time Orson's letter was under consideration, see Horne, *Latter Leaves in the Life of Lorenzo Snow*, 392–93.

26. In his biography of Amasa M. Lyman, author Edward Leo Lyman inaccurately refers to "Apostle Orson F. Whitney's belief in multiple probations or reincarnation, although he never preached this view publicly, proved sufficiently well known that some church leaders could have taken serious offense at them." Herein, we have seen how church leaders dealt with Whitney—who was NOT an apostle at the time he believed the doctrine. See Lyman, *Amasa Mason Lyman: Mormon Apostle and Apostate,* 388. *Bishop* Whitney was not called to the apostleship until long after his watershed season.

27. On July 22, 1900, Orson wrote: "Spent the forenoon in my office. Finished a poem entitled 'Zina' upon which I have been working for some days. Also continued working over old letters, mine and Zina's. A very tender task" (*OFWJ*, under date given).

28. *OFWJ*, July 11, 1900.

29. *OFWJ*, July 14, 1900.

30. *OFWJ*, August 11, 1900. I have been unable to identify Georgiana. Carmon Hardy's list of plural wives in his book *Solemn Covenant*, Appendix 2, contains two plural wife names like Georgiana's, but spelled slightly different. Both have different, later, marriage year dates than the woman that Orson courted and that had secretly married not long before he began courting her.

31. *OFWJ*, August 7, 1900.

32. *OFWJ*, September 17, 1900; see also *OFWJ*, ca. August, 1900.

33. *OFWJ*, October 11, 1900.

34. *TMH*, 232.

35. *OFWJ*, October 30, 1900.

36. *OFWJ*, December 25, 1900.

37. *OFWJ*, January 1, 1901.

38. Roberts' refusal to sign the so-called political manifesto nearly cost him his position as a member of the Presidency of the First Council of the Seventy; see Horne, *Latter Leaves in the Life of Lorenzo Snow*, 246–47.

39. *OFWJ*, January 14, 1901.

40. *OFWJ*, January 22, 1901.

41. *OFWJ*, January 23, 1901.

42. *OFWJ*, February 15, 1901.

43. See *OFWJ*, March 5, 7, and 15, 1901; for further explanation, see *TMH*, 236–38.

44. President Cannon wrote, "His style is somewhat dramatic, but I think that he is without doubt the best orator in the Church—at least I have heard no one that in my opinion equals him in oratory" (George Q. Cannon journal, October 30, 1897; as quoted in Madsen, *Defender of the Faith*, 346, n435).

45. *OFWJ*, March 30, 1901.

46. *OFWJ*, April 12, 1901; see also *TMH*, 239.

47. See *OFWJ*, April 28, May 3, 6, 13, 19, 20, and 22, 1901.

48. *FWJ*, May 23, 1901.

49. *OFWJ*, May 25, 1901.

50. *OFWJ*, June 5, 1901.

51. See *OFWJ*, June 8, 9 and 12, 1901.

52. See *OFWJ*, June 14, 1901.

53. *OFWJ*, July 1, 1901.

54. *OFWJ*, July 13, 1901; see also *OFWJ*, July 2, 1901.

55. See *OFWJ*, July 14, 1901.

56. *OFWJ*, July 15, 1901.

57. *OFWJ*, July 22, 1901.

58. *OFWJ*, September 1, 1901.

59. For a review of B. H. Roberts' work, see Madsen, *Defender of the Faith*, 290–93. See also Horne, *Latter Leaves in the Life of Lorenzo Snow*, 293, 386, 398.

60. *OFWJ*, September 6, 1901.

61. *OFWJ*, September 11 and 12, 1901; see also *OFWJ*, September 10, where Orson was baptized for them.

62. *OFWJ*, ca. September, 1901.

63. *OFWJ*, October 4 to 6, 1901.

64. *OFWJ*, October 9, 1901.

65. *OFWJ*, October 13, 1901; see also TMH, 240.

66. *OFWJ*, October 18, 1901. For a review of events leading to Joseph F. Smith becoming the president of the Church, see Horne, "President Joseph F. Smith's Succession to the Presidency," in *Joseph F. Smith: Reflections on the Man and His Times*, 267–78.

67. For further information on this subject, see Mecham, *Changes in Seniority to the Quorum of the Twelve Apostles of The Church of Jesus Christ of Latter-day Saints*; and Bishop, "The Apostolic Succession of Joseph F. Smith," in *Joseph F. Smith: Reflections on the Man and His Times*, 249–64.

68. *OFWJ*, October 27, 1901.

69. *OFWJ*, November 23, 1901.

70. *OFWJ*, December 16, 1901.

71. *TMH*, 240.

72. *OFWJ*, December 22, 1901.

73. *OFWJ*, December 26 and 27, 1901.

74. *OFWJ*, December 31, 1901.

Chapter 13

1. *TMH*, 243–244.
2. *OFWJ*, September 1, 1900.
3. *OFWJ*, October 27, 1901.
4. *OFWJ*, December 20, 1901.
5. *OFWJ*, January 2, 1902.
6. *OFWJ*, April 17, 1902.
7. *OFWJ*, January 5, 1902.
8. *OFWJ*, February 1 and 15, 1902. In his own diary, President Anthon H. Lund noted, "At the Historian's Office in the morning and had a talk with Bro. Orson F. Whitney about the hymn book. He is willing to work upon its revision" (*AHLJ*, January 31, 1902); further: "Bro. Orson F. Whitney and I talked about the hymn book, and the Presidency agreed with me in the proposition to go over the revision" (*AHLJ*, February 1, 1902); and in March: "The hymn book needing a revision, I have put Bro. Orson F. Whitney at the work. He and I compared a few hymns together" (*AHLJ*, March 11, 1902).
9. *OFWJ*, April 12, 1902.
10. *OFWJ*, April 6, 1902.
11. See *OFWJ*, February 17, May 10, May 15, June 1 and June 23, 1902.
12. *OFWJ*, May 20, 1902. As much as he loved and missed Zina, Orson was also fully mindful of the blessing he had of his other wife May, and wrote, "Today is my dear May's birthday. She is a true, faithful, devoted, and loving wife, and I much appreciate her for her loyalty, integrity, and kindness of heart. I shall be glad to soon place her and the children, as well as myself, in a new house . . . the work upon which is progressing steadily and will soon be done" (December 10, 1902). That June, Orson recorded a curious attempt, perhaps rooted in vanity, to stop the balding process that was gaining noticeable headway: "Began taking treatment for hair and scalp . . . it is thought I can regain my former growth of hair, which was once luxuriant. I began getting bald soon after my return from England in 1883. Mrs. Brown has graduated in San Francisco . . . and is confident she can cure me of baldness, which with me is only partial" (*OFWJ*, June 4, 1902). The treatment did not work.

13. *OFWJ*, September 19, 1902.

14. *OFWJ*, September 19, 1902.

15. *OFWJ*, September 29, 1902.

16. *OFWJ*, September 30, 1902.

17. *AHLJ*, November 3, 1902.

18. *OFWJ*, November 4, 1902.

19. *OFWJ*, December 11, 1902. In the same diary entry, he also wrote, "I have just written for the First Presidency their 'Christmas Greeting' to the Latter-day Saints to be published in the [illegible] No. of the *Deseret News*. I feel very happy in those continued evidences of the confidence and good will of the Authorities." The second and concluding reading of the poem was even more successful: "In the presence of a throng that filled the commodious parlors of the Richards mansion 175 A. St. I gave this, the last reading of the series begun December 10th at Col. Clayton's. . . . All present overwhelmed me with praise and congratulations. I told them I felt more than grateful, but not lifted up a particle, for I did not feel that I had done it, but God to whom I gave all the glory" (January 11, 1903).

20. *OFWJ*, December 16, 1902.

21. See *OFWJ*, December 30 and 31, 1902.

22. *OFWJ*, January 9, 1903.

23. *OFWJ*, January 10, 1903.

24. *OFWJ*, January 24, 1903.

25. *OFWJ*, February 3, 1903.

26. See *OFWJ*, February 9, 1903.

27. *OFWJ*, February 17, 1903.

28. *OFWJ*, February 18, 1903.

29. *AHLJ*, February 16, 1903.

30. *AHLJ*, February 18, 1903.

31. Rudger Clawson diary, February 16–18, 1893; as found in *A Ministry of Meetings: The Apostolic Diaries of Rudger Clawson*, 547.

32. *OFWJ*, February 21, 1903.

33. *TMH,* 247, 249.

34. See *OFWJ*, March 4, 7, and 13, 1903.

35. *OFWJ*, March 17, 1903.

36. *OFWJ*, March 20, 1903.

37. *OFWJ*, May 23, 1903; For a report of the conference, see *Deseret News*, May 25, 1903.

38. See *OFWJ*, June 1, 1903.

39. See *OFWJ*, June 19, 1903.

40. *OFWJ*, July 1, 1903.

41. *OFWJ*, July 3, 1903.

42. *OFWJ*, July 4, 1903.

43. *OFWJ*, July 5, 1903.

44. *OFWJ*, July 13 and 16, 1903.

45. See *OFWJ*, December 24, 1903.

46. *OFWJ*, July 17, 1903.

47. *OFWJ*, July 22, 1903.

48. *OFWJ*, July 30, 1903.

49. *OFWJ*, October 6, 1903.

50. *OFWJ*, ca. October 15, 1903.

51. *OFWJ*, December 7, 1903.

52, *OFWJ*, December 20, 1903.

53. *OFWJ*, December 31, 1903.

54. *OFWJ*, January 1, 1905.

55. For further information regarding Elder Clawson's marriage to Pearl Udall, see Hoopes and Hoopes, *The Making of a Mormon Apostle: The Story of Rudger Clawson*, 215–220, 225–26, 227, 235, 236, 271.

56. See *OFWJ*, January 4, 10, 26 and February 2 and 27, 1905.

57. *OFWJ*, January 3, 1905; See also March 1 and 3, 1905.

58. *OFWJ*, January 5, 1905.

59. See *OFWJ*, March 6, 1905.

60. *OFWJ*, April 6, 1905.

61. *OFWJ*, May 8, 1905.

62. *OFWJ*, April 18, 1905.

63. *OFWJ*, September 27, 1905.

64. *OFWJ*, June 1, 1905.

65. See *OFWJ*, July 3, 1905; see also July 29 and September 16, 1905.

66. *OFWJ*, ca. September 25, 1905.

67. *OFWJ*, July 14, 1905.

68. *OFWJ*, July 29, 1905.

69. *OFWJ*, September 16, 1905.

70. *OFWJ*, October 8, 1905.

71. *OFWJ*, December 6, 1905.

72. *OFWJ*, December 18, 1905.

73. *OFWJ*, January 1, New Year's Day, 1906.

74. *OFWJ*, ca. February, 1906.

75. *OFWJ*, November 20, 1906.

76. See *OFWJ*, January 27, September 30, 1907, and November 6 and 7, 1908.

Chapter 14

1. *OFWJ*, April 6, 1906.

2. Francis M. Lyman in particular had been involved, along with President George Q. Cannon, in public refutations of reincarnation doctrine. Lyman himself had more personal reasons for his awareness and wariness of that and other dangerous doctrines and practices in the Church; his father, Amasa Lyman, had been a member of the Quorum of the Twelve Apostles also, but had become involved in spiritualism, séances, and false doctrine; thereafter being dropped from the Twelve and then excommunicated. See Lyman, *Amasa Mason Lyman: Mormon Apostle and Apostate; A Study in Dedication.*

3. *OFWJ*, April 7, 1906. Elder Whitney's own description of these events stated, "The greatest honor that my life has known came to me in the month of April, 1906, when I was ordained an apostle and called into the Council of the Twelve. This advancement, though a complete surprise to me and mine, fulfilled more than one prediction made concerning me during the previous quarter of a century.

   "Three vacancies had existed in the Council, caused by the death of Marriner W. Merrill, and the retirement [resignation] of two other of the Twelve, John W. Taylor and Matthias F. Cowley, who had found themselves out of harmony with the changed attitude of the Church relative to the further practice of plural marriage. Those vacancies were filled when George F. Richards, Orson F. Whitney, and David O. McKay became apostles.

   "Called at the General Conference in the Tabernacle, on Sunday the eighth of April, we were ordained by President Joseph F. Smith in the Temple, on the day following. Others taking part in the ordinations were Presidents John R. Winder and Anthon H. Lund; Elders Francis M. Lyman, John Henry Smith, Rudger Clawson, Hyrum M. Smith, George Albert Smith, and Charles W. Penrose, of the Council of the Twelve; and Patriarch John Smith. The remaining members of the Council—George Teasdale, Heber J. Grant, and Reed Smoot—were absent on duty elsewhere" (*TMH*, 262).

4. *OFWJ*, April 8, 1906.

5. *OFWJ*, April 9, 1906.

6. *AHLJ*, April 9, 1906.

7. *TMH*, 262,263.

8. *OFWJ*, April 10, 1906.

9. *OFWJ*, April 11, 1906.

10. *OFWJ*, April 12, 1906.

11. *OFWJ*, April 15, 1906.

12. *OFWJ*, April 17, 1906. In this letter, Elder Whitney did not admit to President Smith that the main reason for his debt was because he had given so much money to Charles W. Stayner.

13. *OFWJ*, April 19, 1906.

14. *OFWJ*, April 21, 1906.

15. *OFWJ*, April 24, 1906. Against counsel, Elders Taylor and Cowley had continued involving themselves in matters related to plural marriage after the second manifesto, and their actions brought public trouble upon the Church. Further information about their "trials" (formal disciplining) can be found in Drew Briney, *Apostles on Trial: Examining the Membership Trials of Apostles Taylor and Cowley* (n.p.: Hindsight Publications, 2012). This self-published book by Briney is "fundamentalist" (pro-continued polygamy after the manifesto) in nature and therefore supportive of Taylor and Cowley, and against their being disciplined. See also Hardy, *Solemn Covenant: The Mormon Polygamous Passage*, esp. chapter 7. Historical works often state that Matthias Cowley was disfellowshipped. This is not completely accurate. His son, Elder Matthew Cowley, set the record straight, as well as providing insight into his father's attitude toward the Church: "I was reared in a very unusual home. Because of certain conditions that arose . . . my father was released from the Quorum of the Twelve Apostles. He was not disfellowshipped; he was not excommunicated; but he had to hold his priesthood in abeyance for a number of years until the First Presidency again gave him the green light to go ahead. I suppose he was officially inactive for some 27 or 28 years. At the beginning of that period his children were mostly young. I was just 7 or 8 years of age. He could not officiate in the priesthood in any way. But they couldn't stop him from being the patriarch of his own family—from presiding in his own home. I wouldn't be here today . . . if it had not been for the integrity and the devotion and the loyalty of my father, to The Church of Jesus Christ of Latter-day Saints. During those years of inactivity, he kept his sons on missions for 25 years." ("Put Your Hand into the Hand of God," *BYU Speeches*, October. 20, 1953; the above quotation is a transcription of the audio recording, and is not included in the published version of this talk as found in *Matthew Cowley Speaks*, 295–300. Matthias Cowley died in 1940.

16. *OFWJ*, May 3, 1906.

17. *OFWJ*, May 4, 1906.

18. *OFWJ*, May 8, 1906.

19. *OFWJ*, May 11, 1906.

20. *OFWJ*, May 13, 1906.

21. *OFWJ*, May 16, 1906.

22. *OFWJ*, May 26, 1906.

23. *OFWJ*, May 29, 1906.

24. *OFWJ*, May 30, 1906.

25. *OFWJ*, June 7, 1906.

26. John Henry Smith diary, June 7, 1906; as found in *Church, State and Politics: The Diaries of John Henry Smith*, 569.

27. *OFWJ*, June 8, 1906.

28. *OFWJ*, June 14, 1906.

29. *OFWJ*, June 22, 1906.

30. *OFWJ*, June 23, 1906.

31. See Horne, *Latter Leaves in the Life of Lorenzo Snow*, 213–14, 221.

32. *OFWJ*, July 3, 1906.

33. *TMH*, 265–66

34. *OFWJ*, July 10, 1906.

35. *OFWJ*, ca. April, 1906.

36. *OFWJ*, ca. April, 1906.

37. *OFWJ*, ca. April, 1906.

38. *OFWJ*, ca. April, 1906.

39. *TMH*, 219.

40. *OFWJ*, July 15, 1906. For further explanation of this incident, see *TMH*, 266–67.

41. *OFWJ*, July 19, 1906.

42. *OFWJ*, July 22, 1906.

43. See the Introduction for a statement by President Joseph F. Smith regarding how such alleged items of doctrine should be viewed.

44. *JEHJ*, July 27, 1906.

45. *OFWJ*, July 28, 1906.

46. *OFWJ*, August 13, 1906.

47. *OFWJ*, September 4, 1906.

48. *OFWJ*, September 13, 1906.

49. *OFWJ*, September 15, 1906.

50. *OFWJ*, September 17, 1906.

51. *OFWJ*, September 20, 1906.

52. *OFWJ*, September 26, 1906.

53. *OFWJ*, October 3, 1906.

Chapter 15

1. Conference Report, April 1929, 110. See also *Through Memory's Halls*, 68–69.

2. For instance, President Boyd K. Packer quoted Elder Whitney in his talk, "Our Moral Environment," (*Ensign*, May 1992, 66). President Packer also taught a similar doctrine to a group of mission presidents and their wives, "Many of you are leaving your children and grandchildren. They will be blessed and looked after. And if there is one that has strayed, you be prayerfully patient—you are working with part of His family—He will have someone work with *that* part of your family. And in the course of things—now or beyond the veil—you can rest assured that there won't be empty chairs in your family circle there. That is the pay you get for the extra price it is taking now for you to accept these assignments" ("Remarks" 2005 Seminar for New MTC Presidents and Visitors' Center Directors, January 13, 2005). Elder David A. Bednar addressed this subject and gently corrected an interpretation of Elder Whitney's doctrine as teaching a form of blanket or unconditional salvation for all wayward children of faithful parents in his article published in the March 2014 *Ensign* (see David A. Bednar, "Faithful Parents and Wayward Children," *Ensign*, March 2014, 28–33). For President Lorenzo Snow's teachings on this subject, see Horne, *Latter Leaves in the Life of Lorenzo Snow*, appendix 3.

3. *OFWJ*, February 23, 1902.

4. *OFWJ*, April 21, 1902.

5. *OFWJ*, May 10, 1902.

6. *OFWJ*, December 14, 1903.

7. *OFWJ*, December 25, 1903.

8. *OFWJ*, December 27, 1903.

9. *OFWJ*, December 28, 1903.

10. *OFWJ*, December 31, 1903.

11. *OFWJ*, January 23, 1905.

12. *OFWJ*, January 25, 1905.

13. *OFWJ*, September 16, 1905.

14. *OFWJ*, April 21, 1906.

15. *OFWJ*, April 27, 1906.

16. Clipping from *Deseret News*, missing date, as found in *OFWJ*, April 30, 1906.

17. Ibid.

18. *OFWJ*, June 4, 1906.

19. *OFWJ*, May 22, 1906.

20. *OFWJ*, November 8, 1906.

21. *OFWJ*, November 21, 1906.

22. *OFWJ*, January 5, 1907.

23. *OFWJ*, March 22, 1908.

24. *OFWJ*, March 23, 1908.

25. *OFWJ*, April 5, 1908.

26. *OFWJ*, April 6, 1908.

27. *OFWJ*, April 8, 1908.

28. *OFWJ*, April 9, 1908.

29. *OFWJ*, April 10, 1908.

30. *OFWJ*, April 16, 1908.

31. *OFWJ*, April 14, 1908.

32. *OFWJ*, April 18, 1908.

33. See *OFWJ*, April 19 and 20, 1908.

34. *FWJ*, April 23, 1908.

35. See *OFWJ*, June 15, 16 and July 1, 2, 3, 1908.

36. *OFWJ*, July 11, 1908.

37. *OFWJ*, July 12, 1908.

38. *OFWJ*, July 13, 1908.

39. *OFWJ*, July 14, 1908.

40. *OFWJ*, July 16, 1908.

41. *OFWJ*, July 19, 1908.

42. *OFWJ*, September 15, 1908.

43. *OFWJ*, November 9, 1908.

44. *OFWJ*, November 2, 1909.

45. *OFWJ*, November 4, 1909.

46. *OFWJ*, November 9, 1909.

47. *OFWJ*, November 12, 1909.

48. *OFWJ*, March 13, 1912.

49. *OFWJ*, May 27, 1912.

50. *OFWJ*, May 29, 1912.

51. See *OFWJ*, September 19, 1913.

52. See *OFWJ*, November 23, 1913. For example, of his "actress" daughter, Margaret, he wrote, "April 27, 1917. Lester [Essig] and I walked up City Creek Canyon and over the adjacent hills, talking of 'Mormonism,' etc. He is a fine fellow. Would he were one of us. God grant he may yet be. He and his relatives with Margaret attended the organ recital at the Tabernacle, and later we all met at my daughter Emily's to 'eat the wedding cake.'" And, "April 30, 1907. Margaret's wedding day. The marriage took place at 7:30 p.m. at my daughter Helen's . . . President Richard W. Young performing the ceremony. It was a truly beautiful affair."

53. See *OFWJ*, January 17, 1918; September 18, 1918; February 12, 1931.

54. *OFWJ*, January 1, 1917.

Chapter 16

1. *OFWJ*, October 5, 1906.
2. *OFWJ*, October 8, 1906.
3. *OFWJ*, November 19, 1906.
4. *OFWJ*, December 13, 1906. For further explanation of this story, see *TMH*, 268–69. Whitney therein says that President Smith "was visibly touched" by the gesture.
5. *OFWJ*, December 24, 1906.
6. *OFWJ*, December 25, 1906.
7. *OFWJ*, December 31, 1906.
8. *OFWJ*, January 2, 1906.
9. *OFWJ*, January 3, 1907. For the report as delivered and further history about it, see Clark, *Messages of the First Presidency* 4:133–54.
10. *OFWJ*, January 4, 1907.
11. *OFWJ*, January 13, 1907.
12. *OFWJ*, January 30, 1907.
13. *OFWJ*, February 7, 1907. Further reference to the subject can be found in Roberts, *The Truth, the Way, the Life: An Elementary Treatise on Theology*, 81–84; Top, *The Life Before*, 39–51; Godfrey, "The History of Intelligence in Latter-day Saint Thought," in *The Pearl of Great Price: Revelations From God*, 213–36; and Horne, *Bruce R. McConkie: Highlights from His life and Teachings*, 326–38. This latter work contains material wherein Elder McConkie comments on Elder Roberts's doctrinal theories regarding intelligences.
14. *OFWJ*, February 20, 1907.
15. Many have wondered why President Joseph F. Smith supported Reed Smoot's senatorial ambitions so staunchly in the face of such widespread national Mormon-bashing. In the autobiography of Charles W. Nibley (Presiding Bishop of the Church), we find some of the reasoning: "I recall that in 1906 when we were returning from Europe, (it was just a year or so after the Smoot investigation which had caused such a disturbance in the Church and out of it) one bright moonlit night the sea was smooth and we were enjoying the ocean breeze, standing by the

railing [of the ship], President Smith and I alone, chatting about one thing or the other, I ventured to suggest to him that it would be a wise and prudent thing for Senator Smoot to stay at home. I approached the subject as cautiously and as adroitly as I knew how to do, and presented my facts and arguments and logic in just as smooth a manner as possible. I could see he was listening but with some impatience. Finally, bringing his fist down on the railing between us he stated in these emphatic terms, 'If I have ever had the inspiration of the spirit of the Lord given to me forcefully and clearly it has been on this one point concerning Reed Smoot, and that is, instead of his being retired, he should be continued in the United States Senate.' Now it seemed to me that all the arguments, all the facts, all the logic were on my side, but when he announced what had been manifested to him by the Spirit of the Lord with such positiveness, I withdrew my opposition and from that hour to this (1918) I have loyally and faithfully supported Senator Smoot. The sequel proves how gloriously the inspiration of the Almighty was vindicated as compared with my reason and logic and facts, as I supposed. Everywhere and with one accord the men who do big things in this nation when they have been passing through Salt Lake City and called on the Presidency, have almost without exception, praised in the highest terms the work of Senator Smoot, and urged upon President Smith and others that he be continued in the work that he was so splendidly performing" (*Reminiscences [of] Charles W. Nibley*, 125–26).

16. *OFWJ*, February 26, 1907.

17. *OFWJ*, February 27, 1907.

18. *OFWJ*, March 3, 1907.

19. *OFWJ*, March 4, 1907.

20. *OFWJ*, March 21, 1907.

21. *OFWJ*, March 22, 1907.

22. *OFWJ*, March 31, 1907.

23. *OFWJ*, April 2, 1907.

24. *OFWJ*, April 1, 1907.

25. *OFWJ*, April 5, 1907. For the text read by Whitney to the conference, see Clark, *Messages of the First Presidency* 4:143–55.

26. *OFWJ*, April 7, 1907.

27. *OFWJ*, May 30, 1907.

28. *OFWJ*, June 12, 1907.

29. *OFWJ*, July 21, 1907.

30. *OFWJ*, July 31, 1907.

31. *OFWJ*, August 11, 1907.

32. *OFWJ*, August 25, 1907.

33. *OFWJ*, September 6, 1907.

34. For an instance in which an *important interview* notation in a diary meant a marriage proposal, see Smith and Stewart, *Life of Joseph Fielding Smith*, 254.

35. *OFWJ*, September 18, 1907.

36. *OFWJ*, September 29, 1907.

37. *OFWJ*, October 1, 1907.

38. *OFWJ*, October 2, 1907.

39. *OFWJ*, October 16, 1907.

40. *OFWJ*, October 4, 1907.

41. *OFWJ*, October 5, 1907.

42. *FWJ*, October 6, 1907.

43. See *OFWJ*, October 18 and 30, 1907.

44. *OFWJ*, November 9, 1907.

45. *OFWJ*, November 23, 1907.

46. *OFWJ*, December 4–8, 1907.

47. *OFWJ*, December 11, 1907.

48. *OFWJ*, December 18, 1907.

49. As quoted in *Reminiscences [of] Charles W. Nibley, 1849–1931*, 120–22.

50. *OFWJ*, January 1, 1908.

51. *OFWJ*, January 2, 1908.

52. *OFWJ*, January 21, 1908.

53. *OFWJ*, January 22, 1908.

54. *OFWJ*, January 30, 1908.

55. *OFWJ*, March 17, 1908.

56. *OFWJ*, March 20 and 21, 1908.

57. *OFWJ*, March 30, 1908.

58. *OFWJ*, April 3, 1908.

59. *OFWJ*, April 4, 1908.

60. *OFWJ*, May 12, 1908.

61. *OFWJ*, July 10, 1908.

62. *OFWJ*, August 25, 1908.

63. *OFWJ*, August 26, 1908.

64. *OFWJ*, August 29, 1908.

65. *OFWJ*, September 2, 1908.

66. *OFWJ*, December 3, 4, and 5, 1908.

67. *OFWJ*, April 5, 1909.

68. *OFWJ*, April 6 and 7, 1909.

69. *OFWJ*, May 6 and 7, 1909.

70. *OFWJ*, May 10, 1909.

71. *OFWJ*, May 11, 1909.

Chapter 17

1. For the statement, see Clark, *Messages of the First Presidency* 4:84–85.
2. A standard text reviewing these years is Hardy, *Solemn Covenant: the Mormon Polygamous Passage*; see also Reimann, *Plural Marriage Limited*; Van Wagoner, *Mormon Polygamy: A History*; and Anderson, *The Polygamy Story: Fiction and Fact.*
3. *OFWJ*, July 15, 1909.
4. *OFWJ*, July 22, 1909.
5. *OFWJ*, August 6, 1909.
6. *OFWJ*, August 20, 1909. This is one of a few entries where Orson mentions his personal sympathies regarding new polygamy. See Hardy, *Solemn Covenant*, Appendix 2, #93.
7. See *OFWJ*, September 1, 1909.
8. *OFWJ*, September 2, 1909.
9. *OFWJ*, September 14, 1909.
10. *OFWJ*, September 16, 17, and 18, 1909. The Talmage reference is to him reading his new book, *The Great Apostasy,* to a committee of the Brethren to approve it before publication.
11. *OFWJ*, September 19, 1909.
12. *OFWJ*, September 20, 1909.
13. *OFWJ*, September 27, 1909.
14. *OFWJ*, September 30, 1909. This was not the only occasion for John A. Widstoe to give his thoughts on the document. On October 23rd he wrote a letter to Whitney, stating, "However, let me say that I have read your article on 'The Origin of Man' that you sent me a few days ago. It is undoubtedly an excellent statement of the scriptural view of the origin of man. To me, it is perfectly satisfactory. It is well written, comprehensive and complete. Of course, it does not in any sense deal with the law of evolution or the theory of animal descent as believed in by many evolutionists. . . . As for the article that you have prepared, I cannot understand how any person who understands the Gospel can take issue with it in any way. It certainly would be a good thing to publish. Undoubtedly the comment will be made upon it that it does not after all answer the questions propounded by the evolutionist. I take it that you have not

attempted to do this, except in an indirect way" (Correspondence, John A. Widstoe to Orson F. Whitney, October 23, 1909; Church History Library Archives).

15. *AHLJ*, October 14, 1909.

16. *HLJ*, October 20, 1909. Whitney's diary does not mention this reading.

17. Several authoritative commentators have noted disputations about the declaration; see Packer, "The Law and the Light," in Monte S. Nyman and Charles D. Tate Jr., eds., *The Book of Mormon: Jacob Through Words of Mormon, To Learn With Joy*, 1–31, esp. 22–23; Horne, *Bruce R. McConkie: Highlights from His Life and Teachings*, 258; Horne, *Determining Doctrine*, 187–94; and Joseph Fielding McConkie, "Doctrinal Contributions of Joseph F. Smith," in *Joseph F. Smith: Reflections on the Man and His Times*, 21–23.

18. Clark, *Messages of the First Presidency* 4:205 (200–06). Some have speculated that in preparing this statement, Whitney drew upon his own material from an earlier article he had written entitled, "Man's Origin and Destiny" (see *The Contributor*, Vol. 3, No. 9 [June, 1882]. If so, this was and is common practice among speakers and authors: to reuse, revise, or refine their own former material. Elder Whitney himself was staunchly anti-evolution, firmly believing mankind (Adam and Eve) to be the offspring of Deity, with no animal descent involved.

19. *OFWJ*, September 24, 1909.

20. See Hardy, *Solemn Covenant*, 295.

21. *OFWJ*, September 25, 1909.

22. *OFWJ*, September 26, 1909.

23. See *AHLJ*, September 24, 1909.

24. *OFWJ*, October 3, 1909.

25. *OFWJ*, October 4, 1909.

26. *OFWJ*, October 6, 1909.

27. *AHLJ*, October 15, 1909.

28. *JEHJ*, November 7, 1909.

29. *OFWJ*, January 7, 1910.

30. See *OFWJ*, February 3 and 10, 1910. See also Hardy, *Solemn Covenant*, Appendix 2, #9.

31. *OFWJ,* January 15, 1910.

32. *OFWJ,* January 21, 1910.

33. *OFWJ,* January 27, 1910.

34. For an explanation of the rest of the story, see *TMH*, 392–94.

35. *OFWJ,* March 14, 1910.

36. See *OFWJ,* March 28 and 31, 1910.

37. *OFWJ,* March 18, 1910.

38. *OFWJ,* March 25, 1910.

39. *OFWJ,* April 4, 1910.

40. *OFWJ,* April 6, 1910.

41. *OFWJ,* April 7, 1910.

42. *OFWJ,* April 11, 1910.

43. *OFWJ,* April 15, 1910.

44. *OFWJ,* April 21, 1910.

45. *OFWJ,* May 19, 1910.

46. *OFWJ,* May 20, 1910.

47. *OFWJ,* May 30, 1910.

48. *OFWJ,* May 5, 1910.

49. See Hardy, *Solemn Covenant*, Appendix 2, #198.

50. *OFWJ,* June 15, 1910.

51. See *OFWJ,* June 22, 1910.

52. *OFWJ,* June 26, 1910.

53. *OFWJ,* July 1, 1910.

54. *OFWJ,* July 3, 1910.

55. *OFWJ,* July 4, 1910.

56. *OFWJ,* July 6, 1910.

57. *OFWJ,* July 7, 1910.

58. *OFWJ,* July 8, 1910.

59. Mention of Orson's acquaintance with a woman in 1910–11 is found in two allegedly historical books. Michael Quinn refers to Orson stopping pursuing a woman in *The Mormon Hierarchy: Extensions of Power*, 714; and Drew Briney (a pro-polygamy fundamentalist author), using Quinn as his source, references the same item in his book *Apostles on Trial: Examining the Membership Trials of Apostles Taylor and Cowley*, 234–35; Briney's notes rely on a "Bluffdale Conference" speech given by Quinn. Briney's summaries based on Quinn's inaccurate presentation do not accurately reflect the record for Whitney. These are the only two instances I have located, other than sources cited herein (such as Josiah E. Hickman's diary), that mention Laura (though not by name).

60. *OFWJ*, July 17, 1910. References to Josiah E. Hickman in his educational capacity are scattered throughout *Brigham Young University: The First One Hundred Years*, Vol. 1.

61. *OFWJ*, July 17, 18, and 19, 1910.

62. *JEHJ*, July 21, 1910. In explanation of his own views, which harmonized with Whitney's, Josiah Hickman wrote, "I am troubled at present, over the attitude that is being taken by the Twelve Apostles, especially some of them, in hunting down those who have gone into plural marriage the last few years and are disfellowshipping them. I can't feel that it is God's will, yet I vote to sustain them as prophets, seers, & revelators. . . . We are seeking to make peace with the mammon of unrighteousness. I may be wrong, but it seems that we are buckling to our enemies instead of keeping God's commandments and trusting to Him to fight our battles. . . . I have prayed over this but I can't, so far, feel in my heart to sanction this line of conduct. If it is right I hope to see it. If it is wrong I hope God will over rule things for the good of His cause and give His people their rights" (*JEHJ*, July 7, 1910).

63. *OFWJ*, July 21, 1910.

64. *OFWJ*, July 27, 1910.

65. *OFWJ*, July 28, 1910. At this same time, Orson was also corresponding with "F." which usually meant one of two acquaintances named Francis or Frances (Hickman or Thomasson). It is often hard to distinguish which one he is referring to, since the spelling of the name is inconsistent and hard to read.

66. *OFWJ*, August 7, 1910.

67. *OFWJ*, August 9, 1910.

68. *JEHJ*, August 20, 1910.

69. *OFWJ*, August 29, 1910.

70. *OFWJ*, August 30, 1910.

71. *OFWJ*, September 3, 1910.

72. *OFWJ*, September 4, 1910.

73. *OFWJ*, October 2, 1910.

74. *OFWJ*, October 6, 1910.

75. See *OFWJ*, October 8, 1910.

76. *JEHJ*, October 11, 1910. In his diary, Josiah confused the timing of Whitney's visit with himself eleven months before, with Whitney's visit with his family in Benjamin.

77. *JEHJ*, August 7, 1913.

78. *OFWJ*, October 17, 1910.

79. *OFWJ*, October 18, 1910.

80. See *OFWJ*, September 22, 1910. See also Hardy, *Solemn Covenant*, Appendix 2, #148.

81. See *OFWJ*, October 3, 1910. See also Hardy, *Solemn Covenant*, Appendix 2, #198.

82. See *OFWJ*, October 19, 1910. See also Hardy, *Solemn Covenant*, Appendix 2, #60 and #85.

83. *OFWJ*, October 23, 1910.

84. *OFWJ*, October 24, 2010.

85. *OFWJ*, October 25, 2010.

86. See *OFWJ*, September 29, 1910.

87. See *OFWJ*, November 1, 1910.

88. See *OFWJ*, October 31, 1910.

89. See *OFWJ*, August 18 and 25 and October 15, 1910.

Chapter 18

1. "Presentism" is a term used by historians, meaning to impose modern social and political mores on a historical figure that lived in another time and place, and to judge that person by present (and therefore false) standards, leading to incorrect conclusions.
2. *OFWJ*, September 19, 1910.
3. *OFWJ*, November 5, 1910.
4. *OFWJ*, November 7, 1910.
5. *OFWJ*, November 8, 1910.
6. See Hardy, *Solemn Covenant*, Appendix 2, #185 or 186.
7. *OFWJ*, November 9, 1910.
8. *OFWJ*, November 10, 11, and 12, 1910.
9. *OFWJ*, November 13, 1910.
10. *OFWJ*, November 14, 1910.
11. *OFWJ*, November 15, 1910.
12. *OFWJ*, November 20, 1910.
13. *OFWJ*, November 27, 1910.
14. *OFWJ*, November 28, 1910.
15. See *OFWJ*, November 29 and 30, 1910.
16. *OFWJ*, December 7, 1910.
17. *OFWJ*, December 12, 1910.
18. *OFWJ*, December 13, 1910.
19. *OFWJ*, December 15, 1910.
20. *OFWJ*, December 21, 1910.
21. *OFWJ*, December 22, 1910.
22. *OFWJ*, December 23, 1910.
23. *OFWJ*, December 24, 1910.
24. *OFWJ*, December 25, 1910.
25. *OFWJ*, December 26, 1910.

26. *OFWJ*, December 27, 1910.

27. *OFWJ*, December 29, 1910.

28. *OFWJ*, January 1, 1911.

29. *OFWJ*, January 3, 1911.

30. *OFWJ*, January 7, 1911. See also Hardy, *Solemn Covenant*, Appendix 2, #185.

31. *OFWJ*, January 9, 1911.

32. *OFWJ*, January 11, 1911.

33. *OFWJ*, January 12, 1911.

34. *OFWJ*, January 13, 1911.

35. See *OFWJ*, January 20 and 23, 1911.

36. *OFWJ*, February 3, 1911. The issues over science and evolution at BYU became known as the *modernism controversy*. For a review of this episode, see *Brigham Young University: The First One Hundred Years*, Vol. 1, ed., Earnest L. Wilkinson (Provo, UT: Brigham Young University Press, 1975), 412–512.

37. *OFWJ*, February 5, 1911.

38. *OFWJ*, February 6, 1911.

39. *OFWJ*, February 14, 1911; "Chanticler" and "An Old Sweetheart of Mine," (James Whitcomb Riley) were popular poetic readings of Whitney's day.

40. *OFWJ*, February 16, 1911.

41. See *OFWJ*, February 21 and 22, 1911.

42. *OFWJ*, February 22, 1911. Also, "March 1, 1911: Returned to Salt Lake arriving at 10:20 a.m. In Council at the temple until 5 p.m. on John W. Taylor case." See also Hardy, *Solemn Covenant*, Appendix 2, #191.

43. *JEHJ*, February 22, 1911.

44. *OFWJ*, February 28, 1911.

45. *OFWJ*, March 9, 1911.

46. *OFWJ*, March 10, 1911.

47. *OFWJ*, March 13, 1911. The "White and Blue" was a BYU student newspaper at the time.

"'A Problem in Eve-olution': How big was Adam's apple, Pa, / That halted in his throat, / To show all down the centuries, / Beneath his billy-goat? How happened it that Eve could gulp / And swallow all o' hern, / While Adam could not get his down / By any twist or turn? The reason is, my little lad, / That Adam was a frog, / In throttle just about the size / Of yonder polly-wog. The apple was not over large, / But froggie's throat was small— / No wonder modern science doubts / He got it in at all; / While Eve was woman from the first, / She'd swallow anything— / Apples, gossip, sweets galore, / Whatever luck might bring. This Adam was a rib of hers (A ribbon, it should read; / It beats the deuce how Bible words / Get changed as times proceed). There's been an Eve-olution, but / It's all in Adam's race; / Frog-like he rose by leaps and bounds— / She could not keep the pace. So finally she fell behind, / And, crowding to the van, / This frog became the king of beasts, / And called himself a 'man'" (Whitney's poem, as quoted in Thompson, *Orson F. Whitney: Poetic Writer*, 57).

48. *OFWJ*, March 15, 1911.

49. See *OFWJ*, March 17 and 20, 1911.

50. See *OFWJ*, March 26 and 27, 1911.

51. *OFWJ*, March 28, 1911.

52. *OFWJ*, April 2, 1911.

53. *OFWJ*, April 4, 1911.

54. *OFWJ*, April 6, 1911.

55. *OFWJ*, April 12, 1911.

56. *OFWJ*, April 13, 1911. Such words of commendation from President Smith would seem to indicate that Elder Whitney was not committing any kind of serious sinful immorality.

57. *OFWJ*, April 14, 1911. "M.A." or "M.A.T's." full name is never given, but was evidently a secret romantic interest of Whitney's.

58. *OFWJ*, April 16, 1911.

59. See *OFWJ*, April 22–25, 1911.

60. *OFWJ*, April 29, 1911.

61. *OFWJ*, April 30, 1911.

62. *OFWJ*, May 2, 1911. The word "Seen" (instead of "Scene") is spelled correctly and was used that way on purpose.

63. *OFWJ*, May 4, 1911.

64. *OFWJ*, May 9, 1911.

65. See *OFWJ*, May 10 and 11, 1911. See also Hardy, *Solemn Covenant*, Appendix 2, #56.

66. *OFWJ*, May 15, 1911.

67. *OFWJ*, May 30, 1911.

68. *OFWJ*, June 3, 1911.

69. *OFWJ*, June 4, 1911.

70. *OFWJ*, June 5, 1911.

71. *OFWJ*, June 6, 1911.

72. *OFWJ*, June 7, 1911.

73. *OFWJ*, June 8, 1911.

74. *OFWJ*, June 9, 1911.

75. *OFWJ*, June 10, 1911.

76. *OFWJ*, July 4, 1911.

77. *OFWJ*, July 6, 1911.

78. *OFWJ*, July 7, 1911.

79. *OFWJ*, July 13, 1911.

80. *JEHJ*, July 28, 1911.

81. *OFWJ*, July 15, 1911.

82. *OFWJ*, July 18, 1911.

83. *OFWJ*, July 20, 1911.

84. *OFWJ*, July 21, 1911.

85. *OFWJ*, July 22, 1911.

86. *OFWJ*, August 2, 1911.

87. *OFWJ*, August 5, 1911.

88. *OFWJ*, August 9, 1911.

89. *OFWJ*, August 17, 1911.

90. *OFWJ*, August 18, 1911.

91. *OFWJ*, August 19, 1911.

92. *OFWJ*, August 24, 1911.

93. *OFWJ*, August 25, 1911.

94. *OFWJ*, August 27, 1911.

95. *OFWJ*, August 29, 1911.

96. *OFWJ*, August 30, 1911.

97. *OFWJ*, September 23, 1911.

98. *OFWJ*, September 29, 1911.

99. *OFWJ*, September 30, 1911.

100. *OFWJ*, October 4, 1911.

101. *OFWJ*, October 7, 1911.

102. *OFWJ*, October 8, 1911.

103. *OFWJ*, October 10, 1911.

104. *OFWJ*, October 13, 1911.

105. *OFWJ*, October 17, 1911.

106. *OFWJ*, November 10, 1911.

107. See *OFWJ*, November 22, 1911.

108. *OFWJ*, November 27, 1911.

109. See *OFWJ*, November 28 and December 6, 1911.

110. *OFWJ*, December 7, 1911.

111. *OFWJ*, January 6 and 7, 1912.

112. *OFWJ*, January 17, 1912.

113. *OFWJ*, January 20, 1912.

114. *OFWJ*, January 25, 1912.

115. *OFWJ*, February 5, 1912.

116. *OFWJ*, August 1, 1916.

Chapter 19

1. *OFWJ*, February 29, 1912. Emmeline B. Wells spent her life working for the advancement and improvement of women in Utah and the Church, becoming the General President of the Relief Society and founder of the Women's *Exponent*, a magazine devoted to improving women's minds both intellectually and spiritually. According to a friend, Ethel Lund, Emmeline Wells was blessed to receive a vision of the Lord Jesus Christ in the Salt Lake Temple (See Church History Library Archives, Interviews: Salt Lake City, Utah, 1986 Nov.–1987 May; Lund, Ethel Cecelia Newman 1897–1998), OH 985.
2. Nine years later, Elder Whitney spoke at her funeral, "April, 1921. 'Aunt Em.' Wells died April 25th, 1921 and I was one of the speakers at her funeral, held in the Salt Lake Tabernacle, on the 29th inst."
3. See *OFWJ*, February 13, March 8, May 1 and 3, July 12, November 19, 1912; and March 26, April 25, and August 4 and 5, 1913.
4. *OFWJ*, January 19, 1914. This *Americana* history series was later updated and revised by Roberts and published in 1930 as the six volume *A Comprehensive History of the Church of Jesus Christ of Latter-day Saints.*
5. See *OFWJ*, June 21 and 26, and November 5, 1912.
6. *OFWJ*, May 6, 1913. The Bureau of Information was an early form of what later became visitor's centers.
7. *OFWJ*, March 3, 1913.
8. See *OFWJ,* November 16, 1913. See Orson F. Whitney, *Gospel Themes: A Treatise on Salient Features of Mormonism.* The Preface, which he dated as December of 2013, states, "This little book was written and compiled at the request of the General Priesthood Committee, under the sanction of the First Presidency of the Church, for the use and benefit of the priesthood classes, throughout the stakes and wards of Zion."
9. *OFWJ*, March 21, 22, and 23, 1912.
10. *OFWJ*, March 24, 1912.
11. *OFWJ*, January 13, 1913.
12. *OFWJ*, February 26, 1913.

13. *TMH*, 271–72.
14. *JEHJ*, May 3, 1914.
15. *TMH*, 272.
16. *OFWJ*, May 2, 1912.
17. *OFWJ*, May 14, 1912.
18. *OFWJ*, May 30, 1912.
19. *OFWJ*, June 17, 1912.
20. *OFWJ*, July 8, 1912.
21. See *OFWJ*, July 13 and 17, 1912.
22. *OFWJ*, July 20, 1912.
23. *OFWJ*, April 5, July 28, October 5, 1914.
24. *JEHJ*, January 10, 1915.
25. *OFWJ*, February 11, 1912.
26. *OFWJ*, April 5, 6, and 7, 1912.
27. *OFWJ*, April 21, 1912.
28. *OFWJ*, February 23, 1913.
29. *OFWJ*, April 4, 1913.
30. *OFWJ*, April 27, 1913.
31. *OFWJ*, June 15, 1913.
32. *OFWJ*, April 4, 5, and 6, 1914.
33. *OFWJ*, March 14, 1912.
34. *OFWJ*, January 24, 1913.
35. *JEHJ*, July 13, 1913.
36. *OFWJ*, June 12, 1913.
37. *OFWJ*, December 12, 1913.
38. *OFWJ*, January 18, 1914.
39. *OFWJ*, March 17, 1914.
40. *OFWJ*, July 1, 1914.

41. *OFWJ*, July 3, 1914.

42. *OFWJ*, November 28, 1914.

43. *OFWJ*, December 17, 1914.

44. *OFWJ*, December 22, 1914.

45. See *OFWJ*, December 24, 1914.

46. *JEHJ*, January 5, 1915.

47. See *OFWJ*, January 13, 14, and 20, and June 15, 1914. See also Hardy, *Solemn Covenant*, Appendix 2, #169 and #125. Thomas Clark in not listed.

48. *JEHJ*, March 15, 1914.

49. *OFWJ*, January 27, 1913.

50. *JEHJ*, April 22, 1913.

51. *JEHJ*, August 7, 1913.

52. *OFWJ*, July 2, 1913.

53. *OFWJ*, April 1, 1912.

54. *OFWJ*, July 2, 1914.

55. *OFWJ*, under dates given.

56. See *TMH*, 280–92.

57. *OFWJ*, November 21, 1914.

Chapter 20

1. *OFWJ*, January 27, 1915.
2. *OFWJ*, January 31, 1917.
3. *OFWJ*, July 20, 1917.
4. *OFWJ*, April 9, 1917.
5. *OFWJ*, November 16, 1917.
6. *OFWJ*, December 5, 1917.
7. *OFWJ*, December 13, 1917.
8. *OFWJ*, January 21, 1918.
9. *OFWJ*, June 7, 1918.
10. *OFWJ*, July 1, 1918.
11. *OFWJ*, July 2, 1918.
12. See *OFWJ*, March 16 and April 18, 1915 and July 21, 1916.
13. *OFWJ*, October 26, 1916.
14. *OFWJ*, March 14, 1917.
15. *OFWJ*, March 19, 1917.
16. *OFWJ*, March 22, 1917.
17. *OFWJ*, April 16, 1917.
18. "July 23, 1917. Read ms with Bro. Hyrum M. Smith, from 10 a.m. to 11:15."
19. *Doctrine and Covenants Commentary* is the title that appeared on the spine and front cover, but the title page simply named the book as the Doctrine and Covenants, with an introduction and historical and exegetical notes by Hyrum M. Smith, and came to exactly 1,100 pages. The later 1951 revised edition, came to 900 pages, but was typeset differently. One of the notable differences between the two editions was a revision of the commentary of section 132.
20. See *OFWJ*, May 1 and June 4, 1917.
21. "October 18, 1919. Completed a biographical sketch of President Heber J. Grant to be published in the *National Cyclopedia of American*

Biography. I read the first draft to him yesterday, prior to his departure for the east."

22. *OFWJ*, June 27, 1917.

23. *OFWJ*, June 30, 1917.

24. *OFWJ*, April 8, 1916. These early movies are available on DVD from Church Distribution Services.

25. *OFWJ*, July 19, 1917.

26. *OFWJ*, May 22 and 23, 1920.

27. *OFWJ*, June 29, 1920.

28. *OFWJ*, June 7, 1920.

29. *OFWJ*, July 11, 1920.

30. *OFWJ*, May 1 and 2, 1915.

31. See *OFWJ*, June 7, 1915.

32. *OFWJ*, October 6, 1916.

33. See *OFWJ*, October 9, 1916.

34. *OFWJ*, October 5, 6, and 7, 1917.

35. *OFWJ*, October 25, 1917.

36. *OFWJ*, September 3, 1918.

37. *OFWJ*, October 5, 1918.

38. *OFWJ*, September 23, 1919.

39. *OFWJ*, October 3, 1919.

40. *OFWJ*, October 5, 1919.

41. See *OFWJ*, March 28 and December 31.

42. See *OFWJ*, July 9, 1920.

43. *OFWJ*, January 9, 1921.

44. *OFWJ*, March 2, 1921.

45. *OFWJ*, April 6, 1916.

46. *OFWJ*, April 24, 1916.

47. *OFWJ*, March 24, 1918.

48. *OFWJ*, March 21, 1920.

49. *OFWJ*, July 9, 1916.

50. *OFWJ*, July 10 and 11, 1916.

51. *OFWJ*, July 29, 1916.

52. *OFWJ*, September 27, 1917.

53. See Hardy, *Solemn Covenant*, Appendix 2, #91.

54. Lyman's father Amasa M., as an apostle, became involved with spiritualism to the point that he began teaching publicly that the Atonement of Jesus Christ, and the doctrine of repentance, were not necessary; he also became involved in séances, and was eventually excommunicated. He later joined an apostate organization. It may be that Amasa's problems with spiritualism became one of the reasons Francis became so concerned about, and sensitive, to Orson's dabbling on the fringes of such matters. Francis's son Richard R. would also find himself running afoul of Church discipline, committing adultery and being excommunicated.

55. *OFWJ*, November 20, 1916.

56. *OFWJ*, November 22, 1916.

57. *OFWJ*, November 23, 1916.

58. *OFWJ*, October 3, 1918.

59. *OFWJ*, October 4, 1918.

60. *OFWJ*, October 31, 1918.

61. D&C 138:17; emphasis added.

62. *OFWJ*, November 17, 1918.

63. *OFWJ*, November 19, 1918.

64. *OFWJ*, November 20, 1918.

65. *OFWJ*, November 21, 1918. For information recounting the passing of President Smith, as well as the reception of the vision of the redemption of the dead, see Joseph Fielding Smith, *Life of Joseph F. Smith*, 466–85.

66. *OFWJ*, November 22, 1918.

67. *OFWJ*, November 23, 1918.

68. Further background information on this subject can be found in Horne, *Latter Leaves in the Life of Lorenzo Snow,* 381–83.

69. *OFWJ*, January 1, 1919.

70. *OFWJ*, June 1, 1919.

71. *OFWJ*, March 3, 1921.

72. *OFWJ*, March 10, 1921. For a sketch of the life of Anthon H. Lund, and a large sampling of his diaries, see *Danish Apostle: The Diaries of Anthon H. Lund 1899–1921.*

73. *OFWJ*, March 17, 1921. Elder Widtsoe's personal account of his call and ordination can be found in Widtsoe, *In a Sunlit Land: The Autobiography of John A. Widtsoe*, 156–57.

74. *OFWJ*, February 4, 1917.

75. *OFWJ*, February 5, 1917.

76. *OFWJ*, August 11 and 12, 1917.

77. *OFWJ*, July 4, 1919.

78. *OFWJ*, July 31, 1917.

79. *OFWJ*, January 20, 1918.

80. *OFWJ*, January 24, 1918.

81. *OFWJ*, April 24, 1918.

82. *OFWJ*, October 16, 1918.

83. *OFWJ*, October 19, 1918.

84. See *OFWJ*, October 16, 1918.

85. *OFWJ*, November 11, 1918.

86. *OFWJ*, December 2, 1918.

87. *OFWJ*, December 9, 1918.

88. *OFWJ*, June 2, 1919; see also *OFWJ*, April 5, 1919.

89. *OFWJ*, April 14, 1921. See Whitney, *Saturday Night Thoughts*.

90. *OFWJ*, April 5, 1920.

91. *JEHJ*, April 8, 1920

92. *OFWJ*, April 4, 1915.

93. *OFWJ*, June 17, 1915.

94. *OFWJ*, June 18 and 19, 1915.

95. *OFWJ*, June 21, 1915.

96. *OFWJ*, August 2, 1915.

97. *OFWJ*, August 3, 1915.

98. *OFWJ*, August 10, 1915.

99. *OFWJ*, August 11, 1915.

100. *OFWJ*, January 25, 1916. They had met and visited some months before: "August 13, 1915. Went to Provo on the [train]. Roomed at the Lamar. My friend G. Francis Hickman called on me there." See also Hardy, *Solemn Covenant*, Appendix 2, #91.

101. *OFWJ*, August 19, 1915.

102. *OFWJ*, August 27, 1915.

103. See *OFWJ*, September 15 and 20, 1915.

104. *JEHJ*, March 12, 1916.

105. *OFWJ*, August 1, 1916.

106. *OFWJ*, August 2, 6, 26; September 3, 1916..

107. *OFWJ*, September 14, 1916.

108. *OFWJ*, September 18, 1916.

109. *OFWJ*, September 22, 1916.

110. *OFWJ*, October 17, 1916.

111. *OFWJ*, October 23, 1916.

112. *OFWJ*, November 9, 1916. See also Whitney, *Popular History of Utah*.

113. *JEHJ*, December 4, 1916.

114. *OFWJ*, December 20, 1916.

115. *OFWJ*, April 14, 1917 and *JEHJ*, April 17, 1917.

116. See *OFWJ*, July 10 and September 5, 1917.

117. *OFWJ*, October 19, 1917.

118. See *OFWJ*, May 26, 1918; April 25, May 27 and September 2, 1919.

119. *JEHJ*, October 8, 1919.

120. See *OFWJ*, October 19, November 29, December 15, 1919.

121. *OFWJ*, July 6, 1920; see also *OFWJ*, June 14 and 28, and July 4 and August 6, 1920.

122. *JEHJ*, July 23, 1920.

123. *OFWJ*, March 19 and 20, 1921.

124. *JEHJ*, March 23, 1921.

125. *OFWJ*, May 14, 1921.

126. *JEHJ*, May 17, 1931.

127. *OFWJ*, May 1, 1921.

128. *OFWJ*, May 16, 1921.

129. *OFWJ*, May 19, 1921.

130. *OFWJ*, May 20, 1921.

131. *OFWJ*, May 23, 1921.

132. *OFWJ*, May 24, 1921.

Chapter 21

1. *OFWJ*, June 21, 1921.
2. *OFWJ*, June 26, 1921.
3. *OFWJ*, July 1, 1921.
4. *OFWJ*, July 2, 1921.
5. *OFWJ*, July 15, 1921.
6. *OFWJ*, September 10, 1921.
7. *OFWJ*, September 13, 1921.
8. *OFWJ*, September 16, 1921.
9. *OFWJ*, September 19, 1921.
10. *OFWJ*, October 11, 1921.
11. *OFWJ*, October 14, 1921.
12. *OFWJ*, October 17, 1921.
13. *OFWJ*, October 26, 1921.
14. *OFWJ*, November 11, 1921.
15. *OFWJ*, November 14, 1921.
16. *OFWJ*, December 1, 1921.
17. *OFWJ*, December 9, 1921.
18. *OFWJ*, December 25, 1921.
19. *OFWJ*, January 16, 1922.
20. *OFWJ*, January 18, 1922.
21. *OFWJ*, January 20, 1922.
22. *OFWJ*, January 22, 1922.
23. *OFWJ*, January 23, 1922.
24. *OFWJ*, January 27, 1922.
25. *OFWJ*, January 28, 1922.
26. *OFWJ*, February 5, 1922.
27. *OFWJ*, February 12, 1922.

28. *OFWJ*, February 19, 1922.

29. *OFWJ*, March 5, 1922.

30. *OFWJ*, April 18, 1922.

31. *OFWJ*, May 1, 1922.

32. *OFWJ*, May 2, 1922.

33. See *OFWJ*, May 22, 1922.

34. *OFWJ*, May 24, 1922.

35. *OFWJ*, May 27, 1922.

36. *OFWJ*, June 12, 1922.

37. *OFWJ*, June 13, 1922. In this case, it may well be that the reason Whitney crossed out the wording about kindness is that his nurse later turned on him and became petty and spiteful, no longer proffering the needed kindness. For a review of this difficult time period from Whitney's perspective some years later, see *TMH*, 334–38.

38. *OFWJ*, June 14, 1922.

39. *OFWJ*, June 20, 1922.

40. *OFWJ*, June 21, 1922.

41. *OFWJ*, September 27, 1922.

42. *OFWJ*, September 28, 1922.

43. *OFWJ*, October 11, 1922. For further information about this episode in Whitney's life, see *TMH*, 340–46. The autobiographical account in *TMH* is evidently drawn from this same diary account, but with further commentary and detail.

Chapter 22

1. In his autobiography, Elder Whitney wrote, "At that time I could neither read nor write, nor even think clearly. There was a weight on my brain like an iron clamp, and I felt when walking as if I were lifting great chunks of lead. I doubt if any of the brethren, or even the members of my family fully understood my case or realized what I was passing through. How could they, without a like experience?" (*TMH*, 348).
2. *OFWJ*, under date of October 22, 1922, but obviously covering months. Emotional and mental illness issues, such as those endured by Elder Whitney, have received increasing attention and recognition in the Church as the decades have passed. George Albert Smith, for instance, suffered occasional periods of severe mental illness in his life. See Stubbs, *A Biography of George Albert Smith, 1870–1951*, 106–07, 317–18; *George Albert Smith: Kind and Caring Christian, Prophet of God*, 60–77, and many other references scattered throughout the book. For a more general and contemporary approach to the subject, see Jeffrey R. Holland, "Like a Broken Vessel," *Ensign*, November 2013, 40–42.
3. *OFWJ*, January 27, 1924.
4. *OFWJ*, February 17, 1924.
5. *OFWJ*, February 24, 1924.
6. *OFWJ*, March 9, 1924.
7. *OFWJ*, March 16, 1924.
8. *OFWJ*, March 23 [17], 1924.
9. *OFWJ*, April 4, 1924.
10. *OFWJ*, April 6, 1924.
11. *OFWJ*, April 7, 1924.
12. *OFWJ*, April 1924, no day date given.
13. *OFWJ*, April 10, 1924.
14. *OFWJ*, April 13, 1924.
15. *OFWJ*, April 15, 1924. See also West, *Life of Franklin D. Richards*.

Chapter 23

1. See *OFWJ*, May 15, 1924.
2. *OFWJ*, May 18, 1924.
3. See *OFWJ*, May 25, 1924.
4. *OFWJ*, June 10, 1924. This was not the only occasion when an unusual spirit accompanied the remarks of a Church leader at a funeral for a Cannon family descendant. President George Albert Smith likewise experienced an unusual outpouring of the Spirit of the Lord when he himself spoke at a Cannon descendant funeral; see Horne, *An Apostle's Record: The Journals of Abraham H. Cannon*, 51–52.
5. *OFWJ*, July 13, 1924.
6. *OFWJ*, July 15 and 16, 1924. See also Roberts, *Joseph Smith, the Prophet Teacher.*
7. *OFWJ*, August 30, 1924.
8. *OFWJ*, September 2, 1924. See also Kimball, *Father of a Prophet: Andrew Kimball*, 224–29.
9. *OFWJ*, September 25, 1924.
10. *OFWJ*, September 26, 1924.
11. *OFWJ*, October 27, 1924.
12. *OFWJ*, November 2, 1924.
13. *OFWJ*, December 25, 1924.
14. *OFWJ*, December 28, 1924.
15. *OFWJ*, January 4, 1925.
16. *OFWJ*, February 20, 1925.
17. See *OFWJ*, February 25, 1925.
18. See *OFWJ*, June 3, 1925.
19. *OFWJ*, June 10, 1925.
20. *OFWJ*, June 17, 1925. For another take, besides what is found in chapter one of this book, see Walker, *Qualities That Count*, 61–80.
21. *OFWJ*, July 1, 1925.

22. *OFWJ*, August 9, 1925.

23. *OFWJ*, October 15, 1925.

24. *OFWJ*, January 13, 1926.

25. *OFWJ*, February 20 and 21, 1926.

26. *OFWJ*, March 7, 1926.

27. *OFWJ*, April 4 to 6, 1926. Other diary entries mentioning Whitney's labors on his autobiography include:
"[Ca. Early] March 1927: Have been busy upon my memoirs for some months and they begin to take the shape I desire—quite readable, I think."
"Christmas, 1927: The rest of the week I was busy at my office, and on my memoirs."
"July 8, 1928: A vacation of some weeks followed during which I busied myself working on my memoirs."
"December 31, 1928: Am still busy on my memoirs, and greatly appreciate a brief lull in routine labors during this Holiday season, which enables me to push forward the work."
"New Year's, 1929: Made a few calls during the day, and I worked some on the memoirs."

28. *OFWJ*, ca. July 5, 1926.

29. *OFWJ*, October 4, 1926.

30. *OFWJ*, November 21, 1926.

31. *OFWJ*, November 22, 1926.

32. *OFWJ*, November 14, 1926.

33. *OFWJ*, December 19, 1926.

34. *OFWJ*, December 23, 1926.

35. *OFWJ*, January 3, 1927.

36. *OFWJ*, ca. January, 1927.

37. See *OFWJ*, ca. January, 1927.

38. See *OFWJ*, February 4, 1927.

39. *OFWJ*, ca. early March, 1927.

40. *OFWJ*, April 24, 1927.

41. *OFWJ*, ca. mid-May, 1927.

42. *OFWJ*, June 21, 1927.

43. *OFWJ*, September 3 and 4, 1927.

44. *OFWJ*, October 7, 1927.

45. *OFWJ*, October 23, 1927.

46. *OFWJ*, November 9, 1927.

47. See *TMH*, 357–69.

48. See *OFWJ*, December 18, 1927.

49. *OFWJ*, Christmas, December 25, 1927.

50. *OFWJ*, January 1, 1928.

51. *OFWJ*, February 19 and 20, 1928.

52. *OFWJ*, March 15, 1928.

53. *TMH*, 402.

54. *JEHJ*, April 17, 1928.

55. *OFWJ*, April 6, 1928.

56. *OFWJ*, April 12, 1928.

57. *OFWJ*, May 9, 1928.

58. See *OFWJ*, May 10, 1928.

59. See *OFWJ*, July 8, 1928.

60. *OFWJ*, October 6, 1928.

61. *JEHJ*, October 20, 1928.

62. *JEHJ*, Nov. 17 1928. They had another long talk a few months later: "[*JEHJ*] February 10, 1929: I had a long talk with Apostle Whitney while I was in S.L. He had been in Los Angeles attending conference."

63. *OFWJ*, December 31, 1928.

64. *OFWJ*, December 29, 1929. See also "Latter-day developments: [addresses] . . . over radio station KSL, by Orson F. Whitney."

65. *OFWJ*, January, 1930.

66. See *OFWJ*, April 18 and 20, 1930.

67. A small card with the foregoing inscription, probably written in the handwriting of David O. McKay, was placed in Orson's diary above the date for June 22, 1930.

68. *OFWJ,* August 17, 1930.

69. *OFWJ,* November 28, 1930.

70. *OFWJ,* December 3, 1930. Being a private project, the publishing costs had to be paid. "December 30, 1930: Sent check $500 to Samuel O. Bennion, Independence, Mo., on acct publication of *Through Memory's Halls.*"

71. *OFWJ,* January 1, 1931.

72. *OFWJ,* January 14, 1931.

73. See *OFWJ,* January 15 and 18, 1931.

74. *OFWJ,* February 13, 1931.

75. *JEHJ,* March 11, 1931.

76. *OFWJ,* April 1, 1931.

77. *OFWJ,* April 5, 1931.

78. *JEHJ,* May 17, 1931.

Selected Bibliography

This list is focused on those works that help tell the life story of the subject, and is not meant to be an exhaustive survey of all Whitney-authored or Whitney-related printed items. The most comprehensive bibliographic review I have seen of Whitney's published writings (especially his poetry) is found in Woodruff Thompson's unpublished thesis, "Orson F. Whitney: Mormon Writer," 133–41, as listed below. The below items indicate Whitney's major publications, followed by other sources referenced while preparing this biography. For the more commonly quoted works cited, see the Key to Note Abbreviations. For archival materials, see Orson F. Whitney papers, 1868–1930, Church History Library Archives, Salt Lake City, Utah (MS 1308); see also Orson F. Whitney Diaries, Special Collections and Archives; Utah State University Merrill-Cazier Library, Logan, Utah (MS 188).

Notable Books and Pamphlets by Whitney

Elias: An Epic of the Ages, New York, The Knickerbocker Press, 1904. Authors Jubilee Edition, 1905, limited to 150 copies; Revised and Annotated second edition, 1914.

Gospel Themes: A Treatise on Salient Features of "Mormonism," Salt Lake City, The Church of Jesus Christ of Latter-day Saints, 1914.

History of Utah: in Four Volumes, Salt Lake City, George Q. Cannon & Sons, Vol. 1, 1892; Vol. 2, 1893; Vol. 3, 1895; Vol. 4, 1904 – Biographical. (Volume four contains a sketch of Whitney's life titled, "The Author and His Work," that identifies John Nicholson as author. While his name is on it, evidence indicates that Whitney probably prepared most of it for Nicholson. See pages 703–07).

In Memoriam; Horace G. Whitney: Biographical Sketch, Funeral Ceremonies, Resolutions of Respect, Editorials, Personal Tributes, Salt Lake

City, Utah, n.p., 1920. While no author or publisher is given for this item, it reads like it was prepared by Orson for his brother's funeral.

"Latter-day developments: [addresses] . . . over Radio Station KSL," Church History Library (M247.4 W621w); addresses dated Nov. 24, 1929–Dec 29, 1929; Mar. 10, 1929–June 23, 1929.

Life of Heber C. Kimball, An Apostle; the Father and Founder of the British Mission, Salt Lake City, Published by the Kimball Family at the Juvenile Instructor Office, 1888.

Love and the Light: An Idyl of the Westland, Salt Lake City, The Church of Jesus Christ of Latter-day Saints, 1918.

The Making of a State: A School History of Utah, Salt Lake City, Deseret News, 1908.

"The Mormon Prophet's Tragedy," Salt Lake City, Deseret News, 1905.

The Poetical Writings of Orson F. Whitney: Poems and Poetic Prose, Salt Lake City, Juvenile Instructor Office, 1889.

Popular History of Utah: Complete in One Volume, Illustrated, Salt Lake City, Deseret News, 1916.

Saturday Night Thoughts: A Series of Dissertations on Spiritual, Historical and Philosophic Themes, Salt Lake City, Deseret News, 1921.

Speeches of Hon. O. F. Whitney in Support of Woman Suffrage, Delivered in the Constitutional Convention of Utah, March 30th, April 2nd, and April 5th, 1895, [Salt Lake City], Utah Woman Suffrage Association, 1895.

The Strength of the "Mormon" Position, Zion's Printing and Publishing Co., Independence, MO., 1917.

Through Memory's Halls: The Life Story of Orson F. Whitney, as told by himself, Independence, Missouri, Zion's Printing and Publishing Company, 1930.

Voices from the Mountains, Liverpool, [published by the European

Mission], 1922. This is a collection of many of Whitney's more well-known poems, often mentioned in his diary.

"The Wasatch Literary Association," *Improvement Era* 28 (September 1925).

Works Cited

Anderson, J. Max, *The Polygamy Story: Fiction and Fact*, Salt Lake City, Publishers Press, 1979.

Arrington, Leonard J., *Beet Sugar in the West: A History of the Utah-Idaho Sugar Company, 1891–1066*, Seattle and London, University of Washington Press, 1966.

______, *Great Basin Kingdom*, Lincoln, University of Nebraska Press, 1958.

Bergera, Gary James, "Transgression in the LDS Community: The Cases of Albert Carrington, Richard R. Lyman, and Joseph F. Smith, Part 1," in *Journal of Mormon History* 37: 3 (Summer 2011).

Berlin, G. Elliot, "Abraham Owen Smoot: Pioneer Mormon Leader," unpublished Master's Thesis, Brigham Young University, 1955.

Bitton, Davis, "A Masterwork of Mormon Theology?" in B. H. Roberts, *The Truth, the Way, the Life: An Elementary Treatise on Theology*, ed., John W. Welch, Provo, UT; BYU Studies, 1994.

Black, Susan Easton, and Mary Jane Woodger, eds, *Women of Character: Profiles of 100 Prominent LDS Women,* American Fork, UT; Covenant Communications, 2011.

Brigham Young University: The First One Hundred Years, Vol. 1, ed., Earnest L. Wilkinson, Provo, UT; Brigham Young University Press, 1975.

[Church, LDS, curriculum] *Teachings of Presidents of the Church: Lorenzo Snow*, Salt Lake City, The Church of Jesus Christ of Latter-day Saints, 2012.

Bitton, Davis, and Leonard J. Arrington, *Mormons and Their Historians*, Salt Lake City, University of Utah Press, 1988 (56–68).

Clark, James R., comp., *Messages of the First Presidency of The Church of Jesus Christ of Latter-day Saints*, 6 Vols., Salt Lake City, Bookcraft, 1965–1975.

Compton, Todd M., *In Sacred Loneliness: The Plural Wives of Joseph Smith*, Salt Lake City, Signature Books, 1997.

Doctrine and Covenants, with an introduction and historical and exegetical notes by Hyrum M. Smith (1st ed.), Liverpool, Printed and Published by George F. Richards, 1919.

Douglas, Colin B., "A Survey of Mormon Literary Criticism," unpublished master's thesis, Brigham Young University, 1978.

Ehat, Andrew F. and Lyndon W. Cook, *The Words of Joseph Smith*, Provo, Utah; BYU Religious Studies Center, 1980.

Flake, Dennis D., "Orson F. Whitney's Philosophy of Education," Church History Library (M270.1 W621f).

Gibbons, Francis M., *George Albert Smith: Kind and Caring Christian, Prophet of God*, Salt Lake City, Deseret Book, 1990.

Godfrey, Kenneth W. "Charles S. Whitney's Diary: A Nineteenth-century Salt Lake City Teenager," in *Journal of Mormon History* 27 (fall 2001): 215–51.

______, "The History of Intelligence in Latter-day Saint Thought," in *The Pearl of Great Price: Revelations From God*, Provo, UT; BYU Religious Studies Center, 1989.

______, "Moses Thatcher in the Dock: His Trials, The Aftermath, and His Last Days," *Journal of Mormon History*, 24:1 (Spring 1998), 54–88.

Hardy, B. Carmon, *Solemn Covenant: The Mormon Polygamous Passage*, Urbana and Chicago, University of Illinois Press, 1992.

Hatch, Charles M., and Compton, Todd M., eds., *A Widow's Tale: The 1884–1896 Diary of Helen Mar Kimball Whitney*, Logan, UT, Utah State University Press, 2003.

Hefner, Loretta L., "From Apostle to Apostate: The Personal Struggle of Amasa Mason Lyman," in *Dialogue: A Journal of Mormon Thought*, 16:1 (Spring 1983), 90–104.

Helpful Visions, the Fourteenth Book of the Faith-Promoting Series, Salt Lake City, Juvenile Instructor Office, 1887.

Hinckley, Bryant S., *Daniel Hammer Wells and Events of His Time*, Salt Lake City, Heber J. Grant and the Deseret News Press, 1942.

Holzapfel, Jeni Broberg, and Richard Neitzel Holzapfel, *A Woman's View: Helen Mar Whiteny's Reminiscences of Early Church History*, Provo, UT; BYU Religious Studies Center, 1997.

Hoopes, David S. and Roy Hoopes, *The Making of a Mormon Apostle: The Story of Rudger Clawson*, New York, Madison Books, 1991.

Horne, Dennis B., *An Apostle's Record: The Journals of Abraham H. Cannon*, Clearfield, UT; Gnolaum Books, 2004.

_____, *Bruce R. McConkie: Highlights from His life and Teachings*, 2nd ed., Salt Lake City, Eborn Books, 2010.

_____, *Determining Doctrine*, Salt Lake City, Eborn Books, 2005.

_____, *Latter Leaves in the Life of Lorenzo Snow*, Springville, Cedar Fort, 2012. (A thirty-five page overview of Orson F. Whitney's life is found on pages 21–56 of this volume.)

Improvement Era, LDS Church publication, various early issues as referenced in the notes.

Jenson, Andrew, *LDS Biographical Encyclopedia*, 4 Vols. Salt Lake City, Andrew Jenson History Company, 1901–1936.

Journal of Discourses, 26 vols., London, Latter-day Saints' Book Depot, 1854–1886. This lengthy set is now readily available in public domain online editions. Vol. 26 contains two of Whitney's discourses.

Journal of Mormon History, Vol. 37, No. 4, Fall, 2011.

Kimball, Edward L., *Father of a Prophet: Andrew Kimball*, Provo, UT; BYU Studies, 2011.

Kimball, Edward L., and Andrew E. Kimball Jr., *Spencer W. Kimball*, Salt Lake City, Bookcraft, 1977.

Lyman, Edward Leo, *Amasa Mason Lyman: Mormon Apostle and Apostate; A Study in Dedication*, Salt Lake City, University of Utah Press, 2009.

Madsen, Truman G., *Defender of the Faith: The B. H. Roberts Story*, Salt Lake City, Bookcraft, 1980.

Mancill, Craig K., Brian D. Reeves, Guy L. Dorius, and J. B. Haws, eds., *Joseph F. Smith: Reflections on the Man and His Times*, [2012 BYU Church History Symposium], Provo, UT; and Salt Lake City, BYU Religious Studies Center and Deseret Book, 2013.

Matthew Cowley Speaks, Salt Lake City, Deseret Book, 1954.

Mecham, Travis Q., *Changes in Seniority to the Quorum of the Twelve Apostles of The Church of Jesus Christ of Latter-day Saints*, Utah State University, Unpublished Masters Thesis, 2009.

[Nibley, Charles W.] *Reminiscences [of] Charles W. Nibley, 1849–1931*, Salt Lake City, Stevens & Wallis, 1933.

Packer, Boyd K., "The Law and the Light," in Monte S. Nyman and Charles D. Tate Jr., eds., *The Book of Mormon: Jacob Through Words of Mormon, To Learn With Joy*, Salt Lake City, Bookcraft, 1990.

Poulson, Larry N., "The Life and Contributions of Newel Kimball Whitney," unpublished master's thesis, Brigham Young University, 1966.

Quinn, D. Michael, *The Mormon Hierarchy: Extensions of Power,* Salt Lake City, Signature Books in association with Smith Research Associates, 1997.

Reimann, Paul E., *Plural Marriage Limited,* Salt Lake City, Utah Printing Company, 1974.

Roberts, B. H., *A Comprehensive History of The Church of Jesus Christ of Latter-day Saints*, Salt Lake City, Deseret News Press, 1930.

_____, *History's Apprentice: The Diaries of B. H. Roberts, 1880–1898*, ed. John Sillitoe, Salt lake City, Signature Books & Smith Research Associates, 2004.

Roberts, B. H., *Joseph Smith, the Prophet Teacher*, 2nd ed., Salt Lake City, Deseret Book, 1927.

_____, *The Truth, the Way, the Life: An Elementary Treatise on Theology*, ed., John W. Welch, Provo, UT; BYU Studies, 1994.

Searle, Howard C., *Early Mormon Historiography: Writing the History of the Mormons, 1830–1858,* University of California Los Angeles, unpublished doctoral dissertation, 1979.

Smith, John Henry, *Church State and Politics: The Diaries of John Henry Smith*, ed. Jean Bickmore White, Salt Lake City, Signature Books and Smith Research Associates, 1990.

Smith, Joseph, *History of the Church of Jesus Christ of Latter-day Saints*, B. H. Roberts ed., 7 Vols. Salt Lake City, Deseret Book, 1946.

Smith, Joseph Fielding, *Life of Joseph F. Smith*, Salt Lake City, Deseret Book, 1938.

Smith, Joseph Fielding, Jr., and John J. Stewart, *The Life of Joseph Fielding Smith*, Salt Lake City, Deseret Book, 1972.

Stubbs, Glen R., *A Biography of George Albert Smith, 1870–1951*, unpublished doctoral dissertation, Brigham Young University, Provo; Utah, 1974.

Stuy, Brian H., ed., *Collected Discourses*, Vol. 5, Woodland Hills, UT; B.H.S. Publishing, 1992.

Taylor, Fred G., *A Saga of Sugar: Being a story of the romance and development of Beet Sugar in the Rocky Mountain West*, Salt Lake City, Deseret News Press and Utah-Idaho Sugar Company, 1944.

The Thatcher Episode; A Concise Statement of the Facts of the Case; Interesting Letters and Documents; a Review of M. Thatcher's Claims, Pleas and Admissions, Salt Lake City, 1896.

Thompson, Woodruff C., "Orson F. Whitney: Mormon Writer," Unpublished Master's Thesis, University of Utah, 1959.

Top, Brent L., *The Life Before*, Salt Lake City, Bookcraft, 1988.

Van Wagoner, Richard S., *Mormon Polygamy: A History*, Salt Lake City, Signature Books, 1979.

Walker, Ronald W., *Qualities that Count: Heber J. Grant as Businessman, Missionary, and Apostle*, Provo, Utah, *BYU Studies*, 2004.

______, *Wayward Saints: The Social and Religious Protests of the Godbeites against Brigham Young*. Provo and Salt Lake City, UT; Brigham Young University Press and University of Utah Press, 2009.

West, Franklin L., *Life of Franklin D. Richards*, Salt Lake City, Deseret News Press, 1924.

Widtsoe, John A., *In a Sunlit Land: The Autobiography of John A. Widtsoe*, Salt Lake City, Deseret News Press, 1952.

Index

A

B

C

D

E

F

G

H

Index

I

J

K

L

M

N

O

P

R

S

T

U

V

W

Y

About the Author

Dennis B. Horne was born in Salt Lake City, Utah, and grew up in Bountiful. He served in the Missouri Independence Mission and then attended both Brigham Young and Weber State Universities, earning a bachelor of science in communications. While finishing his degree, he met and married the late Celia Rae (Benson) Horne. They had two daughters together before she passed away. He later met and married Karin Chelsey Nelson, with whom he has one daughter. He worked for a number of years in television broadcasting, and then with the Materials Management Department of the LDS Church as a technical writer. He has lived in several locations in Davis County, Utah, and currently resides in Woods Cross.

He is the author of a number of doctrinally and historically oriented works, including *Bruce R. McConkie: Highlights from His Life and Teachings* (now in 2nd ed.); "*Called of God, by Prophecy*"; *An Apostle's Record: The Journals of Abraham H. Cannon*; *Determining Doctrine*; *Faith to Heal and Be Healed*; and *Latter Leaves in the Life of Lorenzo Snow*; the latter two issued by Cedar Fort, Inc. He has also presented papers at the 2012 and 2014 BYU Church History Symposium.

0 26575 14313 3